ALLIANCE
OF EVIL

ALLIANCE OF EVIL

Russia, China, the United States and a New Cold War

HAS THE MYSTERY OF THE END TIMES FINALLY ARRIVED?

LTC. ROBERT L. MAGINNIS

DEFENDER

CRANE, MO

ALLIANCE OF EVIL: *Russia, China, the United States and a New Cold War—Has the Mystery of the End Times Finally Arrived?*
By LTC Robert L. Maginnis

Printed in the United States of America.

Scripture taken from the King James Version of the Bible unless otherwise noted.

Cover design by Jeffrey Mardis.

ISBN: 978-1-9480-1406-9

Dedication

Dedicated to the Christians living in Russia and China who face persecution because of their faith.

ACKNOWLEDGMENTS

I gratefully acknowledge…

Once again, my wonderful wife lovingly tolerated my absence to work through this volume. I'm blessed to have such a wonderful helpmate.

My Christian brother Don Mercer once again selflessly gave of his time and talent to provide wise counsel and edits as this volume grew. Don, like me, is a retired Army lieutenant colonel and a veteran of the Cold War as well as the hot war in Vietnam.

There were many others who contributed their time by consenting to interviews, and to them I'm indebted.

The Lord put on my heart the idea and the insights to assemble this important work that I pray will serve His purposes.

Robert Lee Maginnis
Woodbridge, Virginia

Contents

Preface

The old Cold War was a frightening time, and I fear the new Cold War will cause just as much anxiety—and, in fact, it could be the catalyst that ushers in the prophetic end times. The fact is I don't know whether the growing tension between the US and its allies and China and its Russian partner is that catalyst, and neither do you. However, what is clear to me and addressed in detail in the *Alliance of Evil* is that the United States and its allies are engaged in a global confrontation on many fronts that I label the "new dual Cold War."

This Cold War is dual because there are two very different opponents—China and Russia. The Russian Federation is on the rise from the ashes of the former Soviet Union. Although it is weakened economically, Moscow, Russia's capital city, still manages to marshal significant resources to mount a serious threat against the West—ideologically, through cyberspace, and militarily, as we see in Ukraine and Syria. Many doubters say this is Moscow's last gasp for significance before it wilts into obsolescence. We'll see in time whether it re-emerges as a true great power, which is Russian President Vladimir Putin's ambition, or whether this period becomes a footnote in Moscow's long decline.

The People's Republic of China is unquestionably a great power with serious regional and arguably global ambitions, and now it is led by an autocrat for life like the former dictator Mao Zedong, President Xi Jinping. It is unwise to dismiss Communist China's rapidly growing economic and military might as only a regional threat, as some analysts do. Economically, it will soon outpace America, and its global network threatens to dominate the world's trade and financial markets.

Beijing is a rising global security threat as well. It will soon host a very significant global-capable blue-water navy; it fields the world's largest expeditionary and credible ground force; it is growing a fleet of fifth-generation jet fighters; it will soon have a fleet of anti-access, long-range hypersonic missiles; it already has a significant offensive/defensive space program; it uses its army of cyberspace warriors to daily attack our vulnerable cyber networks and steal our intellectual property; and it arguably has an edge on artificial intelligence harnessed to big data that could eventually control aspects of all five security domains—land, air, sea, cyber, and space.

I realize some readers will come to this volume with little understanding of the history of the old Cold War that pitted the former Soviet Union against the United States and Western Europe from 1945 to 1991. I know that period well and explore it in some detail in this volume. I not only lived through most of that time, but I served on the front lines of the Cold War on the Iron Curtain in Europe and faced the Chinese and North Korean threat in Asia. I've studied and written extensively about that for decades, and I had the occasion to visit the former Soviet Union and Hong Kong as a young US Army officer.

The old Cold War was a dreadful time in our history; no one who lived through it ever wants to repeat those years. That's why I introduce it to the reader and draw some lessons from those decades of cold conflict for us to consider as we examine the implications of the new dual Cold War. Yes, there are similarities with the old Cold War, but the new dual Cold War has unique aspects as well that may be more dangerous than before.

Admittedly I'm rather pessimistic about America's future, a view I share with many contemporary historians and national security experts. I profile in this book America's misguided and naïve hubris about its place in the contemporary world in order to indicate that we had better stop being so arrogant and become serious about the threats we face; otherwise, America will become irrelevant—aka, lose the new dual Cold War.

I like President Trump's new dual Cold War plan for America in his National Security Strategy, which is thoroughly examined in these pages. Time will tell whether Mr. Trump is able with congressional help to execute that plan and whether it has the effect needed to stop America's decline and the rising opposition to Western values, principles, our geopolitical influence, and economic well-being that the tag team of China and Russia threatens.

I'm somewhat unique among the foreign affairs and national security authors because not only do I have significant geopolitical experience (five decades), but I bring to my writings a thorough understanding of the interworking of the US national security and foreign affairs establishment and do so from an evangelical Christian's perspective. Who else writing on such matters still works within our national security establishment at the Pentagon and teaches at a major military college, much less is openly pro-Israel and studies and speaks about God's prophetic Word?

The final chapter in this work takes a deep dive into the prophetic Scriptures to debunk some of the misplaced speculation and suggests how we ought to consider the present times.

Finally, the *Alliance of Evil* is thoroughly documented. I rely on many other experts for important insights and then weave that material into a tapestry that suggests a compelling scenario that is contemporary, honors the Scriptures, and suggests just where this crazy world appears to be heading: the prophetic end times.

Introduction

America and the democratic West are on an unprecedented path headed for the most dangerous time in world history. The time is so unique that a new phrase must be used to describe it: Dual Cold War.

Twentieth-century America and her North Atlantic Treaty Organization (NATO) allies faced Russia and the Warsaw Pact almost exclusively in Europe during a period we labeled as the "Cold War." (The label belies the fact that there were incidents in which men died on both sides.) In the twenty-first century, we are witnessing the resurgence of a bold, assertive Russian Federation (Russia) and the aggressive military growth and actions by the People's Republic of China (China). Thus we have a dual nature to the new Cold War we are already in, and our adversary is rightly labeled the "Alliance of Evil."

The situation now is far more complex than in the old Cold War. In the past, Russia and her allies produced very little of interest to the democratic West. Now, however, China is an economic giant, and our economy is intricately tied with Beijing. And, as we shall see in later chapters, the dual Cold War comes at a time when America and the West are at the lowest level of military readiness in modern history. Clearly there are serious implications and perils for our collective future.

The most challenging factors in the emerging dual Cold War are questions about America's primacy. Is America past its prime, and can it lead like-minded nations to recover clarity, stability, and dominance over our wayward world to win the emerging dual Cold War? What about the threats of nuclear attacks emanating from North Korea and Iran? How will they affect the dual Cold War as we counter new threats or even move to a hot war with these rogue countries?

Further, is the dual Cold War just the beginning of a slide into a hot war with one or both of our chief antagonists, Russia and China?

Finally, this volume will go where no political military analyst has gone before. Are we on the verge of God's prophesied and promised direct intervention into human events on the planet? Is the dual Cold War pulling the world into specific and detailed prophetic events described in the Bible in the near future that will change the planet? Is the "Alliance of Evil" the catalyst that ushers in those events?

This study explores those questions in seven chapters beginning with the case for the reality of a contemporary dual Cold War pitting the US—and by association, the West—against China and Russia, a conflict that could quickly overheat into World War III.

The second chapter explains why this metamorphosis into a new dual Cold War happened, likely, at least in part, because the US is past its prime, demonstrates naïve hubris, and no longer serves as a global stabilizing force.

The third chapter reviews the original (old) Cold War—the US (West) versus the former Union of Soviet Socialist Republics (USSR) from 1945–1991)—its history, lessons, and the consequences of the USSR's collapse for Russia, China, and by association the entire world. This is an important issue to digest because it is foundational to understanding the implications of the new dual Cold War.

The fourth chapter examines those implications and how the dual Cold War will eventually radically change the world, especially America.

The fifth chapter identifies the four battlegrounds upon which the new dual Cold War will most evidence itself and could mushroom into a real, hot, shooting war.

The sixth chapter recommends what President Donald Trump and America's allies promise to do or at least should do to derail the dangerous implications of the dual Cold War to prevent the anticipated troubling metamorphosis from sparking a global apocalypse, if that outcome isn't in fact God's planned prophetic end state.

Finally, the seventh chapter addresses the prophetic end times, and if the new dual Cold War is the catalyst for the apocalypse, then we must answer the question: What, if any, roles do the US, China, and Russia play in the process that leads to the Tribulation and the Lord's return? Will these geopolitical players usher in global war, the Antichrist, the Rapture of the Church, and the final battle of Armageddon as outlined in Ezekiel, Daniel, and Revelation?

The epilogue to *Alliance of Evil* takes a deep step into informed speculation to suggest just how all the pieces to the dual Cold War might come together leading to the end times. It may read like fact, but for now it is sheer fiction.

CHAPTER ONE

The Case for a New
Dual Cold War

The old Cold War of the twentieth century that pitted the US and the Soviet Union in a death struggle featured covert conflicts, terrorism, and proxy wars that threatened to erupt at any time into global nuclear warfare. That existential challenge, an evil the United States under former President Ronald Reagan ultimately defeated, demanded unflinching fortitude and clarity of aim, and constituted a multigeneration struggle fought on many fronts across the globe. We knew at the time that any appeasement to Moscow was the same as aiding a ruthless enemy.

Those decades of Cold War were incredibly anxious times due to the strategic uncertainty for Americans who were instructed by their government to seek faux safety under school desks and inside backyard cellars (aka fallout shelters) as if those shelters would save them from Soviet nuclear-tipped missiles that threatened to vaporize all of us at any moment. Citizens who remember those years shared the widespread anxiety and especially the tensest close encounters with doom like the 1962 Cuban Missile Crisis and the Able Archer episode, a 1983 US military exercise that narrowly avoided starting a nuclear war when horribly misinterpreted by Russian military analysts.

The old Cold War was not only a time of great anxiety, but it was also incredibly expensive. It cost the US and Russia a combined $18 trillion over four-plus decades, and the political costs were enormous as well. We fought among ourselves over ideologies, viciously argued over allegiances (McCarthyism), and disagreed over President Dwight Eisenhower's warning about the dangers associated with the growing military-industrial complex, which rapidly grew throughout the old Cold War.

That hand-wrenching period in history was extremely destabilizing as the sides made virtually all foreign policy decisions through a Cold War lens. Such decisions brought every world region into the conflict and fueled endless proxy wars, such as Korea and Vietnam.

It is from this background that we must view the emergent new dual Cold War. Unfortunately, the evidence of a new and more existential conflict is lighting up the world stage. It pits the People's Republic of China and the Russian Federation in league against America and her allies, threatening to radically transform our world in previously unfathomable ways.

There are at least sixteen indicators outlined below that demonstrate the US and its covey of allies are very much locked into a new dual Cold War with China and Russia. However, some dissenting voices are included for balance.

It would perhaps be easy to dismiss a few of these markers as not that serious, but when one steps back to consider all sixteen indicators simultaneously, the picture is rather grim. Yes, we are very much in a new dual Cold War with no end in sight.

Indicator #1: Diplomatic

In October 2017, President Trump tweeted that our relationship with Russia "is at an all-time & very dangerous low." Others agree the relationship is bad, but they blame the administration for a lack of a coherent Russian strategy, especially regarding sanctions imposed over Moscow's

2014 annexation of Ukraine's Crimea and continued support for the uprising in Eastern Ukraine.

George Beebe, a former director of Russia analysis for the Central Intelligence Agency (CIA), told CNN: "I think it is very unclear exactly where the administration intends to go in our dealings with Russia or how it intends to put together a coherent strategy for dealing with Moscow." Beebe continued, "I think there is actually a very real risk that we could get into an escalatory spiral that would be difficult for either country to control."[1]

Russian leaders pile on the criticism of the Trump administration as weak. "The Trump administration has shown its total weakness by handing over executive power to Congress in the most humiliating way. This changes the power balance in U.S. political circles," said Russian Prime Minister Dmitry Medvedev in a Facebook post. "The U.S. establishment fully outwitted Trump; the President is not happy about the new sanctions, yet he could not but sign the bill [that imposed sanctions on Russia]."[2]

The attack from Medvedev followed President Vladimir Putin's decision to cut the United States' diplomatic mission in Russia by 755 people, a response to the seizure of Russian compounds and the expulsion of 35 diplomats by the Obama administration, an action intended to punish Moscow for the 2016 presidential election meddling.

The diplomatic kerfuffle over sanctions and the tit-for-tat embassy staff cuts linked to sanctions continues, but more troubling is the unwillingness of our European allies to get tough with Russia beyond a few words and a handful of sanctions. Most insist on clinging to the tired idea that America will always rush to Europe's rescue as it did in World Wars I and II. That view is beginning to shift, however.

In January 2018, German Foreign Minister Sigmar Gabriel gave a sobering warning to his European colleagues that there are no vacuums in international politics, and when—not if—the US withdraws from a region such as Europe, inevitably Russia and China will step in. Gabriel said of Syria, Russia filled a vacuum there in part because the US failed to sufficiently take the lead in that war, and in global trade policy, China is filling gaps left void by Americans. He continued to warn about reliance on the US feeling that it is bound to the North Atlantic Treaty Organization's (NATO) collective defense principles as outlined in Article 5 of the alliance treaty. "We are pleased that Donald Trump and the U.S. have affirmed Article 5 [mutual defense guarantee in the treaty], but we should not test that trust too much. At the same time, Europe could not defend itself without the U.S., even if European structures were strengthened."[3] Gabriel's observation about Europe's weakness and America's resolve is no doubt music to Russian ears given President Trump's past critical statements about NATO.

President Trump, both in his campaign and as a newly minted president, called on NATO members to share the burden of their defense by investing at least the member obligation of 2 percent of their gross national product (GDP) in defense. That isn't happening, however, and as I've heard from European military officers on more than one occasion in recent years, "We [NATO member nations] don't have to build up our militaries, because you Americans are going to protect us." Well, Mr. Trump and the American people are growing tired of footing the bill for our erstwhile NATO allies, and there will come a day when, as German Foreign Minister Gabriel states above, we (Americans) will pack up our tanks and howitzers and head home.

The evident combination of a lack of spine on the part of many NATO allies to properly invest in their security, America's hedging commitment to the alliance, and the lack of a viable American strategy against Russian aggression feed speculation about a new dual Cold War.

The same observation fits our relationship with China. In 2017, Mr. Trump lit a fire in Asia that caught many by surprise. At the Asia-Pacific Economic Cooperation summit, President Trump spoke of the "Indo-Pacific" instead of the "Asia-Pacific," the term used by previous American administrations. The switch in terms changes the mental map that has prevailed since the end of the old Cold War and since China's 1980s "reform and opening" policies. The new term, "Indo-Pacific," as

Trump used it, implies a new configuration in which India and America and other Asian allies—Japan and Australia—are now joined to contain China's growing influence, another indicator of a new Cold War with the Asian giant.[4]

(It is noteworthy that the Pentagon changed the name of the US Pacific Command to the US Indo-Pacific Command to better encapsulate that command's responsibilities. This reflects Congress' push for increased focus on China's activities in the Indo-Pacific and the 2019 defense bill, which includes provisions to counter the rising Chinese influence across both the Pacific Ocean and Indian Ocean regions.[5])

Then US Secretary of State Rex Tillerson made the administration's view about the India and America relationship explicit in an October 18, 2017, speech. "The Indo-Pacific—including the entire Indian Ocean, the Western Pacific and the nations that surround them, will be the most consequential part of the globe in the 21st century. The United States and India are increasingly global partners with growing strategic convergence. Indians and Americans don't just share an affinity for democracy. We share a vision of the future."

Former Secretary Tillerson's statement was a not-so-subtle-criticism of China, a communist regime and a country that doesn't share our "vision of the future." This criticism is confirmed by China's understanding that the US is a global actor that could disrupt—contain—China's rise. Therefore, China pursues a transformation strategy to escape America's containment strategy.

At the Chinese Communist Party's ninety-fifth anniversary in July 2016, President Xi Jinping addressed China's intent to play a larger global role, including shaping a "fairer" global governance system. Mr. Xi stressed that his country will defend its interests and not shy from provocations, which is an obvious counter to US plans to contain the giant.

China evidences this new "global governance system" through a variety of means to seek a higher profile in global institutions and to establish new ones that serve its ambitions. For example, China launched the Asian Infrastructure Investment Bank (AIIB) in January 2016 as a multilateral development bank to promote infrastructure building in Asia. Of course, the AIIB advances China's global trade and investment footprint throughout the world via major infrastructure projects not only in Asia, but also in Africa, Latin America, the Middle East, and parts of Europe. These global investments are known as Beijing's "One Belt, One Road" initiative that loudly indicates China's intentions to use economic means to enhance its global role and advance its foreign policy and strategic goals.

Beijing is also especially assertive in advancing its sovereignty and territorial claims, such as the 2014 claim of sovereignty over the vast South China Sea, which includes established international maritime shipping lanes. China employs coercive tactics such as maritime militia to enforce its claims and advance its interests short of provoking armed conflict.

Notably, Beijing militarized Scarborough Shoal, a cluster of rocks and reefs, more than a hundred miles west of Manila, Philippines. That country's president, Benigno S. Aquino III, said America must fight China over the militarization of the South China Sea. He claims that America will lose "its moral ascendancy, and also the confidence of one of its allies" if it refuses to confront China.[6]

Both Beijing and Manila claim the Scarborough Shoal, which happens to rest in the middle of international sea lanes and atop yet-to-be-tapped oil reserves, as a precious resource for an energy-hungry country like China. Remember that in June 2012, the Scarborough Shoal saw the confrontation of Chinese ships and Filipino fishing boats. The Filipinos never returned after that confrontation, but Aquino called on the US to come to the rescue.

The US positively responded to the Filipino call for help by increasing its presence in the region, and tensions continue to mount to this day. Further, in 2016 the International Arbitration Tribunal in The Hague, Netherlands, ruled in favor of Manila's claim over the Scarborough Shoal, but the judgment was to no effect because it was ignored by the powers in Beijing.

Now China is converting the South China Sea Spratly Island chain—which includes Fiery Cross, Mischief, and Subi reefs—into artificial islands with military-capable docks, barracks, radar, sensors, and airfields to reinforce its territorial claims to the region. Mischief Reef warrants special attention, because Beijing deployed electronic warfare (EW) equipment to prepared positions in early 2018, consisting of thirteen concrete pads located along an airfield. That gear can be used to harass and jam foreign electronic equipment, most likely passing American aircraft and ships. It also is an important tool to position China for continued territorial claims in the region.[7]

The converted reefs are also home for a significant communications suite. To the southeast of Mischief Reef, China constructed a high-frequency, direction-finding antenna array installation used to collect electronic or signals intelligence from passing aircraft and ships. North of Mischief Reef, there is an inter-island communication tower associated with other antenna array on four other reefs. Finally, there is a Doppler, very-high-frequency omnidirectional range (DVOR) radio system adjacent to the Mischief airfield, a system designed to provide navigation information for aircraft without using satellite navigation data.[8]

Beijing's expansion into the region is rapidly worsening. On May 2, 2018, CNBC reported that China increased its threat by deploying anti-ship cruise missiles and surface-to-air missile systems to some of the Spratly reefs. This is the first deployment of missiles to the chain and bolsters China's increased focus on improving its presence and infrastructure.[9] Further, it is evidence that China crossed "an important threshold. Missile platforms present a clear offensive threat," said Gregory Poling, a fellow at the Washington, DC-based Center for Strategic and International Studies. "[The missile deployment] is a pretty clear threat to the other claimants and furthers China's goal of establishing complete control over the water and airspace of the South China Sea," added Poling.[10]

This escalation is just the beginning, according to Collin Koh, a fellow at the Maritime Security Programme at Singapore's S. Rajaratnam School of International Studies. Mr. Koh expects to see future rotational deployment of high-powered assets like fighter jets and bombers at the artificial islands' air bases, such as the H-6K long-range bombers observed practicing against marine targets and then landing on the islets in May 2018. In response to such escalation, US Pacific commander Admiral Philip Davidson testified that his command needs to invest in increased resiliency in its forward-deployed force posture in order to ensure regional security in the South China Sea. Then he said, "U.S. operations in the South China Sea—to include freedom of navigation operations—must remain regular and routine."[11]

Over the past couple of years, US warships and aircraft passing these Chinese outposts were repeatedly and increasingly harassed by Chinese warships and jet fighters. Then, in 2017, Vietnam joined the South China Sea quarrel, and it, like the Philippines, started calling for American help.

Why doesn't Vietnam call on its Russian "friends" rather than the United States to help with the quarrel? After all, Vietnam remains Russia's most trusted ally in Southeast Asia, a reflection of Putin's new policy called "Turn to the East," a foil to former President Obama's 2012 "Pivot to Asia." But Russian officials distance themselves from backing Vietnam's opposition to China's aggression in the South China Sea. A rare explanation of this geopolitical relationship comes from Russian Foreign Minister Sergey Lavrov, who in April 2016 said he hopes to see a solution to the South China Sea dispute without "any interference from third parties or any attempts to internationalize these disputes." He continued to explain that nonclaimants (read "the US") should "refrain from taking sides" and stop using the situation for their own "geopolitical unilateral advantage."[12]

Lavrov's comments are obviously aimed at the United States, which backs Vietnam's claim. Anton Tsvetov with the International Affairs Council, a think tank in Moscow, wrote that the timing of the booming Russia-China partnership could be taking a "toll on Russia's strong ties with Vietnam. This is something the Vietnamese have been concerned about for some time now." Tsvetov explained that Lavrov's comment about not helping Vietnam was to be expected, because Moscow has a policy of noninterference in other nations' affairs—that is, unless it fits President Putin's interests like in Ukraine, Georgia, and Syria.[13]

Eventually, China will have a heavily fortified group of artificial reefs (islets) to strongly contest any outside force in the South China Sea, and then Beijing will have accomplished its hegemonic aim of truly consuming more space and intimidating the entire neighborhood. No telling what area on the globe is next on Beijing's hegemonic game plan.

China has also demonstrated aggressive behavior in the East China Sea, using maritime law enforcement ships and aircraft to patrol near the Senkaku Islands to challenge Japan's claim. Both countries claim the continental shelves and the exclusive economic zone (EEZ) in the East China Sea, which contains natural gas and oil, although that energy source is very difficult to estimate and exploit.

Japan calls on China to observe the midpoint of the EEZ as the extent to which either country will conduct development of oil and natural gas fields. In fact, there was a principled consensus reached in 2008 that both sides would respect an equidistant median line in the East China Sea for resource development. Also, part of the ongoing tension between China and Japan is Tokyo's administration of the nearby Senkaku Islands.

Meanwhile, far away on China's southern border, the communist regime is locked in a land dispute with India over Arunachal Pradesh (a part of an Indian state claimed by China), which Beijing says is part of Tibet, and also over the Aksai Chin region. Both sides accuse the other of frequent incursions and military buildups in the disputed territories. A Border Defense Cooperation Agreement between the nations established procedures for managing the interaction along the Line of Actual Control, but violations are common.

China is bullying its way across Asia, which is an indicator of a new Cold War between the communist giant and her neighbors, many of whom have a growing relationship with the United States, which brings America into the tension-packed power struggle.

Indicator #2: Ideological

There are ideological indicators, but they are very different from the old Cold War and are not necessarily to America's advantage. Further, there are strong dissenting voices as to whether there are any ideological markers of a new dual Cold War.

Condoleezza Rice, former secretary of state under President George W. Bush, describes the old Cold War as "a challenge between two systems that had a view of how human history ought to unfold. They were mirror images of each other. This now is really more great-power politics, great-power rivalry, great-power conflict."[14]

Two other strong voices claim there is no ideological battle with China and Russia today. Dr. Stephen M. Walt, the Robert and Renee Belfer professor of international relations at Harvard University, argues in *Foreign Policy* that "there is no serious ideological rivalry at play today." He explains, at least regarding Russia, that there is no "ideological appeal outside its borders." Then he asserts, "Putinism has appeal only to a handful of oligarchs or would be autocrats."[15] Walt does not address China is his article, however.

Dr. Marek J. Chodakiewicz, the holder of the Kosciuszko Chair as professor of history with the Washington, DC-based Institute of World Politics, argues, "Russia is fully post-Communist, China remains Communist…[and] both powers resort to Marxist dialectics to exercise power. However, Russia no longer invokes Marxism as its guiding light. China does."[16]

Dr. Chodakiewicz does acknowledge the existence of an ideological conflict that disadvantages the West, especially the United States. He explained:

> As we indulge the liberal dictatorship of pleasure, cultural nihilism, and its attendant pathologies, the Russians and Chinese project themselves as champions of traditional Western values, including traditional family and sex (not gender) roles. They

also encourage others to appreciate the apparent normalcy and stability of their systems. They argue that what the U.S. calls democracy leads to chaos, disorder, and social pathology. Their systems are democratic, they assure us, but they are predicated on order and harmony. Those are guaranteed by strong [autocratic] leaders who are continuously re-elected by their grateful fellow citizens.[17]

I understand and respect these voices. However, I firmly believe there is an ideological conflict at play, especially when Moscow interferes with Western democratic elections, such as America's 2016 presidential contest. Granted, the ideological conflict isn't as clear perhaps as the communism-versus-Western democracy battleground of the old Cold War, but it is potentially just as destructive.

The contemporary evidence indicates Russia's President Putin, via his surrogates, attempted to damage the candidacy of former Secretary of State Hillary Clinton, tilting the election for Donald Trump. Why? Evidently, Mr. Putin reacted to Ms. Clinton's longstanding criticism of the Russian leader for suppressing free speech during that country's 2011–2013 protests. Then there is the matter of sanctions imposed by President Obama over Moscow's annexation of Crimea, another unacceptable affront to the Kremlin. Of course, Putin and his cronies deny any attempt to meddle in the American elections, but mounting evidence indicates that the Kremlin orchestrated the entire attack on Clinton without any collusion by the Trump campaign.

Why did the Kremlin really interfere in America's 2016 presidential election? Perhaps it wasn't as outlined above, that the Russians were angry with Clinton and Obama. Rather, Putin, like his Soviet predecessors, is focused on countering America's strategy to "contain" Russia's new adventurism represented by the Kremlin's growing range of military, geopolitical, and economic actions across the globe.

Evidence of Russia's new adventurism abounds. The Kremlin has resurrected old KGB (Komitet Gosudarstveennoy Bezopasnosti—the main security agency for the Soviet Union) tricks not just to manipulate the 2016 US presidential election, but also to influence both world and domestic audiences by confusing and demoralizing them, as well as by using a mixture of true and false information that fits the preexisting view of the intended audience.

The Kremlin set the stage for this manipulation by using tools it created in new law. Those legal changes increased government controls over technology and content, giving Moscow powers to block content, ban websites, monitor online activity, and limit media ownership. The US Defense Intelligence Agency suggests that Russia's ultimate goal regarding online activity is to create a "sovereign Internet," an effort to reduce foreign influence on the Russian media and the population in general.[18]

The Kremlin also pushed through legislation to restrict foreign ownership of Russian media, marginalize foreign non-government organizations (NGOs) supporting Russian media outlets, and force Russian media to account for any foreign support. There are numerous examples of the Kremlin expelling from Russian soil foreign NGOs it perceived as a national security threat, such as George Soros' Open Society Institute.[19]

The newest tool in Russia's information toolkit is cyber-enabled psychological operations harnessed to support both strategic and tactical information warfare objectives. Specifically, these techniques involve compromising computer networks for intelligence information that can be used to embarrass, discredit, or falsify information. Examples of this toolkit are "hacktivists," Russian intelligence services that co-opt or masquerade as other hacktivist groups to conduct cyber attacks such as those on Estonia in 2007 and the hack against the French station TV5 Monde in January 2015. Another group even hijacked the Twitter feed of the US Central Command.[20]

CyberBerkut is a front for Russian state-sponsored cyber activity in support of military operations and strategic objectives especially in Ukraine to demoralize, embarrass, and create distrust in officials. In March 2014, CyberBerkut was implicated in cyber espionage and attacks against NATO, Ukraine, and German government websites.

Another tool in Russia's cyber toolkit is the "troll," a paid online commentator who tries to manipulate or change a story to favor the Kremlin. Moscow's army of "trolls," known as the Internet Research Agency (IRA), is in fact state-funded and operates under the Kremlin's direction. Their goal is to counter negative media and Western influence in the media as well as promote false content, what President Trump calls "fake news."

In February 2018, special counsel Robert S. Mueller III won a grand jury's indictment of thirteen Russian "trolls" and three companies in a sweeping conspiracy to defraud the US and its political system using bogus social media posts and other "information warfare." The US indictment states the IRA, aka "troll factory," was funded by oligarch Yevgeny Prigozhin, who has close ties to President Putin and earned hundreds of millions of dollars in Russian defense contracts, some of which include mercenary operations in Syria.[21]

The "trolls" "came to the factory and thanks to their personal qualities and knowledge of English, they were rapidly promoted," said a former "troll factory" worker Lyudmila Savchuk to the *Associated Press*. "They saw it was simple, well-paid work.... What they wrote was not necessarily how they felt inside," she said. "It was business and nothing personal."[22]

Mikhail Burchik, one of those indicted by Mr. Mueller, was the executive director of the IRA and in charge of operational planning of US activities. Burchik scoffed at the indictments: "If several hundred million Americans are so worried about the activities of an ordinary Russian businessman involved in IT [information technology] and website development, then it seems that the country is facing a grave situation."[23]

It is not surprising that President Putin denies any official Russian involvement in the alleged 2016 presidential meddling. Putin told NBC News that he "could not care less" about indictments issued by Mueller because "they do not represent the interests of the Russian state" and are unrelated to the Kremlin.[24]

"Maybe they're not even Russians," said Putin. "Maybe they're

Ukrainians, Tatars, Jews, just with Russian citizenship, even that needs to be checked."

The cyber-related allegations against Russia grew in mid-March 2018 when the US Treasury issued new sanctions against Russia entities and individuals in response to "ongoing nefarious attacks." Specifically, Russian intelligence services such as the Federal Security Service and the Main Intelligence Directorate were named in the sanctions. The Russians are charged with using cyber tools to target US officials, "including cyber security, diplomatic, military, and White House personnel." Meanwhile, the US Department of Homeland Security announced that nearly one year ago (2017), Russian hackers began targeting American commercial facilities, affecting its nuclear, aviation, water, construction, and manufacturing sectors.[25]

Moscow not only hacks many American cyber networks, but it also manipulates information through the use of "bots," a software application that pushes content on social media. "Bots" can continuously push content in real-life patterns and can drown out unwanted content—anti-regime messages. For example, the Russian regime targeted America's democratic process using "bots" by exploiting and exacerbating America's internal divisions by skillfully using information warfare via the tools of social media such as Facebook. Specifically, Moscow inflamed America's hyper partisanship by pumping fake news through social media outlets to feed American political tribalism—an old, Soviet-era propaganda ploy intended to divide America. Expect Russia to continue such cyber war-making that could lead to very serious confrontations.

Moscow also employs what it calls "information confrontation," or IPb (*informatsionnoye protivoborstvo*), a term for conflict in the information domain, which includes diplomatic, economic, and political, cultural, social, and religious areas. IPb helps shape perceptions and manipulate the behavior of target audiences.

The major difference between Russia and China in this troll-bot-IPb information realm is that the Chinese retain communism as their governing ideology, albeit with nuances to fuel its economy. President

Xi Jinping is a nationalist who set China on a course of bullying its neighbors and confronting America. Xi wields great power because he holds China's top three positions: head of the ruling Communist Party of China; head of state; and, as a chairman of the Central Military Commission, he is China's commander in chief.

President Xi's vision for China is known as "The Chinese Dream," a plan to rejuvenate the nation. His four-part plan includes a Strong China (economically, politically, diplomatically, scientifically, and militarily); a Civilized China (equity and fairness, rich culture, high morals); a Harmonious China (amity among social classes); and a Beautiful China (healthy environment, low pollution).[26]

Mr. Xi intends to see that China is a fully developed nation by 2049, the one hundredth anniversary of the People's Republic. He wants to double the GDP per capita by 2020 and complete urbanization by 2030. However, to accomplish the above, he needs to modernize China by becoming a world leader in science and technology as well as economics and business.

A major challenge for Xi in realizing "The Chinese Dream" is to assert strength and assure control. That's critical to enable reform, which explains his efforts to appeal to nationalistic aspirations by accusing reformers of caving in to Western pressures and inoculate the Chinese against being labeled "pro-Western." Of course, Xi must legitimize one-party rule to perpetuate his governance—a daunting task. He argues that one-party rule (an old communist ploy) is necessary to improve the standard of living, keep the country stable and harmonious, and at the same time rejuvenate the nation.

"Xi does have every intention on restoring China's past glory and very much wants China to excel in every field from economics, military, and academics [The Chinese Dream]," said Dr. Christopher Lew, a Chinese scholar, president of Water Dragons Consulting, a US Army Reserve Major and a senior China Policy Analyst at Science Applications International Corporation, McLean, Virginia. There is an ideological element to contemporary China as well, according to Lew, which "clearly does represent a different system (although not as radical as the contrast between Soviet socialism and Western democratic capitalism) and it hopes to encourage global emulation of that system, but at the same time, it does not necessarily envision completely dismantling the Western system at this time." However, Dr. Lew believes there will come "a time where China has no need for the Western system and will no longer seek to even pay lip service to playing by its rules."[27]

China scholar and author Dr. Steven W. Mosher believes China is very much engaged in an ideological contest with the United States and seeks world dominance, thus, as Dr. Lew said, it no longer "pay[s] lip service to playing by its [Western] rules."

"Xi Jinping's 'The Chinese Dream' is a world under Chinese hegemony, while his propaganda apparatus relentlessly stokes national narcissism to create a sense of cultural, economic, and even territorial entitlement among the population," Mosher asserts. "The Chinese are taught that only America still stands in the way of the achievement of the 'China dream', a claim that the Chinese party-state uses to justify 'unrestricted warfare' against the reigning hegemon, the United States. China is determined to bring this conflict to a successful conclusion and usher in the World of Great Harmony," explains Mosher.[28]

Mr. Xi is essentially pushing a personality cult to try to match the highly popular nationalist Putin in Russia. Both men believe authoritarianism under their popular stewardship is best for their respective countries. That's why they use the powers of the central government to control access to the Internet, especially the content.

Time will tell whether President Xi and his ideology of Chinese nationalism under one-party, communist rule is enough to maintain control over a growing and somewhat disenfranchised population. After all, communist governments historically make big promises, but when reality strikes, the people resist, and then the regime's true nature is exposed, such as in the 1989 bloody protests in Tiananmen Square, an event that is sometimes called the '89 Democracy Movement.

Whether in Moscow or Beijing, the prevailing ideology is authoritarianism, a tradition well known in both countries. Russian authoritarians, whether old Soviets or new populists like Putin, historically clamp down on free speech and use the tools of the state to target both domestic and overseas calls for democratic reform. Beijing is still a relatively closed society, where one-party rule maintains a tight grip on communications with the outside world. Both countries continue to espouse an ideology radically different than the openness evidenced in the United States, and that's another indicator of the new dual Cold War. But there is more, something true and troubling.

Mitigating against the US and the West ideologically is our bankrupt culture. It is a weapon used against us by China and Russia, as Dr. Chodakiewicz explains. Specifically, Chodakiewicz said:

> Some of us defend tradition and stick with the [American] Founding Fathers; others would like to build an egalitarian paradise on Earth premised on post-modernism, deconstruction, and Marxism-Lesbianism. Human rights for us are no longer the sanctity of life and freedom, but pedophilia and other joys of the sexual revolution, including radical individualism. That schizoid character of America leaves us vulnerable. Further, it makes most humanity disgusted at us and our practices as projected by Hollywood and Madison Avenue. Our enemies, including China and Russia, exploit this.[29]

Today's ideological battle is very different but just as divisive and serious for the West in the new Cold War.

Indicator #3: Russian and Chinese Espionage against America

Our top cyber warrior, US Army General Keith Alexander, said, "The loss of industrial information and intellectual property through cyber espionage constitutes the 'greatest transfer of wealth in history.'" What's at stake? The Department of Commerce values our intellectual property (IP) at $5.06 trillion, or 34.8 percent of the US GDP in 2010, and accounts for over forty million American jobs and over 60 percent of United States exports.[30] Obviously, America has a lot at stake.

The loss of our IP through economic espionage is a matter of national security, to the tune of $300 billion per year and 2.1 million jobs, according to the Commission on the Theft of American Intellectual Property. Russia and China are the leading cyber thieves draining America of our competitive advantage and market share. They are literally robbing us of our future. For example, "American oil and gas firms are frequently targeted and subject to theft of trade secrets, business plans, exploration bids and geological data."[31]

The US worked with the Chinese to address the IP theft problem, to limited avail. In September 2015, Beijing agreed with the US to refrain from cyber-economic espionage, but evidence of that promised restraint is hard to find. Reuters reported on that agreement, stating that "neither government would knowingly support cyber theft of corporate secrets or business information. But the agreement stopped short of any promise to refrain from traditional government-to-government cyber spying for intelligence purposes."[32]

Consider the extent of Chinese spying operations against the United States.

Beijing has a worldwide network of clandestine forces—spies. Beijing's spy networks in the US include up to twenty-five thousand Chinese intelligence officers and more than fifteen thousand recruited agents, according to a Chinese dissident with close ties to Beijing's intelligence establishment.[33]

Guo Wengui, a billionaire businessman who severed relations with Red China in early 2017, said he had close ties to the Ministry of State Security (MSS), the civilian intelligence service, and the country's military spy service. "I know the Chinese spy system very, very well," Guo claimed. "I have information about very minute details about how it operates."[34]

Guo claims to have learned the intricacies of Chinese spying from Ma Jian, a former MSS vice minister who ran China's counterintelligence operations against foreign targets—that is, until Ma was imprisoned.[35]

Gua also knew Ji Shengde, the former People's Liberation Army (PLA) military intelligence chief who was implicated in the 1990s scandal involving Chinese funding of Bill Clinton's presidential re-election campaign. China gave Ji a suspended death sentence in 2000 on charges of bribery and illegal fundraising.[36]

China's spying radically increased after the 2012 Communist Party Congress brought the current leader, Xi Jinping, to power. Guo explained that "before 2012, cumulatively China had around 10,000 to 20,000 agents working in the United States…working in a defensive mode [learning about the U.S.]." President Xi put the spy network on the offensive, according to Guo, who said, "I mean [the spy network was] to be ready to destroy the U.S. in ways they can."[37]

China poured a lot of money into that spy network. In 2012, Beijing's intelligence-gathering efforts cost around $600 million annually, but after Xi's surge of offensive spying, the budget accelerated to almost $4 billion annually. Remember, espionage, infiltration, and influence-peddling may be different, but they are all part of Beijing's comprehensive effort to build national power, according to Robert Daly, a former Beijing-based diplomat and director of the Kissinger Institute on China.[38]

A spring 2018 report demonstrates just how pervasive and centrally controlled are Beijing's spying activities. Specifically, the Communist Party of China (CCP) authorized an aggressive program to steal American science and technology information, according to a leaked Party directive obtained by the *Washington Free Beacon*. The directive, which is authorized by the CCP's Central Committee and dated in 2016, ordered the campaign to be carried out by an intelligence unit called the United Front Work Department and states in part that it is a: "working plan on strengthening the intensity of United Front Work in the area of science and technology of the United States in 2017." The document continues: "The United Front Work targeted on the areas of science and technology of the United States is an important measure of our party to deeply divide western hostile forces, to maintain social stability, to ensure national security, to comprehensively advance the rapid development of our own science and technology and economy, to accelerate the construction of national defense modernization, and to consolidate the overseas united front."[39]

Chinese spying even reaches into our higher education establishment. FBI Director Christopher Wray testified before the Senate Intelligence Committee in February 2018 that the Bureau is investigating many Confucius Institutes, the Chinese-funded language and cultural centers located on more than one hundred American universities. The US intelligence community warns that these institutes are potential spy tools and thirteen of them are located on universities that host top-secret Pentagon research, such as Arizona State, Auburn, and Stanford. Wray warned that "naiveté" in the academy aggravates the risks, and he asserts that the Chinese exploit "the very open research and development environment that we have" on college campuses.[40]

Top US intelligence officials also warn that Chinese-made cell phones and other devices present an unacceptable security risk, especially among military personnel. In May 2018, *Military Times* reported that US military exchange stores removed Chinese-made cell phones, personal mobile Internet modems, and other electronic products manufactured by the giant, state-subsidized electronics firms Hauwei and ZTE out of an abundance of concern about the security risk those devices pose.

"Huawei and ZTE devices may pose an unacceptable risk to the Department's personnel, information and mission," a Pentagon spokesman said. "In light of this information, it was not prudent for the Department's exchanges to continue selling them to DoD personnel." The decision to remove the devices from military store shelves was prompted by congressional testimony from government intelligence and security officials who refused to support the private use of the Chinese-made devices by private American citizens. Not surprisingly, Huawei officials told the *Military Times*: "We remain committed to openness and transparency in everything we do and want to be clear that no government [read "Beijing"] has ever asked us to compromise the security or integrity of any of our networks or devices."[41] In spite of made-in-China fake assurances, Beijing's espionage activities in the US are especially critical to the regime's military modernization. China uses a variety of methods to acquire high-technology foreign military and dual-use technologies, including human spies on campuses or within industry, and cyber and exploitation by Chinese nationals who act as procurement agents or intermediaries. For example, in August 2016, the US sentenced a naturalized citizen to prison for conspiring with a Chinese national to violate the Arms Export Control Act. That compromised citizen attempted to acquire and then export jet engines used in the F-35 and F-22 and the MQ-9 unmanned aerial vehicle. The Chinese national admitted to working on behalf of the Chinese military.[42]

Russia is just as aggressive as the Chinese at seeking American IP and other exploitable national security information. Russian cyber warriors soak up American secrets, hurting our competitiveness, and, much like the Chinese, their agents are in America mapping our infrastructure should war become necessary.

Evidently, for the past decade, American counterintelligence agents were asleep while Russian agents significantly ramped up operations against the United States. An American intelligence official told *Politico*, "We've definitely been ignoring Russia for the last 15 years." We've paid a heavy price for being unobservant and sloppy.[43]

An old Cold War tactic was for the Soviets to sit off of America's shores and monitor our military operations. That's happening once again. In March 2018, the US Navy reported a Russian spy ship conducting surveillance operations near an American ballistic missile submarine base in Georgia. "We are tracking the Viktor Leonov's presence off the East Coast, much like we are aware of all vessels approaching the United States," said Navy Commander Bill Speaks, a Navy spokesman.[44]

The Leonov is known for conducting annual forays near sensitive military facilities off the East Coast, such as near Naval Submarine Base

Kings Bay, home to US nuclear missile submarines. Kings Bay is the location of Submarine Group 10 that includes six nuclear-armed, ballistic-missile submarines and two guided-missile submarines. It is also the location of Strategic Weapons Facility, Atlantic, the facility for maintaining nuclear warheads for submarine-launched ballistic missiles.[45]

The Leonov reportedly is equipped with magnetic anomaly sensors, acoustic gear to profile American vessels, and a capability to map the ocean's floor and look for uncharted cables that reach across the ocean.[46]

Another old Cold War Russian trick is cloak-and-dagger spying to include the assassination of enemy personnel and renegade spies. It appears, at least if the British prime minister is to be believed, that Russia was behind the nerve-agent poisoning of a former Russian spy and his daughter in Salisbury, England, on March 4, 2018.[47]

Prime Minister Theresa May told Parliament that it was "highly likely" that Russia was responsible for the attack, which employed a military-grade nerve agent known as Novichok. May said: "Either this was a direct action by the Russian state against our country, or the Russian government lost control of its potentially catastrophically damaging nerve agent and allowed it to get into the hands of others."[48]

"This attempted murder using a weapons-grade nerve agent in a British town was not just a crime against the Skripals [the last name of the former spy and his daughter]," May said. "It was an indiscriminate and reckless act against the United Kingdom, putting the lives of innocent civilians at risk." Further, the prime minister pointed the finger at Moscow based on "Russia's record of conducting state-sponsored assassinations and our assessment that Russia views some defectors as legitimate targets for assassinations."[49]

Nikki Haley, the US ambassador to the UN, agreed that the Russians are responsible for the attempted assassination of a former Russian double agent and his daughter in Britain. "The United States believes that Russia is responsible for the attack on two people in the United Kingdom using a military-grade nerve agent," Haley told the UN's Security Council.[50]

US Army General Curits Scaparrotti, the commander of the US European Command, agrees with Haley. "I think it underscores what they're [the Russians] willing to do. To attempt an assassination on the soil of a sovereign country, I think, it should be very clear to us what they're willing to do in order to further whatever their objective was here," explained Scaparrotti. "And I'll remind you there have been several assassinations in Ukraine, as well."[51]

"This is a government that is violating all the standard norms and international rules and laws, to bring violence onto other nation's soil in order to reach their objectives," Scaparrotti continued. "Amazing, frankly."[52]

Predictably, a Russian foreign ministry spokeswoman denied the existence of the nerve agent Novichok and alleged that the West is trying to "distract attention from what they did in Syria and Iraq" and Britain "needs to somehow show the world that Russia is not in fact a peacekeeper but is playing its own game." Moscow will likely continue such activities as new dual Cold War tensions grow.[53]

China and Russia are waging a war on America, stealing us blind and dusting off old cloak-and-dagger techniques such as assassination. These actions are very important indicators of a new dual Cold War.

Indicator #4: China and Russia Abuse of Trade and Economic Instruments

Russia and China are very different trade and economic Cold War adversaries. Russia is much less complicated than China because the United States and Russia have little trade ($20 billion annually)—and besides, Russia's economy is very narrow, mostly dependent on revenue from energy exports and hampered by an inefficient and corrupt management of industry. That explains why the Kremlin has few economic options when dealing with geopolitical challenges, which may explain more rapprochements with the West.

The past three US administrations patiently tried to develop stronger economic ties with Russia, hoping it would improve diplomatic relations. But the Clinton, Bush, and Obama administrations all found that trade as an engine for improving relations with Russia doesn't work. We are not natural trading partners; in fact, we tend to be trade adversaries.

The United States tried to introduce Russia to the world's marketplace by helping its accession to the World Trade Organization (WTO), but then, after observing Moscow's ongoing misbehavior, Congress passed the Magnitsky Act in 2012 that empowered the American government to clamp down on Russia by withholding visas and freezing assets of Russians thought to have been involved with human-rights violations. The Magnitsky Act was also used to sanction Moscow because of its role in the Ukrainian and Syrian crises.[54]

Russia has demonstrated economic misbehavior by using its vast energy supplies to leverage mostly European political decisions. For years, President Putin declared Russia an energy superpower, and Europeans focused on the threat of Moscow's "energy weapon"—the prospect that the Kremlin would turn off the gas, forcing it to fall in line with Moscow on diplomatic and security issues. However, Russia's energy leverage has fallen off in recent years and is likely to decline further over the coming decade.[55]

Moscow's energy influence is declining in its effectiveness as a political tool for three reasons. First, Europeans are finding alternative sources of energy. For example, Lithuania, which was once totally dependent on Russia for gas supplies, now imports most of its gas from Norway and the United States. Second, there is a global energy supply glut that has driven down prices. That surplus is thanks to China's slowed consumption, American fracking, and increased production in places like Iran, which results in flooded energy markets. Finally, European Union (EU) regulation impacts Russia's "energy weapon" utility. The European Commission pushes the Russians to change their pricing mechanism to increase transparency and decrease prices.[56]

Just as Moscow loses the effect of its "energy weapon," the West (the US and the EU) are applying considerable economic leverage to wring out Russian misbehavior by imposing sanctions for annexing Crimea in 2014. The steady drip of more and more Western sanctions is slowly and surely plunging the Russian economy back into recession.

So, as the West imposes ever more sanctions, Moscow frantically searches for meaningful retaliation. For example, in 2017, when the Trump administration imposed new economic sanctions, Russian Deputy Foreign Minister Sergei Ryabkov promised a response that he surmised would take the erstwhile Cold War foes into "uncharted waters."[57]

Alexey Pushkov, head of the international affairs committee in Russia's parliament, called the mounting Western sanctions "a new stage of confrontation," a clear indication of the new Cold War.

China is a very different trade partner; in fact, it is America's largest—to the tune of $663 billion in 2017, with half of that being a trade deficit that favors Beijing. Currently, Beijing boasts the world's second-largest economy, but in recent years, its growth is slowing due to high debt and accelerating capital flight. In spite of these current challenges, Beijing's economy is expected to overtake the US as the world's largest by 2030-2035, and its global trade is already on top.

Understandably, the US views the trade relationship with China as a national security matter. In December 2017, President Trump wrote in his National Security Strategy (NSS) that China is a strategic competitor, and when it comes to trade, the US "will no longer turn a blind eye to violations, cheating or economic aggression." In fact, the NSS goes on to assert that China does not qualify as a "market economy," according to World Trade Organization (WTO) rules.[58]

The EU agrees with Trump regarding China's WTO position. Both insist the Chinese state's role in its economy remains too large to justify granting it WTO market economy treatment, which could make it subject to higher anti-dumping duties under US trade law.

Meanwhile, China is experiencing slow economic growth as local Chinese governments assume significant debt, which potentially sets up the country for a crash, especially as investors lose confidence in the Chinese currency. There are also warning signs that investors are finding ways to relocate funds outside China—bad news for a struggling economy.[59]

These economic warnings prompted the Beijing government to pursue protectionist policies that discriminate against American businesses. For example, American and other nationality firms that want to do business in China are now pressured to transfer proprietary technology (trade secrets, intellectual property) to Chinese firms as a condition of doing business. As if this isn't enough, the communist regime also targets foreign firms with competition regulations, giving domestic competitors an unfair advantage. These and other practices explain why American corporations feel that China's economic playing field is unfair.

Let's put these "pay-to-play" Chinese requirements into proper perspective. No communist country has ever achieved economic greatness. The propensity of authoritarian communist leaders like President Xi to centrally control everything is the enemy, not the engine, of a great economy. Such behavior stifles creativity and innovation over time, and it becomes inflexible.

But there is one economic area where the system has not totally fallen prey to this communism curse: the military, especially in Russia. Even as the Russian economy deteriorated, Russia was still turning out high-quality military equipment, sometimes better than American. The Russian military production centers paid their workers higher wages, recruited the best and brightest engineers and scientists, and gave them better working and home conditions—even when the economy was at its worst.

The contemporary Chinese military production model is similar to Russia's system, and there is no doubt that China's military hardware quality is highly competitive, not to mention large in numbers. Yet, President Xi, on the other hand, so far seems to be the exception. But his success to date is heavily dependent on cyber warfare, outright theft, and espionage. If America remains lax, Xi could be even more successful.

Juxtapose China's economic challenges and policies with President

Trump's campaign promise to fix the trade imbalance and unfair trade practices with countries like China that rob American jobs by erecting new trade barriers such as limits on Chinese investment in the US or raising tariffs unilaterally. Further, as indicated above, Beijing takes advantage of American businesses by stealing their intellectual property. There are also particular concerns expressed by the US Commerce Department about the national security impact of rising imports of Chinese steel and aluminum.

"There needs to be a fundamental, systemic change and a real commitment to market opening by China," said a Trump administration official to the *Washington Post*. "We want China to stop stealing our stuff, live up to its commitment, and don't distort the international trading system."[60]

President Trump started to take measures to counter China's distorted trade practices by imposing tariffs. In March 2018, President Trump added a 25 percent tax on foreign steel and 10 percent on foreign aluminum in the name of national security. Specifically, the US imports 90 percent of its steel, and China, leading up to the president's decision on new tariffs, was the major problem, because it flooded international markets with cheap steel and aluminum, trying to destroy American steel and aluminum industries.[61]

This is truly a national security issue, because America has become over-reliant on foreign steel and aluminum. America's single-largest need for steel is for ships and submarines. Each submarine needs ten thousand tons of steel, and an aircraft carrier requires sixty thousand tons. Also, steel and aluminum go into all other weapons platforms, including attack helicopters, F-35 jets, jet engines, tanks, and a long list of other weapons and support equipment.[62]

China hasn't voluntarily curbed its production, however. Leo W. Gerard, president of the United Steel, Paper and Forestry, Rubber, Manufacturing, Energy, Allied Industrial and Services Workers International Union, told the House Commerce Committee that China, despite claims of curbing overcapacity, increased steel production by thirty-six million tons in 2016 to one billion tons.[63] Unfortunately, China controls other important products as well, such as microchips (integrated circuits) that, should Beijing limit their sale, could threaten America's security.

Beijing controls much of the globe's microchip market, which means the US "can't build a military aircraft without Chinese chips," according to David Goldman, a columnist for *Asia Times* and who served as a consultant for the US National Security Council and the Department of Defense. "China's share of high tech exports has risen from about five percent in 1999 to about 25 percent at present, while America's has plummeted from about 20 percent to about seven percent," Goldman said.[64]

Such trade disparities prompted Trump negotiators, who met with Chinese trade officials in early May 2018, led by US Treasury Secretary Steven Mnuchin, to issue a lengthy list of demands, a recognition of China's threat to the American economy. Specifically, the Trump administration pursues six key economic themes with Beijing: reduce the trade balance, protect American intellectual property and technology theft, seek lower tariffs and non-tariff barriers, impose Chinese investment restrictions, and recognize that China is a non-market economy. Although China wants to avoid a trade war with the US, Beijing is likely to hold tough and make difficult decisions as well as drag out negotiations.

"The economic fight of the century has now begun," according to Stratfor, a Texas-based geopolitical and intelligence organization. Stratfor soberly warns: "The underlying economic competition between the United States and China…is here to stay. The current trade dispute is just the first round of an economic fight that will last years, if not decades, as the two economic powers lurch forward on their long term collision course."[65] Both China and Russia are waging economic war with the US and the West. This is another indicator of a new dual Cold War.

Indicator #5: Increased Defense Budgets

Military budgets typically rise with escalating tensions, and that's evident among the new dual Cold War adversaries and their neighbors.

On March 5, 2018, China unveiled its largest rise in defense spending in three years, setting a target of 8.1 percent growth for this year, or approximately $175 billion. China will "advance all aspects of military training and war preparedness, and firmly and resolvedly safeguard national sovereignty, security, and development interests," Chinese Premier Li Kequiang told the opening session of the parliament.[66]

China's true defense spending is much larger, because "some spending will be hidden in civilian spending," said one diplomat, who spoke on the condition of anonymity to *Reuters*.

"The pace and scale of this build-up are really dramatic. It is extremely alarming for Australia and many other countries in the region," said Sam Roggeveen, a visiting fellow at the Strategic and Defence Studies Centre of the Australian National University in Canberra.[67]

It is difficult to know exactly how much Beijing spends on its military because the regime is not transparent. Further, China's published defense budget omits important categories of expenditure, such as research and development and procurement. Further, Jane's Defence Budgets anticipate China's defense budget to increase at an annual average rate of 7 percent, growing to $260 billion by 2020. In comparison, the US defense budget outlays for 2018 will reach $700 billion in current dollars, a significant disparity, which, given the high cost of American manpower compared to China, distorts any meaningful comparison.[68]

US Army Chief of Staff General Mark Milley put the US-versus-China defense budget comparison into perspective in his May 2018 testimony before the Senate Appropriations Subcommittee on Defense. "I've seen comparative numbers of U.S. defense budget versus China, U.S. defense budget versus Russia or any other number of countries," Milley said. "What is not often commented on is the cost of labor." He continued, "The cost of Russian soldiers and Chinese soldiers is a tiny fraction. So we would have to normalize the data in order to compare apples to apples and oranges to oranges… I think you'll find that Chinese and Russian investments, modernization, new weapons systems, etc., their R & D—which is all government-owned and also is much cheaper—I think you'd find a much closer comparison." In fact, based on *Breaking Defense*, the Chinese defense budget minus personnel has more spending power than does the Pentagon's budget.[69]

Russian defense spending has also grown over the last decade as well. It spent 4.5 percent of its GDP on defense, which in 2016 was $61 billion. That's quite an increase, considering that in 2006, Moscow spent $27 billion, or 2.4 percent, of its GDP on defense.

Moscow's plan, the Strategic Armament Program (SAP), indicates a sustained effort to rearm. SAP calls for spending $285 billion to modernize military forces through 2020. However, it is not clear how Moscow can reach that stretch goal, given its military spending decrease in 2017, dropping an estimated 20 percent to $66.3 billion, according to a Stockholm International Peace Research Institute (SIPRI) report. That decrease results in an estimated 4.3 percent of the GDP, down from 5.5 percent in 2016.[70]

Years of recession forced Moscow to make significant defense cuts in 2017, which will inevitably impact operations and new procurement. Of course, the decline could be reversed subject to the price of energy, the key Russian export, and other economic decisions under consideration, as well as more belt-tightening by Kremlin leaders.

The real story about defense spending as an indicator of a new Cold War requires that we look beyond the immediate players—the US, China, and Russia. Nations across the world arm up when they sense an increased threat, and that's what is happening.

Total world military expenditure rose to $1,686 billion in 2016, an increase of 0.4 percent in real terms from 2015, according to SIPRI. Defense spending grew in North America, Central and Eastern Europe,

Asia, Oceania, and North Africa. It fell in Central America, the Caribbean, the Middle East, South America, and sub-Saharan Africa.[71]

We need to watch certain nations close to expected flashpoints for indications of a perceived growing threat. For example, the Japanese have steadily increased their defense spending on antiballistic missile systems to defend against North Korea's threat and the rising Chinese threat. Further, in early 2018, Japanese defense minister Itsuanori Onodera expressed concern about the threat posed by China.[72]

"We would like to develop (the system) into a basic infrastructure that will be helpful in comprehensive missile defense and can (intercept) cruise and other kinds of missiles," Onodera said while visiting a missile facility on the Japanese island of Kauai. Japan already announced its intention to purchase the American-made Aegis Ashore, the land-based version of America's anti-missile defense system.

Russia is on the mind of Central European leaders. Overall defense spending in Central Europe grew 2.4 percent between 2015 and 2016. "The growth in spending by many countries in Central Europe can be partly attributed to the perception of Russia posing a greater threat," said Siemon Wezeman, a SIPRI researcher.[73]

Even tiny Denmark is substantially increasing its defense spending to help counter Russia's military activity. "Russia's behavior has created an unpredictable and unstable security environment in the Baltic Sea region," Denmark's Prime Minister Lars Lokke Rasmussen said in January 2018. "When I received (Vladimir) Putin in Copenhagen during my first term as prime minister back in 2010, everybody thought that it would be the beginning of a new and much better and much more friendly cooperation between Europe and Russia. And that we could decrease our military spending," Rasmussen said. "But given the Russian aggression and what happened in Crimea, I think we simply have to be realistic about things and invest more in our security."[74]

The adage "money talks" is especially important in the security arena. The growing investment in arms strongly suggests the emergence of a new dual Cold War.

Indicator #6: The Building of Large, Sophisticated Militaries

China is experiencing a significant military modernization to enhance the People's Liberation Army's (PLA) ability to conduct sophisticated operations: fight short-duration, high-intensity regional conflicts at significant distance from the homeland. Meanwhile, the PLA is undergoing a radical reformation that establishes new structures similar to that found in the United States armed forces: a joint staff department, an overseas operations office, a joint logistics support force and five regionally-based joint theaters very similar conceptually to the United States' geographical combatant commands.[75]

Beijing's modernization campaign targets capabilities aimed directly at countering core US military-technological advantages such as anti-access/area denial systems intended to dissuade, deter, and defeat interventions during theater campaigns such as China's much-anticipated future invasion of Taiwan. Further, these platforms can attack, at long ranges, an adversary that operates in the western Pacific area—read "United States' aircraft carriers."

China is also building a worldwide-capable expeditionary force, which is quickly becoming a near peer with the US armed forces, capable of extensive global air-land-sea-space-cyber (five-domain) operations. For example, China is building a blue-water navy as large or larger than the US Navy in total vessels that added its first aircraft carrier in 2012, its second in 2018, and China started building its third in 2017 at a Shanghai shipyard and anticipates having four operational carriers by 2030. The early carriers use a Soviet-designed ski-jump system to launch aircraft, while the newer carriers will employ catapult systems like that used by the United States Navy.[76]

It is evident that China seeks a global naval force with operations in what Beijing calls the "far seas." That explains the push for aircraft carriers capable of extending air defense umbrellas beyond the range of coastal systems and to project power by protecting important sea lanes from terrorism, piracy, and foreign interdiction such as the United

States. Of course, the world is watching to see how Beijing defines "far seas," as it is expected in time to launch carrier battle groups to places not previously visited.

These developments seriously worry the Pentagon and justifiably so.

A 2018 report from the respected US-China Economic and Security Review Commission concludes the US is falling behind China in the development of advanced weapons and will have to hurry to avoid being overtaken. "The United States has a small window, only a decade at most, to develop new capabilities and concepts for countering China's advanced weapons programs," the report said.[77] Russia is making serious military advances as well.

The Russian Federation is modernizing its military strategy, doctrine, and tactics to include new operations using asymmetric weapons platforms to complement its growing and sophisticated conventional force. That force enables Moscow to project power outside Russia's borders using new, conventional, precision-strike weapons, such as the cruise missiles tested in combat in Syria.

Russia is aggressively building anti-access/area-denial platforms for the same reason as are the Chinese. Those weapons are intended to repel or defend against a Western aerospace attack against Russia using its conventional, nonstrategic nuclear forces.

This major transformation, known as "New Look," emphasizes Moscow's power projection, modern platforms with high-technology weapons, and a focus on readiness checked by no-notice "snap" exercises that include mobilization and deployments. Why?[78] The Kremlin views military power as critical to achieve strategic objectives and global influence, and especially contest US/NATO military superiority in a regional conflict. But it also seeks an out-of-area power projection capability, which explains prioritizing strategic forces, space, precision-guided munitions, and aerospace defense capabilities.

Moscow's expeditionary platforms are especially impressive. Its strategic nuclear triad remains the backbone of the force, but reliance on conventional strategic forces is growing. Russia's long-range aviation includes bombers for operations in the Pacific, the Arctic, and missions as far away as 6,250 miles. The US military reports an increased presence of long-range Russian bombers off Alaska in recent years.

Russian naval forces are now conducting routine operations in the most likely to be contested oceans: Mediterranean, Arctic, and Indian Ocean, and of course the Atlantic and Pacific oceans. Moscow's recapitalization program puts special emphasis on general-purpose submarines and surface combatants to enable continued out-of-area operations. Noteworthy is Russia's focus on enhancing its C4ISR (Command, Control, Communications, Computers, Intelligence, Surveillance and Reconnaissance) capabilities, which improve global targeting using its constellation of space satellites.

Finally, the Kremlin's creation of a modern, expeditionary military reflects its desire to once again become a leader in a multipolar world, and, if possible, recapture its former great power status. Clearly it is capable, if necessary, to intervene in conflicts across the globe, and that ambition is reflected in a subtle way: the retention of the draft. All Russian men are required to register for the draft and must perform one year of military service.

Other nations aligning themselves on either side of the new dual Cold War (US/West versus China and Russia) are accelerating their purchase of sophisticated weapons and new platforms. This is obvious in Eastern Europe, especially among former Soviet satellite countries. Middle East countries like Saudi Arabia and the Gulf emirates are spending hundreds of billions of dollars on mostly US weapons and platforms as they anticipate a future war with the emergent Iran, a Russian/Chinese ally. Then countries around China—such as Taiwan, a country clearly in Beijing's crosshairs—are increasing their military arsenals.

Taiwan's President Tsai Ing-wen promises to make significant and long-term investments in advanced weapons systems, which is understood as that country's growing determination to forge a stronger deterrent against an anticipated Chinese attack. Taiwan's immediate priorities include new missiles, drones and electronic warfare systems, fighter warplanes, and ballistic missile defenses, according to the Ministry of National Defense.

"If there are three weapons systems that China's high command really wants to keep out of Taiwan's hands, it is submarines, fighter jets and ballistic missile defenses," said Ian Easton, a research fellow at the Project 2049 Institute. "Taipei is smartly investing in all three."[79]

It is also important to note the significant weapons investment by China's largest neighbor to the south, India, a country opposed to Beijing's bullying and aligning itself ever closer with the United States.

India is the world's fifth-largest military spender, with outlays of $55.9 billion, according to SIPRI. India's military spending has averaged an annual increase of 10 percent during the past three years, and much of that is going to buy big-ticket platforms like Rafale fighter jets, Apache attack helicopters, and modern howitzers.[80]

India's modernization push, and especially its nuclear strike capabilities, seems to be motivated by China. Although India's declared policy is no first nuclear strike, its modernization program, particularly its ballistic missile program, shows that India is intent on bringing the whole of China into its strike range. Further, the Arms Control Association estimates that India's nuclear stockpile has at least 130 warheads, making it the seventh largest in the world.[81]

There is good reason India is suspicious of China's geopolitical intentions.

Tensions between China and India are on edge, and Beijing is preparing for a future confrontation in unique ways. For example, the *Asia Times* reported in May 2018 that Beijing spent $236 million to construct the seldom-used Yading commercial airport in the frigid wilderness of the Tibetan Plateau, at an elevation of 14,471 feet above sea level where the air supply is 30 percent less than at sea level. Evidently, the investment is worth the cost, given the PLA's use of the facility to test a new generation of jet-fighters (J-20 stealth fighter) to fend off missile threats from the Indian Ocean. The high-perched airfield allows the PLA unobstructed observation of every movement at Indian installations in the Bay of Bengal, such as US and Indian submarine activities, and is a potential launch site for the world's highest mid-range anti-ballistic missile defense system.[82]

Both Russia and China are investing in sophisticated weapons systems that challenge America's past dominance, another indicator of a new Cold War. Further, the rest of the world sees that conflict and is arming up as well.

Indicator #7: China and Russia Identifying the US as an Enemy

Virtually every Chinese defense-related strategic statement identifies the US as China's adversary. President Xi's "China Dream" of national rejuvenation includes a major military transformation modeled on countering the American armed forces. It seeks to replicate American high-technology capabilities via what it calls "winning local wars under informatized conditions." It fields anti-access systems to defend against American naval (read "aircraft carriers") and air forces (read "long-range stealth bombers") that might interfere with China's hegemonic activities in the vast East China Sea, the South China Sea, against Taiwan and in support of its ally North Korea.

Beijing adopted America's "net-centric" warfare strategy to use advanced information technology and communications systems to gain advantage over an adversary (read "United States"). It also has doctrine that calls for the use of a "coercive approach," a tactic short of armed conflict to advance its interest. This approach seeks to enhance China's influence without provoking the US into open conflict. We have already seen this tactic played out in the maritime sovereignty dispute in the South and East China Seas.

China's navy developed a strategy on how best to deal with the US via what it calls "far seas protection," a reflection of the regime's expanding interest overseas. This communicates the intention to increase its global role, which is becoming evident with China's first overseas military base in Djibouti (North Africa). It is not a coincidence that facility is very close to an American naval facility located at the same harbor.

Moscow's 2015 National Security Strategy identifies the US and its NATO allies as Russia's main threat. That strategy accuses the West of pursuing a policy of "containment" against Russia in order to dominate the international order, thus deprive Moscow of its rightful place in the world. Specifically, the strategy states: "The Russian Federation's implementation of an independent foreign and domestic policy is giving rise to opposition from the United States and its allies, who are seeking to retain their dominance in world affairs."[83]

The strategy identifies three specific threats: NATO's buildup along the Russian border, the deployment of US anti-missile systems in Poland and Romania, and the American development of precision weapons (in Europe) as a serious threat to Russian security. Moscow is evidently also fearful of American non-nuclear weapon speed and accuracy, another justification given for reserving the right to use nuclear weapons should it face an existential threat presumably from the US and/or NATO.

Even US Army Lieutenant General Ashley, director of the Defense Intelligence Agency (DIA), testified in March 2018 before the Senate Armed Services Committee that Russia and China believe we are already in a conflict. Ashley answered his rhetorical question about Russian and Chinese threat views: "So the line of which you declare hostilities is extremely blurred, and if you were to ask Russia and China, 'Do you think you're at some form of conflict with the U.S.?' I think behind closed doors their answer would be yes," Ashley testified.[84]

The identification of the US as China and Russia's primary enemy is a strong indicator of a new Cold War.

Indicator #8: China and Russia's Military Posture

A nation postures its military forces in locations to best defend its interests. The Russians understood this view back in 1952 when the Soviet government under Joseph Stalin secretly communicated with Western officials that German reunification was possible if they agreed that "all armed forces of the occupying powers [mostly US] must be withdrawn from Germany…all foreign bases on the territory of Germany must be liquidated."[85] Of course, the West didn't believe the Russians, and the deal became a footnote in Cold War history.

Today, China and Russia would welcome news that the US pulled all its forces out of Europe and Asia. However, that is unlikely to happen because of American interests in those regions, which therefore impacts where Beijing and Moscow posture (station and operate) their armed forces at ports and airfields or in a variety of locations to equip warriors with sophisticated weapons platforms to communicate their readiness to fight.

Consider their growing footprint across the world.

Russia maintains significant military posture just inside its territory along international borders with former Soviet satellite states. Defense Minister Sergei Shoigu said Russia would build up its military forces on its western borders and blames NATO's "anti-Russia course" for the worsening security situation, which prompted Moscow to form twenty new units on the western frontier opposite the Baltic states and Poland.[86]

Those forces routinely engage in readiness exercises along the common border as a reminder that the Russian Bear is watching closely and could spring an attack at any moment, much as it did when it seized Crimea in 2014 and two provinces of the Republic of Georgia in 2008. Those exercises and Russian operations prompted the US to launch the ongoing Operation Atlantic Resolve, "a demonstration of continued US commitment to collective security through a series of actions designed to reassure NATO allies and partners of America's dedication to enduring peace and stability in the region in light of the Russian intervention in

Ukraine." That operation began in April 2014 with the US Army Europe conducting continuous, enhanced multinational training and security cooperation activities with allies and partners across Eastern Europe.[87]

Russian expeditionary operations have also increased over the past few years, another posture indicator. For example, Russia has forward-stationed troops in ten countries: Armenia, Belarus, Georgia, Kazakhstan, Kyrgyzstan, Moldova, Tajikistan, Ukraine (Crimea), Vietnam, and, most notably, in war-torn Syria. Russia operates high-visibility military facilities supporting the Syrian regime at Hmeimim Air Base near the city of Latakia and at a naval facility near the Syrian port city of Tartus.[88]

The presence of Russian forces in Syria added a layer of complexity to the West's response to Assad's April 7, 2018, chemical-agent attack that affected hundreds of innocent civilians in the town of Douma. The Pentagon confirmed that normal de-confliction was performed with the Russians before the April 14 American cruise missile attack. However, the US did not notify Moscow of target sites in advance, according to US Marine General Joseph Dunford, the Chairman of the Joint Chiefs of Staff. Further, the general said the US sought targets that would limit any involvement with Russian military forces in Syria.[89]

On other fronts "Russia views the Arctic [region] as vital to its national security," testified DIA Director General Ashley. "Over the past 5 years, Russia has strengthened its military presence in the Arctic, refurbishing once-abandoned Soviet-era installations and developing new dual-use facilities to support civilian and military operations. These efforts include construction of airfields, naval ports, search and rescue centers, and radar installations. Russia has also created new Ground Forces units, air defense units, and coastal missile units to improve security of Russia's northern border."[90]

"If you look at what they're putting in place, they would have the capability in the next two to three years to control the Northern Sea Route," said US Army General Curtis Scaparrotti, the Supreme Allied Commander Europe, in testimony before the Senate Armed Services Committee in March 2018.[91]

Russia is not only building up its military presence in the Arctic, but laid claim to much of that region. In 2015, Russia formally claimed a large portion of the Arctic Ocean to include the true North Pole, even planting a Russian Federation titanium flag on the sea floor at that point under the thick ice. Moscow's claim includes oversight on economic matters, including fishing and oil and gas drilling based on the UN convention, the Law of the Sea.[92]

Another posture indicator is Moscow's routine deployment of long-range bombers along the Alaska-to-California coastlines, the Arctic, and even into the Caribbean. Russia also conducts naval operations in the Mediterranean, the Arctic, and more recently in the Western hemisphere (North Atlantic) and the Indian Ocean. It is especially noteworthy that Russian submarines and surface ships with miniature submarines aboard have been seen operating along sea lanes that trace critical undersea communication cables as well as hugging the US East Coast, an old Cold War operation to surveil American communications.

Posturing forces includes the demonstration of long-range-weapons effects that impact outside one's borders, such as the Kremlin's sobering firepower demonstration in support of the Damascus, Syria, regime. In recent years, Moscow launched at Syrian opposition forces Kalibr land-attack cruise missiles from naval platforms in the Caspian and Mediterranean Seas, demonstrated an air-launched, cruise-missile capability from its Tu-160ML Blackjack, Tu-95MS Bear heavy bombers, and forward-staged Tu-22M3 Backfire bombers from an Iranian air base.[93]

China's military posture is rapidly outpacing the Russians. Beijing is growing its military posture within the Asia-Pacific region and overseas, which communicates intent and acts as a warning to the countries near those forces that the communist giant may have unannounced malevolent intentions.

Beijing's increasing confrontations throughout its periphery is a loud posture statement to those neighbors: Vietnam, Philippines, Malaysia, Singapore, Thailand, and all nations to include the United States that use the East and South China Seas' international maritime shipping routes. The growing presence of heavy combat units operating from islets (reefs) in disputed areas far from the Chinese mainland is a serious posture statement.

Further, the explosive growth of China's expeditionary military forces—aircraft carriers and "far sea" major warships—is a posture statement, especially now that Chinese service members are more evident than ever before throughout the world conducting counterpiracy, peacekeeping, humanitarian assistance missions as well as military exercises as faraway as places such as the Baltic Sea in Northern Europe.

Beijing also appears to be poised to establish military bases in countries with longstanding, friendly relationships, such as the new (2017) facility in Djibouti (at the horn of Africa) supposedly designed "to help the navy and army further participate in United Nations peacekeeping operations, carry out escort missions in the waters near Somalia and the Gulf of Aden, and provide humanitarian assistance."[94]

China's posture is pretty broad elsewhere, with military personnel and "security personnel" known to operate in Afghanistan, Laos, Myanmar, Thailand, South Sudan, Ethiopia, and Iraq. Some of these locations are due to China's growing economic internationalization, known as Chinese Outward Foreign Direct Investment (COFDI).[95]

The UN Conference on Trade and Development shows an explosion of COFDI's reach in less than two decades. In 2000, annual COFDI was less than $2.3 billion compared to 2015, when it reached a whopping $135.6 billion in a diverse mix of sectors.[96]

China is also expanding its access overseas to pre-position logistics support to sustain its "far-seas" strategy, such as in the Indian Ocean (read "Pakistan"), Mediterranean Sea (read "Syria"), and the Atlantic Ocean (read "Panama and Cuba"). Beijing is playing a very sophisticated game of geopolitical chess as it grows access overseas.

China is crafting leverage using its "far-seas" strategy as well as its COFDI internationalism by remaining on the sidelines of the Syrian civil war as Russia and the US exchange verbal and occasional kinetic blows in the seven-year-old war. Specifically, Logan Pauley, a China relations fellow with the East Asia Program at the Stimson Center, writes, "Syria was once the Western terminus of China's ancient Silk Road, and today its geographic position is again important for Beijing. Syria sits at a crucial point along one of the six corridors that make up Beijing's sweeping Belt and Road Initiative, offering direct access to the Mediterranean Sea. China also has promising contracts with Syrian oil companies and telecommunications infrastructure."[97]

China's overseas ambitions motivate Beijing to keep Syria's dictator President Bashir al-Assad in power and to call for, as China's ambassador to the UN, Ma Zhaoxu, said, a solution to the civil war that requires a "Syrian-owned and -led political process." That is an example of China playing both sides of the Syrian problem by not blaming either the US or Russia for the chaotic situation; rather, Beijing is pledging financial and development help for post-civil war Damascus, such as commitments to rebuild Syria's railroad system and its telecommunications system and develop its private business sector. That's a smart and strategic place to be for the hegemonic Beijing.[98]

Not surprisingly, Beijing will potentially reap significant benefits from such investment promises without paying a price by letting Russia and the US do all the dirty work. Pauley cited a view about the conflict attributed to Yitzhak Schichor, a professor at the University of Haifa, Israel, who explained that China's strategy in Syria reflects a Mandarin proverb: "Sitting on the hill while the tigers fight." Translation: Beijing projects an image as a "newfound bastion of multilateralism and protector of peace," explained Pauley. China will milk the Syrian proxy war between the US and Russia by nurturing a relationship with Assad, who will likely welcome Chinese investment, thus making Beijing the real winner in that country's civil war.[99]

Beijing's nuanced geopolitical play vis-à-vis the Syrian conflict is complemented by its growing expeditionary military forces and its growing economic interests overseas. That expanding overseas footprint is likely to be the precursor for foreign policy activism, and although Beijing denies malevolent intentions, great power history means the US and the balance of her partners must watch Beijing's accelerated foreign adventures with a jaundiced eye. Those foreign adventures include a significant increase in overseas military diplomacy using PLA uniformed officers in at least 110 embassies worldwide. This deployment indicates China's growing global interest in building partners overseas through security cooperation (exercises, capacity building, exchange of information, relationship building) as well as collecting intelligence on those countries.

Beijing's expeditionary military forces and a growing armed presence appear to expand with its overseas investments as well. Thus, it is reasonable to expect this tightening grip over its foreign infrastructure and resources to be followed by foreign policy activism. Although Beijing denies malevolent intentions, great power history means the US and the balance of her partners must skeptically watch Beijing's foreign adventures.

Another telling posture indicator of the new dual Cold War is the United States' recognition that it faces specific regional missile threats from Russia and China, which require forward stationing of anti-ballistic missile systems. This new policy marks a shift from a prior strategy that focused only on rogue nations like North Korea and Iran, and now America recognizes the need to consider missile threats from Russia and China.[100]

The *Stars & Stripes*, for example, reports that "Russia's thousands of missiles easily could overwhelm existing U.S. missile defenses in the event of a full-scale war." Therefore, the United States will not attempt to field a shield against that threat; rather, it will rely instead on its own vast nuclear arsenal as the deterrent. However, according to the *Stars & Stripes*, the new nuclear posture "policy will more discretely look at ways the United States can better deal with burgeoning missile threats from Russia and China in regional theaters such as Europe and Asia, where the two countries' systems have alarmed the American military."[101]

Russia and China's growing global military posture indicates the reality of a new Cold War that contests America's past dominance.

Indicator #9: Chinese and Russian Nuclear Actions
Suggestive of War

In 2015, at the Lennart Meri conference, then Estonian President Too-
mas Hendrik Ilves asked a panel of experts addressing the topic "Thinking the Unthinkable" an important question: Should the barrage of
recent Russian nuclear threats be taken seriously or dismissed as mere
posturing? A US diplomat named Alexander Vershbow, who was then
NATO's deputy secretary general, responded: "Yes: a short answer is
yes."[102]

Russia maintains a giant strategic (nuclear) force. Under the New
Strategic Arms Reduction Treaty (START), it is limited to no more
than 1,500 deployed warheads on 700 triad platforms. Those platforms
include a fleet of bombers (mostly Tu-95 Bear and Tu-160 Blackjack),
intercontinental ballistic missiles (ICBM) (SS-18, SS-19, SS-25, and
expect newer, road-mobile and silo-based systems by 2020) and 10
nuclear-powered ballistic missile submarines. Moscow plans to invest
$28 billion by 2020 to update its triad.[103]

This nuclear triad has until recently been Russia's post-Cold War
security guarantor, only to be used in a last resort. However, that view
seems to be changing, which makes nuclear war more likely. After all,
Russia's new military doctrine anticipates a first use of nuclear weapons "in the event of aggression against the Russian Federation with the
use of conventional weapons when the very existence of the state is in
jeopardy."[104]

Nuclear war also seems to be more likely with President Putin in
the Kremlin. Every recent Russian large-scale exercise (such as the 2017
Zapad, "West" along the East European frontier) includes a scenario of
a limited nuclear strike against NATO, dubbed Moscow's "escalation to
de-escalate" concept. Instances of simulated nuclear strike exercises are
reported to have targeted Warsaw, the Stockholm archipelago, and the
Danish island of Bornholm.[105]

Moscow's "escalation to de-escalate" doctrine seems more credible when one considers that Russia has in recent years acquired an edge over NATO in tactical nuclear weaponry, apparently another violation of the 1987 Intermediate-Range Nuclear Forces Treaty, as well as the means to deliver small nuclear payloads aboard highly accurate cruise missiles. That combination of tactical nuclear weapons and greater range, accurate delivery systems makes Russian talk about limited nuclear war scenarios worrisome and believable.

The Baltic region of Europe is especially concerned about Russia's growing regional superiority in conventional forces, anti-access/area denial platforms, and the threat of limited nuclear use. The problem for the West in this region is it relies on a strategy of deterrence, but Russia already has sufficient military posture in place to quickly overwhelm, seize entire small countries (like Estonia and Lithuania), and then defend them against a slow NATO response by issuing credible nuclear threats.

This is a repeat of an old Cold War confrontation strategy—but worse, if the Russians expect they can limit the use of nuclear weapons. The problem, as former US Deputy Defense Secretary Robert Work testified in 2015, "Anyone who thinks they can control escalation through the use of nuclear weapons is literally playing with fire. Escalation is escalation, and nuclear use would be the ultimate escalation." But Russia appears to believe it has the upper hand and is ready to use its nuclear arsenal under the right circumstances.

A veteran Russian politician indicates that the Kremlin will use nuclear arms if the US or NATO moves against the Crimean Peninsula or eastern Ukraine and, likely, against any future Russian move on the Baltics or other former Soviet satellites. Vyacheslav Alekseyevich Nikonov, a member of the Duma, Russia's lower house of parliament, told attendees of the 2017 GLOBSEC Bratislava Global Security Forum in Slovakia that "Russian forces would need to utilize some form of nuclear warfare to deter US or NATO forces from invading Russia should they decide to enter Crimea or eastern Ukraine."[106]

"On the issue of NATO expansion on our borders, at some point I heard from the Russian military—and I think they are right—if U.S.

forces, NATO forces, are, were, in the Crimea, in eastern Ukraine, Russia is undefendable militarily in case of conflict without using nuclear weapons in the early stage of the conflict," Nikonov said.[107]

This view is supported by the Military Doctrine of Russia, which was last updated in 2014. That doctrine states Moscow reserves "the right to use nuclear weapons in response to the use of nuclear and other types of weapons of mass destruction against it and/or its allies, as well as in the event of aggression against the Russian Federation with the use of conventional weapons when the very existence of the state is in jeopardy."[108]

It is important to understand that Russia developed nuclear capabilities far beyond what is necessary to protect the state and in some rather unexpected ways. Specifically, the Kremlin created an underwater nuclear drone capable of carrying a 100-megaton nuclear warhead, a discovery announced in a leaked draft of the Pentagon's *Nuclear Posture Review*. That draft reported by the *Huffington Post* indicated that the weapon, an autonomous underwater vehicle officially known as Ocean Multipurpose System Status-6 and nicknamed "Kanyon," was reportedly tested in 2016 after being launched from a Sarov-class submarine. The Kanyon reportedly has a range of 6,200 miles, with a top speed in excess of 56 knots and can dive to 3,280 feet below sea level.[109]

Moscow's growing nuclear arsenal and its evident willingness to do the "unthinkable," employ that arsenal in a future war, explains the Trump administration's desire to substantially increase the US' nuclear stockpile and match some of Russia's new nuclear capabilities.

The likelihood of a nuclear attack by China is more opaque. China maintains a "no first use" policy and indicates it would use nuclear weapons only in response to a nuclear strike against its homeland. There is some ambiguity to China's policy, however. Some PLA officers have announced in military publications the need to outline the conditions under which China might need to use nuclear weapons first, such as if an enemy's conventional attack threatened the survival of China's nuclear force or the regime.[110]

The PLA Rocket Force (PLARF) has a full range of ballistic missiles to deliver nuclear warheads. The DF-26 is an intermediate-range ballistic missile, which is capable of conducting conventional and nuclear precision strikes. It also has a new multiple independently targetable reentry vehicle (MIRV) capability, maneuvering warheads, decoys, chaff, jamming, thermal shielding, and road-mobile ICBM, the CSS-X-20 (DF-41).

The PLARF continues to make enhancements to its ICBM force to address survivability and mobility. China's CSS-10 Mod 2, with a range in excess of seven thousand miles, can reach the entire United States. More recently, China tested new, more capable weapons. In April 2018, there were press reports about China's flight-testing of a nuclear-capable air-launched ballistic missile (ALBM) along with a new, long-range strategic bomber to launch the missile. That report, which appeared in *The Diplomat* is evidence of China's promised new generation of long-range strategic bombers, and the new missile, the CH-AS-X-13 is expected to be ready by 2025 to threaten the contiguous United States, Hawaii, and Alaska. "These capabilities are being augmented with two new air-launched ballistic missiles, one of which may include a nuclear payload," according to DIA director, General Ashley.[111] An important part of China's nuclear triad is its four Jin-class nuclear-powered ballistic missile submarines, armed with the JL-2 submarine-launched ballistic missile. Also, the PLA Air Force is developing a new strategic bomber that is expected to have a nuclear mission as well, rounding out China's first credible nuclear triad.[112]

China is believed to have a nuclear arsenal of up to 260 warheads.[113]

Any analysis of the nuclear threat isn't complete without acknowledging the other nations with nuclear power and/or atomic weapons. At least two dozen nations have nuclear power, and nine are known to have actual nuclear weapons: Russia, the United States, China, India, Israel, France, North Korea, Pakistan, and the United Kingdom. Together, according to the Ploughshares Fund, a global security foundation, there are more than fifteen thousand nuclear weapons around the world, and nearly two thousand nuclear weapons are ready to launch at any given time.[114]

The prospect of nuclear war appears to be increasing, given the global rhetoric and the growing availability of warheads especially with Russia, China and their proxies—another clear indicator of a new dual Cold War.

Indicator #10: China and Russia Identifying the United States as a Security Threat

Russia considers the United States its primary threat, according to DIA director, General Ashley. As a result, it is "developing a modern military designed to defeat all potential threats to the Russian homeland and accomplish its larger foreign policy objectives."[115]

Evidently, President Putin's effort to reassert Russia as a great power on the global stage is a response to what he perceives is a lopsided international order that favors America. As a result, Putin seeks to promote a multi-polar world with Russia playing a significant role—albeit also preventing the US from dominating. That explains Moscow's fixation on rebuilding a robust military to project power, adding credibility to Russian diplomacy.

These views are clearly documented in Russia's published national security strategy. Specifically, that strategy identifies the US and its NATO allies as Russia's main threat and accuses the West of trying to "contain" Russia (an old Cold War concept), thus depriving it of its rightful place on the world stage. The document states that the "Russian Federation's implementation of an independent foreign and domestic policy are giving rise to opposition from the United States and its allies, who are seeking to retain their dominance in world affairs."[116]

The Russian strategy goes even further to indicate NATO's buildup in Eastern Europe near the Russian border, the deployment of American anti-ballistic missile systems in former Soviet satellite countries, and America's pursuit of strategic, non-nuclear, precision weapons all threaten Moscow's security and give Russia the rationale to vigorously counter the perceived and growing threat.

Moscow also accuses America of waging a campaign to impose its values, which threatens Kremlin power at home and abroad. That is evidence, according to the Russians, that the US is laying the groundwork for a regime change in Russia, an existential threat, a view expressed by a leading American intelligence agency.

A 2017 Defense Intelligence Agency report indicates Moscow's "deep and abiding distrust of U.S. efforts to promote democracy around the world and what it perceives as a U.S. campaign to impose a single set of global values."[117]

"The Kremlin is convinced the United States is laying the groundwork for regime change in Russia, a conviction further reinforced by the events in Ukraine," the report states, a clear reference to Putin's claims that the US engineered the popular uprising that ousted Ukraine's Russia-friendly president, Viktor Yanukovich, in 2014. Then, in response, Russia annexed Crimea and fueled a separatist uprising in eastern Ukraine.[118]

Moscow also "worries that US attempts to dictate a set of acceptable international norms threatens the foundations of Kremlin power by giving license for foreign meddling in Russia's internal affairs," so states the DIA report, *Russia Military Power*, the first such report since the 1991 demise of the former Soviet Union.[119]

China shares Russia's view of the United States.

China views the US as its primary threat, which is reflected in its statements and publications as well. That explains its ambitious agenda of military modernization and organizational reforms to transform its force into one capable of conducting advanced joint operations against its primary adversary, the United States.

America as China's primary threat is evident, given Beijing's close studies of US military operations and equipment, and then its preparations specifically tailored to counter those threats. For example, in 1993, then president Jiang Zemin directed the PLA to "prepare for conflict under modern, high-technology conditions after observing US military operations in the Gulf War."[120]

The PLA embraced the US military's concept of "net-centric" warfare. China's navy also fielded an array of cruise missiles to counter an adversary fleet's intervention with multi-axis, high-intensity attacks. Further, China's fielded CSS-5 ASBMs are specifically designed to hold adversary (read "US") aircraft carriers at risk when inside 1,500 kilometers.[121]

There is no doubt, based on Chinese and Russian statements and written defense materials, that both nations consider the US their primary threat, yet another indicator of the new dual Cold War.

Indicator #11: China and Russia Forming an Alliance-like Relationship to Oppose the United States

An experienced Sovietologist believes the US and Russia are locked in a new Cold War because of the lack of a mutually accepted agenda as a basis for negotiations and the fact the contemporary leaders (Trump and Putin) are very different than those (Reagan and Gorbachev) who ended the old Cold War's "struggle for ideological and military dominance." In fact, "the political obstacles in the United States and the level of distrust in Russia are higher today" than during the old Cold War, according to Dr. Ray Smith, a thirty-year US State Department veteran who worked on Soviet/Russian affairs and arms control and the author of *Negotiating with the Soviets*.[122]

Dr. Smith asserts that the motivation behind the new Cold War is in part explained by the fact that "Russia believes its efforts to participate meaningfully in the post-Cold War system…have been rejected." A major result of that perception, according to Smith, is Moscow's growing potential to form an "alternative alliance structure built around other countries" such as China, Iran, Syria, and even Turkey.[123]

Further, the US and Russia have returned to policies similar to those followed during the old Cold War, according to Dr. Robert Legvold, a Russia expert and professor emeritus at Columbia University. Legvold traces this view to such divisive decisions as the NATO-Russia Council's decision not to give a maritime escort to a ship bound for Syria on a mission to neutralize chemical weapons in 2014, which ended up being a ruse that backfired in 2018 when Syria's dictator once again used chemical munitions to kill innocent civilians.

Legvold says that as the new Cold War progresses, both parties will prioritize their international politics, which will make Russia "increasingly dependent on its relationship with China."[124] That is an outcome that supports the view of a dual Cold War, an idea rooted in the not-so-distant past, and one that supports the view that a new alliance might be in the making.

Russia and China started coalescing their new "alliance" of mutual interest beginning in late 2012 with the first of at least seventeen visits between Chinese President Xi Jinping and President Vladimir Putin in Beijing. In June 2017, the two presidents adopted three joint statements at one of those meetings, including one aimed at challenging Western interpretation of international law regarding issues such as the growing instability in Northeast Asia (North Korea) and disputes over sovereignty in the South China Sea. The joint stance is a first for China and Russia, whose warming ties show that a new dual Cold War has begun, wrote Zhejiang University's Korean studies expert Li Dunqiu in a commentary published in the *China Youth Daily* on July 30. Professor Li wrote that the new Cold War had begun with the US rebalance to the Asia-Pacific in 2012, an integral aspect of President Obama's national defense strategy.

A Russia-China alliance really started to become evident after the fall of the Soviet Union, because communist China sought Russian arms—in part because Moscow was a willing merchant, but also because Russian arms were compatible with China's Soviet-era equipment.

The favorable China-Russia arms ties helped those nations overcome areas of distrust leading to the current military-to-military cooperative relationship. In fact, in 1996, Beijing and Moscow cemented that relationship with a "strategic partnership of coordination" agreement that established high-level, ongoing talks on military affairs.[125]

Evidence of the close military relationship between China and Russia grew over the subsequent years. The most visible demonstration of their cooperation is a very active bilateral military exercise schedule. In 2015, the Russian defense minister Sergei Shoigu explained the rationale for those exercises. "The most important issue of the Russian-Chinese military cooperation is the…military exercises. They contribute to improving combat training of the armed forces of [the] two countries, and demonstrate our readiness to counteract modern threats."[126]

The target of that statement about counteracting "modern threats" is the United States and its Western military counterparts, such as the North Atlantic Treaty Organization (NATO). After all, and for example, in July 2017, China and Russia conducted their first-ever joint naval drills in the Baltic Sea (Northern Europe), called the "Joint Sea" exercise. A People's Liberation Army Navy (PLAN) flotilla, consisting of a destroyer, a frigate, and a replenishment ship, joined Russia's Baltic fleet off the coast near the city of St. Petersburg. China's *Xinhua News Agency* reported the drill was designed to "consolidate and advance the Sino-Russian Comprehensive Strategic Partnership of Coordination, and deepen friendly and practical cooperation between the two militaries."[127]

Russia and China are closely cooperating on end-use technology and equipment, making their weapons compatible or, in military parlance, "interoperable," which is critical for effective coalition operations—the primary focus of military alliances. The West seeks much the same outcome among its allies. But the Russia-China weapons interoperability, according to the Stockholm International Peace Research Institute (SIPRI), is especially outstanding. SIPRI found that since the end of the Cold War, nearly 80 percent of China's total arms imports have been Russian, and more than a quarter of all Russian arms exports went to China.[128]

The arms transfers slowed over the past decade, mostly because China's own military industrial complex can now satisfy its weapon demands, but also because the Chinese are concerned about Russian quality control. Yet, these partners continue arms sales and technology exchanges, such as the 2016 Russian sale of 24 Sukhoi Su-35 fighter aircraft to China and the anticipated 2018 Russian delivery of the S-400 surface-to-air missile defense system. Both systems, according to the SIPRI report, demonstrate increased Sino-Russian cooperation and are intended to overcome the threat posed by US capabilities present in Asia.

Deepening defense ties between Russia and China have also accelerated, especially since 2012, when Chinese President Xi Jinping and Russian President Putin concluded it was in their mutual best interest to cooperate against US-led efforts to "contain" them as evidenced by the Obama administration's rebalance to Asia policy (2012) and NATO's expansion into Eastern Europe.

Further, a 2017 report by the US-China Economic and Security Review Commission states since the end of the old Cold War, Beijing and Moscow's military and defense establishments "have steadily worked to minimize and overcome" their differences, and now their defense ties are among "the most important components of the overall [bilateral] relationship."[129]

In fact, the Chinese and Russian defense ministers met in Moscow in April 2018, when they affirmed their cooperation and opposition to the United States. General Wei Fenghe, China's new defense minister, said in a meeting with Russian Defense Minister Sergei Shoigu that he chose Russia for his first trip abroad to "show the world a high level of development of our bilateral relations and firm determination of our armed forces to strengthen strategic cooperation." Shoigu responded that Wei's visit "underlines a special character of relations between Russia and China," which deepens their militaries' relationship and described their "strategic partnership" as in opposition to the "unipolar" world, a reference to alleged US global domination.[130]

The drumbeat of deepening military-to-military relations between

Russia and China was once again evidenced at the late April 2018 meeting of the Shanghai Cooperation Organization between Russian Defense Minister Sergey Shoigu and Air Force General Xu Qiliang, deputy vice chairman of China's Central Military Commission. Shoigu praised "the privileged character of intergovernmental ties" evidenced by the frequent meetings between the Russian and Chinese presidents, and then he said the two nations were continuing "their strategic course towards further boosting friendly and trustworthy ties in the defense sphere." General Xu reportedly said "the Sino-Russian relationship has reached new heights, thanks to a strong push by leaders from both countries." Sino-Russia bilateral relations are now at an all-time high, characterized by deepening strategic mutual trust and expanding cooperation.[131]

These partners may not be an official alliance like NATO cemented by a formal treaty relationship, but they share common weapons, doctrine, and views about the US and the West. They exercise together, seek to be interoperable, and routinely talk at senior military levels as evidenced above. Collectively, they demonstrate all the particulars of an alliance, and that is how the United States and the West ought to understand their dual Cold War relationship.

Indicator #12: Chinese and Russian Forces Confronting US Military at an Increasing Rate

The Russians resurrected their old ways to welcome a new Cold War. Russian tanks and troops once again are on the march into sovereign nations such as Crimea, Ukraine, and the Republic of Georgia. The re-emergent Russian Bear plays high-risk military games of chicken with American nuclear bombers, jet fighters, and ships sailing through international waters. Of course, some of the Kremlin's actions are in response to our movement of troops into Eastern Europe, Washington's decision to supply Javelin anti-tank missiles to Ukraine, and antiballistic missile defense systems installed in Poland and Romania, all clearly antagonize Russia.

Confrontations between Russian forces and the US Navy are especially significant in the Black Sea, a regular event. American warships usually sail into the Black Sea for allied exercises, such as the destroyer USS Carney. "Returning to the Black Sea and Odessa is a familiar mission," said Commander Peter Halverson, commanding officer of the USS Carney. He explained, "We look forward to improving our cooperative capability with the Ukrainian navy" as well as protecting international waters that hold economic and military importance.

Other Russian-US military encounters take place on a regular basis in the Northern Pacific off Alaska, in the North Atlantic, the Batlic Sea, along America's coastlines and elsewhere. The frequency and associated danger of these confrontations put American forces on high alert for encounters that could escalate.

There is also the real fear that a confrontation could turn into a hot war and, as we saw earlier, Putin and his field marshals have already announced their willingness to use their robust nuclear arsenal early in the conflict to overcome any conventional force shortfall or to stop what Russia may perceive as an unacceptable threat to the Federation. That declaration alone should give the US and its allies pause before launching operations against Putin or his proxies. But count on it: Eventually, given the right opportunity, Putin fully intends to give Washington a bloody nose to restore the greatness of the former Soviet empire. No, a full-up, major war isn't on the immediate horizon, at least without a broader alliance that includes China.

China is very aggressive against the US and other militaries as well. It constantly harasses American warships and reconnaissance aircraft and is a bully when it comes to the militaries of smaller neighbors such as Vietnam and the Philippines.

Beijing deploys its growing and sophisticated giant military to confront neighboring countries and the US at sea and in the air. This is especially evident in the Taiwan Strait.

Taiwan has been a special problem for Beijing since the Communist Revolution in 1949. The communist giant managed to isolate the nationalist government on Taiwan by using Beijing's UN Security Council seat and by taking punitive measures. China maintains a territorial claim to Taiwan and could well invade the island nation, which might provoke armed conflict with America because Washington supports its democratic partner in Taipei, as evidenced by a new law.

A new American law is a stick in the eye to the communist regime in Beijing regarding China's long-standing claim over Taiwan. As evidence of the new Cold War, in March 2018, President Trump signed a bill increasing high-level visits with Taiwan, an act that followed the administration's announcement to impose tariffs on imports of steel and aluminum products and that primarily targets China.[132]

The Chinese Communist Party newspaper, *Global Times*, said the new law would trigger one of China's conditions for using force to reunite the island with the mainland. However, in an effort to draw a line in the geopolitical sand, Senator Marco Rubio (R-FL), a key sponsor of the law, said, "Taiwan is a fellow democracy and important partner in the Indo-Pacific region." He added, "It is critical the United States to strengthen our ties with Taiwan, especially as China increases efforts to isolate Taiwan and block its participation in international organizations."[133]

China is working hard to isolate Taiwan from the world by persuading nations to withdraw their recognition of the island nation, a possible pretext to Beijing's using force to capture the island, an action that could lead to a US-Chinese military confrontation. For example, in April 2018, *Bloomberg* reported that the island nation of the Dominican Republic formally established diplomatic relations with the Peoples Republic of China, a blow to Taiwan as Beijing continued to isolate the self-governed island. This move reduced to nineteen the number of countries that formally recognize the government in Taipei—the latest success in China's effort to marginalize Taiwanese President Tsai Ing-wen. Not surprisingly, China lured the Dominican Republic with money. A spokesman for the Dominican Republic said ties with China creates "immense" opportunities in areas from finance to technology, tourism, education, and energy. Previously, in June 2017, China won over Panama and, once again at Beijing's coaxing, in May 2018, another nation, Africa's Burkino Faso, cut ties with Taipei.[134]

It is noteworthy that the RAND Corporation updated a six-year-old study this past year (2017) that considered the chances of a US-China war, *Conflict with China Revisited*. That report examined a number of the contemporary scenarios—South China Sea, Taiwan, East China Sea—that might prove to be catalysts for such a confrontation. The RAND report states: "We still do not believe that a Chinese-US military conflict is probable in any of the cases, but our margin of confidence is somewhat lower than it was six years ago."[135]

Chinese scholar Dr. Christopher Lew, president of Water Dragons Consulting, said, "If Beijing believes it is being backed into a corner and will not survive domestic upheavals or public disapproval, then the likelihood that they will resort to a foreign war will increase."[136]

Confrontations between the two sides—US versus China and Russia—are increasing, which is another indicator of a new dual Cold War.

Indicator #13: Russian and Chinese Citizens and Experts Believing a New War Is Underway with the United States

Most (61 percent of) Americans consider Russia an enemy of the United States, and a plurality, 36 percent, worry the US will become engaged in a major war in the next four years, according to a 2017 survey by *NBC News*.[137] That view is mutual among Russians.

Moscow's view that America is its enemy is widely shared among Russians. A January 2018 poll among Russians found that 68 percent name the US as their top foe, according to Russian pollster Levada Center. In fact, one in four respondents said Russia "is surrounded by enemies on all sides." Ukraine earned 29 percent of the vote for their primary enemy, while the balance (14 percent) of Russians named the European Union its top foe.[138]

Russia's president encourages the anti-American view, which in part explains his popularity. President Putin is incredibly popular (77 percent reelected him on March 18, 2018) among the Russian people, even though he rules that country with an iron fist very similar to his Cold-War communist predecessors. Putin's popularity is perhaps because of his confrontational approach to foreign policy that is spun in the Russian media as a win for the Kremlin against the White House. Unfortunately, the seriousness of the significant ongoing confrontation with the West is likely missed by most Russians. After all, Sergei Karaganov, a hawkish member of the Russian foreign-policy community, told *Bloomberg*: "The current situation is just like that in the 1960s, when the world was on the brink of war…the possibility of war is definitely there, which could be triggered by minor mistakes."[139]

Even though the average Russian and American believes our countries are enemies, the concept of a new Cold War is only mentioned on the sidelines by mostly the academic and media communities. For example, Oleksandr Danylyuk, the chairman of the Center for Defense Reforms in Ukraine, warned in 2016 that Russia has "been carrying out not only information operations but also other clandestine and special operations against Ukraine for more than a decade." Danylyuk concluded: "Russia is not preparing for war with the West; the war is already being actively conducted—on Russia's terms."[140]

"It's no doubt, at least for me, that Russia and the West are in the situation of [a] new Cold War," said defense analyst Alexander Golts, deputy editor of *Yezhednevny Zhurnal* [*Weekly Journal*] in Moscow. "[The] Cold War is a situation when you have a problem that cannot be solved…[not] diplomatically [or] militarily. This problem is Ukraine."[141]

The situation is intractable from a Russian perspective, Golts said. Moscow cannot pull back from its war in Ukraine, and until that happens, NATO won't cooperate. Thus the tension continues to escalate.[142]

Other scholars agree with Danylyuk and Golts that the US and Russia have "entered a new Cold War." Robert Legvold, professor emeritus at Columbia University, is a leading expert on Russia.[143] He said we have seen a "historic shift in international politics." But rather than the politically driven Cold War of the twentieth century, Legvold explained the new Cold War will instead be fueled by the dispute over "basic civilizational values." The "overarching framework is…adversarial," he continued. Today, each side no longer sees the other as "neither friend nor foe," and the relationship was until recently unclear. However, now that the US-Russia relationship is clear, "the ambiguity is gone."[144]

The US and Russia both reached back to the last Cold War, Legvold said, citing several examples, including America's decision to stop negotiations about missile defense (the 1972 Anti-Ballistic Missile Treaty) and the NATO-Russia Council's decision not to give a maritime escort to a ship bound for Syria on a mission to neutralize chemical weapons.

The new Cold War is warping foreign policy as well, Legvold said. He predicts that as the conflict progresses, the US will prioritize new Cold War activities over others, such as the global war on terror and the threat of weapons of mass destruction landing in rogue hands. Further, Legvold anticipates that as the new Cold War heats up, Russia will be "increasingly dependent on its relationship with China."

President Putin's State of the Nation address on March 1, 2018, fanned the embers of the new dual Cold War. An editorial in the *Vedomosti* (a Russian business daily), "The New Terrifying and Comfortable Russia of Putin," states, "This address [Putin's State of the Nation address] is about presenting a new political construction for the world." The editorial continued, saying that Putin's speech is "an actual invitation to form a new Warsaw Pact [a military alliance]."[145]

Russian political expert Evgeny Minchenko heard much the same message from Putin. "Apparently, this [Putin's speech] will provide a new impulse for the U.S. Army rearmament program…. So, for the 'hawks' in the U.S. it's more of a gift than a kind of sobering signal."[146]

Vyacheslav Smirnov, the head of the Institute of Political Sociology in Moscow, said of the Putin speech: "The upcoming decade will take place under the Cold War flag. Whatever happened today, or a year or two ago, during the Crimea accession, is just the beginning. It will be worse, tougher, just as in the 80's."[147]

Russian intellectual Fyodor Lukyanov responded to President Putin's March 1, 2018, State of the Nation speech by calling the president's new policy "proactive deterrence." Lukyanov said the US has been playing at reviving the Cold War, and now Putin pushed back in the speech. "Ok, if you say it's the Cold War, let it be the Cold War," said Lukyanov. He stressed that the new Cold War is governed by a new axiom: "Russia is stronger than the West."[148]

Meanwhile, the Chinese media refers to escalating global tensions as *xin leng zhan*, or the "new Cold War." Kor Kian Beng with the *Straits Times* wrote: "Chinese analysts are also interpreting issues through a 'new Cold War' lens that pits China, Russia and North Korea against the U.S., Japan and South Korea."[149]

Fan Jishe, an American studies researcher with the Chinese Academy of Social Sciences, told a Singapore conference in 2017 that the Association of Southeast Asian Nations (ASEAN) might have to soon "pick sides" between Beijing and Washington, further fueling speculation about the emerging new Cold War.[150]

Zhang Baohui, a political science professor in Hong Kong, said in the wake of the publication of the 2017 American National Security Strategy (NSS), the hoped-for partnership between Presidents Trump and Xi "is dead."

"China has invested huge diplomatic capital in securing that relationship," Zhang said. Until the NSS, the leaders appeared to be getting along well, especially during Trump's 2017 Beijing trip.[151]

"Now his foreign policy (is returning) to the standard posture of the U.S. in world affairs since 1945 [the start of the Cold War], which is that it is bent on maintaining primacy and sees other great powers as challengers," Zhang speculated. The NSS shows, according to Zhang, "that the two countries are on a long-term collision course."[152]

Public opinion shouts that we are in a new dual Cold War. Most citizens on either side based on recent surveys indicate a new Cold War is underway, and that view is shared by many scholars and those in the media.

Indicator #14: American Chinese and Russian Governments and Their Leaders Suggesting a New Dual Cold War

Immediately after the collapse of the Soviet Union, China declared "war" on the United States, according to Dr. Steven W. Mosher, the president of the Population Research Institute and an internationally recognized authority on China as well as an acclaimed author.[153]

"When the Soviet Union collapsed, [then chairman of the Central Advisory Commission] Deng Xiaoping told the CCP [Chinese Communist Party] Politburo, 'The old Cold War between the Soviet Union and America is over. The New Cold War between China and America has begun.' China has been at war with us [the United States] across all domains—stealing our intellectual property, stealing our factories and jobs, opposing us internationally, warring against us in cyberspace, building a military specifically designed to combat American strengths—ever since," Mosher states.

Mosher continued: "If your enemy says you are at war, you are probably at war, whether you want to be or not." President Trump appears to subscribe to that view, according to his 2017 National Security Strategy (NSS). That document describes both China and Russia as "revisionist powers" who want "to shape a world antithetical to U.S. values and interests."[154]

Predictably, a Chinese foreign ministry spokeswoman referenced the NSS and then called on the United States to abandon Cold War thinking. Hua Chunying urged the US to "abandon its Cold War mentality and zero-sum game concept," as reflected in the NSS. She continued to warn that failure to do so "would only harm itself as well as others."[155]

"China will resolutely safeguard its sovereignty, security and right to develop," she said. "No one should have the fantasy of expecting China to swallow the bitter fruit of harming its own interests."[156]

China is engaged in a Cold War with the US, and according to President Trump's former national security adviser, so is Russia. US Army Lieutenant General H. R. McMaster, Trump's former adviser, said the US has "failed to impose sufficient costs" on Russia. In a speech to the Atlantic

Council, just days prior to his departing the White House, McMaster said, "For too long, some nations have looked the other way in the face of these threats.... Russia brazenly and implausibly denies its actions and we have failed to impose sufficient costs." Then the general said, "Mr. Putin may believe that he is winning in this new form of warfare. He may believe that his aggressive actions...can undermine our confidence, our institutions, and our values."[157] Yes, Putin, according to McMaster, believes we are engaged in a "new form of warfare," a new Cold War.

The NSS warns that Russian nuclear weapons are "the most significant existential threat to the United States." Kremlin spokesman Dmitry Peskov said Russia "cannot accept" being described as a threat to US security. He continued, "The imperialist character of this document [NSS] is obvious, as is the refusal to renounce a unipolar world, an insistent refusal."[158]

In February 2016, Russian Prime Minister Dmitri Medvedev was asked whether there is a new Cold War between Russia and the West. He denied saying that a new Cold War has begun, but said: "I said that NATO's decisions are pushing us toward a new Cold War." He continued to explain that the NATO secretary general called for containing Russia by increasing the alliance's defenses along the Russian border. "If this isn't preparing for another Cold War, what is it for then? For a hot war? Such is the reality," Medvedev said.[159]

In February 17, 2018, Russian Foreign Minister Sergey Lavrov spoke at the annual Munich Security Conference, summarizing Russia's foreign policy. He used the occasion to claim that "the post-Cold War order" (liberalism) "has come to an end." He said Russia rejects the "liberal world order," which he defined as a model that serves "an elite club of countries." He implored the leaders at the conference to choose "a post-Western world order," in which countries develop their own "sovereignty" with respect for each country's identity. He added that the Western world order was similar to the Third Reich's policies, as evidenced by the efforts to isolate Russia.[160]

The view that Russia and the US are in a new Cold War resonates in Washington as well.

Republican Senator Richard Burr (NC), who chairs the Senate Intelligence Committee, believes "we are" in a "new Cold War." He continued, "It mirrors very much what we saw in the 1980s, except for the fact that Russia, just like China, has used technology to leverage what they can do offensively in a way that even the United States hadn't leveraged." Burr continued, "We have a very antiquated procurement process in the military. They have bypassed that and they've truly taken this birth of technology and they've incorporated it in their offensive R&D [research and development] of weaponry."[161]

On March 1, 2018, former CIA deputy director Michael Morell told CBS News, "We are again in a Cold War." His statement followed President Putin's announcement in his State of the Nation speech about an array of new strategic nuclear weapons that the Russian claimed can't be intercepted by US defenses.[162]

"There should be no doubt in anyone's mind that after the invasion of Georgia, the invasion of Ukraine, the intervention in Syria, the meddling in our election, the attack last week by Russian mercenaries on U.S. forces in Syria [February 2018], that we are again in a Cold War," Morell said.[163]

It is also noteworthy to consider what top US military officials say about global tension leading to the new Cold War. In early 2018, US Marine Corps Commandant General Robert Neller, during a visit to Norway, spoke with US Marines on rotation in that country to be ready for a "big-ass fight" at all times. "I hope I'm wrong, but there's a war coming," Neller continued. "You're in a fight here, an informational fight, a political fight, by your presence."[164]

NATO's secretary general agrees with General Neller that something like a new Cold War is brewing. Secretary General Jens Stoltenberg spoke at a NATO meeting in Romanian to say "We are concerned by… [Russia's] lack of transparency when it comes to military exercises." He was referencing a Russian-Belarus operation in September 2017 involving thousands of troops, tanks, and aircraft held in Belarus. Then Stoltenberg said: "Russia is our neighbor…we don't want to isolate Russia. We don't want a new Cold War."

The United Kingdom's former ambassador to Moscow says we are living at the most "dangerous" time since the end of the Cold War. Sir Tony Brenton, who spent thirty years working for the British foreign office, said "in my experience…the relationship [US and Russia] has never been as dangerous as it is today."[165]

"They are fighting in effect, the United States and Russia, a proxy war at the moment in Syria and it is quite striking that in the context of exchanges last autumn where the chairman of the U.S. Joint Chiefs told Congress that they could have no fly zones in Syria if they were willing to go to war with Russia and the Russians put nuclear-tipped-capable rockets on display in Kaliningrad to show the Americans where this thing might go," Brenton warned.[166]

He continued, "I don't think anybody seriously wants a confrontation but the real worry is that you have an accident and then nobody can walk back from the consequences of that accident."[167]

The government in Sweden is alarmed enough about the prospects of war with Russia that in May 2018 it reissued a handbook, *If Crisis or War Comes*, the first significant revision of that publication since the midst of the Cold War a half century ago. The handbook warns Swedish citizens to be prepared for a host of problems to include war with a certain big neighbor to the east. Sweden and its neighboring countries are concerned about what they perceive as provocative actions by Russia, particularly since Moscow's annexation of Crimea in 2014.[168]

American, Chinese and Russian leaders tend to agree, something like a new Cold War is taking place today.

#15: Fractured Nuclear Agreements between the US and Russia

Former Soviet leader Mikhail Gorbachev warns that fractured nuclear pacts have reached a "dangerous point." "I don't want to give any concrete prescriptions but I do want to say that this needs to stop. We need to renew dialogue," the former leader warned.[169]

Gorbachev is rightly concerned about obvious violations of a number of critical arms agreements by the Russians. The New Strategic Arms Reduction Treaty (New START) was intended to replace the arms-control treaty that expired at the end of 2009 and was to be fully implemented in 2018. That agreement requires both Russia and the US to limit their deployed nuclear arms to 1,550 aboard no more than 700 bombers and missiles. Unfortunately, that agreement does not limit tactical nuclear weapons and rail-mobile intercontinental ballistic missiles, flaws according to many members of the US Congress.

Those "flaws" were highlighted in testimony by DIA Director General Ashley. The general told Congress the Russians declared 1,444 warheads on 527 deployed ICBMs, submarine-launched ballistic missiles (SLBMs), and heavy bombers. But in addition, "Russia has an active stockpile of up to 2,000 nonstrategic nuclear weapons" that include air-to-surface missiles, short-range ballistic missiles, gravity bombs, and depth charges for medium-range bombers, tactical bombers, and naval aviation."[170]

Another concern is that Russia violated the New START in a number of important ways. It continues to increase the number of deployed warheads, a clear violation of the agreement. It has also modernized its weapons stockpile by replacing older warheads under the provisions of the treaty with new ones not covered. Further, the US State Department claims Russia has been exceeding the number of allowed nuclear warheads, stating that now Russia has hundreds more than the United States.

Russia is also in violation of the 1987 Intermediate-Range Nuclear Forces Treaty (INF), according to US Air Force General Paul Selva, Vice Chairman of the Joint Chiefs of Staff, who testified in March 2017 that Russia violated the INF with the fielding of the SSC-8 ground-launched cruise missile (GLCM), which violates the treaty ban on ground-launched ballistic and cruise missiles with ranges of between 500 and 5,500 kilometers.[171] General Selva explained, "The system (GLCM) itself presents a risk to most of our facilities in Europe, and we believe that the Russians have deliberately deployed it [one or more battalions of GLCMs] in order to pose a threat to NATO and to facilities within the NATO area of responsibility."[172] Harvard nuclear arms expert Gary Samore testified at the same Senate hearing that heard from General Selva about Russia's violation of the INF. Samore said Russia could do the same with the 1987 INF Treaty that the US did with the Anti-Ballistic Missile (ABM) Treaty. The US withdrew from the 1972 ABM Treaty on June 13, 2002. "But in typical Russian fashion, instead of doing the above-board thing, which is to withdraw from the treaty just like we withdrew from the ABM Treaty, the Russians do it by cheating and denial. And that's the practice we've seen," Samore testified.[173]

The Russians evidence a long a history of not being trustworthy treaty partners. It's noteworthy that Suzanne Massie, a writer in Russia, met with former President Ronald Reagan many times. Massie advised President Reagan that "the Russians like to talk in proverbs. It would be nice of you to know a few. You are an actor—you can learn them very quickly." The Russian proverb that Reagan famously embraced applies to arms-control agreements with the Russians: "Trust, but verify."[174] Unfortunately, given today's tensions with Russia, we can't trust them because they refuse to comply with active agreements.

Indicator #16: Proxy Conflicts

A characteristic of the old Cold War was the proxy conflict, such as in Vietnam, Korea, Cuba, and elsewhere. Similar proxy conflicts between the US/West and both Russia and China are taking place across the world today and more are likely to emerge.

It is unlikely that Russia will elect to go toe to toe with the US militarily, at least in the near term. No, Moscow will keep the new Cold War conflict on the margins through new proxy wars by illegally annexing sovereign territories such as Crimea, the two Republic of Georgia provinces (South Ossetia and Abkhazia), and re-establishing a dominant role in the Middle East by protecting a brutal dictator with Russian (and mercenary) forces operating from an air base and port in Syria. Further, it will manipulate frozen conflicts in places like Moldova, Azerbaijan, and Armenia. Moscow's new Cold War isn't limited to its near neighbors either; all former satellites of the defunct Soviet Union are at risk, as are distant former clients.

President Putin's decision to seize Crimea from Ukraine, then annex it and launch a civil war in southeastern Ukraine, violated all established post-World War II norms of national sovereignty. The trigger for this proxy war was Putin's anger over Ukraine's decision to sign a pact with the European Union, but Ukraine was not part of the Russian Federation, therefore Putin's protests about a sphere of influence being infringed by the EU is untenable.[175] Of course, the US and the EU responded to Putin's aggression by imposing sanctions and started to assist Kiev, which made the ongoing conflict a true proxy war. The US upped the ante by sending military aid to Ukraine—lethal (Javelin anti-tank missiles) and non-lethal (food, vehicles, drones)—to sustain Kiev's military and push back against Russian aggression.

Other proxy conflicts involving Russia are emerging as well. The US has been fighting the Taliban in Afghanistan since 2001, but there is growing evidence over the past two years that Russia is arming the Taliban to sustain the fight with the US/NATO. Further, the Syrian regime under President Bashar al-Assad is backed by Russia, and the rebels fighting Assad enjoy US support, another classic proxy conflict.

Consider a common example of Russian proxy forces fighting Americans and the US' own proxies, albeit with US advisers.

On February 7, 2018, a fire fight in northeast Syria provided a stark example of the ongoing proxy war between Russia and the United States. Russian mercenaries contracted to the Wagner Group, a Kremlin-associated private military company, attacked a Kurdish force advised by US special operations soldiers. Those American special operators called in US air strikes and artillery fire that repelled the assault and reportedly killed many fighters to include Russian mercenaries, according to a variety of sources.[176]

In April 2018, Secretary of Defense James Mattis acknowledged giving the order to attack the Russian mercenaries. Mattis testified before the Senate Armed Services Committee that the "irregular forces" [read "Wagner Group mercenaries"] were in conflict with US forces and "the Russian high command in Syria assured us it was not their people, and my direction to the chairman was for the force, then, to be annihilated. And it was." In fact, according to then CIA Director Mike Pompeo, the US killed "a couple hundred Russians."[177]

CBS News reported that the Wagner mercenaries involved in the Syria firefight worked for Russian oligarch Yevgeny Prigozhin, a close ally of Putin and the same man accused of running a cyber "troll" factory that targeted the 2016 US presidential election. Prigozhin was in contact with both Syrian and Russian officials before and after the assault, according to *CBS News*. Prigozhin's private mercenary army joined the fight a couple years ago to help the Russian military rescue dictator Bashar al-Assad's forces.[178]

An American general confirmed the US-Russia fight and expressed concern that more might follow. On March 14, 2018, US Army Brigadier General Jonathan Braga, director of operations for the US-led anti-Islamic State coalition in Syria, confirmed that his opposition includes many Russian mercenaries. The general described the February 7, 2018 clash between his forces and the pro-Bashar al-Assad fighters that included Russian private military contractors. This was the first time in at least fifty years that Americans and Russians have engaged in direct combat.[179]

General Braga confirmed previous media reports that between two hundred and three hundred Russian mercenaries died in the February attack. Those figures are "close to our estimates," said the general who indicated that the fire fight lasted six hours. He continued that he was "absolutely concerned" that the clash will lead to a larger confrontation with Russia.[180]

Although the Kremlin denies that Russian civilians fighting in Syria are sponsored by the Kremlin, at least on three separate occasions in 2018, groups of men returning from Damascus, Syria, immediately headed to Molkino, a Russian military base, upon landing in that country, as reported by *Reuters*. Molkino is the home of the Russian 10th Special Forces Brigade. *Reuters* reports the Russian defense ministry would not respond to inquiries when asked why civilian fighters in Syria returned to a Russian military base. More than two thousand Russian contractors are believed to be fighting with President al-Assad's forces in Syria, according to *Reuters*.[181]

Russia's use of mercenaries is evident elsewhere as well. In early 2018, Stradfor, a private intelligence firm in Austin, Texas, reported that the Kremlin hired the Wagner Group to deploy to Sudan to construct a military base on the Red Sea to "counteract U.S. interference in the area." Sudan's request to the Russians follows similar requests by nearby Eritrea, Djibouti, and Somalia. Further, in November 2017, Sudan became the first Arab country to receive the fourth generation of Russia's Su-24 fighter jets, part of a $1 billion arms deal.[182]

Moscow's new interest in Africa doesn't stop with Sudan. Other reports indicate that the Wagner Group may help the Kremlin in the Central African Republic. After all, in December 2017, Russia successfully lobbied the UN Security Council to permit the shipment of light arms and ammunition to the Central African Republic despite the 2013 arms embargo. Russia anticipates gaining business opportunities and more influence from that renewed relationship.

Although the Kremlin's use of a private security firm to reopen doors in Africa doesn't mean a full-scale military return to Africa, it does mean Russia is paving the way for more robust involvement on the continent and the real likelihood of a return to the proxy wars of the past.

China is fighting a proxy war with the United States via the North Korean nuclear and ballistic missile threat as well. After all, North Korea is being used as a buffer by Beijing between the West and its border. China's part in this proxy war is its behind-the-scenes support of North Korea in spite of its promises and UN sanctions to do otherwise.

China's ongoing support to North Korea over United States' objections and in spite of UN sanctions is evidence of a proxy war, according to retired US Army Brigadier General Anthony Tata on Fox News. "Well China, normally when they agree with us, they abstain from a UN vote and now they are trying to put a good face forward on this.... They're probably funneling things to North Korea that they shouldn't and they're fighting a proxy war with us through North Korea."[183]

It is noteworthy that US satellite images aired on *Fox News* showed proof of Chinese tankers transferring fuel to North Korean ships at least thirty times in 2017, despite UN sanctions to prevent trade with Kim Jong-Un's regime.

There is far more to the China-North Korea relationship than just a few tankers of fuel circumventing UN sanctions. In early March 2018, Kim Jong Un invited and President Trump accepted to meet to resolve the tension between the US and North Korea regarding Pyongyang's nuclear and ballistic missile programs. Leading up to that proposed meeting, it is important to note, President Xi hosted the North Korean leader once in Beijing and again in May in Dalian, Liaoning province, China for consultations. Part of those consultations likely included a discussion of the important year 2035.

"People have to understand why Xi talked to Kim about 2035, and what it means in the context of the power struggle between the U.S. and China," said a source familiar with the two-country relationship as reported by the *Nikkei Asian Review*. That consultation is part of the ongoing proxy war between the US and China.

Rewind to the October 2017 Chinese Party National Congress, at which the Chinese Communist Party drew up a grand blueprint for building China into a great modern socialist country by 2035. Project 2035, a plan to overtake the US by that year, is focused on both economic and military outcomes. The *Nikkei Asian Review* proposes an answer to the question: "What is Xi's reason for sharing China's long-term development vision [Project 2035] with Kim?" Perhaps Xi's message to his fellow communist "leader for life" is that he (Xi) is someone to be trusted and he will not budge from office until China overtakes the US economically and perhaps militarily by 2035. Also, the message might be: "You are young. Don't you think it would be wiser to follow China, a nation that will soon be the world leader, than to gamble on a deal with Donald Trump, who can only serve two terms?"[184]

The Trump-Kim summit took place on June 12, 2018, among great celebration by both sides. Whether follow-on negotiations produce tangible results that transform North Korea is certainly orchestrated in part by President Xi, who has a long view that puts China on top and the United States vis-à-vis the long proxy war over North Korea and its nuclear arsenal.

China is also involved in other proxy fights, but with the US as the proxy for its Asian partners. Earlier in this chapter, I described the ongoing crisis in the South China Sea between China and the nations of Vietnam and the Philippines. Those nations reasonably expect China to use force to back up their claims to the South China Sea, and Hanoi and Manila want the US to fight China for them. The US Navy has on numerous occasions intervened in a show of force to back up claims by both Vietnam and the Philippines.

Expect more proxy wars to emerge as both Russia and China expand global operations and sense American unwillingness to engage.

Conclusion

Does President Xi's new aggressiveness and China's growing close relationship with Putin's Russia pitting them against the United States in a new dual Cold War mean a future hot war is inevitable? No, but war with the US is far from unthinkable. That conclusion prompted the US Army to commission the RAND Corporation to consider a study of an "unthinkable" war between at least China and the United States, described in part above.

Clearly, the aforementioned sixteen indicators of the new dual

Cold War tee up the possibility that the RAND Corporation studied in 2016. Briefly, such a war between the US and China would be ruinous for both countries and the region—and the world economy would be seriously rocked.[185] After all, both the US and China with their allies have large concentrations of military forces throughout the Asia-Pacific region (perhaps as many as four hundred facilities) and, should hostilities erupt, both militaries have ample means to destroy both man and machine across vast domains: land, sea, air, space, and cyberspace. The scope and consequences of World War II in the Pacific and a possible hot US-China war is an appropriate historic comparison.

Although the consequences of such a hot war are difficult to predict exactly, what's certain is that there would be steep losses on both sides, and the US should not expect to control a conflict it arguably cannot dominate militarily. The days of unquestioned American dominance against a Chinese military are gone, and it is clearly a toss-up which side would win such a war. In fact, the worst consequence, assuming little or no Russian involvement, could leave Russia as the dominant single power: a unipolar world under the authoritiarian Putin or even a renewed communist-light Moscow.

Further, making such a confrontation—a probable World War III—more complex is the emergence of an alliance between China and Russia. This twenty-first-century "alliance of evil"—Russia and China—will inevitably play a key role in the prophetic end times and may become the catalyst for the much-anticipated final, bloody, global war.

Yes, the new dual Cold War is very real, and World War III is a real possibility that may usher in the prophetic end times. That outcome may be encouraged by the decline of America as a global stabilizing force, the subject of the next chapter.

CHAPTER TWO

America's Hubris Makes the Dual Cold War a Reality

The new dual Cold War comes at a time when there are serious questions about America's resilience as a counterbalancing world force. Until recently, America played a critical stabilizing role across the world; after all, it defeated the former Soviet Union, thus emerged as the singular dominant world power. Unfortunately, America's steady geopolitical hand is declining as other powers like China and Russia bully their way forward to grasp the reins from a weakened US and her allies.

The evidence of America's decline is sobering: a weakening military, dwindling foreign influence, government corruption and arrogance, declining economic prowess, cultural/moral implosion, diminished scientific competitiveness, and much more. A Pentagon study echoes this stark and frightening assessment.

A 2016 Army War College study claims the US-backed international order that followed the Second World War is rapidly "fraying" and may even be "collapsing," which could mean America loses its position of "primacy" in the world after more than seven decades of dominance. That means, according to the War College study, the United States "can no longer count on the unassailable position of dominance, supremacy, or pre-eminence it enjoyed for the 20-plus years after the fall of the Soviet Union."[186]

The study does not state that America has suddenly become a toothless tiger, however. No, the United States still retains global political, economic, and military power, but it no longer enjoys an unassailable position versus its competitors, especially China and Russia. The conclusion is that unless our decline is stopped and hopefully reversed, the consequences for the West—and America in particular—are stark.

The study labels our dual Cold War protagonists Russia and China as "revisionist forces" that benefitted from the past US-dominated international order, yet they "seek a new distribution of power and authority commensurate with their emergence as legitimate rivals to the U.S. dominance." The authors indicate that Russia and China "are engaged in a deliberate program to demonstrate the limits of U.S. authority, will, reach, influence, and impact." As a minimum, Russia and China want to reorder the status quo to be more favorable to their core objectives and unseat America as the unquestioned dominant world force, thus the emergent new dual Cold War.[187]

This chapter will examine what that decline means for America and her adversaries. However, the loss of primacy does not necessarily mean the US can't regain the upper hand over China and Russia, nor does it mean America's many very favorable virtues are in ruins. After all, America is a resilient country that overcame past significant setbacks such as the 1861–65 Civil War, the Great Depression, and the post-Vietnam War era. Therefore, even in the face of compelling threats from China and Russia, we must not undervalue America's fundamental strengths and its proven ability to overcome adversity.

Yes, America is at a tipping point in its 250-year history as it faces down the new dual Cold War. Consider the evidence suggesting the US is in decline, thus granting an opportunity for China and Russia to bully their way into a dominant role. Then consider in mitigation our resilient strengths, which, if harnessed correctly, might just reverse the decline.

Before considering the specific evidence of America's decline, it is useful to set the stage by establishing that America indeed decades ago became a great power—some say a modern-era "empire." Appreciating that status—"great power" and/or "empire"—is seldom disputed, but that is important to acknowledge, because it provides an opportunity then to consider from world history whether lessons from the fall of other past great powers and empires might be instructive for contemporary America and in particular the new dual Cold War.

America the Great Power: "Empire Status"

America became a great power after the Second World War and added to that status to become the world's sole superpower with the fall of the Soviet Union in 1991. It is noteworthy that during the old Cold War (1945–1991), both the US and the Soviet Union, although militarily great powers, never claimed to be empires even though both demonstrated classical characteristics of past empires. In fact, each made derogatory statements about the term "empire" and used "empire" as a disparaging remark about the other, such as President Ronald Reagan's reference to the Soviet Union as an "evil empire" in a March 1983 speech to the National Association of Evangelicals.[188]

The fact is both superpowers fit the classic definition of "empire," which, according to the *New Oxford Living Dictionary*, is "an extensive group of states under a single supreme authority, formerly especially an emperor or an empress."[189]

Consider the case for classifying the post Second World War United States as an empire.

The US consists of an "extensive group of states," fifty to be precise, as well as territories such as Puerto Rico, Guam, the US Virgin Islands, and, for a period in the twentieth century, the Philippines. Arguably, control over these territories qualifies America as an empire, but there is more. America also exercises considerable influence over other areas vis-à-vis its alliances such as the one with the North Atlantic Treaty

Organization (NATO) (a twenty-nine-nation European alliance), and it exercises considerable influence over much of the Western Hemisphere, thanks to its influence from the Monroe Doctrine, a nineteenth-century proclamation by President James Monroe that warned European nations to no longer get involved in American political matters because that was the exclusive domain of the United States.

Past empires such as the Ottoman, Roman, and Persian were also autocratic, while the contemporary American political system is republican, a representative form of government. Even though America has never had an emperor or empress, that fact alone doesn't disqualify it from empire status. Arguably, America became like past empires: a dominant state, due to its significant economic and military power over global affairs, much as other empires dominated many states in their time. In fact, American presidents, especially after the Second World War, exercised considerable influence internationally, which makes them similar to past emperors.

Former Secretary of State Henry A. Kissinger explained America's unusual empire-like status in his book *World Order*:

> Imbued with the conviction that its course would shape the destiny of mankind, America has, over its history, played a paradoxical role in world order: it expanded across a continent in the name of Manifest Destiny while abjuring any imperial designs; exerted a decisive influence on momentous events while disclaiming any motivation of national interest; and became a superpower while disavowing any intention to conduct power politics. America's foreign policy has reflected the conviction that its domestic principles were self-evidently universal and their application at all times salutary; that the real challenge of American engagement abroad was not foreign policy in the traditional sense but a project of spreading values that it believed all other peoples aspired to replicate.[190]

We can disagree as to whether America is a true empire. However, the United States has certainly demonstrated characteristics common with past empires, and as a result, it is instructive to consider the factors that brought about the demise of former empires to ascertain whether they apply to modern America's decline.

Rise and Fall

World history chronicles the rise and fall of past great powers (empires) such as Egypt, China, Greece, Rome, Persia, and the Soviet Union. Their eventual decline is evidenced by a number of symptoms: corruption, natural disasters, social conflict, resource-draining wars, overwhelming debt, and loss to external powers (wars). But there is something underlying these and other symptoms that significantly contributed to their demise, which may be key to understanding the current times for America as well.

J. Rufus Fears, professor of the classics at the University of Oklahoma, identifies perhaps the most persuasive reason past empires ultimately failed. He cites the work of the Greek historian Herodotus, who illustrates the underlying cause of the demise of the Persian Empire to illuminate the point.

In 490 BC, Persian King Darius preemptively attacked Athens' army at a plain near Marathon (the namesake of the popular 26.2 mile run today), and even though the Persian army was three times larger, better equipped, and better trained than the Athenians, it lost the battle, which, according to Herodotus, began the decline of the Persian Empire.

Professor Fears wrote: "The battle of Marathon was the most decisive battle in the history of freedom and the most decisive battle in the history of the United States." Fears connects the Persian-Athenian battle with the US because of what was at stake in the broadest sense.[191]

"Had the Athenians failed at this great challenge, the word 'democracy' would be lost in history. The values of Europe, above all individual and political freedom, would have been lost to history," Professor Fears argued. You see, Herodotus understood "that the war against Darius was part of the never-ending-struggle of the values of Europe against the Middle East: freedom vs. despotism." Fears explained that outcome inspired America's founders, who faced their own daunting adversary: the mighty British fleet and His Majesty's army. So, what is the lesson for modern America, according to Fears?[192]

Herodotus was skeptical about the typical explanations for the fall of empires. After all, in the case of the Persian Empire, the problem wasn't wealth, because that empire was an economic superpower. The empire covered a vast area (Spain to China), and it was a creditor nation with a gold-filled treasury. Provincial taxes paid for the king's vast army, and the historical records indicate that the Persians governed their empire efficiently. The problem, according to Herodotus, was poor leadership.

The Persian Empire failed because of King Darius' leadership, specifically his "hubris." The term "hubris" in Greek means "outrageous arrogance," or the abuse of power. "The Greeks believed that hubris was preceded by moral blindness that makes you believe that you can do anything you want to and there will be no consequences from either gods or men," according to Professor Fear. It was hubris that led King Darius to attack Athens and his moral blindness that convinced him that he would never see defeat. Hubris has long been the enemy of good leadership and the seed that crumbles empires.

Is America falling prey to the same "sin of hubris" that infected the Persian king? After all, in the wake of the collapse of the Soviet Union, America was on top of the world: economically, politically and militarily supreme—the sole world superpower. Americans were incredibly optimistic, self-confident after the fall of the Iron Curtain and full of pride thanks to President Reagan's inspiring leadership. What happened? This "pride" should remind Christians of the Scripture verse, "Pride goeth before destruction, and a haughty spirit before a fall" (Proverbs 16:18, KJV).

Professor Fears suggests that if the ancient Herodotus were present today, he would say America's current decline from the heights of sole superpower status is attributable to the fatal flaw of hubris—thinking it to be undefeatable. Herodotus would look around our contemporary world to observe that American hubris contributed to China's superpower rise. He might say that Russia exited the old Cold War utterly disillusioned, but thanks to American hubris, it is now coming back worse than ever—chauvinistic and armed with a modern arsenal itching for battle.

Why did this happen? That's evident as we look back in time. The US and much of the West cashed in common sense at the end of the old Cold War to focus inward, and we let down our guard. We made very poor decisions and mostly ignored history, believing that superpower America was undefeatable. Further, our loss of focus on the important things encouraged an unlikely alliance to form—Russia, China, Iran, North Korea, and others—that evidently now smells "American blood in the geopolitical water" and is aligned against America in a new dual Cold War.

American hubris over the past few decades led to many incredibly bad decisions. Our leaders accepted an overwhelming national debt ($20+ trillion) and issued massive amounts of fiat currency (backed no longer by gold or silver but by the "full faith and credit" of the US government). They led us into preventive wars (Vietnam, Iraq, and Afghanistan) and failed to stop millions of illegal immigrants who now drain our wealth from entering the country. Further, we naively pretend that our globally capable military can be sustained on serial, continuing-resolution funding streams fueled by an overtaxed mostly service-oriented economy. That's the height of hubris!

Herodotus wrote his history to urge Athenians to learn from the decline of the Persian Empire. They didn't have to repeat history. He urged them to recapture the values that made them great: patriotism, courage, and financial and political common sense. Then Herodotus gave them a sobering warning: Empires that fall never rise again.

America is seriously infected with hubris manifested in our culture, economics, national security, and government. Those symptoms clearly point to the underlying disease (hubris), and if not quickly arrested, it will kill the patient and America will never rise again.

Symptoms of Hubris in American Culture

America's culture has experienced a meltdown thanks to the Boomer generation (those born between 1946 and 1964) and their sin of hubris, but their incompetence as cultural custodians is mostly masked by technology and empty words divorced from reality—a cultural façade pushing a vicarious life advanced by West Coast elite who are full of themselves.

Imagine what Herodotus might say about our twenty-first-century American cultural mess. Likely, the Greek historian would study the headlines in our media to see that our elites are mired in excess, and while safe in their exclusive enclaves, demonstrate unconscionable hubris over our decaying cultural institutions such as Hollywood.

Herodotus would be especially critical of the role played by the entertainment elite. He would likely eviscerate the infamous Holly-wood-mogul-Harvey-Weinstein-serial-sexual-abuse-alleged-rape episode as emblematic of America's cultural implosion. He would endorse the view expressed by Victor Hanson of the *National Review*, who wrote, "The [Boomer] generation that gave us the free-love and the anything-goes morals of Woodstock discovered that hook-up sex was 'contrary to nature.'" Weinstein, according to Hanson, "got into his head that the fantasy women in his movies who were customarily portrayed as edgy temptresses and promiscuous sirens were reflections of the way women really were in Los Angeles and New York—or the way that he thought they should be." Weinstein is suspected of assaulting and harassing many women, and in the spring of 2018, he was charged by the Manhattan district attorney with two counts of sexual misconduct and rape—a true ingrate tolerated by the cultural elites until his public shaming.[193]

Hanson submits that "Weinstein [also] reminded us, especially in his eleventh-hour medieval appeals for clemency [after many accusers came forward] by way of PC attacks on the NRA [National Rifle Association] and Donald Trump, that mixing politics with art was, as our betters warned, always a self-destructive idea." But that's what our culture has become: a platform for moral relativists to excuse criminal and immoral behavior.

Hanson nailed the coffin shut on the entertainment cabal when he exposed what most observers have already concluded: that slimy Hollywood "ran out of original thought about three decades ago, and the people noticed and so [they] keep avoiding the theaters." He goes on to cite examples of the lack of imagination, the high-brow embrace of social justice by Hollywood elite, and the infatuation of the acting community with political correctness to serve their radical progressive and faux elitist struggle on race and gender against so-called bad racists and sexists (read "the rest of America"). Their hubris is literally dripping with hypocrisy.

The National Football League (NFL) is another cultural institution that is, like Hollywood, in moral freefall. The NFL, according to Hanson, reveals generational symptoms of exhaustion. Specifically, the owners, players, and their stable of announcers on television (especially *ESPN*) and elsewhere totally lost sight of their original mission: athleticism, sports commentary, inductive thinking, civic education, and disinterested inquiry. Rather, their money and self-adulation puffed up those faux Olympians who do little more than grandstand against their patrons, the fans who fund their often-exorbitant lifestyles and platform for their sanctimony.

He goes on to attack the NFL cabal's inconsistencies and fragilities that ram their political agendas down the throat of America. Hanson concludes that politics are destroying the NFL, and you can "thank in part the [80 percent African-American] twentysomething, half-educated multimillionaires who think they are our moral superiors." These young men need a lesson on patriotism to stand on their feet rather than taking a knee to political correctness. That's another example of cultural hubris gone amok.

America's news media is another cultural icon overflowing with hubris, states Hanson. Today's "journalists graduate with majors that confer thinly disguised degrees in different sorts of activism" rather than training on objective journalism. He indicates that the problem with most journalists today is their politically driven ignorance and activism. No wonder President Trump labels many of them "fake news" because they too evidence hubris in the name of journalism.

Our educational system gets special attention because it also has become politically correct and Stalinistic on our campuses, Hanson explains. Our so-called higher education establishment empowers ignorance by watering down curricula with activist courses like "white racism" rather than tough academic courses like math, engineering, and English composition that might possibly contribute to our collective betterment. No, our higher educational establishment politicizes mediocrity to advance ignorance and arrogance—all in the savaged name of free speech.

The classic manifestations of that ignorance and arrogance are tearing down the statue of American Civil War leaders like General Robert E. Lee without understanding a shred of his background, much less the history of that war. Others torch or at least violently disrupt conservative speakers on campuses, like at the University of Connecticut, which hosted conservative speaker Ben Shapiro in January 2018. Shapiro said the college restricted access to his speech and offered formal counseling to any student "hurt" by the fact he was visiting the campus. "Something has to be done about a system where a few crazed leftists don't want me to speak," Shapiro said.[194]

Our hubris-infected, radically liberal, higher-education culture has an Orwellian language that masks its anti-democratic reality on many American campuses with a frightening PC lexicon: "safe spaces" (means "segregation"), "affirmative action" (means "implicit racial quotas"), "theme houses" (means "race-based apartheid"), "diversity" (ensures orthodoxy of expression), and much more. Gone are the days when all views were debated on a reasonably level playing ground.

Worse, America's PC-infatuated, higher-education establishment ensures that the formerly coveted Bachelor of Arts degree has become almost worthless because it no longer includes science, math, history, and how to write a cogent thesis—all skills American businesses need in the workforce. Further, even the elite colleges like Harvard, Yale, and Princeton can be worse, because they too have lost sight of their obligation to educate the next generation and now tend to produce graduates with little more than giant debt and heads full of worthless hubris.

No wonder America is ranked number seven in education across the world. We are rapidly losing our competitive edge against the likes of China because we are producing a new generation whose educational attainment is lower than their parents and grandparents in terms of content and value.

A brief comparison between American and Chinese university degrees is quite sobering and in part explains America's declining competitiveness.

"China produces four times as many science, technology, engineering, and mathematics (STEM) bachelor's degrees and twice as many STEM Ph. D's as the United States," according David Goldman, a columnist for *Asia Times* and a Pulliam Distinguished Visiting Fellow in Journalism at Hillsdale College. Goldman continued, "Only six or seven percent of U.S. college students major in engineering. In China that number is 30–40 percent."[195]

No wonder American competitiveness and perhaps survival are at risk, thanks in part to a totally corrupted higher-education establishment. A May 2018 Pentagon report on American Industrial Capabilities sounds alarms about long-term trends that "continue to threaten the health of the industrial base, limit innovation, and reduce U.S. competitiveness in the global markets." This is especially evident thanks to our lack of STEM graduates in the aerospace and defense industry, which faces "a shortage of qualified workers to meet current demands as well as needing to integrate a young workforce with the 'right skills, aptitude, experience, and interest to step into the jobs vacated by senior-level engineers and skilled technicians' as they exit the workforce."[196]

Our schools and media are also robbing America of its patriotism and love for the country. Contemporary public educational institutions teach a history that most Baby Boomers wouldn't recognize, and our media never misses an opportunity to bash America, much less distort our rich heritage and sacrifice. No wonder only half of US adults told Gallup in a survey that they are "extremely proud" to be Americans; that's down from 70 percent in 2003. Further, patriotism is especially rare among American young adults; it's now at 34 percent. Why? Our culture pumps them full of ideas that run counter to being patriotic and loving their country. That's faux self-focused hubris and dangerous for our collective future.

Herodotus would look beyond the cultural institutions of Hollywood, sports, journalism and education to see a much deeper problem with a hubris-soaked America. No doubt the Greek historian would also point his finger at us, the American public. After all, Americans like to blame our cultural institutions (Hollywood, media, education) for the current mess and claim victimhood as if we are blameless for our slimy culture. That's false hubris.

Most of us deny any accountability for the mess much like King Darius blamed others for his loss at Marathon. We too are blinded by hubris regarding the real culprit for the current state of affairs: ourselves. Look around yourself and draw your own conclusions.

Who supports the cultural institutions we are so quick to blame? Do you support Hollywood, professional sports, the liberal mainstream media, and our educational establishment who collectively trash America? If you are honest, the answer is a resounding yes. It gets worse. You and I also elect the people who endorse these culture-changing institutions by the laws they pass and the government policy they oversee.

We vote into office crooks and charlatans and then expect their politics to reflect our values: pro-life, pro-family, and pro-faith. That's foolishness. We wonder why the American family is imploding from divorce, fatherlessness, moral bankruptcy, lack of faith, and apathy. It is because we made bad choices and turned a blind eye to the facts and elect politicians who ignore those facts. That's hubris on our part. We are too busy with our lives to get involved, and the culture goes to hell as a result.

Sure, many of us are angry about our slimy culture, but it doesn't go much farther than a few muffled words of discontent to a confidante. That anger raises our blood pressure but seldom motivates us to step out of our comfort zone and do something!

We don't exercise common sense in our interactions either, and we pretend ignorance about the facts. But there is no excuse for ignorance in a modern world with access to instant facts thanks to our pocket computers. No, we too often put our heads in the sand, electing to remain uninformed, naïve, and apart from meaningful solutions so desperately needed. The American Christian community is worse than the secular culture. We claim to read our Bibles, and therefore should know better, because God's Word is clear about the issues sliming our culture. Like King Solomon writes in Proverbs, we are fools for following the ways of the world when we know better, and like Jesus' disciple Matthew who wrote that the unfaithful Christian is as tasteless salt, we are worthless in the face of evil.

The fact is our culture reflects deep moral anarchy similar to what the Scripture describes in Judges 21:25: "In those days Israel had no king; everyone did as he saw fit." Today our society embraces similar moral relativism where right is in the eyes of the beholder and unfortunately the church is no better than the secular world.

Many Christians can't seem to even distinguish false teaching from biblical truth, because too few believers understand the basics of their faith. We even have some in Christian ministries engaged in outright blasphemy and no one calls them out. No wonder most (two-thirds) of youth leave the Christian church behind for spiritual journeys, such as new age or atheism, and never return. That's evidence of cultural hubris in the Christian church.

America's culture is overwhelmed by the sin of hubris, which contributes to our decline.

Symptoms of Hubris in American Economics

Empires and great powers may not have fallen solely because of economic reasons, but economic decisions laced with hubris have certainly accelerated their fall. There is a lesson here for America.

The Persian Empire in its prime was the center of a global economy, a rich creditor nation backed by a giant armed force and an efficient bureaucracy with a postal service made famous by the motto: "Neither rain nor snow nor gloom of night shall keep these couriers from their appointed route."[197]

Even though the Persians fell to the Athenians at Marathon, the empire continued for most of a century as it slowly weakened, in part due to oppressive economic policies. The Persian leaders imposed oppressive taxation, which sparked economic depression and revolt. Further, the kings hoarded gold and silver, which is an indicator of economic hubris that contributed to turmoil, because the precious metals were the currency for doing business.[198]

Economic hubris contributed to the fall of the Roman Empire as well. Rome lasted as an empire for over a thousand years to become an adaptive civilization that eventually split into eastern and western portions governed by separate emperors. That alone contributed to the fall, as did factors that include the introduction of Christianity, decadence, monetary troubles, and military challenges. Like all others, there was plenty of evidence of imperial incompetence (mostly due to hubris), and that's especially true in the case of Rome's economic policies that contributed to the empire's fall.

The Roman government's economic policies should sound familiar to modern Americans. The primary economic factors associated with Rome's fall appear to be inflation, over taxation, and feudalism. However, contributing to these factors was the hoarding of bullion by Roman citizens, looting of the treasury by barbarians, and a massive trade deficit. These issues created significant stress that no doubt impacted the fall.[199]

Emperor Nero created a lack of confidence in Rome's reliability by debasing Roman currency when he ordered the removal of precious silver and gold from the coinage in order to increase the supply. That meant the coin's intrinsic value went from 100 percent silver in a denarius to only .02 percent, thus creating a fiat currency, a move the US made in 1971 by abandoning the gold standard and underpinning the currency's value by the strength of the government. Rome's move to a fiat currency led to inflation, and it didn't help that luxury-loving emperors like Commodus depleted Rome's imperial coffers, leaving them empty by the time of his assassination.[200]

Initially, the Roman Empire acquired wealth through conquering new lands. Once those conquests stopped, it turned to confiscating the estates of the wealthy, and eventually it taxed the poor (feudalism). Of course, the poor farmers were already accustomed to being taxed by the rich landlords.

Before Rome imposed federal taxation, the provincial landlords made their money by taxing the middle-class farmers, who eventually abandoned their property due to high taxes and moved to the cities where they became dependent upon the state. That resulted in growing social dependency, forcing the Roman government to first deplete the elites' resources and then turn to the poor to pay the state's bills. The Roman (an early version of the Internal Revenue Service) tax collectors were the Praetorian Guards and other military troops who depended on those tax receipts for their income.

In 476 CE, Romulus, the last Roman emperor, was overthrown by barbarians, ending the empire's millennial reign and beginning what is known as the Middle Ages. Contributing to Rome's ultimate collapse were economic policies such as high inflation, unacceptable taxation, massive government welfare, and a marginalized (fiat) currency. These symptoms of Rome's fall reflected a leadership failure, hubris.

Like ancient Romans, contemporary Americans tend to be dissatisfied with their government's economic policies as well, and much of that discontent is attributable to hubris with good reason.

It took America two hundred years to produce its first $1 trillion budget, and now Washington runs annual deficits twice as large. Our Social Security and Medicare programs are broken, progressive entitlement programs that threaten to soon subsume the entire national GDP. Further, America's federal unfunded liabilities are now approaching a breathtaking $100 trillion.

Our economy wasn't always failing. For many years, Congress responsibly kept spending under control—that is, until it suffered budget deficits every year from 1970 through 1997. Then in 1998, President Bill Clinton broke the cycle with a surplus that was repeated each year until 2001.[201] Fiscal year 2018 began with a series of stop-gap spending resolutions and no annual budget, and we can reasonably expect yet another giant budget deficit each year for the foreseeable future.

How did we get into this economic mess? We can thank hubris. Bad decisions mired us in preventable wars that vanquished our long-expired surplus. What did our leaders do then? Like the Romans, they expanded the money supply in an attempt to reinflate the bubble. One author said that's "akin to downing a fifth of vodka in order to drown a hangover." It was sheer criminal hubris.

No one doubts that 2008 was a bad economic year (Great Recession), a crisis created by government hubris. We let our political class borrow unlimited amounts of money just like past failed empires. They spent that money wildly on highly questionable programs, and meanwhile, our central bank operated with practically no boundaries on its size, budget, and dominance over our financial markets.

Why did our "leaders" decide to give the Federal Reserve the authority to become the primary financier of the federal debt? Hubris. America couldn't fail, they assumed. Let others buy our debt.

The record speaks for itself. The Federal Reserve, in its "wisdom," oversaw the decline of the dollar's value by 90 percent in the 1970s, which drove capital out of America. That sounds like something Roman emperor Nero did two thousand years ago, which contributed to Rome's ultimate fall.

Washington's hubris also squandered our global advantage in living standards as per capita income stagnated in dollar terms and declined when measured in monetary standards of China and Europe. That is why in part our global leadership in innovation, wealth, and clout are fading and our industry moves assets and profits abroad.

Our founders never dreamed our government would borrow trillions of dollars to sustain itself, much less issue fiat currency. Yet our federal government now consumes almost half of America's GDP, a very dangerous message and one that robs the confidence of our citizenry and allies.

David Smick, author of *The World Is Curved: Hidden Dangers to the Global Economy*, argues that economics is dead because of hubris, an apt conclusion given the state of America's economy as outlined above.

Smick writes that hubris is the common currency of the economic policy world, and that is bad news. He states: "In the 1960s and 1970s… liberal economists believed they could eliminate all poverty. In the 1980s, conservatives thought tax policy could permanently raise the savings rate. It turns out other factors also influence a person's decision to save."[202]

Earlier this century, central bank economists made similarly bad policy. They thought they could engineer monetary policy to eliminate the US business cycle by deregulating the financial industry as well. All wrong. That effort allowed banks to engage in hedge-fund trading with derivatives that ultimately led to the global financial crisis, the so-called Great Recession of 2007–2008.

Alan Greenspan, the man who ran the Federal Reserve until January 2006, admits some culpability for the subprime-fueled housing boom crisis that triggered the Great Recession. He admits to mistakes in his book, *The Map and the Territory: Risk, Human Nature, and the Future of Forecasting.* He wonders "how we all got it so wrong, and what we can learn from the fact that we did." He explained that before the crisis, "macroeconomic modelling unequivocally failed when it was needed most.... The Federal Reserve's highly sophisticated forecasting system did not foresee a recession until the crisis hit."[203]

During congressional testimony, Greenspan explained why he and others were wrong. He responded as follows to the simple question "Were you wrong?":

> Partially...I made a mistake in presuming that the self-interest of organizations, specifically banks, is such that they were best capable of protecting shareholders and equity in the firms.... I discovered a flaw in the model that I perceived is the critical functioning structure that defines how the world works. I had been going for 40 years with considerable evidence that it was working exceptionally well. The overall view I take of regulation is, I took an oath of office when I became Federal Reserve chairman. I'm here to uphold the laws of the land passed by Congress, not my own predilections.[204]

Similar economic hubris infected Europe as well. European economists thought they could contain Greece's debt problems, and Italian policymakers were infected with hubris, believing their government-bond interest rates would remain unaffected by the Greek crisis. Wrong. Italy's long-term rates skyrocketed.

Keynesians (those who embrace the theory that economic output is strongly influenced by aggregate demand), according to Smick, have insisted that massive new government spending has excess capacity, thus debt doesn't matter. President Obama followed that model through his $1 trillion stimulus package, which created a limp economy. Meanwhile, conservative economists called for fiscal austerity, hoping that would attract capital, but it really does quite the opposite.

Central bankers have a terrible track record as well. They demand that we trust their typical rosy economic forecasts that predictably underperform. No wonder most Americans sense something is fundamentally wrong, because the traditional fiscal and monetary tools the economists use simply don't work anymore.

Smick concludes that the field of economics is dying. It has become less a science and more an art—an informed guessing game with our futures. Over the last decade, after ample fiscal and monetary stimulus, global public and private debt exploded and the stock market capitalization jumped, yet the world economy is slowing.

Smick asks: "How do we survive a global capital system with ever expanding oceans of money and seemingly few rules of the road? Are central bankers irrelevant? Is eye-popping financial volatility, therefore, the 'new normal'?"

Greenspan asks why "virtually every economist and policymakers of note was so off about so large an issue [policies that led to the Great Recession]?" But not everyone agreed with Greenspan, such as Robert Shiller, a 2013 Nobel Prize in Economics recipient who warned about "irrational exuberance." That and other warnings fell on deaf ears, however. Economist hubris ruled the day and led us over the cliff.

Author Stephen King wrote in the *London Times* that Greenspan should more appropriately have asked: "Why [were] those who subscribed to the conventional wisdom treated anyone who suggested otherwise with, at best, amused detachment and, at worst, utter contempt?" There were plenty of warnings leading up to the Great Recession of 2007–2008, but most economists chose to ignore the skeptics.

It's time to rethink our economic policy before it is too late and to begin that process by abandoning hubris. We haven't much time to wrestle back out-of-control federal spending and a deficit that promises global default. Hubris is our internal subversive enemy. It begins with a moral slide gathering momentum and can lead to a surprise destruction.

Symptoms of Hubris in American National Security

The sin of hubris often afflicts national security vis-à-vis government and military leaders who, though evidencing sometimes great leadership, abuse their power to gratify their own vanity and ambition. One of the best examples of leader hubris is Achilles in Greek mythology, the greatest warrior of the army of Agamemnon in the Trojan War. Achilles asks the Greek leaders for his fair share of the booty and sulks until his beloved Patroclus is killed, then Achilles rejoins the fight, evidencing the worst sin of leadership: hubris. The curse of this overwhelming pride is a common failing in Greek mythology, as it is today for some who oversee the defense of our country.

Hubris is incredibly dangerous in the context of national security because it needlessly risks lives and entire countries to satisfy the leader's self-glorification, arrogance, overconfidence in one's ability, and right to do whatever he or she wants, to the point of disdaining the cardinal virtues of life.[205] Unfortunately, wars over the ages have been won and lost due to the excesses of hubris, or what some call "overreach."

A brief review of the role hubris has played in the outcome of past battles and wars is instructive as we consider America's future and especially the new dual Cold War with China and Russia.

Complacency, writes the British historian Alistair Horne, is indicative of hubris, "a first step on the path to ruin." German Chancellor Otto von Bismarck once said: "A generation that deals out a thrashing is usually followed by one which receives it." History validates Bismarck's view, according to Horne, such as the French World War I victory of Verdun that left that nation with hubristic self-confidence that they "would be safe behind the super-Verdun-like fortress of the Maginot line." The 1940 Nazi Blitzkrieg into France at the outset of World War II demolished Paris' hubristic complacency and faux trust in the Maginot line.[206]

Horne poses an interesting question for those overseeing military operations: "Why don't successful generals know when to stop?" His answer is simple: "It is hubris itself which blinds generals." Below are historical examples of top military and government leaders who demonstrated blinding hubris, a lesson for contemporary American leaders facing down a new dual Cold War. Then we briefly consider a contemporary institutional example of how hubris infects an entire government and the armed forces.

Napoleon Bonaparte

Napoleon Bonaparte (1769–1821), also known as Napoleon I, was a French military leader who seized power through a coup d'état in 1799 and then went on to conquer much of Europe. He was a skilled strategist who successfully expanded his empire through waging war. However, Napoleon didn't know when to stop, thanks to hubris, which cost him the throne. He was then exiled to Elba, an island off Italy's west coast in the Mediterranean Sea.

In June 1812, Napoleon led his Grande Armée to attack Russia. He hubristically expected to dispatch the Russians in short order like he had other armies, which explains why the French army carried only summer gear into battle.

There is an explanation for Napoleon's hubris. He rose from being a Corsican outsider to the position of emperor of France and then conquered much of Europe. As emperor, he was widely known as a brilliant military tactician, which evidently went to his head—especially when he confronted the Russians. On June 24, 1812, Napoleon invaded Russia with his five hundred thousand-soldier army, the largest European military force ever assembled to that date. A reputation as a successful conqueror and a massive army created a "Thucydides trap" for the hubristic emperor.

That metaphor is associated with the fifth-century BC Greek historian Thucydides and represents the dangers when a rising power rivals a ruling power like Sparta in ancient Greece. Most such contests tend to end badly, and it does for Napoleon.

The Russians withdrew before the French, refusing to engage Napoleon's superior force. As they withdrew, General Mikhail Kutuzov, the Russian commander, ordered his forces to destroy every village as he retreated ever deeper into Russia, thus denying the French foraging opportunities. On September 14, Napoleon arrived in Moscow after the indecisive bloody Battle of Borodino. Once in Moscow, the French found the city set ablaze and almost the entire population evacuated. At that point, the French army found itself without supplies just as the harsh Russian winter started. Shortly thereafter, with the Russians refusing to surrender, the French campaign turned into a retreat and a disaster for the emperor.[207]

Napoleon's retreat was disastrous due to the continual harassment by the Russian army, the lack of food, and attacks by spear-wielding Cossacks. Finally, remnants of the French army reached the Berezina River, which is in modern Belarus, where Napoleon lost another thirty-six thousand troops in the November crossing that was blocked by the Russians. It is noteworthy that the word "Berezina" is used even today in the French language as a synonym for "catastrophe."

Napoleon's retreat from Moscow became a rout, and on December 8, 1812, the emperor left the remnants of his Grand Armée to return to Paris. Meanwhile, six days later, what was left of the Armée escaped Russia—but not until it suffered the loss of more than four hundred thousand men overall.

All told, more than a million people, soldiers and civilians, died due to Napoleon's hubris.

Adolf Hitler

Adolf Hitler could have invented the word "hubris." Days after he became Germany's new chancellor, he gave a speech to a gathering of senior generals. He spoke for two hours, and not a person left or interrupted the presentation, during which Hitler outlined his ambitions to destroy both democracy and Marxism and conquer the "living space in the east."[208]

Hitler quickly seduced the military leadership, known for their traditionally conservative values that embraced the new chancellor's grandiose vision for Germany to be restored to its "rightful place" in the wake of defeat in the First World War. Hitler promised the German brass a modern, mechanized army with plenty of promotions and increased influence. No wonder the Wehrmacht quickly gave Hitler its "unconditional obedience" and the Führer's (German for "guide") hubris went on to infect most of the German officer corps as well.

Leading up to the Second World War, the Wehrmacht developed a savage reputation, great confidence (hubris), and a tactic known as the Blitzkrieg, German for "lightening war." Little wonder one general boasted, "We have the best armed forces in the world!" That view was soon validated as Nazi troops invaded Austria in 1938, then Poland in the fall of 1939.

After Hitler impressively overran France in the spring of 1940, few doubted that the Wehrmacht was invincible, especially the German generals. In 1941, General Heinz Günther Guderian boasted that the devil could "fricassee [cut up for a stew] him" if he wasn't in Moscow in eight days' time. He made that declaration in Minsk, four hundred miles away.[209]

Germany's early victories fostered a belief in its invincibility, but that view was mostly in the minds of the leaders, not of the average soldier. One exhausted soldier wrote home from the front: "Weeks of endless grinding slog…blazing sun, cold nights, foot-high sand and swamps…. Only those who have fought in [this] campaign can grasp how much this has cost us in nerves, sweat and effort."[210]

The Blitzkrieg brought early success, but soon Germany's enemies learned to counter the strategy, which turned success into a bloody slog. The "end of the beginning," according to British historian Alistair Horne, began with Moscow in 1941. That battle was the first time Hitler's so-called invincible panzers (tanks) were stopped, defeated, and then forced to retreat, not all that different than what had happened to Napoleon more than a century earlier.

The outcome of Hitler's hubristic decisions cost the Russian people millions of lives and led to a post-WWII divided Europe known as the Cold War. It also made the Russian leader, the murderous Joseph Stalin, an omnipotent war leader who, with those who followed him at the Kremlin, brought the world to frequent nuclear standoffs.

Douglas MacArthur

Noted author David Halberstam in his book, *The Coldest Winter,* exposes why General Douglas MacArthur's hubris cost so many lives.

America's intervention in the Korean War did reverse the communist thrust into South Korea, but left half the peninsula impoverished to this day and a Stalinist state seeking nuclear weapons that threaten the United States.

The Korean War is noteworthy for some very bad decisions, arguably because of skewed military intelligence. Evidently, according to Halberstam, American military officers massaged the facts they reported to civilian leaders. Halberstam said the manipulation of the facts set a "most dangerous" precedent: "The American government had begun to make fateful decisions based on the most limited of truths and the most deeply flawed intelligence in order to do what it wanted to do for political reasons, whether it would work or not."[211]

Halberstam points out three major reasons for these bad decisions. First, the command relied on "massaged" intelligence, and second, the commanding general, Douglas MacArthur, ran the war from the luxury of his Tokyo hotel. Third, he (MacArthur) was unanswerable to anyone, Halberstam said, and his "willfulness was unyielding, abetted by pseudo-intelligence subserviently packaged by staff toadies in Tokyo."[212]

MacArthur's hubris led him to a tragic miscalculation. He claimed that Chinese leader Mao Zedong would be intimidated if the US inserted an army by sea at Inchon, South Korea. Further, he was certain that the Chinese would never intervene in the Korean War. Yes, the September Inchon landing was an initial success…but then came the winter.

After Inchon, MacArthur made a victory lap in Korea, where he confidently boasted: "The war is over. The Chinese are not coming... the Third Division will be back at Fort Benning [Georgia] for Christmas dinner." Just as quickly as he came, MacArthur flew back to his Tokyo hotel (no roughing it overnight for him), and, as one colonel said, no one doubted the five-star general because "it would have been questioning an announcement from god."[213]

Winter came early that year, and so did hordes of Chinese soldiers. The US forces were divided after Inchon when the Chinese struck hard, forcing the Eighth Army to retreat, and the X Corps withdrew to the frozen, death-trap Chosin Reservoir, a reservoir in northeastern Korea known historically by the Japanese pronunciation of the Korean place name Changjin.

The Chinese Second Offensive (November–December 1950) intended to drive the United Nations out of North Korea and the Chosin campaign was directed against the 1st Marine Division. That campaign succeeded in forcing the X Corps to withdraw to South Korea but failed to isolate the Marines.

It wasn't until April 1951 that MacArthur's hubris caught up with him, and belatedly, President Harry Truman sacked the arrogant MacArthur by replacing him with Lieutenant General Matthew Ridgway. Halberstam said the general's ouster took so long because MacArthur continued to stretch his mandate and openly criticize the strategy to contain the war in Korea. What really scared the leaders in Washington was that MacArthur's hubris could have horrific consequences, because by then, Russia's Stalin, a North Korean ally, had the atomic bomb.

Lyndon Johnson and Robert McNamara

The Vietnam War was a trying time for America, in part, because our leaders failed to exercise good judgment. President Lyndon Johnson accelerated the war he inherited from President John F. Kennedy by making decisions for the wrong reasons. He demonstrated yet another tragic example of hubris.

President Johnson felt political pressure to be perceived as strong against communist aggression; as a result, he expected domestic political consequences. He quipped, "If I don't go in now and they show later I should have gone, then they'll be all over me in Congress.... They'll push Vietnam up my ass every time. Vietnam. Vietnam. Vietnam. Right up my ass!" Author David Halberstam explained that Johnson was especially afraid that not taking a tough stand in Vietnam might lead Congress to deny funding to his political defining Great Society programs.[214]

Vietnam also presented a personal challenge to Johnson. He believed North Vietnam's leader Ho Chi Minh was challenging him, a Texan who wouldn't allow himself to be pushed around. Johnson aimed to show Ho his mettle and toughness, and only then would they talk. Johnson's hubris ultimately cost America fifty-eight thousand lives and a war defeat.

President Johnson chose a man for the Pentagon also given to hubris. Robert McNamara was Johnson's secretary of defense who, in his memoir on the Vietnam war, *In Retrospect: The Tragedy and Lessons of Vietnam*, admitted: "We were wrong, terribly wrong...not in terms of values and intentions but of judgments and capabilities." Once again, another leader demonstrated hubris that cost American blood and treasure.[215]

America joined the Vietnam War with its superior technology, firepower, mobility, and air supremacy, but was ultimately defeated by a smaller, less well-equipped foe much like the Persian-Athenian matchup that disgraced Darius. Vietnam was a proxy fight and thus unwinnable due to the Cold War, because had America taken the steps to prevail, it risked escalation and confrontation with the Soviet Union and/or communist China. However, although the strategic realities of the war contributed to the outcome, it was McNamara's hubris that deserves most of the blame.

McNamara's hubris was evident in his mismanagement, not his assertion that the war was inherently unwinnable, which was arguably true. McNamara came to the Pentagon with a liberal and naïve optimism that any problem could be solved by the application of proper management techniques and the social sciences. This is a progressive view traceable to the likes of nineteenth-century German philosopher Georg Wilhelm Friedrich Hegel and President Woodrow Wilson, who believed there was nothing that a government run by the "best and the brightest" could not accomplish, and that included saving Vietnam from communism.

McNamara wrote in his book that despite having protested twice to the president, he was not qualified to be secretary of defense. He wrote: "I had no patience with the myth that the Defense Department could not be managed... I had spent fifteen years as a manager identifying problems and forcing organizations—often against their will to think deeply and realistically about alternative courses of action and their consequences."[216]

McNamara tried to replace military strategy with a management and economics approach that doomed the US in Vietnam. Ben Schemmer, who served as director of land force weapon systems on McNamara's staff, said the secretary would intensively study the Southeast Asia statistical digest hoping to avoid making hard strategic choices by naively insisting he be provided more data on the issues. Schemmer wrote, "He was the consummate nit-picker" and "he was like a surgeon awash in hemorrhaging arteries who busied himself band-aiding capillaries while the patient bled to death."

Secretary McNamara evidenced hubristic incompetence to the highest order, and he failed to accept full responsibility for the tragedy on his watch. No, he blamed the Army and Marine Corps, who favored different strategies in the war. (The Army stressed a "search and destroy" strategy and the Marines favored a counterinsurgency approach.) "The military never fully debated their differences in strategic approach, or discussed them with me in any detail," McNamara admits. That's a lame excuse for a man at the head of the Pentagon charged with the lives of so many young Americans.[217]

George W. Bush

For President George W. Bush, the Iraq War was personal. He remarked in a speech on September 26, 2002, "After all, this is the guy [Iraq's

Saddam Hussein] that tried to kill my dad at one time." Not long after that comment, he rhetorically asked congressional leaders, "Do you want to know what the foreign policy of Iraq is to the United States?" Bush raised his hand, thrust his finger in front of a US Senator, and said, "F… the United States! That's what it is—and that's why we're going to get him!"[218]

At least Bush was consistent about his intent to go to war. Another account indicates a reporter at a White House press conference asked about possible reasons to go to war with Iraq. Bush responded by asking his aide, "Did you tell her I don't like motherf[***]ers who gas their own people? …Did you tell her I don't like assholes who lie to the world? … Did you tell her I'm going to kick his sorry motherf[***]ing ass all over the Mideast?"[219]

The president's predetermined decision to go to war set the tone for his administration and dangerously ignored contrary views and information. The authors of *Hubris: The Inside Story of Spin, Scandal, and the Selling of the Iraq War*, soberly reveal how the Bush administration used faulty intelligence to sell the case for war. Michael Isikoff and David Corn, the authors of *Hubris*, wrote that "Bush and his aides were looking for intelligence not to guide their policy on Iraq, but to market it. The intelligence would be the basis not for launching a war but for selling it."

The president used every opportunity to sell his go-to-war plan. Bush's 2002 "State of the Union" speech labeled Iraq as part of the "axis of evil," making Saddam Hussein part of the sinister and wicked trilogy with Iran and North Korea. In that speech, Bush alleged Hussein abetted terrorists, possessed weapons of mass destruction (WMD), and had the means to strike the United States.

Bush surrounded himself with sycophants who echoed the president's go-to-war enthusiasm. An insider said: "The president was clearly in charge. I think the president wanted to do it [go to war]. He didn't want to get a lot of advice. He didn't want a lot of debate. He informed his secretary of state [Colin Powell] that we were going to war; he didn't ask him."[220]

Isikoff and Corn cite examples of Bush's misuse of intelligence to justify the Iraq War. One of those reasons was the threat of Hussein's WMD. David Kay, a former United Nations weapons inspector who investigated Iraq's WMD programs, agreed to lead a post-invasion search for the WMD and afterward testified to the Senate Armed Services Committee: "We were almost all wrong—and I certainly include myself here." Further, the administration's own investigation report concluded that "the intelligence community was dead wrong in almost all of its pre-war judgments about Iraq's weapons of mass destruction. This was a major intelligence failure."[221]

Yes, the intelligence was wrong, but in part because the administration didn't like contrary opinions. On October 1, 2002, the Central Intelligence Agency delivered a National Intelligence Estimate (NIE) to Congress that Isikoff and Corn wrote "came to symbolize the entire WMD foul-up." But even the NIE included dissenting views that were ignored by the administration. Then in time, other dissenting views came to light—but too late.[222]

Paul Pillar of the CIA later wrote in *Foreign Affairs* magazine, "The Bush administration would frown on or ignore analysis that called into question a decision to go to war and welcome analysis that supported such a decision."

He continued, "Intelligence analysts...felt a strong wind consistently blowing in one direction. The desire to bend with such a wind is natural and strong, even unconscious."[223]

Witness to the Trap of Hubris

I fell into the same trap. Beginning in October 2002, I participated in many Pentagon meetings hosted by Secretary Donald Rumsfeld that often included Deputy Secretary of Defense Paul Wolfowitz and General Richard Myers, Chairman, Joint Chiefs of Staff. I consistently heard from those officials over the five months preceding the Iraq War that the intelligence supported going to war. They consistently agreed with President Bush's assertions that the threat was real and imminent.

Just before we launched operations into Iraq (March 20, 2003), I sat through a classified briefing at the Pentagon on Iraq's WMD and heard from the uniformed briefer the same message pushed by Rumsfeld: Hussein has plenty of WMD. I was shown a series of satellite images allegedly proving the existence of WMD and lists of deadly materials inside Saddam's bunkers. Meanwhile, I had compelling and contrary information about the WMD threat, which I shared with the Bush administration.

In early 2002, I was introduced to Iraqi exiles living in America who maintained contacts in the Baghdad military. One such man was Fawzi al-Shamari, a former three-star general under Hussein in Iraq who, over the course of the months leading up to the 2003 invasion, repeatedly insisted to me that Hussein no longer had a WMD arsenal; it had all been destroyed. He said military officials in Baghdad were willing to cooperate with the US, and the Iraqi exile community was ready to help.

I spoke with key Pentagon and White House officials about the contrary information and questioned the reliability of some of the administraiton's sources such as Ahmed Chalabi, whom my Iraqi friends said was working for Tehran. Consistently, top officials refused to listen. I had the distinct firsthand impression that they thought they knew better.

My account is a matter of record. I spent hours being interviewed by the Department of Defense Inspector General after congressional Democrats complained that the Bush administration was improperly manipulating media analysts (I was a *Fox News* analyst at the time) to promote a go-to-war narrative to the American people. Clearly, the Bush administration in hindsight manipulated the intelligence and ignored contrary views to advance a go-to-war agenda.

In our defense, we (the media) analysts who enjoyed great access to Pentagon leaders did ask tough questions and even disagreed on occasion. More often than not, we were briefed by uniformed officers who insisted that the facts on the ground were such and such. Unfortunately, those facts in many cases were tainted by an overzealous administration.

The hubris displayed by President Bush—don't confuse me with the facts, full-steam ahead to war—is a sobering lesson. Even those in the Bush administration who should have known better failed to listen to alternative views (like mine) that ultimately allowed the nation to go to war that cost the US more than 4,400 lives and $1 trillion.

Leader hubris and the tendency by subordinates to "bend with the wind" dishonor us all. Hubris infects not just individual leaders, but can be dangerous when an entire armed force embraces a view that leads to overreach.

American Technological Hubris in War

America's warfighting technological edge is fading, and so should the hubris, which has crept into the military's culture, a view that our armed forces are the best in the world and therefore can't be defeated.

President George H. W. Bush (41) said in the glow of America's success in the 1990–1991 Gulf War, "The specter of Vietnam [failures] has been buried forever in the desert sands of the Arabian Peninsula." That may be true, but in its place, the military shifted to a dangerous overconfidence (hubris) in technology.[224]

Admiral William Owens, the former Vice Chairman of the Joint Chiefs of Staff, echoed that naïve optimism. He said:

> Technology could enable U.S. military forces in the future to lift the "fog of war".... Battlefield dominant awareness—the ability to see and understand everything on the battlefield—might be possible. When you look at areas such as information warfare, intelligence, surveillance, reconnaissance and command and control, you see a system of systems coming together that will allow us to dominate battlefield awareness for years to come.... And while some people say there will always be a "fog of war,"

I know quite a lot about these programs. The emerging system of systems promises the capacity to use military force without the same risks as before—it suggests we will dissipate the "fog of war."[225]

Owens' views reflect what Robert McNamara tried which failed in Vietnam. It is the belief that American technological superiority will allow our forces to always achieve quick, easy victories with few casualties. We see this especially among the high-technology advocates even today who suggest: "The power of the new information systems will lie in their ability to correlate data automatically and rapidly from many sources to form a complete picture of the operational area, whether it be a battlefield or the site of a mobility operation." The conclusion: Victory is assured because of the digitization of the battlefield that replaces the old ways taught by Prussian strategist Carl von Clausewitz, the father of modern warfare and the most important of the classical strategic thinkers.[226]

The academic world echoes the view about technology regarding the military's understanding of its importance for the modern battle-field. Admiral Owens collaborated with the dean of the Kennedy School of Government at Harvard, Joseph S. Nye, Jr., on an article about bat-tlespace dominance to the world of international affairs:

> This information advantage can help deter or defeat traditional military threats at relatively low cost.... [It] can strengthen the intellectual link between U.S. foreign policy and military power and offer new ways of maintaining leadership in alliances and ad hoc coalitions.... America's emerging military capabilities... offer, for example, far greater pre-crisis transparency. If the United States is willing to share this transparency, it will be better able to build opposing coalitions before aggression has occurred. But the effect may be more general, for all nations now operate in an ambiguous world, a context that is not entirely benign or soothing.[227]

Such thinking is misguided and nothing more than sheer hubris. Yes, technology can offer our military substantial leverage. The problem is our opponents are catching up quickly (especially the Chinese), and besides, Americans have a long track record of overestimating our technological superiority and underestimating our enemies.

Former US Army Chief of Staff General Ray Odierno cautioned against relying too much on the twenty-first-century high-technology tools of warfare. "There's a thought process out there that technology can solve our problems, it's a clean way to conduct war," said General Odierno. "I understand what people like about this. You use technology, you don't have casualties, you don't have injuries, you don't have people dying as much."[228]

Then the general made a cautionary statement: "That's not a solution. It's about influencing, it's about compelling, and it takes personal interaction. In some cases it takes people on the ground in order to be able to do that."

We clearly need less of the hubris of the Admiral Owens of the military and more of the pragmatism expressed by those who agree with General Odierno.

Hubris is dangerous among military leaders and commanders in chief. It distorts what is possible to include technology's limitations and blinds those leaders to the sobering realities of the battlefield. Unfortunately, America historically has had a problem with hubris within its military ranks and among the top civilian leadership, which contributes to our decline.

Hubris in American Government

Americans want strong, wise, and yet self-effacing, humble leaders and public servants who keep the best interests of the citizens always foremost in their thoughts and intentions. That outcome, according to historian Peter Turchin, happens only when "the degree of solidarity felt between the commons and aristocracy" is close, which is critical to success, what he calls vertical integration.[229] Unfortunately, that's not what America enjoys with Washington's elite political class.

Turchin explained that the Roman Empire enjoyed close vertical integration, the key to its long success. He wrote: "Roman historians of the later age stressed the modest way of life, even poverty of the leading citizens. For example, when Cincinnatus was summoned to be dictator, while working at the plow, he reportedly exclaimed, 'My land will not be sown this year and so we shall run the risk of not having enough to eat!'"[230]

How many of America's current political class ever actually worked to grow food for their families, much less held real jobs before coming to Washington? Their numbers are small and dwindling. We have a professional political class running this country that is far removed from the average citizen.

Vertical integration is a feature of all successful empires, writes Turchin. He argues that the "lack of glaring barriers between the aristocracy [read "political class"] and the commons [average citizens] seems to be a general characteristic of successful imperial nations during their early phase." However, once those barriers between commoners and the elite political class become impassable, the empire is doomed.[231]

Contemporary America's government and the political class has steep barriers separating them, along with a cabal of deep-pocketed political influencers—lobbyists, rich donors, think tank members, and academia—and the liberal mainstream media in support, from the average American citizen. The days of the average citizen getting elected to national office like the 1939 comedy-drama *Mr. Smith Goes to Washington*, much less influencing the direction of the country, are becoming very rare if not nonexistent.

Turchin's view seems to be supported by the eighteenth-century Scottish economist Adam Smith, who saw grave danger for a citizenry thanks to political power coupled with hubris. Smith said that for a government official "to insist upon establishing, and upon establishing all at once, and in spite of all opposition, everything which [his] idea may seem to require, must often be the highest degree of arrogance."[232] Yes, a politician's hubris can corrupt moral judgment and encourage destructive behavior. We've seen this outcome time and again as politicians go to jail for corruption, leave office in disgrace, and/or make horrendous, costly mistakes that impact all of us and, in some cases, as seen earlier in this chapter, waste the blood of our youth.

Someone familiar with former President Franklin Roosevelt issued a sage warning about political leaders and the danger of their hubris for good government: "The problem of restraining power has always been the central problem of government.... Power is dangerous. It grows by what it feeds upon, dulling the perception, clouding the vision, imprisoning its victim, however well-intentioned he may be, in that chill of isolation of a self-created aura of intellectual infallibility which is the negative of the democratic principle."[233]

The pervasive nature of hubris among America's political class distorts our national psyche as well, especially as it redefines the original meaning of American exceptionalism.

For much of the history of America, our leaders described the United States as an "empire of liberty," "the best hope of earth," and the "leader of the free world." There is always a place in presidential candidate speeches—except in the case of President Barack Obama—to express American exceptionalism as if we are special among all nations.

Stephen Walt, a Harvard professor, writes in *Foreign Policy* magazine that American exceptionalism presumes that our values, political system, and history are universally admirable, that the US is a very special nation destined to play a distinct and positive role on the world stage. Walt writes that those claims are a myth, although he admits that America has some unique qualities, but our infectious and pervasive political hubris—self-talk—blinds us to the fact that we are a lot like everyone else: flawed.[234]

Our flaws are warts on our history. Like most other nations, our wars and financial problems, thanks to greed and corruption, squandered our privileged position. The more appropriate assumption made that God is on America's side, as many contend, is to heed Abraham Lincoln's advice that our greatest concern should be "whether we are on God's side."

Yes, our early history was blessed by God, but in recent decades, all but a remnant of that specialness has rapidly crumbled, thanks to hubris.

Unfortunately, contemporary American exceptionalism exhibits a dangerous hubris that infects Americans, persuading them to argue that the US, by dint of its unique geography and the superiority of its democratic values, can and should pursue a loftier policy. This sense of a special mission drove American policy toward a crusading impulse to make the world safe for democracy. That may be an admirable goal, but we need to be careful not to over react.

Professor Walt wrote:

> Far from being a unique state whose behavior is radically different from that of other great powers, the United States has behaved like all the rest, pursuing its own self-interest first and foremost, seeking to improve its relative position over time, and devoting relatively little blood or treasure to purely idealistic pursuits. Yet, just like past [other] great powers, it has convinced itself that it is different, and better, than everyone else.[235]

We need to be careful to acknowledge that the opportunity to make our world a better place should not be poisoned by false pride, hubris. Yet, that appears to be the case in the recent past, when we justified unilateral military action and believed what good America does justifies all means (moral relativism). This is simply a false justification, even though battlefield results are heavily in our favor.

The problem with our new exceptionalism is that it leads to abandoning prudence and moderation in exchange for triumphalism. That attitude led the US to liberate itself from former constraints like the 1972 Anti-Ballistic Missile Treaty, an outcome that frees America to exercise its power for world order, which, according to policy analyst Robert Kagan, makes the nation "a behemoth with a conscience."

Unfortunately, contemporary American exceptionalism echoes the progressive language of President Woodrow Wilson, who said, "We will actively work to bring the hope of democracy, development, free markets, and free trade to every corner of the world." Those are fine words, but accompanying those outcomes are elitism, feudalism, and humanism—all part of the radical progressive agenda, something antithetical to the intent of our founders.

No wonder French scholar Pierre Hassner called American exceptionalism "Wilsonianism in boots." This is the presumed promise to replace tyrannical regimes like Saddam Hussein's Iraq, Basher al-Assad's Syria, and Muammar Gaddafi's Libya with democracies. Those efforts haven't been very productive, however.[236]

The problem seems to be our commitment to investing time and resources. We suffer from battle fatigue for peacekeeping and nation building. Of course, that battle fatigue didn't stop us from invading Iraq and Afghanistan, where, like it or not, we remain today.

The hubris of American exceptionalism is dangerous yet still present among many of our so-called elite leaders and generally across the population. Although America is bound to remain a major power long into the future, it must act with caution, because the competition will inevitably increase as the new dual Cold War matures.

Mitigating Factors against Decline

America has many very positive virtues and resources, but to reverse its current decline, our leaders must abandon hubris. We can do that much as we overcame the Great Depression, the alleged primacy of the Japanese, and the rise of the European Union as a world power. It begins by humbly recognizing just how blessed we are and then focusing on being good stewards, not blindly arrogant.

We must never forget that we are blessed through no success of our own making. America has a very strong military, a very productive workforce, and a growing population. We still account for 21 percent of the world's GDP, and our GDP per capita outpaces that of Red China by more than seven times. Our economy remains the world's largest, and besides, we have deep capital markets, we hold the world's predominant reserve currency, and we enjoy being the world's third-largest exporter of goods and services.

Our natural resources are significant, with enormous oil and gas reserves and vast yet-to-be-developed lands. We are also one of the world's leading agricultural producers.

Our Silicon Valley is the world center for high technology, and we are well positioned to continue to benefit from cutting-edge technologies. America is the home of the top ten tech companies in the world: Apple, Google, Microsoft, Exxon, Berkshire Hathaway, General Electric, Facebook, Amazon, Wells Fargo, and Johnson & Johnson.

We are rich in nonmaterial factors as well. The world turns to America when disaster strikes, and millions still seek to come to our shores every year. Our research universities are unmatched, and they enroll a higher percentage of the best international students of any country, and most (two-thirds) of those graduates remain here to help fuel prosperity.

We have a strong tradition of rule of law, liberty, and democracy. Our political process is generally responsive to our diverse population, an enviable strength in spite of corruption in some places.

America's strengths are not immutable, however. We have serious problems outlined above, but arguably the worst is our hubris that taints almost every aspect of our lives. Yes, we face serious problems, but there is no reason this mess can't be turned around.

President Reagan taught us that the decline of America experienced under the failed leadership of President Jimmy Carter could be turned around. What we need today is similar leadership to grasp a vision for renewal and move forward, not full of cocky hubris, but full of sober optimism that guides our path to overcome challenges associated with the new dual Cold War.

Conclusion

The best is yet to come for America if we put our collective minds to the task. Hubris is not attractive in leaders or in nations and is a key factor in America's decline, which must be abandoned if we are to win the new dual Cold War.

CHAPTER THREE

Old Cold War

The Causes, Impact, and Consequences

Writer and philosopher George Santayana provided sage advice: "Those who cannot remember the past are condemned to repeat it." That is why it is appropriate to look back at the old Cold War before looking forward to the implications of the new dual Cold War. We don't have to "repeat" past mistakes.[237]

This chapter will answer four questions about the old Cold War. (1) What was the old Cold War? (2) What caused the old Cold War? (3) What was the impact of the old Cold War for the US, the USSR, and the balance of the world? and (4) Why did the Soviet Union collapse and what are the consequences of that "black swan" event?

The old Cold War has been extensively studied and documented by hundreds of historians and policy analysts who often disagree about the causes, impacts, reasons for the end, lessons, and consequences. In writing this volume, I reviewed hundreds of sources and filtered the often-conflicting views through my personal prism of experience as an old Cold War warrior and student of world history.

Readers who grew up in the 1950s and 1960s will share with me memories about that stressful period in American history. The old Cold War left an indelible impression on most of us.

I recall as a young child in public school in the late 1950s and early 1960s hearing my public school teachers talk about the feared Soviet nuclear threat. While I was living in Florida, my class even practiced evacuating the school grounds by private cars driven by moms who convoyed us to so-called safe places (presumably underground fallout shelters), and we also practiced ducking under our classroom desks—all thanks to the perceived Russian nuclear threat. The paranoia was very real, which left a deep impression on my young psyche.

I studied Cold War policy and history at the United States Military Academy (1969–1973), where professors and guest lecturers alike addressed the Soviet threat. I recall Harvard Professor Graham Allison, author of the *Essence of Decision*, who lectured at West Point's South Auditorium about the Cold War decision-making associated with the 1962 Cuban Missile Crisis, which for me was the closest we ever came to a nuclear war.

The old Cold War impacted Asia almost as much as it did here. As a new Army second lieutenant, I served in then-Lieutenant Colonel Colin Powell's battalion, 1st Battalion, 32nd Infantry (the Buccaneers) in 1973–1974, where we continued to "fight" the proxy Korean War pitting communists (North Korea backed by Red China and Soviet Russia) against Western democratic nations aligned with the United Nations. The tensions even in the 1970s with the North Koreans were real, and so were the occasional casualties along the demilitarized zone. Also, I visited Southeast Asia (Thailand and the Philippines) in July 1974, and Hong Kong as well. That entire region at the time was transfixed by the ongoing proxy Vietnam War, and so was the perception that America was losing the global Cold War to our enemy's sponsors, Communist Russia and Red China.

In 1979, I joined the 8th Infantry Division in West Germany, where I experienced firsthand the Cold War, which included preparations to fight the Soviets who were arrayed shoulder to shoulder in East Germany opposite our combat formations and who were reportedly ready to attack at a moment's notice. At the time, I studied Soviet tactics and

Russian intelligence operations, and my unit even guarded the Iron Curtain, a real no-man's land filled with barbed-wired fences and anti-personnel mines that separated West and East Germany. We observed the enemy from our watchtower near the Fulda Gap, the ground zero location of the much-anticipated and threatened Soviet attack led by thousands of Soviet T-62 main battle tanks.

While stationed in Germany, I also visited the former Soviet Union as a tourist in 1982, where I was watched closely by the KGB. Briefings by US Army intelligence officials before I went into Soviet Russia prepared me for what to expect, especially warnings to never let down my guard. That was good advice. Yes, I was closely watched and questioned.

That experience confirmed for me much of what I'd heard and read about the Red Menace. Although I was understandably circumspect while in the Soviet Union, I vividly recall the people, their sad faces, the poorly constructed buildings, the poor services, the bland food, their empty boasts, and much more. I will never forget the sense of suspicion and danger I felt, and yes, I truly celebrated and felt the pressure lift off my chest once the Aeroflot airliner landed at Frankfurt International Airport (Frankfurt am Main) after more than a week of stressful travel behind the Iron Curtain.

Also, in 1999 I had the opportunity to visit the post-Cold War, former Soviet satellite nation of Ukraine, where I participated in a conference with former East Bloc military officers, which included Russian military officials. At that conference, the former Soviet and satellite nation officers were anxious to learn from Western officers, and the people of Kiev were optimistic about their future.

Since the Ukraine visit, I have on numerous occasions, thanks to my Pentagon work with other armies, visited with former Warsaw Pact officers and gleaned from those conversations rich confirmation of many of my long-held views of the former Soviet threat.

It is important to understand the old Cold War before moving ahead with an examination of the implications of the new dual Cold War. That is why I have prepared answers to the four questions outlined above. For some readers, this will be a review of the history, but for others it may be a first exposure to the history and challenges associated with the twentieth century's Cold War.

1. What Was the Old Cold War?

Hollywood parodies an answer to this question with the 1966 Academy Award-winning movie, *The Russians Are Coming, The Russians Are Coming.* The film, based on the comic novel, *The Off-Islanders,* by Nathaniel Benchley, depicts the chaos in the wake of a Soviet submarine running ashore near a New England vacation island during the Cold War. A series of hilarious misunderstandings occurs as the villagers realize they have been "invaded."

Hollywood's light-hearted depiction of the Cold War in the movie is cynically typical of the progressive crowd, who oversees the entertainment industry. Certainly, Hollywood and the average American understand that the Cold War was not a laughing matter. In fact, the US Congress answered the question (What was the Cold War?) when it directed the Pentagon to create a Cold War certificate of recognition for all twenty-seven million American veterans and countless civilians who served during the Cold War. That certificate defined the Cold War as "a global competition between two ideologies, the free world, led by the United States, and the communist world led by the Soviet Union." The period of the Cold War, according to Congress, started the last day of World War II, September 2, 1945, and ended December 26, 1991, the last day the flag of the former Soviet Union was lowered at the Kremlin in Moscow, Russia.

Of course, that definition may work for a government-issued certificate, but in reality, the Cold War was much more complex and encompassing. Former Secretary of State Madeleine Albright wrote a thoughtful definition of the Cold War:

It was a time of relentless and institutionalized tragedy; of proxy wars that destroyed lives in every continent, of barbed wire stretched across Europe's heart; of gulags and forced confessions; and of countless thousands killed while trying to escape. Above all, it was a time of fear—of showdowns in Korea, Berlin, and Cuba.... Each night we knew that within minutes, perhaps through a misunderstanding, our world could end and morning never come.[238]

Let me back track a bit at this point to provide context to help those new to the Cold War's history. World War II ended in 1945, and America's leaders anticipated that the Soviet Union would continue the level of cooperation enjoyed during the war years. After all, President Franklin Roosevelt, an ideological progressive, believed the partnership that defeated the Axis Powers, which included Russia, would coalesce around his vision of a United Nations that would prevent future world wars. Roosevelt's dream for the United Nations is traceable to his progressive ideological brother, President Woodrow Wilson, a man who shared a similar ambition after World War I in the form of the League of Nations. The League failed, thanks to Republican senators suspicious of international entanglements, and Roosevelt's grand hope for a "true war-preventing international organization" really never materialized after the Second World War, because Roosevelt's United Nations ultimately became little more than a toothless, empty-headed debating forum on the Hudson River in Manhattan, New York.

The United States inherited from the Second War the global leadership mantle, a role it was ill prepared to fulfill. It quickly saw a rising Soviet Union that must be stopped, and therefore it embraced containment as the only viable strategy. But that containment strategy was primarily a military power exercise that created mutual defense alliances that became little more than an anti-communist alliance and spurred an arms race.

The term "cold" became associated with the American containment strategy's "war" because there was no large-scale fighting between the antagonists, even though both supported proxies in regional wars like Korea and Vietnam. In fact, the term "cold war," according to Harvard University Professor Odd Arne Westad, was first coined by author George Orwell in 1945 "to denote the capitalist-socialist antagonisms between the United States and the USSR after the defeat of Nazi Germany."[239]

The Cold War as an ideological clash between socialism and capitalism was born from the global economic, social, and technological transformations of the late nineteenth century and peaked "between 1945 and 1989 against the backdrop of the geostrategic confrontation between the world's two superpowers and the rise of a bipolar international system," according to Westad.[240]

The Cold War became known for its horrific human cost, according to former Soviet leader Mikhail Gorbachev. He said the Cold War "made losers of us all," which claimed millions of lives in Korea and Vietnam, destabilized numerous Third-World countries, militarized our economies, abused our civil liberties, and posed an existential threat for us all.[241]

Undoubtedly, the worst aspect of that bipolar confrontation was the nuclear competition whereby Americans and much of the world lived in constant fear of annihilation because the two superpowers each had massive nuclear arsenals and on more than one occasion came close to using them.

The twentieth century's Cold War ended in 1991 after the ideological clash went through a process of slow decline and then death.

2. What Caused the Old Cold War?

The collapse of the Soviet Union in 1991 was a "black swan" event—something completely unexpected. That wasn't the case with the beginning of the war, however. There was plenty of evidence of the forthcoming

Cold War long before it officially started in 1945. In fact, the seeds of that future war can be traced from the publication of the Communist Manifesto in 1848 to the uprisings and strikes to the conflict that began with the Russian Revolution of 1917 overthrowing Tsar Nicholas II, which marked the end of the Romanov dynasty and centuries of Russian imperial rule.

The ensuing Russian Revolution pitted the "Red" (color of revolution) Army of the Bolsheviks, led by Marxist Vladimir Lenin, and the "White" (the color of royalty) Armies of the tsarists, capitalists, and supporters of democratic socialism. Eventually, the Bolsheviks won in 1923, with Lenin's Red Army claiming victory and establishing the Soviet Union. Meanwhile, and likely a surprise for many in the West, the United States and its allies invaded Russia in 1918 to aid the White Russians against the Bolsheviks (read "communists"), which seeded the underlying mistrust with the Russian population that eventually contributed to the Cold War.[242]

Americans opposed Bolshevism, according to David Foglesong, who teaches at Rutgers University, because of fear of immigrants, anti-Semitism, and racism. Foglesong argues that Jews, immigrants, and militant American blacks were associated with the Bolsheviks, a perceived internal and external threat to America.[243]

Washington was thus hostile to the Bolshevik seizure of power, according to Foglesong. Immediately after the Russian Revolution, President Woodrow Wilson cut off American funds to the new Soviet government, and then extended the World War I maritime blockade of Germany to include the new Soviet Russia. US Secretary of State Robert Lansing said at the time the Bolsheviks were "dangerous—more so than Germany. They threatened us with revolution."[244]

Soon the American government undertook a series of covert actions against the Bolsheviks' Soviet government. After all, Secretary Lansing had longed for a military dictatorship since the August 1917 Revolution, hoping the American government could help to "restore order." By 1918, the United States and her allies recognized the anti-Bolshevik movements in Russia, which helped motivate their collective desire to join the fight against the Red Army.[245]

In July 1918, a British-led force with the French and joined by five thousand US Army troops, the "American North Russia Expeditionary Force, took the Russian city of Arkhangelsk and another 8,000 soldiers, organized as the American Expeditionary Force Siberia shipped to Vladivostok from the Philippines and California."[246] These American forces, along with our allies, fought alongside the White Russian Army, actions taken by President Wilson without congressional consent, thus the label "Midnight War" became associated with the action.

The American role in the "Midnight War" made a lasting impression on the Soviets' psyche and was in fact a move opposed at the time by the US Army commander in Siberia, General William S. Graves. General Graves was alarmed by the move, which he labeled the most "flagrant case of flouting the well-known and approved practice in states in their international relations, and using instead of the accepted principles of international law, the principle of might makes right."[247]

Historian D. F. Fleming wrote that few Americans are even aware of the US intervention in Russia, but for the Soviets and much of the Russian population, it "was a time of endless killing, of looting and raping, of plague and famine, of measureless suffering for scores of millions." That tragic experience was "burned into the very soul of the [Russian] nation, not to be forgotten." In fact, that troubling memory was evident years later in an address in New York City on September 17, 1959, when then Russian Premier Nikita Khrushchev reminded the world of the American intervention when he said "the time you [Americans] sent the troops to quell the revolution."[248]

President Wilson opposed the Bolsheviks' revolution in part because the Soviets nationalized American investments worth $658.9 million.[249] The Soviets' move motivated Wilson, an established proponent of US international interventionism, to join the multinational invasion, as outlined above. In fact, Wilson labeled the October 1917 revolution a "desperate attempt on the part of the dispossessed to share in the bounty of industrial civilization." Wilson's progressive view also prompted him to call for a "strong commanding personality to arise [in Russia]…and [to] gather a disciplined military force [capable of] restoring order and maintaining a new government."[250]

America and her allies looked for Wilson's "strong commanding personality" and what young John Foster Dulles, the future secretary of state under President Dwight Eisenhower, described at the time as the "white hope of Russia." These leaders came to believe they found that person in Admiral Aleksandr Vasilyevich Kolchak, a famed Russian Arctic explorer, who launched a coup in November 1918 in Omsk, Siberia, aimed at restoring an "orderly existence." Kolchak was known at the time for his rash temper, which led him "beyond the limits of the law."[251]

The US and its allies rushed military aid to Kolchak only to end up fueling what the American Ambassador to Japan, Rowland Morris, called an "orgy of arrests without charges; of executions without even the pretense of a trial; and of confiscations without the color of authority. Panic and fear has seized everyone. Men support each other and live in constant terror that some spy or enemy will cry Bolshevik and condemn them to instant death."[252]

The Russians never forgot the West's invasion, support for Kolchak, and the consequences of that campaign, but most Americans did forget. In May 1972, President Richard Nixon boasted during a visit to the Soviet Union about having never fought one another in war. President Ronald Reagan made a similar mistake in his 1984 State of the Union address. Evidently, presidential ignorance about our Russia invasion history is shared by the vast majority of Americans as well, for in 1985 a *New York Times* poll found that only 14 percent of Americans were even aware that in 1918, the US joined an invasion of Russia.[253]

The mistrust seeded by America's 1918 invasion of Russia was an underlying issue that exacerbated other causes that led to the twentieth century's Cold War. Unfortunately, those causes are not universally accepted, and in fact, there are numerous competing camps regarding the actual causes of the Cold War.

Former US Ambassador to the Soviet Union George F. Kennan believed Soviet behavior sparked the Cold War. That behavior was best understood as a continuation of tsarist policies meant to grow the Russian empire, according to Kennan. That rather simplistic view spawned the revisionist camp, which portrayed the Soviet Union as weakened by the Second World War and only interested in secure borders and peace, but was forced into the Cold War by American aggression.

The realist camp argues that Washington is guilty of the lion's share of the blame for causing the Cold War, because it failed to grant the Soviets their own sphere of influence after World War II, and then the US should have backed out of trying to control events outside the American sphere of influence. Had America not interfered, the worst aspects of the Cold War were preventable, according to the realist camp.

The post-realists are yet another historical-record-interpreting camp that believes the Cold War antagonists joined in a bipolar global network of thoughts, actions, and talk. Professor Westad, a post-realist and noted Cold War scholar, believes the Cold War was an ideological clash between socialism and capitalism born from global economic, social, and technological transformations that peaked between the US and Russia during the traditional Cold War years (1945–1991).[254]

The Second World War had little to do with the emergence of the Cold War, according to Westad. After all, the US and Russia were consumed with one another's reaction to World War II developments like the atomic bomb and the Soviet response to the 1944 Warsaw uprising rather than with what the Axis Powers in Berlin and Tokyo thought.[255]

Westad goes on to argue that the United States and the USSR were "accidental allies" in the Second War. Their relationship was more of a "shotgun marriage influenced by immediate needs." In fact, Westad wrote, the East-West mistrust dating back to the 1918 Revolution was never far away, as evidenced by Soviet leader Nikita Khrushchev's perspective that he "believed that communism was on the up [rise] worldwide, and that his historic role was to steer the Soviet Union through a period in which, through the laws of history itself, the global balance of forces tipped in its direction." However, Khrushchev also knew that a nuclear holocaust threatened Russia's achievement, thus he tempered his celebration because he did not want to "eulogize [that achievement] at its funeral pyre," observed Westad.[256]

Another perspective on the Cold War causes comes from people in the revisionist camp who argue that American leaders wanted to accommodate Stalin to avoid further confrontation. Leaders such as Vice President Henry Wallace (1941–1945) and President Roosevelt's chief diplomatic advisor Harry Hopkins believed that had America pursued a "stand-back policy" with the Soviets, there would have been peace, not a Cold War.[257]

The revisionist view is not supported by Robert Gellately, a Canadian scholar who is one of the leading historians on the Cold War era with books on Lenin, Stalin, and Hitler. Gellately mined the post-Cold War Soviet Union's archives in Moscow to find many historical jewels. Specifically, he discovered that "Stalin started, and tried to manage, the Cold War in an attempt to reach his never-abandoned goal of spreading communism throughout the world, with an aim to final victory."[258]

Gellately's archive research portrays Stalin as a leader "whose every move was based on his sustained belief in Marxist-Leninist ideology." In fact, Stalin, according to Gellately, "made all the first moves and [the West] if anything…was woefully complacent until 1947 or 1948, when the die was already cast [thus starting the Cold War]."[259]

Revisionist proponents like President Roosevelt and British Prime Minister Winston Churchill were wrong and naïve about Stalin, someone they believed was open to compromise. Gellately wrote that Roosevelt "consistently sought to understand and sympathize with the Soviet position and he bent over backwards to ignore or downplay Stalin's horrendous methods of rule and obvious ambitions." Even Churchill wrote, "I like him [Stalin] the more I see him."[260]

Gellately's research at the Soviet archives after the Cold War demonstrated that Stalin's strategy "was to bide his time by doing whatever was necessary until the final showdown between the capitalist west and the communist east." That view explains Stalin's incremental takeover of Eastern Europe, and then he hoped to take over Western Europe and eventually the entire world. He sincerely believed that communism would inevitably triumph, and the only question was how long it would take, according to Gellately.[261]

Gellately explained why Stalin rejected the American offer during the post-World War II era to extend the Marshall Plan aid program to the Soviet Union and its East European satellites. Evidently, Stalin "believed that any aid would lead to rapid economic health, thus undermining his determination to communize the entire region," according to Gellately. Of course, this view was foreign to then Secretary of State George Marshall, who "deplored the emotional anti-Russian attitude" in America and promoted a policy that ignored ideology, a view that helped Stalin, who genuinely believed the United States wanted to dominate the world.[262]

The Russians have an ambivalent view of their Stalinist past, according to Gellately. "The struggle between the anti-Stalinists and the Stalinists is still going on in Russia [today]."[263]

The revisionists also claim that the Cold War struggle was inevitable, because "even intelligent and reasonably well-intentioned policymakers move inexorably toward conflict and hostility. The father of the atomic bomb, Robert Oppenheimer, described the [inevitable] conflict as two scorpions in a bottle, each impelled to fight the other to the death."[264]

Both the realists and the revisionist camps agreed that Moscow is mostly to blame for the intensity and duration of the Cold War. Soviet aggressiveness was spawned by fear and insecurity rooted in past goals of tsarist expansion, assert these camps.

The so-called new left camp sees a completely different, polar opposite cause for the Cold War. One new left proponent said: "The United States has not really been Santa Claus." Rather, it acted in self-interest when causing the Cold War. The new left sees the Soviets on the defensive and blame American "aggression" as responsible for the post-World War II Cold War. Allegedly, America's inherently expansionist political economy and idealism transformed into an evangelical form of anti-communism. America's motivation, according to the new left view, was to create a trading open-door world that provided markets for American products and granted it access to raw materials.[265]

The post-revisionist camp allegedly is another voice led by John Lewis Gaddis, a Yale University history professor, and Meleyn P. Leffler, a University of Virginia history professor, who believe that both the US and the Soviet Union more or less share responsibility for the onset of the Cold War. Leffler argues in his book *Preponderance of Power* that Soviet policies were mainly "reactive." Specifically, Leffler writes, "The establishment of the Cominform [Information Bureau of the Communist and Workers' Parties], the strikes and demonstrations in France and Italy, the coup in Czechoslovakia, and the blockade of Berlin were responses to the western offensive." In particular, the Truman Doctrine, the Marshall Plan, and the affirmative program in western Germany threatened Russia.[266]

Gaddis, unlike Leffler, easily assigns responsibility for the Cold War to the Soviets alone. He wrote in *We Now Know* "that as long as Stalin was running the Soviet Union a Cold War was unavoidable." Gaddis continued, "I find it increasingly difficult, given what we know now, to imagine the Soviet Union or the Cold War without Stalin. For the more we learn, the less sense it makes to distinguish Stalin's foreign policies from his domestic policies or even his personal behaviour."[267]

So, after reviewing the various views regarding the causes of the Cold War, I came to believe the following. First, the Cold War really dates back to the West's 1918 invasion of Russia, when it sided with the White Army to oppose the Soviets. Then, even though Russia joined the West in World War II, that geopolitical anomaly is evidence of the fourth-century BC Indian statement, "The enemy of my enemy is my friend." However, that partnership of convenience didn't last. It soon reverted to a hostile relationship that worsened once Germany and Japan surrendered and both sides scrambled for post-war booty and policies.[268]

The enduring mistrust of the West evidently solidified Stalin's ideological determination spawned under Lenin, which grew through the subsequent Soviet leaders until the very end of the USSR. Stalin's cause that carried forward was ideological and continued for three-quarters of a century, which reminds me of a warning by America's Ambassador to Russia David Francis (1916–1917): "If these damned Bolsheviks are permitted to remain in control of the country, it will not only be lost to its devoted people but Bolshevik rule will undermine all governments and be a menace to society itself."[269]

Ambassador Francis correctly predicted that Bolshevik rule would be "a menace to society itself." That is why the preponderance of the evidence places the blame for the Cold War squarely on the shoulders of the Soviets under Stalin, given his confirmed global ambitions and the overwhelming evidence of that regime's negative impact for the world.

3. What Was the Impact of the Cold War for the US, the USSR, and the Balance of the World?

The Cold War came on the immediate heels of the Second World War as a roaring lion with no end to challenges and serious impacts for US global interests: Soviet armies were in Iran, the Russians controlled Poland and much of Eastern Europe, the Soviets demanded privileges in Manchuria, Greek communists supported by Moscow launched an insurgency to take over the Athens government, the Berlin Blockade isolated the city from West Germany, and a major spy case involving many Soviet agents rocked Canada and by association the entire West. However, the most powerful indicator of the Cold War was the Soviets' test of their first atomic bomb in 1949, which caught most Western experts by surprise. As if this list of urgent challenges wasn't enough, events in the year 1950 left absolutely no doubt about the emergence of the twentieth century's Cold War.[270]

In 1950, there were at least seventy-six significant indicators of the

Cold War, creating an overwhelming sense of danger that consumed America. A few of those 1950 indicators were:[271]

- On January 14, the People's Republic of China seized the US consulate in Beijing, and to the south, Ho Chi Minh founded the Democratic Republic of Vietnam, which was immediately recognized by Red China and Soviet Russia.
- On January 21, Alger Hiss, an American government official, was convicted of perjury in connection with the charge of being a Soviet spy.
- On February 2, Emil Julius Klaus Fuchs, a German theoretical physicist, was arrested for supplying the Soviets with information from the Manhattan Project, the American atomic weapons program.
- On February 9, Senator Joseph McCarthy, a Republican from Wisconsin, charged that 205 communists were working for the US State Department.
- On February 14, the Sino-Soviet Treaty of Friendship, Alliance, and Mutual Assistance was signed, which for some was proof of a worldwide communist conspiracy.
- On June 25, the US joined the war with North Korea and the People's Republic of China, although China had at this point not sent troops.
- In November, Chinese troops crossed into North Korea, overwhelmed United Nations forces led by American commanders in one of the worst defeats in US military history, and then drove the American forces out of North Korea.
- On November 30, President Harry Truman announced he was prepared to authorize the use of atomic weapons in order to achieve peace in Korea, a clear message to then Peking's intervention and Soviet Russia.
- Father Edmund Walsh, vice president of Georgetown University, called for a war with the Soviet Union.

- New York Governor Thomas Dewey called for total national mobilization and a third of our productive capacity dedicated to national defense.
- The National Security Council Paper NSC-68, a top-secret report dated April 7, 1950, recommended measures necessary for fighting the Cold War: quadruple US spending on defense, form alliances with non-communist countries around the world, and convince the American public that a costly arms buildup was imperative for the nation's defense.[272]
- Congress passed the McCarran Internal Security Act, which required communist organizations to register and established a board to investigate persons suspected of engaging in subversive activities or otherwise promoting the establishment of a "totalitarian dictatorship."[273]

That was a scary time for Americans. So how does one understand this surge of Cold War activity? Harvard Professor Westad explained that to understand the Cold War, we should consider three paradigms "as patterns of interpretation, which…signify a particular approach—an angle of view…to the complex problems of Cold War history." Westad called his presentation of this concept "Three (Possible) Paradigms," which provide considerable insight into the impact of the Cold War for both the main antagonists—the United States and the Soviet Union—as well as the world in general. Those paradigms are ideology, technology, and the Third World.

Ideology

Ideology is understood "as a set of fundamental concepts systematically expressed by a large group of individuals." Professor Westad argues ideology as a paradigm helps better explain "single [historical] events" as opposed to "causes and consequences of larger historical shifts." Further, it is my view that this approach also helps understand the aggregate impact of this paradigm as well.[274]

Westad illustrates the utility of the ideology paradigm using the June 4, 1961, meeting between President John F. Kennedy and First Secretary of the Communist Party Nikita Khrushchev. Both men, according to Westad, came to the Vienna, Austria, meeting briefed on the necessity to seek common ground on issues such as nuclear war. Unfortunately, but predictably, the leaders' encounter was marked by "sharp confrontation and the summit itself probably contributed to the increased tension that followed, culminating in the Cuban Missile Crisis the following year."[275] Why?

Two differences between the leaders were evident going into that meeting. Each leader pursued issue outcomes that were fundamentally in conflict, and they had "disharmonious personalities." But that was not the critical difference, according to Westad. The basic ideological perception of each leader was critical to understanding the outcome of that meeting and the ultimate impact on the Cold War.

Khrushchev entered the talks with Kennedy sincerely believing that "his society and political thinking were in ascendance, and that Kennedy, as a class representative of the U.S. 'monopolists,' could be brought to recognize this historical necessity," according to Westad.[276]

Kennedy came to the meeting focused, according to Westad, on assuring "the survival and success of [global] liberty." The young president meant to pursue US ideological hegemony in the world.[277]

As this example illustrates, according to Westad, both sides in the Cold War were in fact driven by their discrete ideologies. Westad also cautioned against a common misperception that only one side was ideological and the other was driven by logic and self-interest. He said that view is "one of the main post-Cold War fallacies of U.S. international historians."[278]

Now consider the ideology paradigm's impact on the Cold War.

American leaders like Kennedy were ideologically predisposed to advance American values such as freedom of expression, freedom of ownership, and freedom of capitalist exchanges. They advanced those values via major foreign policy efforts such as the Marshall Plan, the Truman Doctrine, and support for European integration.

The Marshall Plan, also known as the European Recovery Program, invested $13 billion to help Europe recover from World War II. It successfully sparked economic growth, restored confidence among Europeans, and reinforced the values Americans hold dear. Revisionist historians challenge that assertion to argue that the Marshall Plan's real objective was to provide markets for American goods and to remake the European economy in the image of the US economy.[279] There is some truth to that view, but after all: Why shouldn't America try to recover its losses from the war?

Mikhail Narinsky, a Russian scholar with the Moscow-based Institute for Universal History in 1996, said that Stalin "became convinced that the U.S. [Marshall Plan] aid was designed to lure the Kremlin's East European neighbors out of its orbit and to rebuild German strength." Thus Stalin refused to participate and prevented the Soviet satellite nations from taking part as well.[280]

The Truman Doctrine was an ideological tool used to counter Russia's influence. In 1947, President Truman established that the US would provide political, military, and economic assistance to all democratic nations under the threat of authoritarian forces—by which he meant Soviet Russia.

President Truman introduced that "Doctrine" before a joint session of Congress on March 12, 1947, as a response to the British government's decision to no longer provide military and economic assistance to the Greek government, then engaged in a civil war against the Greek communist party. Truman used the speech to ask Congress to support both the Greek and Turkish governments, which had previously been dependent on British aid, as well as a host of other indicators of Soviet mischief.

Truman evidently believed that the Soviet Union backed the Greek communist insurgency, and thus that war could potentially deliver Athens to the Soviet camp. Complicating the perceived Russian involvement in Greece was the Soviets' failure to withdraw from northern Iran as per the Tehran Declaration of 1943, a Moscow decision to pressure Iran into granting it oil concessions. Additionally, the Soviets forced the

Turkish government into granting them base and transit rights through the Turkish Straits, and Moscow also rejected the Baruch Plan for international control over nuclear energy and weapons in June 1946.

Truman's speech to Congress requested $400 million in aid to the Greek and Turkish governments and for the deployment of American civilian and military personnel and equipment to the region. He argued that Russian interference in those countries would undermine the political stability of the Middle East and create an immense strategic problem for US national security. Truman also made the ideological argument that the US was compelled to assist "free peoples" in their struggles against "totalitarian regimes" (read "the USSR"), because the spread of Russian ideology would "undermine the foundations of international peace." As a result, the Truman Doctrine became "the policy of the United States to support free peoples who are resisting attempted subjugation by armed minorities or by outside pressures."[281]

Anders Stephanson, a Columbia University history professor, argues that it was American ideas (ideology) and their influence on the populations, not just our military aid programs that made the conflict a Cold War. The Soviets lacked the same level of influence because Russia didn't enjoy America's level of international hegemony. America's purpose has long been global domination of its ideas, Stephanson asserts.[282]

The US wasn't just waging the Cold War against communism, but it was engaged in that war to change Europe, as seen above through the mechanism of the Marshall Plan. Washington used its aid program not just to rescue the war-torn countries, but to change both Europe and Japan in the direction of US ideas and models—remake them in the image of America.

Remaking Europe and Japan explains the successful alliance systems that emerged in those countries as well as their rapid political, social, and economic transformation. Specifically, over a fifty-year-plus period, the US helped transform the former Axis Powers—Germany, Italy, and Japan—into its own image. Those changes in policies, social stratification, and economic foundations that the United States' presence inspired gradually created systems of alliances based on compatible geopolitical views that would survive conflicts of interest (unlike those countries in the Soviet Bloc).

The ideological war was almost religious in nature. A former Central Intelligence Agency employee, Harry Rositzke, wrote, "The Cold War became a holy war against the infidels, a defense of free God-fearing men against the atheistic communist system." He further observed, "The Cold War prism created in the minds of diplomatic and military strategists a clear-cut world of black and white. There were no grays."[283]

In fact, the official US view in the Cold War accepted no neutral agents—nonbelievers. "America's policy is global," Secretary of State Dulles told President Muhammad Sukarno of Indonesia, one of the neutralist leaders he and his brother abhorred. "You must be on one side or another. Neutralism is immoral." Two perceptions shaped Dulles' approach to the world. First, he considered "neutralist leaders to be enemies who were secretly in league with the Kremlin." Second, he believed that the "Soviet threat—and by extension the threat from neutralist countries—was so great that it justified any counter-operations, no matter how violent or extreme."[284]

"It is now clear that we are facing an implacable enemy whose avowed objective is world domination by whatever means and at whatever cost," US Army General James Doolittle, a World War II hero, wrote in a secret 1954 report to President Dwight Eisenhower. "If the United States is to survive, longstanding concepts of 'fair play' must be reconsidered.... It may be necessary that the American people be made acquainted with, understand and support this fundamentally repugnant philosophy."[285]

Eisenhower agreed. "I have come to the conclusion that some of our traditional ideas of international sportsmanship are scarcely applicable in the morass in which the world now flounders," the president wrote.[286]

The ideological war was marked by semi-hysteria and war psychosis at home. The war of words and ideology pitted Americans against one another, such as the Wisconsin US Senator Joseph McCarthy-inspired "witch hunts" and mass persecution of political radicals.

Frank J. Donner, a civil liberties lawyer known as an expert on the use of government surveillance, wrote in 1961:

> The obsession with anti-Communism…became a routine feature of our lives. Witness the sedition prosecutions under the Smith Act, the intimidations of the FBI [Federal Bureau of Investigation], the rash of loyalty oaths, the security-screening apparatus which blankets American industry, the emergence of the informer as hero, the wave of deportation and denaturalization proceedings against the foreign-born, the restrictions on the right to travel, the manifold attacks on organizations and on the freedom of association, and the congressional witch hunts.[287]

Concerns about anti-communism resulted in groups such as the US House Un-American Activities Committee to become prominent in 1950. Senator McCarthy is known for his battle against communism whereby he targeted individuals within America who were suspected communists. In fact, on February 9, 1950, McCarthy announced he was aware of 205 card-carrying members of the Communist Party who worked at the US State Department.[288]

Cold War McCarthyism became known as the practice of making accusations of disloyalty, subversion, or treason without proper regard for evidence. The obsession with communists was even associated with Dr. Martin Luther King Jr. At one point, FBI director J. Edgar Hoover sought permission to tap Dr. King's telephone because there were two suspected communists in his camp, New York lawyer Stanley Levison and Jack O'Dell. Hoover wanted to see whether they were trying to influence Dr. King and his movement on behalf of the Soviet Union. Evidently, Dr. King at some point was persuaded to get rid of the alleged communists, lest their presence be used to smear him and his civil rights movement.[289]

Years later, a reporter spoke with Jack O'Dell, who confirmed that he had been a member of the Communist Party. He explained, "Of course I was. They [the Communists] were the only people doing anything about Jim Crow, lynching, the poll tax." O'Dell explained that he joined the Communist Party because "he thought that civil rights would come before socialism came, and he wanted to be part of the movement to make that happen."[290]

Unfortunately, culture was a victim of Cold War confrontation, especially in the case of cinema, a highly effective ideological tool. Soviet leader Joseph Stalin was often quoted as saying, "Cinema in the hands of the Soviet authorities constitutes an inestimable force." His view of the utility of cinema resulted in the formation of the Ministry of Cinematography in 1946, a creation that increased its efforts when Hollywood became a serious opponent.[291]

Both the US and USSR officials recognized that cinema was critical in the struggle for hearts and minds. Sarah Davies, a history professor at Durham University in Durham, England, said Soviet cinema was "engaged in a permanent 'dialogue' with its U.S. counterpart, using Hollywood as its primary point of reference as well as a source of self-definition."[292]

Both sides of the cinema propaganda war recruited leading directors, actors, screenwriters, and composers to the Cold War effort, especially those in the Soviet Union where there was no choice but to become part of the state's propaganda campaign. Ivan Bolshakov, the Soviet minister of cinematography, wrote in 1947, that "a certain section of film industry workers admires bourgeois [Western] cinematic art and some of its practitioners. This is reflected in the uncritical…borrowing of directing and screenwriting techniques."[293]

The Kremlin controlled cinema with the help of the Communist Party's Department of Culture and Department of Propaganda and Agitation by directing "Soviet" and "non-Soviet" approaches to making films. One such clarification known as the Orgburo Decree "on the film *The Great Life*" stressed the movie "ascribes to Soviet people morals and manners that are completely alien to our society. For instance, while wounded Red Army soldiers are left without any help on the battlefield, a miner's wife (Sonya), walking nearby, displays absolute indifference to them."[294]

The Soviet Union forced their cinema to portray America as the enemy from the mid-1940s onward. They were to characterize the USSR with the image of "capitalist encirclement" always pushing the theme of US imperialism.[295]

The Soviets cut "smutty scenes" from Western films and encouraged the "masses" to report suspect films to the authorities. In a 1949 Soviet decree, "The Plan for the Reinforcement of Anti-American Propaganda in the Near Future," the Kremlin called for the unmasking of "the idiocy of bourgeois culture and morals in contemporary America." The document outlined thirty-seven themes in Soviet anti-American propaganda, including the "propaganda of amorality and bestial psychology in the USA." Western moral decline was the cornerstone of Soviet propaganda.[296]

Melvyn P. Leffler, a history professor at the University of Virginia, wrote in *Foreign Affairs* a few years after historians studied the Soviet archives to better understand the Cold War. Professor Leffler concluded that "ideology played an important role in shaping their perceptions, but Soviet leaders were not focused on promoting worldwide revolution.... [T]hey felt threatened by a United States that alone among the combatants emerged from the war wealthier and armed with the atomic bomb.... [N]othing the United States could have done would have allayed Soviet suspicions in the early years of the Cold War. Nevertheless, U.S. words and deeds greatly heightened ambient anxieties and subsequently contributed to the arms race and the expansion of the Cold War into the third world."[297]

Technology

Technology is a paradigm that provides considerable insight into the Cold War. David Holloway, a political science professor at Stanford University, said nuclear technology was at the core of the conflict. In fact, technology in general was the epitome of both ideologies. Professor Westad of Harvard University states "the future of socialism depended on the Soviet Union matching the technological achievements of the imperialist states. Without a Soviet bomb, the socialist world would be inherently weak and under constant pressure."[298]

Technology became a Cold War battleground, which began long before the end of the Second War. In fact, the Cold War foes battled for technological supremacy as early as 1933 in space.

In November 1933, two American military officers flew their balloon, the Century of Progress, to fifty-nine thousand feet, but were discouraged days later by a telegram from the Soviet pilots of USSR-1, which reached sixty-two thousand feet in September 1933. The Soviet pilots wrote: "Hearty congratulations on your great achievements.... May both our countries continue to contest the heights."[299]

This competition was a foretaste of the coming Cold War's technological competition. The short-lived (two year) "space race" advanced balloon flights, including capsule pressurization and carbon dioxide scrubbing, mission-control communications, and scientific experimentation during flights.[300]

Competition for technology took on a more serious role as the Cold War began in earnest. In October 1945, Secretary of War Robert Patterson said, "The laboratories of America have now become our first line of defense." A decade later, half of America's public and private spending was on industrial research and development associated with defense projects.[301]

Technology competition was vicious from the start, which included navigation systems, space exploration, genetics, nuclear technology, and much more. The Soviets faced a tough, uphill battle, because Russia was significantly behind the US in technology in even simple everyday items like telephones, but by the mid-1970s, the Russians had communications satellites, a result of enormous investments in space technology.[302]

The American atomic bomb was a technological wake-up for the Russians. The Soviets faced the reality that the Americans had the bombs and were willing to employ them, as demonstrated at Hiroshima and Nagasaki to end the war in the Pacific.

Stalin learned about the Manhattan Project through Soviet espionage, yet he felt betrayed by President Truman for not revealing the new weapon, which Professor Holloway wrote led Stalin to believe the US intended to use the bomb as an instrument of political pressure against the Soviet Union.[303]

At the July 1945 Potsdam conference to negotiate terms for the end of World War II, Andrei Andreyevich Gromyko, the Soviet minister of foreign affairs, recalls Stalin saying to him that Washington and London "are hoping we won't be able to develop the bomb ourselves for some time. And meanwhile, using America's monopoly…they want to force us to accept their plans on questions affecting Europe and the world. Well, that's not going to happen."[304]

Stalin would not be intimidated by the Americans; thus, he secretly launched a nuclear weapons program. In August 1949 the Soviets tested their first atomic device, which launched the Cold War's arms race.

The Kremlin soon learned that America's determination to keep the lead in nuclear arms forced Moscow to match or surpass US capabilities just to safeguard its own position. Eventually, the frantic nuclear arms race resulted in the building of at least seventy thousand nuclear weapons between the adversaries.

At the height of the Cold War, the adversaries were poised to utterly destroy the other at any moment. In fact, President Kennedy was astonished the Eisenhower administration had driven the US "into a corner where the only choice is all or nothing at all, world devastation or submission."[305]

The early 1960s were an especially frightening time because of the nuclear standoff. American B-52 bombers constantly flew circular patterns near Russia, ready to launch at any moment given the proper coded message from the White House. Other bombers sat on runways, ready to launch in case of a Soviet strike. Missile crews stood around the clock alert, deep inside missile silos, while nuclear-tipped ballistic missiles were constantly at the ready aboard submarines that remained submerged for months at a time.

Another major technology that emerged from the Cold War was the development of computers. The first computers were exclusively for military purposes, and in the US, one company had the lead: International Business Machines (IBM). Its revenues initially came from the analog-guidance computer built for the B-52 bomber and from the SAGE (Semi-Automatic Ground Environment) air defense system. Then IBM's chairman and CEO, Thomas J. Watson, said: "It was the Cold War that helped IBM make itself the king of the computer business."[306]

Initially, the Soviets were not far behind the US in computer technology—that is, until the Pentagon started to look elsewhere. The Pentagon's search led to the technological marriage of the military establishment, industry, and the academy—the military-industrial-academic complex came of age. That marriage led to crucial breakthroughs and, before long, commercially available personal computers, something the Soviets could not match.

The military had the need to link computers at different research centers, what became known as ARPAnet—the Advanced Research Projects Agency Network, the technical foundation of the contemporary Internet. This was the most important technological innovation of the Cold War.[307] And no, there is no evidence that any politician invented the Internet; it was always a military innovation.

The Internet soon linked the capitalist centers of the world more closely in terms of business, trade, education, and culture. It was responsible for the market revolution of the late twentieth century, all thanks to the Cold War competition in technology.

The creation of the Internet left the Soviet Union and its satellite states in the technological dust, isolating them from the rest of the world. Certainly, by the late 1980s, most of the world was moving away from interacting with the Soviets and closer to the West, in part because of the cyber revolution. That reality put an overwhelming challenge on the communists, and in the end, Soviet President Mikhail Gorbachev's perestroika project was about not being left behind in a world moving in a very different technological direction.

Professor Westad admits that making technology a key aspect of the Cold War history is confusing; after all, technology is in its essence politically and ideologically neutral. But he argues that we must admit that "the links between military priorities and technological development and to be open to the suggestion that innovation in some key areas during the past fifty years moved in directions it would not have taken had it not been for the Cold War."[308]

The Cold War profoundly impacted not just new technologies, but science-state relationships as well. Technology and the supporting science became more international, more formalized. It helped mankind remake not only tools for warfare but also the world, state, and society in ways that might not have been possible without the deadly threat brought about by the Cold War.

Third World

Moscow's fear of Washington's power and ideological assumptions about global ambitions pushed the Soviets well beyond Europe. In fact, the Soviet Ambassador to the US, Nikolai Novikov, wrote in 1946 that the United States considered the USSR an implacable foe that must be contained. Novikov stressed America's alleged imperialist motivations and urged Moscow "to be vigilant in protecting national security."[309]

The Soviets' misunderstanding of American intentions launched Moscow on a campaign, which Westad refers to as the third Cold War paradigm, the concept of three worlds. The First World consisted of the main capitalist states (mostly the US and West European countries), the Second World was the Soviets and their allies, and the third was everyone else. Professor Westad said the Cold War made the Third World the victim in the bipolar world, tearing countries apart through proxy wars.

Westad properly states that "the Cold War was made hot in the third world in part through superpower interventions, either directly or via proxies." For the US, these interventions were largely preventive to "reduce the probability of a long chain of events that might someday reduce U.S. security and prosperity."[310]

Certainly, that view was fed by popular justification at the time, such as in "the absence of intervention many more dominoes would indeed fall"—and then the resulting new communist regimes would be stable and support Moscow, thus fueling the bipolar rivalry.[311]

America's impulse to transform the world to make it ultimately secure grew out of a sense of power and immediate security, said Westad. It's noteworthy that the Soviets demonstrated a similar motivation, likely, as Westad suggests, in order to compete geopolitically with the US and realize their Marxist vision. Therefore, as Soviet leaders' confidence in their massive nuclear arsenal and material capability to project power in the late 1960s and 1970s grew, they began to deploy forces to Southeast Asia, south and east Africa, the Persian Gulf, and Afghanistan.[312]

The sad consequence of this geopolitical competition was the human toll for the Third World. Westad argues that this competitive interventionism started with "American ideological insistence that a global spread of communism would, if not checked, result from the postwar extension of Soviet might that made the rivalry between the two powers into a Cold War." Not to be outdone, by the early 1960s, "Soviet ideology had already reached a stage where the competition for influence in the third world was an essential part of the existence of socialism," a staple of Sovietology by the 1970s and 1980s.

The Third World elites jumped at the opportunity to align with one or the other Cold War ideologies, which invited domestic damage through warfare and social experiments. That alignment tended in some cases to delegitimize those elites from their population, forcing the elites to rely more on their superpower partner of choice to help wage war on their own people in order to maintain power. It was indeed a vicious cycle.

An unfortunate aspect of the Cold War was also the willingness of the Third World elites to adopt Cold War ideologies for their domestic purposes. That outcome resulted in untold damage not only through warfare—proxy wars—but through social experiments, thanks to socialist and capitalist ideologies. For example, there were Soviet-inspired rural resettlement programs, five-year plans, and collectivization efforts— much like Soviet programs in Russia—that, when applied in Third World countries, claimed a social and human toll that tended to alienate unwilling societies, thus sparking continuous insurgencies between the ruling elite and the peasantry.

The Cold War competition in the Third World also resulted in a series of larger proxy wars, often characterized as the struggle between communism and democracy. The Korean War (1950–53) was the first and best known next to the Vietnam War.

In 1950, North Korean forces, backed by the Soviets and Communist Chinese, fought the US and South Korea, joined by some United Nations forces, to a bloody stalemate. That war might never have happened if not for Stalin's authorization, however.

Chinese historians like Shu Guang Zhang and Jian Chen and the opening of the Russian archives after the Cold War revealed that North Korean leader Kim Il Sung, the contemporary Kim Jung Un's grandfather, was dependent on Moscow and thus needed Stalin's authorization to attack South Korea to seize the entire peninsula. Stalin hesitated to give his permission, fearing an American response, and only after becoming convinced that the Americans would not intervene did Stalin grant Kim's request.[313] That mistake, along with MacArthur's miscalculation concerning Chinese entry, resulted in higher costs in terms of treasure and lives. That war's cost was significant.

The US joined South Korea in an effort to repel North Korea on June 25, 1950, and fighting continued until an armistice on July 27, 1953. The war cost at the time $30 billion—an estimated $276 billion in today's dollars. However, the cost in blood was significant, with 36,000 Americans killed and more than 100,000 wounded. Meanwhile, the two Koreas lost 620,000 warriors and 1.6 million civilians.[314] Further, an estimated 180,000 Chinese soldiers were killed in the Korean War.[315]

America's intervention in Vietnam is another example of great power miscalculation based on viewing the region through a Cold War ideological prism. Vietnam's Ho Chi Minh was a communist by convenience to curry Soviet aid, but was a nationalist against outside incursions, as we saw in his fight with the French, Americans, and, lastly, the Chinese.

Vietnam's nationalist colors were evident after America's withdrawal from the war in 1975 after unnecessarily sacrificing 58,000 young Americans. Following the US military withdrawal, Vietnam went to war against communist Cambodia, which led to a confrontation with communist China. Now in 2018, Vietnam has come full circle and welcomes the US armed services back as a partner against the communist Chinese.

The world saw the same Cold War ideological distortions in the Middle East, with governments and political movements masquerading as aspirants of socialism or capitalism to gain influence with one or the other Cold War superpowers. Leaders like Egypt's Gama Abdel Nasser cared less whether socialism or capitalism would dominate; rather, national interests and not ideological fervor explained his alignment.[316]

Even the long-standing Arab-Israeli conflict was at the time considered a Cold War subplot. But that's a distorted view, much as it was to consider the Indian-Pakistani tensions as a product of the Moscow-Washington Cold War. Those regional tensions continue in 2018, decades after the end of the former Soviet Union and the Cold War.

During the 1970s, then US Secretary of State Henry Kissinger charged the Kremlin with using Cuban surrogates to support Soviet adventurism in Africa, especially in Angola. Kissinger's accusations failed when information from archives in the post-Cold War Moscow demonstrated that Cuban leader Fidel Castro was in the forefront of the black liberation movements in Africa. Castro began supplying arms and advisers to the popular movement for the liberation of Angola as early as 1965.[317]

Soviet archives indicated that the Kremlin did not know about or authorize Cuba's initial deployment to Angola, which took place aboard old passenger aircraft and pre-revolutionary cruise ships. However, in time, Russia supported the Cuban operation only because Moscow feared losing influence against rivals China and the United States.

The last major Third World Soviet war was in Afghanistan, a fight to bolster a communist leadership threatened by Isalmists, not American capitalists. The Soviet's Afghan allies earned significant aid from Moscow while defying advice to avoid policies that engendered widespread unrest. By the late 1980s, Moscow had enough of Afghanistan and withdrew its forces, leaving that country to metastasize into a terrorist haven until the US committed forces in 2001, where it remains bogged down today.

The bipolar nature of the Cold War created an international system, kept in check by robust nuclear arsenals, while Europe enjoyed peace and the killing was confined to mostly the Third World.

The three paradigms—ideology, technology, and Third World—illustrate the impact of the Cold War for the primary adversaries and for the entire globe. It was a dangerous time for all that eventually, for a variety of hard-to-anticipate reasons came to an end in 1991.

4. Why Did the Soviet Union Collapse, and What Are the Consequences of That "Black Swan" Event?

The collapse of the Soviet Union was arguably the most transformative shift of the late twentieth century, a classical "black swan" event. Many historians speculate about the underlying reasons for that collapse, while others continue to identify the consequences. I will provide a summary of a few of both, as well as offer a glimpse at the political infighting in 1991 that led to the actual collapse of the Soviet Union.

The preponderance of historical evidence suggests that the West won the Cold War primarily because of a series of complex challenges facing the Soviet Union in the late 1980s. Those complex challenges include: nuclear stalemate, imperial overstretch into the Third World, long-term

Soviet command economy decline, US military pressure (especially the introduction of America's Strategic Defense Initiative or "Star Wars"), governing incompetence, corrosive power of nationalism, success of the Russian democracy movement, and—probably the most important, at least ideologically—the Kremlin's failure to catch up with and overtake the capitalist West.

Professor Westad, one of the foremost experts on the Cold War, argues that the West won the Cold War because it was materially, not ideologically, stronger than the USSR. There is significant evidence to support Westad's view as well as other compelling contributions, which are summarized below. We shall begin with the economic challenge.

By the late 1980s, it was clear that the Soviet economy could not compete with the capitalist West. The USSR sank under the weight of an incompetent, government-run economy with state-owned industries routinely turning out inferior products such as tractors that didn't work, and as a direct result, Soviet farmers watched their crops rot in the fields for lack of transport to market. Worse, Kremlin bureaucrats with no marketing experience decided what to manufacture, while the population waited years to buy the necessities of life and Moscow lacked products for a growing and increasingly competitive globalized market place.

There was an ideological component to the collapse of the Soviet Union as well. Specifically, Western ideas flooded the Soviet population through contacts and exchanges with the West, which increased its influence among the Russian people and especially the intelligentsia. Western voices were popular in the USSR and the Soviet satellite nations because of daily radio transmissions from the *Voice of America*, *Radio Liberty*, Germany's *Deutsche Welle*, and the *British Broadcasting Corporation*.

The West's ideological influence seeded unrest among USSR populations and fueled their calls for democratic reform, thanks to those Western broadcast media. As a result, and by the late 1980s, protests broke out across the Soviet satellite states as well as inside Russia.

President Ronald Reagan encouraged the USSR's democratic reform movement when he traveled to Berlin, a city separated by a wall—the

Iron Curtain—built by communists in August 1961 to keep Germans from escaping communist-dominated East Berlin into democratic West Berlin. On June 12, 1987, Reagan made history when he said:

> Behind me stands a wall that encircles the free sectors of this city, part of a vast system of barriers that divides the entire continent of Europe.... Standing before the Brandenburg Gate, every man is a German, separated from his fellow men. Every man is a Berliner, forced to look upon a scar.... As long as this gate is closed, as long as this scar of a wall is permitted to stand, it is not the German question alone that remains open, but the question of freedom for all mankind.... General Secretary Gorbachev, if you seek peace, if you seek prosperity for the Soviet Union and Eastern Europe, if you seek liberalization, come here to this gate.
>
> Mr. Gorbachev, open this gate!
>
> Mr. Gorbachev, tear down this wall![318]

Reagan's message was intended to be a psychological shot in the arm to the democratic reform movement in East Europe as well as Soviet Russia. By 1989, protesters in Germany tore down the Berlin Wall, the symbol of the Soviet's Iron Curtain that separated communist from democratic Europe. Meanwhile, the Soviets failed to quiet the growing dissent across the fifteen Soviet states by imprisoning many and fighting those democratic movements in the streets across the USSR.

Eventually, massive demonstrations came to Moscow as well. On March 28, 1991, a democratic movement demonstration stalled traffic in Moscow with the largest ever crowd of five hundred thousand participants supporting President Mikhail Gorbachev's fledgling reform efforts known as *perestroika*.

Gorbachev's policies of *glasnost* ("openness") and *perestroika* ("restructuring") and his strategic plans focused on ending the decades of Cold War. Those efforts included removing the Communist Party from governing the state, a very high-risk undertaking.

By the mid-1980s, the economic strain of Russia's very expensive military overreach was especially tough, a major reason to end the Cold War. The strain increased significantly once the newly minted President Ronald Reagan committed the US to increased resources for defense and introduced his bank-breaking "Star Wars" initiative, an expense the Kremlin was unprepared to match.

The Star Wars proposal came as Russian coffers were being drained by the war in Afghanistan as well as Moscow's imperialist-like reach elsewhere across the globe. The Soviet's Afghan war that began in the early 1980s proved to be Moscow's Vietnam, a no-win war costing the nation dearly in blood and treasure. Of course, the United States contributed to that cost by equipping Afghan insurgents with American weapons. Further, the Russians were viewed by the Muslim world as invaders and infidels, which drew battlefield recruits from across the Middle East and ultimately cost Russia fourteen thousand soldier lives and wounded another fifty thousand before Moscow withdrew all forces in 1989.

These and many other complex challenges collided with Gorbachev's recognition that he must reform the USSR if it was to survive. He moved quickly to thaw relations with the West by bringing about glasnost and an effort to jump-start his command economy with perestroika's free-market reforms.

Gorbachev's reform efforts met significant opposition from the conservative wing of the Communist Party.

In April 1991, there was an attempt at a peaceful coup d'état, which failed when conservative communist forces attempted to depose Gorbachev from the position of general secretary at the Joint Plenum of the Central Committee and the Central Supervisory Commission. Gorbachev offered to resign at the time, but the conservatives backed down. That failed effort continued, albeit in secret.

Then, in July 1991, Gorbachev became the first Soviet leader to implicitly abandon Marxism. He urged the Soviet Communist Party to push Marxist ideology to the sidelines, which had seized power in the name of the proletariat (working-class people), and then ruled for nearly three-quarters of a century. Gorbachev called on fellow communists to get rid of "ossified dogmas," and warned that without such dramatic changes in the party's philosophy, its disintegration would accelerate and the country's many crises would deepen.[319]

Gorbachev knew he was provoking party conservatives who fought his reforms. He called on those members to leave the party rather than compromise perestroika. "There are forces in the party that have openly declared war on [*perestroika*]," he said. He denounced them, stating "these forces put into doubt all the party's current policies."[320]

Gorbachev proved to be too much for conservative communists, as evidenced by the April peaceful coup d'état. Meanwhile, he made a strategic mistake by steadily emasculating the Communist Party through his reform efforts. He should have maneuvered the communists into supporting and perhaps co-leading his reforms until enough of a new system was in place. Unfortunately, his ham-handedness eroded and humiliated the communists, which provoked strong elements and forced an alliance to form against his reforms.

The conservatives struck again on August 20, 1991, with a real coup d'état attempt known as the "August Coup" or "August Putsch." That effort was overthrown in three days, but as before, the hardliners never went away. The coup leaders were the same hard-liner members of the Communist Party of the Soviet Union who had opposed Gorbachev's reforms during the April peaceful coup d'état. However, and looking into the future, the "August Putsch" attempt is widely considered to have contributed to the eventual dissolution of the Soviet Union a few months later.

The coup diminished Gorbachev's power and propelled Boris Yeltsin and the democratic forces to the forefront of Russian politics. Meanwhile, President George H. W. Bush condemned the coup as "extra-constitutional." Soon Gorbachev resigned as the head of the Communist Party, separating the power of the party from the presidency of the Soviet Union.[321]

As political events in Russia continued to heat up, the Bush administration prioritized the prevention of nuclear catastrophe, the curbing of ethnic violence, and the stable transition to new political leadership. Meanwhile, US Secretary of State James Baker met with Gorbachev and Yeltsin to shore up the economic situation and develop an economic plan, as well as determine ways to allow for more political reforms.

On Christmas Day 1991, Mr. Gorbachev spoke to the Soviet people in a television address to announce: "I hereby discontinue my activities at the post of President of the Union of Soviet Socialist Republics." He was to be the last leader of a totalitarian empire that was undone across his six-plus-year tenure.[322]

"We're now living in a new world," Mr. Gorbachev declared in recognizing the rich history of his time in office. "An end has been put to the Cold War and to the arms race, as well as to the mad militarization of the country, which has crippled our economy, public attitudes and morals. The threat of nuclear war has been removed."[323]

On Christmas 1991 at 7:32 p.m. Moscow time, the Soviet Empire officially collapsed with the lowering of the floodlit crimson hammer-and-sickle Soviet flag at the Kremlin and the hoisting of the white, blue, and red Russian Federation's tricolor. On that fateful day, the Russians found themselves living in a new country, one disfigured by decades of Soviet repression and no leaders with a clue as to how to take the country forward.

In his Christmas Day address to the nation, Gorbachev said, "I am concerned about the fact that the people in this country are ceasing to become citizens of a great power and the consequences may be very difficult for all of us to deal with." That was an understatement.

The post-Gorbachev Russia faced a massive, complex, and painful transformation. Russia, with its 150 million people and its satellite states, had to figure out how to morph from being authoritarian to becoming democratic states governed by the rule of law, and from state-controlled to market-based economies. Those challenges were especially difficult for the national political classes that only knew the Soviet system of government and were mostly too timid to do the necessary work to make the transition.

The consequences of the collapse were immediate and far reaching, and not necessarily welcomed by the United States.

Many in the West feared that the consequences of the Soviet collapse would be potentially catastrophic, for not only would it unleash all sorts of possible dangers, ranging from weapons of mass destruction (radiological, chemical, biological) proliferation to outbreaks of irredentist wars, it would also make economic reformation much more difficult.

National security advisor Brent Scowcroft, under Presidents Gerald Ford and George H. W. Bush, warned, "Our policy [regarding the failed Soviet Union] has to be based on our own national interest, and we have an interest in the stability of the Soviet Union. The instability of the USRR would be a threat to us." Scowcroft was right; the Soviet collapse led to considerable instability.

In hindsight, the Cold War's nuclear standoff arguably brought stability, a long peace that author George Orwell explained. Nations with the atomic bomb were, according to Orwell, "unable to conquer one another, [therefore] they are likely to continue ruling the world between them, and it is difficult to see how the balance can be upset except by slow and unpredictable demographic changes." Orwell also suggested the nuclear stand-off "is likelier to put an end to large-scale wars at the cost of prolonging indefinitely a 'peace that is no peace.'"

Historian John Gaddis agreed with Orwell. Gaddis said the Cold War produced a "long peace," the result of bipolarity and the calming effect that nuclear weapons had upon great power behavior. Gaddis argued the reality was that the Cold War had evolved to produce its own kind of peace order.

President Bush sought to maintain as much stability as possible in the wake of the collapse of the Soviet Union. He met with President Boris Yeltsin of the Russian Federation in February 1992 at Camp David, where they discussed politics, economic reforms, and mostly security issues. Bush's paramount concern was securing Russia's nuclear arsenal and making certain nuclear weapons did not fall into the wrong hands. In fact, Secretary James Baker offered funding to secure nuclear, chemical, and biological weapons. Later that year, the Nunn-Lugar Act established the Cooperative Threat Reduction Program to fund the dismantling of weapons in the former Soviet Union.[324]

The dissolution of the USSR left the United States as the world's sole superpower, a significant strategic consequence for the United States. Unfortunately, the US failed to leverage its new status by welcoming the Russian Federation to join our ranks. What the West ended up doing were half measures that were unsatisfying, and ultimately mostly abandoned Russia to the ravages of corruption.

America and her Western allies focused on cashing in on their Cold War victory by naively embracing a concept first coined by the prophet Isaiah (2:4): "Beat their swords into plowshares and their spears into pruning hooks." That collective decision was historically naïve because it failed to put in place mechanisms to prevent the re-emergence of a new Cold War.

Yes, Russia quickly abandoned communism as an ideal and central planning as an economic tool and morphed the nation into somewhat of a market economy, with the state continuing to play important economic roles such as controlling the two largest money-making enterprises: petroleum and arms sales.

Moscow also pursued and won a significant trade relationship with Europe. It would provide mostly resources like petroleum and gold, but few finished goods. Although Russia had a great talent pool for producing finished goods, that sector wasn't quickly harnessed, and as a result, with limited exceptions, it doesn't compete internationally in that sector today. Failure to transform Russia's talent pool at the end of the Cold War was in hindsight a tragic mistake exacerbated admittedly, at least from a Western perspective, by Moscow's reputation for debt default, the tendency to nationalize companies, and massive corruption, which kept outside investors away.

America's victory over Soviet communism did not lead to dealing with the complexities of postwar planning. The Cold War ended, but

America's hubris remains and will go down in history as a missed opportunity by the West.

Conclusion

Nations seldom have the opportunity to learn from their past failures and then get it right the next go-around. The new dual Cold War need not become yet another example of failing to understand the lessons of history, which could lead the United States to repeat the failure to capitalize on the collapse of the former Soviet Union. After all, former great nations have crumbled, and America may in fact be on the same fast track to the global ash heap as well, because it, too, failed to learn from history.

Yes, America won the Cold War with the Soviet Union, but its failure to shape the outcomes of that conflict resulted in squandering a long-term peace and invariably contributed to the rise of the current dual Cold War.

CHAPTER FOUR

Implications of the
New Dual Cold War

The new dual Cold War ushers in an era of great power competition that introduces a renewed alliance—China and Russia—that will create a very different kind of Cold War. It will certainly have similarities with the old Cold War, such as an arms race, proxy wars, and a divided world encouraged by ideological differences. But the new dual Cold War will become known as well for a mixture of competition and cooperation in political and military spheres, welcomed economic cooperation, and considerable cultural connectivity, but also the real risk for a kinetic war across all domains, especially thanks to radically new high technologies.

The 2017 US National Security Strategy (NSS) sets the stage for the new dual Cold War by declaring that "China and Russia challenge American power, influence, and interests, attempting to erode American security and prosperity," which are indications of the rising great power global competition. The NSS goes on to label China and Russia "revisionist powers" that have "increased efforts short of armed conflict by expanding coercion to new fronts, violating principles of sovereignty, exploiting ambiguity, and deliberately blurring the lines between civil and military goals."[325]

The NSS states: "China and Russia want to shape a world antithetical to U.S. values and interests." Specifically, China intends to displace the United States in the Indo-Pacific region (formerly the Asia-Pacific region) by expanding its state-driven economic model and reordering the region in its favor.[326]

Former Secretary of State Henry Kissinger, an acknowledged China expert, points out that "not since it [the United States] became a global power in the wake of the Second World War has the United States had to contend with a geopolitical equal." Kissinger continued, "Our relations with China will shape international order in the long term. The United States and China will be the world's most consequential countries. Economically, this is already the case. Yet both nations are having to undergo unprecedented domestic transformations."[327]

The former secretary of state then warns that we must be vigilant. Chinese hardliners, according to Kissinger, are dangerous and at the ready to strike the United States. They claim that "the Americans are visibly declining. We will win. We can afford to be tough and look at the world with sort of cold war-ish attitudes."[328]

Russia has hardliners as well ready to pounce on perceived weaknesses in the West. The Kremlin zealots in President Putin's inner circle are former Soviet Union Communist Party functionaries such as Sergei Ivanov, Sergei Shoygu, and Igor Sechin, the so-called "Siloviki," a reference to the uniformed security services.[329]

Consider the evidence of a renewed great power competition, and how this new competition is once again dividing the world into two camps characterized by an emerging alliance between China and Russia.

Evidence of a Great Power Competition

A major factor in the new great power competition is the leadership at the helm of these countries. Both China and Russia are headed by autocrats who test international order just as the United States seems to be losing its way as outlined in chapter 2 of this volume.

Russia's President Vladimir Putin seems immune if not somewhat irritated by Western sanctions over his seizure of Crimea in 2014 and his ongoing misadventure in eastern Ukraine, which some label a civil war. Putin responded to Western sanctions with disinformation campaigns against Western elections, significant saber-rattling along Russia's Western border with former satellite states, and increased harassment of NATO and US military vessels and aircraft across the world.

Chinese President Xi Jinping is an autocrat as well with a great vision for a modern, global armed forces and an economic arm reaching broadly, thus pushing China's influence abroad seeking to dominate the globe's democratic regions, a view shared by China experts in testimony before the House Permanent Select Committee on Intelligence. "The Chinese Communist Party is engaged in a total, protracted struggle for regional and global supremacy," said retired Navy Captain Jim Fanell, a former Pacific Fleet intelligence chief who testified in May 2018. "This supremacy is the heart of the 'China Dream.' China's arsenal in this campaign for supremacy includes economic, informational, political and military warfare." Rick Fisher, a China expert with the International Assessment and Strategy Center, testified that this poses "grave challenges" for American security and warned the US has "about a decade" to take action to counter the threat.[330]

In the face of this confrontation, the West seems feckless at stopping Putin's and Xi's great power ambitions, efforts driven by their authoritarian personalities and evidently accepted and cheered by their domestic power bases.

President Xi is the most powerful ruler in Beijing since Mao Zedong, acknowledged by at least thirteen titles (such as General Secretary of the Central Committee of the Communist Party) and the 19th Party Congress in October 2017, which enshrined "Xi Jinping Thought" as sacred in the nation's constitution. Further, Mr. Xi's purge of lesser wayward officials virtually guarantees his long reign and a loyal court of sycophants. And, thanks to a March 2018 modification to the Chinese constitution by that country's National People's Congress, Xi can rule as long as he likes, president for life.

"This is a very significant move toward China transforming into a one-man system," said Jude Blanchette, a Beijing-based researcher with the Conference Board, a nonprofit business membership and research group. "It's hard to overemphasize what a big deal this is for the future of China and the world," Blanchette explained. Until now, China's ruling Communist Party has governed through institutionalization: the party with no one person holding the reins of power. However, since 2013, Xi has removed safeguards while increasing authoritarian oversight through censorship and jailing lawyers and activists.[331]

One-man rule was not supposed to happen again like the time under Mao, thanks to reformer (then chairman of the Central Advisory Commission) Deng Xiaoping. He introduced collective leadership around the party executive and created presidential term limits, but Xi dismantled these protocols. But "this [one-man rule] is a several thousand-year-old problem for China," said Blanchette. Then she asked, "How long does the emperor stay in power, and how does he exit?"[332]

Dr. Steven Mosher, author of the 2017 book, *Bully of Asia: Why China's Dream Is the New Threat to World Order*, said: "Xi Jinping is the new Chairman Mao, a thoroughly Communist dictator who has managed to seize control of the Party, the Army, and the Government. The new Red Emperor, as we should call him, is likely to be in power for decades to come. And he is not our friend. He is carrying out a new Cultural Revolution in China. Communist Party leader Xi's China 'Dream' is the world's nightmare. Xi 'dreams' of overturning the current U.S.-led world order and replacing it with [a new world order]…dominated by China. A world dominated by China would be less free, less democratic, and less safe, not only for Americans, but for the Chinese people themselves. Xi believes that international law and agreements are, as he has said, just 'waste paper,' or better put, 'toilet paper.'"[333]

Then US Navy Admiral Harry Harris, commander of United States forces in the Pacific, and, at the time of this writing, Mr. Trump's nominee to become ambassador to South Korea, appears to agree with Dr. Mosher. Harris said China's constitutional change to make Xi Jinping president for life is a harbinger of the authoritarian nation's direction and a strategic threat to America.

"China has taken advantage of our openness," Harris told the Senate Armed Services Committee in March 2018. "Our hope in the past has been that if we bring China into organizations like the World Trade Organization and include China in our military exercises and the like, and that somehow China will become like us."[334]

"The reality is that's simply not true. China has taken advantage of our openness…to continue the path that they've always been on and we're seeing that play out now in 2018. Certainly over the next 20 years or so that will be a concern," Harris said.[335]

Admiral Harris explained that Beijing seeks regional hegemony and intends to oust America from Asia. It is developing the means to do that via systems such as the hypersonic glide weapons and stealth fighters. Besides, the admiral expressed concern about China's militarization of islands in the South China Sea and its acquisition of icebreaker ships, although it has no Arctic coast.[336]

Russia's Putin isn't far behind Xi's march for one-man rule and the resurrection of a new version of the old Soviet empire. Leading up to Russia's March 18, 2018, presidential election, Putin delivered his annual State of the Nation speech with bellicose rhetoric similar to that of the communist dictators of the old Cold War. Putin used that speech to threaten Western nations with a new generation of nuclear weapons, including an "invincible" intercontinental cruise missile that he claims can reach virtually anywhere in the world.[337]

Announcing the new weapons was good politics. "He's giving people the image of a desired future, of a future for Russia, and that's appealing for his domestic audience," said Aleksei V. Makarkin, the deputy head of the Center for Political Technologies in Moscow. Putin's Russia-can-do-it-all speech was designed to reassure voters that their president is their best hope for making Russia a superpower again.[338]

"People may say Russia depends on oil, Russia doesn't have the money, but the population at large doesn't care about that," Mr. Makarkin said. "They just want to know that we are a superpower."[339]

Putin's two-hour speech addressed future development of the country and then quickly moved to an extended threat to the West. Gleb O. Pavlovsky, a political analyst and former Kremlin consultant, said, "From tales about progress, the speech flowed into an open-ended declaration of world war [on the West]."[340]

President Putin ended his speech with comments about the perceived disrespect shown him by the US, the world's superpower. "Nobody listened to Russia," Putin said, and then to a resounding applause, he said, "Well, listen up now."[341]

Putin was reelected in March 2018 by a large (77 percent) majority, an indication of his popularity and an endorsement of his vision for the Russian Federation. Keep in mind Putin announced to the world years ago that the collapse of the former Soviet Union was "the greatest geopolitical tragedy of the 20th century."[342] He's anxious to restore Moscow to its former greatness as he suggested in his State of the Nation speech.

On May 7, 2018 Putin was inaugurated for his fourth term, ushering in yet another six years as his country's president making him second only to Josef Stalin in length of service at the helm of Russia. He used the occasion to praise his country as a "strong, active and influential participant in world affairs," further reflecting on his ultimate aim—returning to superpower status.[343]

Let's put Mr. Putin's long-term ambition for Russia into perspective. In the shadow of Russia's seizure of Crimea in 2014, former US Ambassador to the UN, John Bolton, under President George W. Bush and President Trump's current national security adviser, said, "I think Putin knows that he has the high cards, militarily, economically and politically, and he's prepared to use them." Bolton continued, "It's clear he [Putin] wants to re-establish Russian hegemony within the space of the former Soviet Union. Ukraine is the biggest prize, that's what he's after. The occupation of the Crimea is a step in that direction."[344] Those actions have the former Soviet satellites guessing which of them is next on Putin's list of countries to occupy and reclaim.

Retaking lost influence won't be easy, however. Stability long-term under an authoritarian figure like Putin may prove to be difficult, thanks to troubling factors like the centralized management of Russian finances. Further, shrinking revenues from Moscow's oil production, which collapsed in 2015, remain low and are taking a toll on Putin's grasp of Russia's eight-three provinces, republics, autonomous okrugs, krays, federal cities, and autonomous oblasts due to a decline in government subsidies.[345]

President Xi's global ambitions are a true challenge to the US and, like Putin, Xi is not without internal problems that in time might undercut his ambitions as well. Those problems are significant: rising income gaps, draconian birth-control policies, environmental degradation, rising inequalities, demographic imbalance, domestic terrorism, abuses of power, corruption, and dismal human rights.[346]

Inevitably, Putin and Xi will respond to growing domestic and international pressures by further consolidating their power, which will inevitably generate tyrannical measures to silence their opposition. Their approach may work for the near future, but in time, all authoritarian regimes run into trouble and then their fall is ugly.

What's not in question at the moment are the courses Putin and Xi set for their respective countries. Xi's China is rapidly emerging as a great power, and Putin's Russia is re-emerging from a post-Cold War slump to try to recapture its former great power stature, an unlikely outcome without significant outside help.

Consider evidence of both countries' progress to great power status.

Former French Emperor Napoleon Bonaparte declared, "When China awakes, the world will shake."[347] China is awakening, and it is becoming a great power to challenge the United States, which since the end of the old Cold War has enjoyed unipolar super power status.

The current situation between the US and China can be compared to that of ancient Rome when it was challenged by Carthage—a "struggle for power like two gladiators doomed to be an increasingly globalized combat until one side fades."[348]

Many people across the world believe the US is already fading and it won't be long before China is the dominant power in the world. The Pew Center's Global Attitudes Project concluded in 2013: "Regardless of which country is seen as the economic powerhouse today, many publics believe China will eventually replace the US as the world's leading superpower, if it has not already done so."[349] Majorities in most (thirty-three of thirty-nine) countries surveyed agreed America is waning and China is winning—even among her best allies such as the United Kingdom.

Consider some sobering facts about China's emergence as a great power. The most obvious examples of that rise regard military and economic power.

Contemporary China is now projecting a sophisticated and expeditionary military capability across the world. It has a growing nuclear arsenal; an emergent, giant, blue-water navy; a growing space program; the world's largest standing army (3,712,500 active and reserve personnel); and a large, sophisticated air force; and it is conducting military exercises literally across the world.[350]

China is also expanding its military bases overseas as outlined in chapter 1 of this volume to a facility in Djibouti (North Africa), and others appear to be on the horizon. Further, and never forget, Chinese overseas commercial enterprises are really extensions of the Beijing government; more often than not, they are run by "businesses" owned by the People's Liberation Army.

Even China's military leaders are talking like a confident great power. One well-spoken colonel in the People's Liberation Army, Liu Mingfu, wrote in his book, *The China Dream*, "In the 21st century China and the United States will square off and fight to become the champion among nations."[351] China's military is focused like a laser on every way to defeat one adversary: the United States armed forces.

Beijing's world-capable military is reinforced in terms of national power by China's significant economic prowess. China's economic expansion is truly impressive. It is the world's current second-place economy and is soon (2030 to 2035) expected to surpass the United States—and that outcome is in part thanks to a refreshed ancient idea.

China's ancient Silk Road, the four thousand-mile caravan tract, linked Xi-an (Sian) with the West, bringing together the two great civilizations of Rome and China. The new land and sea version of the Silk Road or China's "Belt and Road Initiative" has much the same intention to link China with the rest of the world. The new project started in 2013 aims to promote infrastructure development in sixty-eight countries, covering 55 percent of the world's gross national product, 70 percent of the global population, and 75 percent of known energy reserves.

Beijing's hidden rationale for the initiative appears to be mainly economic, according to Zhuang Jianzhong, vice director of Shanghai Jiao Tong University's Center for National Strategic Studies. It "has political and strategic components and implications, [however]."[352] It also appears to be part of Beijing's effort to internationalize its official currency, the *renminbi*, and to globalize its geopolitical influence. That effort includes significant overseas acquisitions spanning the entire world. (The "renminbi" is the official name of China's currency, which means "the people's currency." "Yuan" is a unit of renminbi currency.)

In late March 2018, Beijing requested that financial institutions prepare for pricing China's crude oil imports in yuan, according to *Reuters*. "Being the biggest buyer of oil, it's only natural for China to push for the usage of yuan for payment settlement. This will also improve the yuan liquidity in the global market," said someone briefed by Chinese authorities and reported by *Reuters*. This effort is designed to eventually dethrone the American greenback, according to an unnamed source reported by *Reuters*.[353]

Beijing, through its state-owned surrogates, is gobbling up port infrastructure literally across the world, from Singapore to the North Sea, through aggressive acquisitions that are redrawing the global trade maps and by association altering Beijing's political influence on every continent. For example, deep-pocketed Chinese behemoths like Cosco Shipping Ports and China Merchants Port Holdings are snapping up shipping terminals in the Indian Ocean, the Mediterranean Sea, and across the Atlantic rim to include crown jewels like the terminal in Zeebrugge, Belgium's second-largest port, as well as facilities in Spain, Italy, and Greece. Today, Chinese shipping firms control at least one-tenth of all European port capacity.

Beijing's geopolitical aim is clear, according to Frans-Paul van der Putten, a China expert with the Netherlands Institute of International Relations. Putten explained, "The fundamental goal seems to be to decrease China's dependence on foreign elements and increase China's influence around the world."[354]

Europeans are rightly concerned about China's growing ownership of European assets. European Commission President Jean-Claude Juncker warned about foreign purchases (read "Chinese") of ports, as did French President Emmanuel Macron, who while visiting Beijing, said, "China won't respect a continent, a power, when some member states let their doors freely open."[355]

China is making major inroads into Latin America as well. Beijing launched a decade-long, Latin American "Marshall Plan" with an infusion of $250 billion for infrastructure investments announced in 2015 by President Xi at a summit in Beijing for the Community of Latin American and Caribbean States, a thirty-three-nation organization. Beijing's aim, according to Latin America expert Juan de Onis "is to double the level of trade between China and Latin America," mostly in commodities like petroleum, soybeans, iron, and copper.[356]

China's reach into the Middle East is impressive as well. Trade with that region shot up tenfold over the past decade and is still climbing. Beijing imports more than half of its energy products from Middle-Eastern oil suppliers.

Beijing is also aggressively seeking more influence in the South Pacific, says Professor Anne-Marie Brady, an academic at New Zealand's

Christ Church-based University of Canterbury. The professor testified that she was warned with a threatening letter and her office was broken into as well by suspected Chinese operatives following the publication of her report, *Magic Weapons: China's Political Influence Activities under Xi Jinping*. That report details Chinese tactics to exert influence in the South Pacific through bodies like the Communist Party United Front Work Department. That group is a Beijing proxy that discredits and even neutralizes opponents of the regime and cultivates foreign political friends.[357]

Professor Brady said China is focusing on New Zealand because it is a member of the so-called "Five Eyes" intelligence-sharing alliance comprised of the United States, the United Kingdom, Canada, and Australia. "Breaking New Zealand out of these military groupings and away from its traditional partners, or at the very least, getting New Zealand to agree to stop spying on China for the Five Eyes, would be a major coup for China's strategic goal of becoming a global great power," Brady wrote.[358]

New Zealand is also an influential player among the smaller Pacific island nations: Cook Islands, Niue and Tokelau and Tonga, Somoa and Tuvalu. Leveraging of New Zealand to influence the patronage of those nations to China's benefit is another Beijing objective.

This is a serious challenge to the United States in the region. "It's clear what's happening: Australia [America's best ally in the South Pacific] is betting on a continued U.S. role in the region—and its 2016 Defense White Paper says so—but New Zealand is keeping its options open," security analyst Mark Thompson told the *Asia Times*.[359]

China also seeks to establish a naval base to counter the strategic advantage of the United States' military facilities at Guam, an American territory in the Western Pacific. Yu Chang Sen, deputy head of the National Center of Oceanic Studies at Guangzhou's Sun Yat-sen University, said China views Guam as part of America's strategic effort to encircle China.[360]

"It's impossible to say where each will be in five or 10 years, but, as the least committed of the pair, New Zealand is at greatest risk of becoming a Western ally with Chinese characteristics."[361]

By comparison, Russia is unlikely to regain the full stature it enjoyed during the height of the old Cold War. However, no one should under estimate President Putin.

Putin aims to weaken the West's influence by dividing its allies and views the North Atlantic Treaty Organization (NATO) and the European Union (EU) as threats to Russia's sovereign influence, especially along the nation's periphery, the former Soviet satellite nations of Eastern Europe.

One way Putin is gaining influence is by taking geostrategic risks in places like Syria. In December 2017, Putin claimed victory over the Islamic State in Iraq and Syria (ISIS)—a faux victory for Moscow, because Putin's chief goal was really ensuring the survival of ally Bashar al-Assad, the Syrian dictator, whose demise was all but assured until Putin's intervention that became a focus of US policy in Syria. Putin's real victory was to undermine American interests in the Middle East while establishing Russia once again as a major power broker in the region. What's the evidence?[362]

Russia never cared much about ISIS because, as its military operations demonstrated, propping-up Syria was the aim. Specifically, in 2016, Russia bombed the second-largest Syrian city of Aleppo, deliberately targeting civilian areas, including hospitals and US-backed opposition forces. Stephen O'Brien, the UN undersecretary-general, called that bombing operation "our generation's shame." Russia called it smart politics, which demonstrates that Moscow is back in as a power broker.[363]

Russia is also undermining United States' influence in Syria by stoking the conflict, according to US Army General Joseph Votel, commander of US Central Command, who testified before the House Armed Services Committee in February 2018: "I'm being very serious when I say they [the Russians] play the role of both arsonist and fireman—fueling tensions and then trying to resolve them in their favor." Votel insists that Moscow is pushing alternatives to US-led political solutions in both Syria and Afghanistan, and the Russians are also trying to fracture the long-standing strategic relationship between the US and Turkey.[364]

The brewing problems with Turkey provide a perfect opportunity for Moscow to undermine the West. Specifically, Turkish President Recep Tayyip Erdogan is angry that the Trump administration refuses to extradite Fethullah Gulen, a former preacher it accuses of treason. There is also the matter of America partnering with Syrian Kurds in the ISIS fight, which Turkey opposes as terrorists. So Erdogan turned to Putin, who was happy to undermine the US and NATO by courting a strategic ally. In late 2017, Erdogan thumbed his nose at the US by purchasing a Russian-made air-defense system, the S-400. Then in early April 2018, Erdogan appeared at Putin's side in an Ankara press conference to declare "We have made an agreement regarding the S-400. That subject is closed. It's a done deal." Putin then said, "We have decided to speed up the delivery of those highly efficient systems."[365]

Putin used the same trip to Turkey to announce the construction of Turkey's first nuclear power plant, which will be built by Russia near the Mediterranean coast at Akkuyu. The leaders said the reactor will be operational by 2023 and constructed by Russia's state-run nuclear power company, Rosatom. It is noteworthy that Moscow constructed the first reactors for both North Korea and Iran; those countries then extracted the plutonium residue for use in their nuclear weapons programs.[366]

Although the sale of the S-400 air-defense system and a nuclear reactor won't necessarily fracture the US-Turkey relationship, it evidences more Cold War-like behavior by Russia and feeds President Erdogan's agenda to grow regional influence.

Moscow's foreign adventures are backed by significant investments in modernizing its armed forces to give it great power credibility. Over the past decade, Mr. Putin has guided the Kremlin's reinvestment in many new nuclear systems that represent a credible and existential threat to the United States. Russia also refreshed its navy and especially its submarine fleet, which almost matches the US fleet in both size and capability. Further, its strategic aims include an array of subversive operational capabilities to destabilize its adversaries' domestic political affairs—not just in Europe, but also here in the United States.

Moscow's shortfall in recapturing great power status is likely its anemic economy, which lacks a globally competitive industrial base and is much too dependent on the sale of raw materials, especially energy resources. That shortfall may hurt the average Russian, but count on Putin sustaining his investment in the armed forces to feed his dream of renewing Moscow's great power status.

For these reasons and perhaps more, the Trump administration made the right decision to identify China and Russia as major US competitors in the new National Security Strategy and National Defense Strategy. It was about time the American government sounded the alarms about these near peer and great power threats. This was the first time since the terrorist attacks on September 11, 2001, that great power competition, rather than global terrorism, is considered America's number-one national security priority.

A logical follow-up to this discussion of the emergence of great power competition is the growing likelihood that China and Russia will formalize their relationship in a true alliance. As alliance partners, China and Russia could form a very capable counter to the US and her Western allies, thus the concept of a new dual Cold War takes on a very real military threat.

China-Russia Alliance

The United States should worry that China and Russia may form an alliance, because such a relationship makes fighting the new dual Cold War much more difficult and dangerous, as you will see in this chapter. A China-Russia alliance isn't necessarily certain, but it could materialize in the next few years.

An alliance is defined as a relationship—in this case, between nation states that unite for mutual benefit for a common cause, either explicitly through an agreement (such as a treaty) or by working on common purposes. Alliances form for a variety of reasons: political, military and business.

A formal military alliance is not required for states to become co-belligerents, as in the case of the allies of World War I and those who fought the Axis Powers of World War II. More recently, the US used the term "allied forces" when referring to co-belligerents to describe coalition partners in the 1990–91 Gulf War, the 2003–2011 Iraq War, and even in the ongoing war against the Taliban in Afghanistan. Only NATO members among these modern coalition partners are true "allies," because they are part of an alliance, a treaty-based organization.

China and Russia have a spotty history of cooperation, and they never formed a true treaty-based military alliance in the past. In fact, their past relationship has had a precarious and at times volatile history marked by three hundred years of border clashes over the area north of the Amur River. Sporadic fighting continued until Russia and China struck a treaty relationship in 1689, when the Treaty of Nerchiansk took effect, and then later, in 1727, with the Treaty of Kiakhta, which addressed disputes over their common border.[367]

Under the iron fist of the tsars, Russia's influence spread eastward, and in the nineteenth century Moscow was ascending while China's power decayed, thanks to constant infighting. Then in 1858, during the Second Opium War, China and Russia set aside their prior two border treaties (Nerchiansk and Kiakhta) to form a new treaty to delineate the Russo-Sino border granting Russia sovereignty over 185,000 square miles of previously contested territory.[368] It wasn't until the following century that the nations became serious about formalizing something like an alliance, however.

It helped Soviet Russia that Marxism gained popularity in China soon after the end of the Second World War, quickly followed by the founding of the People's Republic of China (PRC) in 1949 under Mao Zedong. In February 1950, Mao signed a Treaty of Friendship and Alliance, a mutual defense and assistance treaty, with the Soviet Kremlin and then Mao declared the link between the communist nations a force that was "impossible to defeat."[369]

On February 17, 1950, just prior to his departure from negotiating that treaty in Moscow, Mao said:

> It is plain to see that the unity of the people of the two great countries, China and the Soviet Union, solidified by the alliance treaty, will be permanent and inviolable, and one which cannot be put asunder by anyone. Moreover, this unity will not only influence the prosperity of these two great countries, China and the Soviet Union, but will surely affect the future of humanity and the triumph of peace and justice all over the world.[370]

It is noteworthy that an article in the *New York Times* at the time declared the PRC a new Soviet "satellite" as a result of that treaty. But that relationship frayed by the late 1950s, when the Chinese charged that the Soviets had compromised Marxism-Leninism by demonstrating an attitude of "peaceful coexistence" with the West.[371]

The Central Intelligence Agency (CIA) provides an in-depth analysis of historic trends, which includes a paper available in the CIA's library entitled "Calling the Sino-Soviet Split." The paper details the infighting within the US government over decades regarding whether China and Russia were cooperating. The paper examines the China-Russia relationship throughout the 1950s and most of the 1960s to conclude:

> Finally, our Sino-Soviet story has meaning beyond that of filling in some of the historical record. Its events may be a generation old and a world apart from ours, but they continue to speak to today's intelligence problems. Since 1950, China has passed from being an uneasy junior partner of the USSR, to an enemy of the USSR, to a burgeoning power cooperating with the new Russia in certain respects benefiting each side's interests. Their two presidents have met cordially, at least outwardly; they have jointly pledged to try to reduce America's influence in the world; and Russia now makes considerable modern weaponry avail-

able to China. These two powers are highly unlikely to become formal allies again, but they remain the two great entities that in the future could seriously menace America's security. Hence, developments in that Sino-Soviet future will continue to require close, high-priority intelligence attention, plus the courage, where applicable, to challenge any outmoded assumptions.[372]

In fact, the relationship between China and Russia improved after the end of the old Cold War. American scholar Joseph Nye explained:

With the collapse of the Soviet Union (1991), that de facto U.S.-China alliance ended [the "peaceful coexistence" accusation above], and a China-Russia rapprochement began. In 1992, the two countries declared that they were pursuing a "constructive partnership"; in 1996, they progressed toward a "strategic partnership"; and in 2001, they signed a treaty of "friendship and cooperation."[373]

The 2001 China and Russia strategic partnership on major international affairs is known as the Treaty of Good-Neighborly Friendship and Cooperation. However, that treaty does not name the United States as the adversary, the real reason that brought them together in the post-Cold War era.

The treaty bound China and Russia to jointly oppose the framework the US erected after the old Cold War. Specifically, the treaty's twenty-five articles formally oppose the United States' missile plans and places Russia firmly behind China's claim of sovereignty over Taiwan, which Beijing labels as a breakaway province. The agreement also strengthens military cooperation while rejecting NATO's intervention in the Balkans, an event that took place in 1999.[374]

There is also the Shanghai Cooperation Organization (SCO), which includes Russia and China as member states. That organization, which formed in 2001, acts as a security apparatus, or a type alliance to counter unspecified threats. The SCO's charter states that it exists "to strengthen mutual trust, friendship and good-neighborliness between the member States," which encourages mutual cooperative defense in areas such as terrorism and countering extremists, but SCO is not a mutual defense alliance.[375]

Since 2003, China and Russia have participated in at least twenty-five combined military exercises, and ten of those exercises were under the auspices of the SCO focusing on antiterrorism. These exercises helped the PLA gain valuable experience and information about their partners to improve military interoperability.[376]

Russia and China are also members of the BRICS (Brazil, Russia, India, China, and South Africa) organization. BRICS focuses on coordination in multilateral fora, with a focus on economic and political governance, such as the Financial G-20, International Monetary Fund, and World Bank. This association serves as a benchmark of evolving relations between Russia and China, which acts as both an economic and political grouping, but it is not a treaty-based alliance.

China is now Russia's second-largest trading partner, hitting $84 billion in 2017. The volume of China-Russia trade is expected to reach $200 billion by 2020.[377] Their trade partnership has proven mutually beneficial, especially regarding energy supplies.

In 2014, Moscow and Beijing struck a $400 billion supply deal for up to 38 billion cubic meters of Siberian natural gas to China over the next three decades. This deal links producer and consumer—especially given the $70 billion pipeline infrastructure project—and took the sting out of Western threats to cut Russian gas imports in the wake of Moscow's Crimea annexation.

Russia is also developing its Arctic energy resources to bolster trade with China. Beijing contributed $12 billion to help Moscow build the Yamal gas project, and China will become Russia's biggest liquefied natural gas customer. Arctic shipments will help China meet its huge energy demand by the time the Yamal project reaches its full capacity in 2020.[378]

China and Russia also have other significant bilateral agreements

signed by Putin and Xi. In March 2013, for example, President Xi
told President Putin that Beijing and Moscow should "resolutely support each other in efforts to protect national sovereignty, security and
development interests." Further, the Chinese president promised at that
meeting to "closely coordinate in international regional affairs."[379]

President Putin said at the same meeting that "the strategic partnership between us is of great importance on both a bilateral and global
scale."[380] That seems to suggest a growing recognition the nations must
cooperate more. They are certainly cooperating in regards to the sale of
sophisticated weapons.

Russia sold China Su-35 fighter jets, which began to arrive in
December 2016. Those sophisticated fighters will help the PLA contest
US air superiority and "provide China with technology that could help
accelerate the development of its own advanced fighters, and serve as
a valuable training and learning platform before China fields its next-
generation aircraft," according to the 2017 U.S.-China Economic and
Security Review Commission report.[381]

Also, Russia sold the S-400 surface-to-air missile defense system
to China, which is expected to begin arriving in 2018. This will "help
China improve capital air defense and could assist the PLA in achieving
increased air superiority over Taiwan if deployed to the Eastern Theater
Command."[382]

The US shares some responsibility for pushing China and Russia
closer together. Specifically, American and European Union sanctions
on Russia for its actions in Crimea and eastern Ukraine, among other
actions, cemented a growing autocratic China-Russia coalition. That
view is shared by former syndicated columnist Charles Krauthammer,
who wrote: "China and Russia together represent the core of a new coalition of anti-democratic autocracies challenging the Western-imposed,
post-Cold War status quo. Their enhanced partnership marks the first
emergence of a global coalition against American hegemony since the
fall of the Berlin Wall."[383]

The "emergence of a global [China-Russia] coalition" warrants close attention, because if they form a real security alliance, that coming together could pose a threat to America's current global role and make the new dual Cold War much more challenging. After all, China is already in a unique position as a near-peer competitor with the US in terms of both economic and military power. Even though Russia is still very powerful militarily, it is economically in decline at the moment. So, Moscow would benefit economically while Beijing would benefit militarily from a formal alliance.

How likely is a China-Russia alliance? China, as a nation-state, has limited historical success with alliances. However, that will likely change with its new great-power status, because it needs military depth, something Russia can provide, to oppose the US much as America has bought depth with its NATO alliance.

There are counters that Beijing no doubt will weigh in on any decision to form an alliance with Russia, however.

Specifically, China and Russia have a long history of mutual mistrust, a shaky foundation for any true alliance. Further, unlike in their history together, their roles today are reversed. China no longer needs Russian technology, and Moscow is suspicious of Chinese investment in Siberia's energy resources, which makes them geostrategic competitors.

There is lingering mistrust due to mutual xenophobic views as well. Many Russians hold animosity for the Chinese due to a contentious history and China's growing influence on the Russian economy. Some Chinese hold negative perceptions of Russians as well, which also stems from long-held historical grievances involving Russian harassment of Chinese citizens while in Russia.[384]

Yet there are compelling reasons that China might align with Russia. They share common interests, such as similar regime types (authoritarian); both are great powers with large militaries; they are both often at odds with the US on similar issues; and they share a long common border. They also both face challenges to the legitimacy of their rule, thanks to domestic ethnic and religious minorities. Further, they are very suspicious of Western influence in their political systems, because they know the US and much of the West will never stop promoting freedom and democracy to their populations, which are concepts ultimately hostile to both Xi and Putin.

China and Russia additionally face a "dual containment" policy by the US and its allies, which the Trump administration implicitly identifies in both the 2017 NSS and the 2018 NDS. Further, as evidence of the growing tension with the US, China and Russia want to reshape a global political and economic system, which earned them the "revisionist" label introduced in President Trump's NSS.

Yu Bin, a professor at Wittenberg University, explained the reaction to Trump's "revisionist" label. "China and Russia's discomfort with the existing world order has more to do with their respective interactions with the West [read: "the US"] than their separate 'national identities,' Yu said. "It is an issue of [common] interests rather than identity." Once again, the United States' containment policy is the glue pulling China and Russia closer.[385]

Although officially the regimes deny that an alliance is in the works, there are credible voices to the contrary.

Leading Russian commentator Andranik Migranyan makes a compelling statement that there might be "a greater convergence in Russian and Chinese interests on the matter of containing Washington's arrogant and unilateral foreign policy that attempts to dominate the world."[386] Certainly, the significant increase in Chinese-Russian joint military exercises, as outlined in chapter 1, is another indicator of an emergent alliance.

Yan Xuetong is a leading international relations scholar at Tsinghua University in Beijing. He argues that China will formally align itself with Russia, stating that China and Russia have no option to join the West, primarily because the US will never accept either country as an ally— and besides, if America were to invite Russia to join NATO, that alliance would crumble.[387]

The Chinese scholar also believes US pressure on China and Russia will increase and thus push China and Russia closer together. Yan speaks of "strategic pressure" (*zhanlue yali*), a term used in Chinese strategic discourse. He reasons that, as America inevitably backs out of the wars in the Middle East (Syria, Iraq) and Central Asia (Afghanistan), it will relocate those forces to Europe and Asia, thus creating more pressure for China and Russia.[388]

There is also the matter of the immediate influence of China's and Russia's authoritarian leaders. After all, Russian President Putin won his fourth term, which now guarantees that he will remain in office at least until 2024, which will ensure continued tension in the US-Russian relationship. Much the same is true for President Xi, who is incredibly powerful, who has global goals for his nation, and who is likely to remain in office for the balance of his life, as confirmed by the Chinese Communist Party, which amended the constitution abolishing term limits. That move paves the way for Xi to lead the country into the indefinite future.

There are clear benefits for both nations to form an alliance. An alliance with Russia ensures the stability of China's northern and western border regions, which allows Beijing to focus on its south and east, the Western Pacific. Further, as we saw in the old Cold War, China and Russia vote in lockstep at the UN Security Council, something that will certainly happen in the new dual Cold War as tensions mount.

Of course, a mitigating factor in any alliance decision is that both Moscow and Beijing will consider the likelihood that one or the other will drag any future alliance partner into unwanted wars. After all, Moscow created problems with the Republic of Georgia in 2008 with an invasion and with the annexation of Ukraine's Crimea in 2104. Either action could and still might result in a broader conflict, which could force any alliance partner into the fight as well. Beijing creates similar tensions along the first island chain, where it constantly confronts US and neighboring nations like the Philippines, Japan, and Vietnam in the air space and on the seas around contested island groups in the East and South China Seas.

Russia benefits in a number of ways from an alliance with China. Moscow is more concerned about an American military threat than any from China, and besides, it needs China's economic help and China needs Russia's vast energy products. However, "So far, a limit has been set—neither Russia nor China want to create a full-fledged alliance aimed at the West, at the US," Sinologist Yakov Berger of the Far East Institute in Moscow posits.[389]

Yes, China and Russia appear close to forming a new alliance that will challenge the American-led international system via a new dual Cold War. They are focused on revising that system and pushing America to the sidelines. They are formidable alone, but if they are paired, they have a chance of success and global dominance, their shared goal.

New Dual Cold World Realignment

Expect the new dual Cold War to create a new world realignment much like the old Cold War arrangement. A review of that period is instructive for the likely forthcoming reordering.

Following World War II, European and North American nations aligned themselves against future aggression, either in anticipation of a resurgent Nazi threat or, as it turned out, the growing Soviet aggression.

The West's post-World War II alliance began forming in 1947, with Britain and France signing the Treaty of Dunkirk, the first significant post-war military alliance, which was soon joined by Belgium, Luxembourg, and the Netherlands. The Treaty of Brussel's preamble aimed to preserve a Western-style freedom: to "fortify and preserve the principles of democracy, personal freedom and political liberty, the constitutional traditions and the rule of law," the "common heritage" of the signatory nations.[390]

The new threat was soon evident to the Western alliance. Soviet forces initiated a blockade of Berlin, an act of aggression that led to the formation of the Western defense organization. By that time, the Europeans had demobilized their World War II forces, and as a result, judged themselves unprepared to deter the rising Soviet aggression. That collective observation led the Western European nations to appeal to Washington to form a trans-Atlantic military alliance, the beginning of what became the North Atlantic Treaty Organization (NATO) in April 1949.

The new NATO recruited members starting with all five of the Brussels Treaty nations, then Canada, Denmark, Iceland, Italy, Norway, and Portugal soon joined. Some nations decided to remain neutral: Finland, Ireland, Sweden, and Switzerland. Others entered the alliance during the subsequent decades. Of course, given the concern at the time about a possible Soviet invasion, the critical and attractive part of the treaty was Article 5, the provision that an "armed attack" against any of the signatory nations was to be "considered an attack against them all."[391]

In 1954, the Soviet Union officially asked to become a NATO member, a move Moscow never expected to be granted. Predictably that request was rejected by NATO members, who said "the unrealistic nature of the proposal does not warrant discussion." That brush-off prompted Moscow to form its own alliance. In May 1955, the Kremlin convened a conference in Warsaw, Poland, to draft and then sign the Treaty of Friendship, Cooperation and Mutual Assistance, known as the Warsaw Pact. The Pact's eight member-states were the USSR, Poland, East Germany, Albania (until 1968), Bulgaria, Czechoslovakia, Hungary, and Romania. Predictably, the USSR called the shots and controlled all appointments, much like the US played and continues to play a controlling role with the NATO.[392]

NATO and the Warsaw Pact were the primary Cold War alliances, but the balance of the European countries aligned with one or the other as outlined in chapter 3. Then again, as the bipolar world emerged, the rest of the world also geopolitically attached itself to either the West (the US) or the Soviet Union. Those alignments either in Europe or in the Third World were mostly self-serving relationships that benefited the elite rulers and often disadvantaged their populations because the people were often subjected to social experiments and proxy wars pitting the US against Soviet surrogates.

The reordering of the world in the coming era of the new dual Cold War will be similar. Specifically, a China-Russia alliance will attract a few smaller partners, but realignment is pretty predictable.

Already, China is recruiting new partners mostly by virtue of its economic outreach. Beijing will use its extensive overseas port infrastructure to influence host nations to either identify with it or remain acceptably neutral. China's recruits are a direct reflection of Beijing's Belt and Road Initiative.

Consider China's significant economic acquisitions starting in the far north.

China is rapidly expanding global markets, especially in the Arctic from Canada to Greenland to Russia. Mark Rosen, the co-author of a 2017 CNA report, *Unconstrained Foreign Direct Investment: An Emerging Challenge to Arctic Security*, advises observers to "follow the money" to ascertain China's northern ambitions. Specifically, China's investment in Greenland's economy is 12 percent of its gross domestic product, according to Rosen. Further, China has invested $90 billion in a host of projects above 60 degrees north and more are to follow.[393]

Mr. Hong Nong with the Institute for China-America Studies cites China's white paper on the Arctic that makes clear Beijing's quest for "a polar or ice silk road," similar in purpose to its Belt and Road Initiative that affects at least sixty-eight countries. Beijing is building airports in Greenland, working with the Russians to expand facilities on the Transpolar (Northern Sea) Route for natural gas exports to Asia and building infrastructure in Canada's Northwest Territories to expand fur and diamond exports to the Chinese market.[394]

There are sovereignty and military issues related to China's Arctic reach as well. Mark Nevitt, a law professor at the University of Pennsylvania, explained there is limited enforcement authority in the Arctic compared to the Antarctic, where activities are overseen by a forty-three-nation treaty. But there is no similar agreement regarding the Arctic, which in part raises concerns, given Russia's buildup of military infrastructure throughout the region and its work on icebreaking corvettes (ice class patrol ships). In fact, China is reportedly hardening submarines and some surface ships for northern operations at the same time as it is building an icebreaker.[395]

The US recognizes the coming global realignment, and the Arctic region is just the tip of China's global economic "iceberg." In fact, former US Secretary of State Rex Tillerson said China is trying to make inroads even in Latin America. "Today China is getting a foothold in Latin America. It is using economic statecraft to pull the region into its orbit. The question is: at what price?"[396]

Secretary Tillerson explained that China's Latin America approach is focused on gaining access to commodities from countries such as Brazil, Venezuela, Argentina, and Peru. But the secretary made it clear: "Latin America does not need new imperial powers that seek only to benefit their own people."

"China's state-led model of development is reminiscent of the past," Tillerson said. "It doesn't have to be this hemisphere's future."[397] The suspicion is that China wants much more than access to markets and raw materials.

There will be plenty of proxies for both sides, which are already identified by ongoing conflicts. Clearly, North Korea will remain aligned with China and Russia, while South Korea and Japan will remain firmly in the American camp. Once the dual Cold War is widely recognized, other countries will flock to one side or the other.

Europe is mostly aligned already, which is unlikely to change, except perhaps if President Putin decides to use force with another country— say Hungary or Poland—much as he did in annexing Crimea. However, Putin is making inroads with Eastern Ukraine, which could break from Kiev, and Turkey's long-term alignment with the West is also somewhat questionable, given its economic deals with Russia and the purchase of the S-400 air defense system, which is a matter of considerable concern among NATO member nations.

Meanwhile, Russia already counts some nations within its camp because it maintains military facilities in those countries—Belarus and Moldova—and it occupies Crimea, out of which it operates its Black Sea fleet.

The Middle East is likely to be divided between the two sides as well. Iran and Syria (what's left of it) will align with the China-Russia alliance (because Putin put his full weight behind Syria's Bashir al-Assad). Russia has military facilities in Syria, and over the past years, it used air fields in Iran to launch operations into Syria. Specifically, the Russians maintain a naval facility in Tartus and the Khmeimim air base at Latakia, Syria. It is also possible that Iraq, with its extensive Shia-influenced government, could align with Iran and thus by association with China-Russia. The balance of the region should remain mostly pro-West, however.

Central Asia is up for grabs as well. Russia has military facilities in Armenia, Georgia, Kazakhstan, Kyrgyzstan, and Tajikistan. Further, on May 1, 2018, Islamabad expressed interest in forging a strategic partnership with Moscow, a sign that Pakistan's relationship with the US is deteriorating primarily due to that country's support for militant proxies battling NATO-backed forces in Afghanistan.[398]

Meanwhile, China is developing more infrastructure projects across Asia, especially in strategic ports and transit corridors. These projects generally begin as joint efforts but often end up in Chinese hands.

"The Chinese are using their abundance of labor, capital and workforce to project their influence," said Mira Rapp-Hooper, a scholar at Yale Law School. She added that these projects are "mostly taking place in countries where the US does not have a lot of influence or give a lot of aid," but they are also in countries where China is seizing the geopolitical initiative from the US, such as in Pakistan.[399]

China has a growing relationship with Pakistan, which ramped up its association with Beijing because its relationship with the US began decaying due to Islamabad's unwillingness to fully cooperate by controlling insurgents' use of its territory for mounting operations inside neighboring Afghanistan. Meanwhile, China is also working with the Kabul government by providing significant aid and constructing a military base at the border with China's tense Xinjiang region. Chinese and Afghan troops even perform joint patrols in Afghanistan's remote and mountainous Wakhan Corridor.

President Xi seeks to extend Beijing's influence by pouring billions of dollars in infrastructure projects into South Asia, which includes Afghanistan. In fact, in January 2018, Beijing revealed that it would build an offshore naval base near a strategic Pakistani port.

The new Chinese naval base will be in Gwadar Port, in the Pakistani province of Baluchistan. A new facility is necessary, according to Chinese officials, because current docking is unable to supply the services and logistical support for Chinese warships.[400]

"Chinese investment in Pakistan [alone] is expected to reach over $46 billion by 2030 with the creation of a [China-Pakistan economic corridor] connecting Baluchistan's Gwadar Port on the Arabian Sea with Kashgar, in western China," said Harrison Akins, a researcher at the Howard Baker Center who focuses on Pakistan and China.[401]

China is also reportedly building a military base in Pakistan's Jiwani Peninsula, which is near Gwadar and close to the border with Iran. The construction of a base there would require local residents to be displaced to make room for a security zone, but critical for China to use as a facility for loading Iranian oil arriving by pipeline.

China is also funding a Sri Lankan port project through a secured loan "with a hefty coupon [a ninety-nine-year lease]," according to Navy Secretary Richard Spencer in March 2018 testimony before the House Appropriations Committee. Spencer called such overseas investments "weaponizing capital." "They're doing that [investing] around the globe. Their open checkbook keeps me up at night," Spencer explained.[402]

Marine Corps Commandant General Robert Neller agrees with Spencer. He says the Chinese are playing a long game that features a global reach. "Everywhere I go, they're there," Neller testified. "Their concern for human rights is not there, and they've got big bags of cash."[403]

China, as identified earlier in this volume, opened its first offshore military naval base last year in Djibouti, a small French- and Arabic-speaking country on the horn of Africa. The base is described by the Chinese as a logistic facility and another of China's "string of pearls" military alliances and assets ringing India, including Bangladesh, Myanmar, and Sri Lanka.

President Xi visited the Djibouti base to instruct those forces to improve their combat capability and readiness for war, according to a Chinese ministry official. Xi said progress in joint operations was needed because the troops must train under combat conditions.[404] The ministry statement did not specify the threat, however.

It is possible that the threat President Xi references comes from the United States. In early May 2018, the *South China Morning Post* reported that US pilots warned of possible attacks by Chinese military personnel armed with lasers and others aboard spy drones. The US military, which operates facilities in Djibouti, issued a Notice to Airmen of multiple events "involving a high-power laser" just 2,400 feet from China's base in the Djibouti port. Further, multiple intelligence sources report that the Chinese garrison in Djibouti is suspected of operating a high-power laser weapon to temporarily blind pilots at the base or on a ship offshore, according to a report in *Jane's Defence Weekly.*[405] The top US military commander of troops in Africa is suspicious about China's growing presence on the continent and especially at Djibouti. Marine General Thomas Waldhauser testified before a congressional committee that China could theoretically cut off supplies to a US base in Djibouti if they "took" the port there.[406]

"If the Chinese took over the port, then the consequences could be significant," Waldhauser testified. "There are some indications of [China] looking for additional facilities, specifically on the eastern coast [of Africa].... So Djibouti happens to be the first—there will be more," the general said.[407]

China and America are competing to reshape the economies and political systems across much of Asia in their own image. The US still dominates militarily in Asia, while China is growing its military power and using its economic leverage to reshape the region. China is being successful, in that every Asian country now trades more with China than with the US by a factor of two to one. And even though many Asian economies rely on Beijing, their security relies on the United States, as demonstrated by arms sales, which bind those militaries to the American military.[408]

Many Asian nations thus find themselves caught between Beijing and Washington. "These countries don't want to have to choose sides," said Tanvi Madan, an Asia specialist at the Brookings Institution. Therefore, they try to thread the geopolitical needle by pursuing strategies that draw maximum benefit from both the US and China, while maintaining their independence, a very different outcome, at least for now than what happened in the old Cold War, which was divided cleanly by the two sides.[409]

Southeast Asia is of particular interest for the Chinese. Beijing continues to build islets in the South China Sea and then stations military forces with advanced weapons there to protect what they claim as their sovereign sea area. Beijing has similar hegemonic ambitions for the East China Sea as well, which includes Taiwan and a number of islands claimed by Japan.

The so-called break-away province of China, Taiwan, although aligned with the US, is a target for takeover by President Xi. Beijing's military now has significant anti-access weapons designed specifically to counter American aircraft carriers. In the minds of many Chinese analysts, it is just a matter of a few years before Beijing launches an attack to retake Taiwan.

On March 19, 2018, President Xi reaffirmed China's intention to stop any attempt to formalize Taiwan's independence from Beijing. "All acts and schemes to split China are doomed to failure and will be condemned by the people and punished by history," Xi told China's National People's Congress in Beijing. "The Chinese people have the firm will, full confidence and sufficient ability [read military might] to defeat all activities to split the country," Xi affirmed to the Parliament.[410]

"This is an official warning from China's top leader to the U.S. and Taiwan," said Wang Jiangyu, a law professor at the National University of Singapore. "It's an announcement that China will never compromise on Taiwan-related issues."

That is a view shared by the Chinese military. A scholar at the Institute for Security Policy at Germany's Kiel University said a senior Chinese naval official wrote, "We should do what Putin did in Crimea to Taiwan." In 2014, Putin annexed Crimea, and by inference, Beijing should do the same with Taiwan, which would then grant China direct access to the Western Pacific and extend its influence in the East and South China Seas. However, so far, Beijing has followed a hybrid path of military operations by constructing bases on coral reefs, increasing its naval operations, using drones, and harassing other nations using the contested water.[411]

Beijing's hostility towards Taiwan rose since the 2016 election of President Tsai Ing-wen, a member of the country's pro-independence Democratic Progressive Party.[412] Then in support of democratic Taiwan, the US signaled a tougher line against Beijing when, on March 16, 2018, President Trump signed the Taiwan Travel Act into law. That act encourages visits between American and Taiwanese officials "at all levels"—an act, according to Chinese officials, that "seriously contravenes" the understanding between China and the US over Taiwan.[413]

"The recent 'Taiwan Travel Act' is a mine that America buried and one day it will blow up," said Xu Shijun, a former director of the Institute of Taiwan Studies at the Chinese Academy of Social Sciences.[414]

It is noteworthy that a 2018 survey of Taiwanese found that most citizens will resist Beijing's efforts to retake the island nation. The *Asia Times* reports that mainland Chinese leaders' favorite platitude about Taiwan is that "blood is thicker than water," an expression used by communist newspapers to report that Taiwan's politics were hijacked by a small cabal of hardliners and the truth is that most Taiwanese favor unification with the mainland. That's not true, according to nearly 70 percent of respondents to a survey conducted by the Taiwan Foundation for

Democracy, which found that most Taiwanese said they would resist any effort should the mainland attempt to annex Taiwan by force.[415]

The Russians have an interest in Asia as well.

In 1979, the then-Soviet Union signed a twenty-five-year lease for the use of Cam Ranh Base for the Soviets' Pacific fleet. It became for the Soviets the largest naval base for forward deployment outside the Warsaw Pact during the old Cold War.[416]

In 2014, Russia signed a new agreement with Vietnam to use the port at Cam Ranh. It is noteworthy that Moscow enjoys frequent use of that facility today, while other foreign navies are limited to only one annual ship visit to Vietnamese ports.

Russia is a token player in Asia, but China is becoming dominant. A troubling view expressed by a former top Australian official indicates that Beijing has already filled the US leadership role in the region. Hugh White, a professor at the Australian National University in Canberra, believes America's era of primacy has ended and China is taking its place.[417]

White indicates that America's Asia allies don't want to choose between the US and China, but "nobody in the region wants to make an enemy of Beijing. All the more so because officials increasingly doubt the U.S. will be there in the end."[418]

The professor doesn't subscribe to the view that a war between the US and China is imminent, however. "Clearly China and America face an economic equivalent of mutually assured destruction. For each side the economic consequences of a rupture are so immense as to be almost unthinkable.... Beijing believes that America will blink first to avert a crisis because its interest in Asia is, in the long run, less important than China's. And I think they are probably right."[419]

Yes, the world will realign to fit the new reality: a new dual Cold War. Some countries will naturally gravitate to one side or the other because of ongoing and historic relationships. However, much depends on their national interests, such as economic incentives offered by either side.

Conclusion

This chapter established that China and Russia are now great powers and will likely form something like an alliance in the near future, but there is reason to question just how long such an alliance might last. After all, Russia and China share a similar ambition: world dominance. Further, the world's countries recognize the bipolarity of the emerging geopolitical world and are aligning themselves accordingly.

The next chapter establishes that, much like what happened during the old Cold War, the adversaries will fight on many fronts. Those coming fights are profiled in four contemporary battlegrounds.

CHAPTER FIVE

New Dual Cold War's Four Battlegrounds

Retired US Army Lieutenant General William G. "Jerry" Boykin, a former deputy undersecretary of defense for intelligence under President George W. Bush, said, "The Cold War never ended. We went into a different era. Yes, there is a Cold War with China and Russia today but it is not the same. It deals with cyber, economic issues and information. I think it is no less dangerous than the old Cold War. This war is being fought on different plains and in different ways."[420]

Dr. Chodakiewicz, with the Institute of World Politics, acknowledges that China and Russia "are about world domination but they express themselves in economic and cultural rivalry without our rivals resorting to claims of ideological supremacy.… Instead, both the Russians and the Chinese juxtapose their 'sovereign democracies," or more precisely, post-Communist autocracies, to America's pathologies of cultural nihilism."[421] That in itself seems to be an ideological fight—post-Communist autocracies versus Western cultural nihilism.

"Crystal ball grazing is a pernicious sport," warns Chodakiewicz, but he does expect proxy irregular wars in the future. He anticipates that China and Russia will "test our resolve; and they will continuously threaten our alliance system by bullying or bribing its members. There will be active measures and all sort of monkey business in the intelligence world. Above all, we will have no minute of peace in cyberspace; there cyberwar will be peace by other means."

Indeed, the old Cold War was fought on three primary plains, or battlefields: ideology, technology, and the Third World, as outlined in the previous chapter. The new Cold War ratchets up the intensity of the fight in terms of volume, sophistication, and domain. It will be fought on at least four very intense battlegrounds.

First, the new dual Cold War will take place on the ideological battleground, but not pitting the old Cold War's communism ideology against the West's democratic values. No, the US may still advocate the same Western values promoted during the old Cold War, but the new Russia is very different today, far more ideologically complex than before, and China is not just a communist front anymore, either.

Second, the world changed for both the better and worse with the introduction of the Internet (cyber domain)—a new global battleground. In many ways, the new dual Cold War cyber battleground is already very hot and littered with many figurative corpses. In fact, the cyber domain could potentially become the most dangerous of the four battlegrounds in the dual Cold War.

Third, great power economic competition is a new battleground because it's about the global competition for jobs, talent, access to natural resources, and intellectual property. Every American's livelihood is at stake, and on this battleground, the world's top economic powerhouses—the US and China—must somehow cooperate without destroying one another.

Finally, the new dual Cold War will experience an arms and technology race of grave proportions, the fourth battleground. It will be incredibly expensive, and given the mind-blowing technologies right at our doorstep, the lethality and finality of new high-technology weapons are truly frightening. Missteps by either antagonist on this world stage places all our lives at risk.

New Cold War's Ideological Battleground

First, ideology will once again be a battleground between the great powers, but this time the evil of communism as we knew it won't necessarily be as virulent.

Ideology, as defined in chapter 3, is "a set of fundamental concepts systematically expressed by a large group of individuals." In an earlier chapter, I cited Professor Westad's illustration of ideology to explain what motivated President Kennedy and First Secretary Khrushchev at their 1961 meeting in Vienna, Austria. I explained that the basic ideological perception of each leader was critical to understanding the outcome of that meeting and the impact that had for the old Cold War, especially the Cuban Missile Crisis.

I believe the same approach is appropriate regarding the new dual Cold War. Therefore, we need to study the leadership's ideology motivating Russia's Putin and China's Xi to appreciate the ideological fight ahead.

These leaders evidence a different ideology than encountered during the old Cold War—and, for that matter, the West—and the US in particular has changed its ideological drivers to a certain extent as well.

Let me briefly profile America's prevailing ideology and then consider the ideologies evidenced by the Putin and Xi regimes.

America has four primary ideologies evident within its culture. Each plays a role in our government and society in general and is evident in our foreign policy—that is, how we respond to other countries and in particular how we might react to Russia and China in the new dual Cold War.[422]

America's four primary ideologies are socialism, liberalism, conservatism, and libertarianism. A mixture of two—liberalism and conservatism—is particularly influential regarding the role of government, the economic principles America applies across the world marketplaces, and our collective responses to social issues and civil liberties at home and abroad.

Classically, liberals believe in the role of government as a "safety net" that helps meet needs through social welfare programs. They do not believe in government control of society, except they do tend to endorse regulating both capital and businesses. However, in the foreign policy realm, idealist traditions are basically political liberalism, which argues that states should intervene in other sovereign states in order to pursue liberal objectives, such as via military interventions and humanitarian aid. Their goal is to achieve global structures that are inclined towards promoting a liberal world order.

Classical conservatives believe in smaller government, reduced social welfare, and little government interference in business. They tend to be realists who promote beliefs that nation-states are primarily motivated by the desire for military and economic power or security and interests, not by ideals and ethics. We will explore "realism" in more detail in the next chapter.

A mixture of these ideologies is overseen by different politicians representing one or the other who influence America's foreign policy by advocating our foundational values. Traditionally, America has advanced values like freedom of speech and faith, human dignity, justice, equality, opportunity, and treatment of others. These values are fundamental; they're found in our Bill of Rights and are evident in our foreign policy through the centuries.

These American values tend to guide our support overseas for democratic movements and human rights organizations and motivate us to rush aid to those who suffer due to their race, faith, speech, and natural disaster. They also prohibit American companies from using unscrupulous behaviors, such as the bribery of foreign officials to secure business deals, and they demand transparency in reporting overseas operations. Those same values play an important role, protecting our intellectual property against countries like China and seeking to eliminate corruption at home and abroad.

President Trump's 2017 National Security Strategy (NSS) evidences those values and the ideological challenges posed by China's rise and

Russian interventionism. The president vows in the NSS to enhance American influence and restore a balance of power in the global marketplace, thanks in part to the influence of our value system.

Trump outlines in the NSS the ideological challenge posed by the new dual Cold War adversaries. "China and Russia challenge American power, influence, and interests," argues the NSS. "They [China and Russia] are determined to make economies less free and less fair, to grow their militaries, and to control information and data to repress their societies and expand their influence." Beijing maintains a "repressive vision," it corrupts elites in Africa and seeks to pull countries in Europe and Latin America "into its orbit." Both nations are "revisionist powers" seeking to "shape a world antithetical to U.S. values and interests."[423]

Just what are the ideologies represented by Putin and Xi? Below I profile their distinctive ideologies and then address them within the context of the new dual Cold War.

There are at least two views regarding President Putin's ideology. One is expressed by Jochen Bittner, a political editor for the German weekly newspaper *Die Zeit*. Bittner says that Russia's new ideology under President Putin is "orderism."[424]

Bittner explains that the basic political premise of "orderism" is that liberal democracy and international law have not lived up to their promise, which resulted in inequality and chaos in the post-Cold War Russia. Further, "orderism" claims the status quo leads to open borders—a progressive ideal—and global trade has robbed Russians of jobs and invited mass migration, as well as the loss of traditional values and leniency that allows free sale of marijuana, permits same-sex marriage, and tolerates militant Islamism within western borders. This epidemic of moral weakness, "orderism" cautions, is the very thing that led to the fall of past empires.

Putin's "orderism" "prioritizes stability over democracy and offers an alternative to the moral abyss of laissez-faire societies." Bittner claims that Russia presents a new social contract built on patriotism, traditional gender roles, orthodox Christianity, military strength, and a benevolent leader who will faithfully deliver to the people.[425]

"Orderism," according to Bittner, will deliver cohesion and common spirit, making certain the "orderly nation" outlives the inevitable downturn of the "disorderly west." That is why "orderism" as an ideology is appealing but, as Bittner warns, it "hides something much darker."

Bittner explains that "orderism" is attractive until it "stifles, represses." "Unchecked autocrats turn on the weakest and most vulnerable as scapegoats, and lash out in foreign misadventures to divert attention from problems at home," writes Bittner.[426]

Putin's use of "orderism" is not that different from what voters in America sought by electing Donald Trump. He promised to get tough on corrupt overseas businesses robbing American jobs, reduce the size of government, reduce the flow of illegal immigrants into America, defeat the Islamic State jihadi, and much more. "Part of the difficulty in dealing with 'orderism,'" explained Bittner, "is that it is ideological without being an ideology. It is mercurial, pragmatic and cynical; its meaning and values change to fit the circumstances."

Some will argue that what Putin is doing is no different than what Marie Le Pen of France did and what Donald Trump did in America. They appealed to populist sentiment for traditional values, security, and a brighter future without massive government. That approach works in Russia, evidently worked in the US, and is slowly tearing at the fabric of the European Union. It is a hard ideology to fight for in the West, which faces a similar challenge.

T. S. Tsonchev provides an intriguing alternative perspective of Putin's ideology in his article, "The Kremlin's New Ideology," in the *Montreal Review*, which he publishes. Tsonchev begins with a revealing quote from Russia's first democratically elected president, Boris Yeltsin: "In Russian history during the 20th century, there have been various periods—monarchism, totalitarianism, perestroika, and finally, a democratic path of development. Each stage," Yeltsin noted, "had its own ideology.... But now [the stage of the democratic path of development] we have none."[427]

Tsonchev explains that after the fall of communism, Russia quickly embraced the Western parliamentary system and its own "democratic path of development," but Russia still lacked a true ideology. Evidently, according to Tsonchev, Western ideology didn't work for Russia. It only fed the sense of defeat and humiliation while the country disintegrated.[428]

Then along came Russia's "savior" (my words), Vladimir Putin, who helped Russia rediscover the exceptionality of the Russian political model. Today, the head of the Russian Orthodox Church credits Putin's reformation of the Russian model for bringing back prosperity and stability as "a miracle of God."[429]

Putin didn't resurrect the discredited communist ideology, nor did he put in place Western democracy and liberalism or the ideology of the Russian monarchy. Rather, the former Cold War Komitet Gosudarstvennoy Bezopasnosti (KGB) operative who became president embraced orthodox Russian Christianity as the most convenient and useful source for national, political emancipation for Russians. After all, for centuries the Russian Orthodox Church had been exceptional. According to famed Russian author Alexander Solzhenitsyn, who wrote while a prisoner of the gulag, "Men have forgotten God. That is why all this [the Bolshevik Revolution and, for the same reason, the post-communist destruction] happened."[430]

Putin's solution for post-Cold War Russia was to advance patriotism rooted in Christianity as Russia's ideological solution, which helped him legitimize his authority and rebuild the country. He is a smart politician, who rediscovered the power of the Russian "pravoslavie," orthodoxy, or literally, "true belief."

Evidently, Putin got the idea of harnessing the church for political purposes from Ivan Ilyin, author of *Our Tasks*. Ilyin, a Russian religious philosopher, preached during his nineteenth-century life a "renewal" and "rebirth" of the fatherland. The current leader of the Communist Party, Genadyi Zyuganov, according to Tsonchev, admits that Ilyin "made a very significant contribution to the development of the Russian state ideology of patriotism."[431]

Nikita Mihalkov, the most famous Russian filmmaker today,

described Ilyin as the only philosopher who truly lived for Russia. Mihalkov, who is an ardent supporter of President Putin, likes to quote Ilyin's advice that a person "should live for the things for which he could also die."[432]

Putin put Ilyin's philosophy into practice. "The Russian Orthodox Church," Putin said in a speech, "works tirelessly to bring unity, to strengthen family ties, and to educate the younger generation in the spirit of patriotism." In another speech, Putin argued that the West rejected the "Christian values that constitute the basis of Western civilization," implying that Russia, in contrast, began to cultivate and defend them. That is evident in the very significant rise among those self-identifying as orthodox Christians (from 31 to 72 percent) and those who say they believe in God (from 38 to 56 percent).[433]

Tsonchev writes that Putin managed to fuse religion and politics to formulate Russia's new ideology, sort of a Christian empire under the iron-fist control of the Kremlin.

What's not in doubt is Putin's popularity. He won the March 18, 2018, popular election for the presidency with an overwhelming 77 percent of the vote. Clearly, Bittner and Tsonchev are onto something between their views on "orderism" and the amalgam of orthodox Christian values and politics, and it has real grassroots support.

Even teachers at a music school in Astrahan, Russia, anecdotally evidence the personality cult growing up around Putin. Those teachers sang a song glorifying Putin at a birthday celebration for one of the teachers. The 2014 song, written by local poet Tatiana Klenkova, includes lyrics such as: "Putin—he never gives up," "we are invincible," and "we stand with our president and with all of Russia." The song went viral on Russian social media, evidencing the groundswell of support for Putin.[434]

Russia's new ideology under Putin's leadership will be tough to fight in the new dual Cold War because it will enjoy popular support—that is, until, as Bittner properly warns, "unchecked autocrats [like Putin] turn on the weakest and most vulnerable as scapegoats, and lash out in foreign misadventures to divert attention from problems at home."[435]

Time will tell whether Putin's misadventures in eastern Ukraine, Syria, and perhaps elsewhere become a diversion to increased problems at the Kremlin.

China's Xi Jinping is a bird of a different color than Putin, and especially Xi's new ideology for the Chinese people. However, both men are very authoritarian at the root of their leadership style.

The October 2017 19th Chinese Communist Party Congress was a window into China's future and Xi's leadership and the ideology he promotes. A major outcome of that session was not just the reappointment of Xi for another term, but the tacit endorsement for Xi to continue to rule as long as he desires. Then, on March 11, 2018, President Xi received the official and overwhelming endorsement to become president for life.

On that day, the National People's Congress (NPC) voted 2,964 to 5 to change the country's constitution, removing the restriction that had limited the presidency to two consecutive five-year terms.[436] The 64-year-old President Xi was already considered the most powerful Chinese leader since Mao Zedong, and the NPC's endorsement was welcomed by Xi, who called the decision a reflection of the "common will of the party and the people."[437]

China watchers said the NPC's decision to embrace Xi reflects the president's character. "He's a bit of [a] bulldozer—and there's no other senior politician who could or want to stand up to him," said Duncan Innes-Ker with the Asian office of the Economist Intelligence Unit. Innes-Ker continued, "The trouble with being the clear leader of everything is that everyone knows where the buck stops if something goes wrong."[438]

Not only did Xi garner the NCP's endorsement to be president for life, but it also revised China's constitution to include "Xi Jinping Thought," which elevated him to the level of previous, much-revered leaders Mao Zedong and Deng Xiaoping.

"Xi Jinping Thought" is little more than another version of Marxism in the Chinese context, backed by a personality cult surrounding

President Xi. That was evident because regime sycophants since the 2017 congress have frequently echoed the phrase "Xi Jinping thought on socialism with Chinese characteristics for a new era."[439]

President Xi's enthusiasm for Marxism was in full bloom just prior to Karl Marx's two hundredth birthday (May 5, 2018). *Deutsche Welle* reported President Xi praised Marx as the "greatest thinker of modern times" and called Marx's theories on communism a tool for China to "win the future." Marx's name is "still respected all over the world," Xi said, adding that "his theory shines with brilliant light of truth." Those statements were made at the Great Hall of the People in central Beijing, marking the bicentennial of the German philosopher's birth. Marx is the "teacher of revolution for the proletariat and working people all over the world," Xi explained. He called on all party members to read Marxist works and adopt his theories as a "way of life" and a "spiritual pursuit."[440]

The fourteen principles associated with the "Xi Jinping Thought" emphasize the communist state's ideals and evidently a lot of Marxism. Those principles include a call for "complete and deep reform," "new developing ideas," the promise of "harmonious living between man and nature," "absolute authority of the party over the People's Army," and emphasis on the importance of "one country two systems and reunification with the motherland."[441]

Xi aims to rebuild the regime's legitimacy in the wake of increasing vulnerability to economic slowdown and public anger over corruption, income gaps, and terrible pollution, among the many ailments facing the authorities in Beijing.

Xi's refreshed ideology is an interesting mixture of communism, nationalism, and Leninism with the goal of rejuvenation. This means that the former communist utopian ideology is dead. It lost its legitimacy. Nationalism is now part of Xi's ideological campaign to try to recapture the Chinese people's loyalty to the Communist Party state, making criticism of the party unpatriotic. After all, the Chinese people have consistently rallied behind the state when it defended China's national interests and rejected democratic reform on the grounds that liberal democracy would welcome turmoil and political instability.

There will also be an ideological tightening on China's youth, focusing on the party's increasing efforts within universities and in the Communist Youth League. Education will be dedicated to the "Xi Jinping Thought," much as were the youth in Mao's era to his *Little Red Book* of teachings—a clear ideological campaign.

Quotations from Chairman Mao Tse-tung is a book of statements from speeches and writings of Mao Zedong. It was best known in the West as the *Little Red Book* and was published from 1964 to about 1976. This author was in Hong Kong in 1974, where he was given an English copy of Mao's *Little Red Book*.[442]

Mao-like savagery and ideology will continue under President Xi, especially regarding the battle against people of faith, who evidently threaten the communist Chinese. "Any political party that is willing to kill 400 million of its own unborn citizens—as China has in the one-child policy—will stop at nothing to achieve its goals," said Dr. Steven Mosher, a China expert and practicing pro-life Catholic. "Crosses are currently being ripped off the top of churches, and home church leaders are being arrested and tortured. Catholics have been warned not to bring their own children to Mass, and Christians have been forbidden to teach their children about the faith, or to home school them at all. That would interfere with the Party's plan to turn them all into good little atheists," Mosher said.[443]

The Chinese Communist Party is dead set on clamping down on all expressions of religious faith. Specifically, on March 22, 2018, China placed all "religious affairs" under the control of the Communist Party's United Front Department, an organization created by Chairman Mao Zedong to control non-communist organizations during the Chinese civil war but was later re-tasked by the Party's leadership to coerce various groups.[444]

The United Front Department will aim to consolidate the Party's direction on religion and ensure that religious activities are consistent with socialism. After all, President Xi said in his October 2017 speech to the National People's Congress that "United Front work is an important magic weapon for the victory of the Party's cause." That means, according to Professor Yang Shu of Lanzhou University, "enhance[d] efficiency and centralized power…and management of religious affairs."[445]

"Management of religious affairs" evidently means that churches, according to Yang, will be tightly managed by the state. Already, the February 1, 2018, new "Regulations for Religious Affairs" forbid students and Party members from participating in religious activities. Meanwhile, no wonder Chinese churches continue to be defaced, crosses and statues removed, clergymen required to register with the government, and the sale of Bibles banned except for a "Sinicized," Party-approved version of God's Word. Further, sermons are expected to praise the Chinese leadership, especially President Xi Jinping, and the government is expected to try to annihilate the large Underground Church.[446]

China's ideological campaign also reaches into American campuses as well, according to the Central Intelligence Agency (CIA). Specifically, the Chinese Communist Party funds American universities and policy institutes to push a pro-China viewpoint and coerce Western academic publications to self-censor. Senator Marco Rubio (R–FL), cochair of the Congressional-Executive Commission on China, called on Florida educational institutions to terminate support for Confucius Institutes amid reports that the Chinese government uses those programs to limit discussion on topics that government finds sensitive, such as the 1989 Tiananmen Square Massacre.[447]

The Chinese also provide America ideological advice as if that country is a global moral arbiter. Specifically, the Chinese communist dictatorship called on the US to ban guns in an editorial in a state-run media outlet.

That editorial, "China can offer lessons to U.S. in protecting human rights," ran in the *Global Times*, a mouthpiece for the communist government, on February 22, 2018 after the high school shooting in Parkland, Florida. The editorial applauded American protests that called on government to disarm the citizens. This call comes from a regime that brutally slaughtered hundreds of unarmed protesters during the 1989 Tiananmen Square protests.[448]

The article goes on to argue the US was "founded on the use of firearms," but then the article states that America is now "different from that of more than 200 years ago." "There is an urgent need for the U.S. to impose harsh restrictions on gun purchases nowadays," the editorial continued. "The U.S. has witnessed mad proliferation of guns and rampant gun violence."[449]

China's hypocrisy knows no end. The editorial declares "The right of life is the most fundamental human rights," and that from a country that embraces forced abortions and a well-documented history of flagrant human rights violations, such as the nearly 100 million people murdered by the dictator Mao Zedong.[450]

The editorial ends with: "The U.S. should learn from China and genuinely protect human rights. If the U.S. does not control its guns, problems caused by firearms in the foreseeable future will continue plaguing U.S. society."[451]

In conclusion, the ideological fight is in full bloom today, especially from the Russian and Chinese camps. The evidence is even heard in the open at the annual Munich Security Conference. In 2017, Sergey Lavrov, the Russian foreign minister, rejected "the allegations of those who accuse Russia and the new centers of global influence of attempting to undermine the so-called 'liberal world order.'" Lavrov said that model "was conceived primarily as an instrument for ensuring the growth of an elite club of countries and its domination over everyone else. It is clear that such a system could not last forever." Rather, countries like Russia and China increasingly present a mix of autocratic leadership and capitalism, an alternative ideology to the Western model, and it is attracting a lot of attention.[452]

The ideological mix of autocratic leadership and capitalism is gaining attention because of China's investments and trade as well. "No country today has developed as effective a global trade and investment strategy as Beijing," wrote the risk consultancy Eurasia Group. "China's model generates both interest and imitators, with governments across Asia, Africa, the Middle East and even Latin America tacking more toward Beijing's policy preferences." Further, behind the trade and investment is the ideological fight, which German Foreign Minister Sigmar Gabriel properly warned. The Chinese are gaining influence by pressuring governments that "no longer dare to make decisions that run counter to Chinese interests." Why is that? China leverages its growing and significant economic power to get its geopolitical way and the entire world understands. That is very significant![453]

The new dual Cold War with Putin's Russia and Xi's China present a very challenging ideological battleground veiled by nationalism, capitalism, authoritarian leadership and mixed with some progressive globalist thought. The US and much of the West need to re-evaluate their foundation and what they have to offer or risk losing badly in this emerging battleground.

New Dual Cold War's Cyber Battleground

Second, the five dimensions of the new dual Cold War battleground are: land, sea, air, space, and cyber. The old Cold War was known for proxy fights on land such as Korea and Vietnam; sea confrontations (above and below the surface); air encounters between Soviet and American fighter jets, and the space race. Similar confrontations are already becoming commonplace once again, as indicated in chapter 1, and could well escalate—especially as the arms and technology race picks up momentum as expected. However, the newest battleground dimension is in the cyber domain, which has already caused very serious problems for both sides, will undoubtedly increase in intensity, and could very well become the most decisive dimension in the new dual Cold War. In many ways, cyber is already a hot war with no end in sight and could potentially do as much damage as any ground or even nuclear war.

The nature of the cyber threat is front and center for the American government. President Trump's 2017 National Security Strategy (NSS) issues a stark warning about the cyber threat: "Today, cyberspace offers state and non-state actors the ability to wage campaigns against American political, economic, and security interests without ever physically crossing our borders."

Cyber attacks are potentially silent killers that can "seriously damage or disrupt critical infrastructure, cripple American businesses, weaken our federal networks, and attack the tools and devices that Americans use every day to communicate and conduct business," according to the NSS. Cyber attacks also threaten our national security by disrupting "military command and control, banking and financial operations, the electrical grid, and means of communication."[454]

The NSS states that cyber attacks are cheap killers of people and undermine trust in the institutions of government. "Such attacks have the capabilities to harm large numbers of people and institutions with comparatively minimal investment and a troubling degree of deniability. These attacks can undermine faith and confidence in democratic institutions and the global economic system."

The two biggest culprits of cyber attacks on America today are China and Russia, according to Mr. Daniel Coats, director of national intelligence in testimony before the Senate Select Committee on Intelligence.

"Russia is a full-scope cyber actor that will remain a major threat to the U.S. government, military, diplomatic, commercial, and critical infrastructure," testified Director Coats in 2017. He continued, "Moscow has a highly advanced offensive cyber program, and in recent years, the Kremlin has assumed a more aggressive cyber posture. This aggressiveness was evident in Russia's efforts to influence the 2016 U.S. election, and we assess that only Russia's senior-most officials [read "Putin"] could have authorized the 2016 U.S. election-focused data thefts and disclosures, based on the scope and sensitivity of the targets."[455]

"We assess that Beijing will continue actively targeting the U.S. government, its allies, and U.S. companies for cyber espionage," according to DNI Director Coats. "Private-sector security experts continue to identify ongoing cyber activity from China, although at volumes significantly lower than before the bilateral Chinese-U.S. cyber commitments of September 2015. Beijing has also selectively used offensive cyber operations against foreign targets that it probably believes threaten Chinese domestic stability or regime legitimacy."

The cyber threat posed by China and Russia will likely get worse as the new dual Cold War heats up. The following are areas of particular vulnerability in this new battleground.

Internet Infrastructure

The US and the West in general depend on the Internet for virtually all electronic operations. Therefore, any threat to the Internet's infrastructure, such as to the undersea communication cables that connect the continents, is something to take especially seriously.

The most vulnerable aspect of the cyber domain for the West are the two hundred undersea fiber-optic cables, which Russia and China are focusing on as rich sources of intelligence and clear targets in the ongoing cyber war. These cables that crisscross international waterways are vulnerable to submarines, underwater drones, robots, and specialized ships and divers.[456] This aspect of the dual Cold War has already started.

The Russian navy is alleged to operate an advanced spy ship called the *Yantar* to tap into undersea Internet cables. The *Yantar* "can host two deep submergence submarines for undersea engineering mission," wrote H. I. Sutton, the author of an article posted at the website Covert Shores. "These missions are thought to include cable cutting, laying of taps on undersea cables, removing other countries' taps ('delousing') and related intelligence missions. She may also perform other special missions such as recovery of sensitive equipment from crashed aircraft or test missiles." An expert at the University of Calgary's Center for Military Strategic Studies said, "If the Russians have this [capability], it would be highly likely that both the Chinese and Americans have the same ability."[457]

National Security Networks

The Trump administration's 2018 Nuclear Posture Review (NPR) warns that Russia and China are pursuing asymmetric ways and means to counter US conventional and strategic security capabilities, which include offensive cyberspace capabilities to deter, disrupt, or defeat American forces dependent on computer networks. Those cyber activities include attacking vulnerabilities in our nuclear command, control, and communications (NC3) system.

"China and Russia, who we see as peer and near-peer competitors in cyberspace, remain our greatest concern," testified Admiral Mike Rogers, the director of the National Security Agency (NSA), before the Senate Armed Services Committee on February 27, 2018.

Several years ago, Chinese cyber hackers inflicted what NSA called "serious damage to [Defense Department] interests." Specifically, Chinese hackers were traced to thirty thousand incidents, and at least five hundred of those incidents were labeled "significant intrusions of DoD systems" against sixteen hundred network computers and sixty thousand user accounts.[458]

Chinese defense industrial cyber espionage targets America's technological crown jewels, including the B-2 bomber, F-22 and F-35 fighter jets, the space-based laser, and other sensitive systems.[459]

"Today we face threats that have increased in sophistication, magnitude, intensity, volume and velocity, threatening our vital national security interests and economic well-being," Rogers said.[460]

Robert Soofer, deputy assistant secretary of defense for nuclear and missile defense policy, is one of the authors of the NPR, and shares Admiral Roger's concerns. Evidently, the press acquired a draft of an early version of the NPR, which allegedly stated that the US would consider using nuclear weapons in response to a major cyberattack on America. Specifically, on page 16 of the leaked draft of the NPR, according to the *Washington Free Beacon*, the document reportedly reads that "the president will have an expanding range of limited and graduated options to credibly deter Russian nuclear or non-nuclear strategic attacks, which could now include attacks against U.S. NC3, in space and cyber space." That line was eliminated in the published version of the NPR. However, Soofer answered "yes" when he was asked if a "debilitating" cyber attack on the US could trigger a nuclear response.[461]

"We are looking at strategic attacks, non-nuclear strategic attacks that cause catastrophic effects. If the attack could, say, cause thousands of U.S. casualties in a city, adversaries need to know that could elicit a nuclear response. That's a deterrent effect," Soofer said. "We're not excluding it, no."[462]

Cyber also has a military tactical dimension that is just beginning to take shape. However, the Pentagon has a complicated relationship regarding authorities and cyberspace operations, especially at the tactical battlefield level.

The US Army is fielding a cadre of cyber warriors while it sorts out the authorities. Specifically, Army leaders want tactical commanders to control cyber capabilities on the battlefield and are piloting a program called Cyber and Electromagnetic Activity (CEMA) Support to Corps and Below (CSCB).[463]

Army leadership wants to put the CEMA capability at the brigade combat team level, whereby such units can use social media to affect mission and maneuver. US Army Lieutenant General Paul Nakasone, commander of Army Cyber Command, told reporters that social media is a powerful medium that has the potential to dominate local communication. Therefore, according to the general, the Army intends to develop capabilities to disrupt our enemies' use of social media platforms such as Twitter or Facebook to our advantage.[464]

General Nakasone added that is a real mission for a brigade combat team. For example, the brigade might want to prevent an enemy from talking to others, or it might want to track an enemy as he makes his way past a number of different cameras that the brigade's tactical cyber unit could hijack in order to monitor enemy progress.[465]

The national security uses of cyber are significant from both a defensive and offensive perspective, and across all levels of operation.

Domestic Infrastructure

The West's infrastructure is a target of Chinese and Russian cyberattacks.

In January 2018, Britain's defense secretary warned that a Russian cyber attack on Britain's electricity supply could cause "thousands and thousands" of deaths. Secretary Gavin Williamson revealed that Moscow has photographed power stations in Great Britain and may be planning to damage the country's economy and infrastructure.[466] Count on the fact that both China and Russia have done the same in the United States as well.

Mr. Williamson suggested that Russia could target interconnectors, which link power between countries, thus leaving millions in the dark. "The plan for the Russians won't be for landing craft to appear in the South Bay in Scarborough and off Brighton Beach. They are going to be thinking: 'How can we just cause so much pain to Britain?' Damage its economy, rip its infrastructure apart, actually cause thousands and thousands and thousands of deaths, but actually have an element of creating total chaos within the country."

"What they [the Russians] are looking at doing is trying to spot vulnerabilities, because what they want to do is they want to know how to strike it, they want to know how they can kill infrastructure, and by killing that infrastructure, that means hurting Britain and the British people," according to Ciaran Martin, chief executive of GCHQ's (The Government Communications Headquarters) National Cyber Security Center.

The United States is just as vulnerable to a massive cyber attack on our electric grid, a view backed by many senior US officials who make it clear this threat is one of the most serious faced by the nation.

In 2017, for example, ninety-nine nuclear power plants licensed by the Nuclear Regulatory Commission (NCR) were affected by a cyber attack aimed at the energy grid. Fortunately, according to the NRC, the incident had no operational impact on the transmission of electricity. However, that illustrates the increased threat of electronic and computer-based assaults on our critical infrastructure.[467]

It is noteworthy that Energy Secretary Rick Perry said a prolonged cyber attack "demonstrates exactly why" he created an Office of Cyber Security and Emergency Response. That office will "combat the growing nefarious cyber threats we face," he said.[468]

Richard B. Andres, a professor at the US National War College and senior fellow at the Institute for National Strategic Studies, explains the potential catastrophic impact of a cyber attack that cripples our electric grid:

> In the first few minutes of a national outage, virtually all commerce would cease as electronic systems went down. Gasoline pumps would stop. Telephones, including those used by government and emergency responders, would quickly cease functioning. Cities that use electricity to pump water would lose water pressure, and sewage systems would back up into fresh water. Fuel pipelines would cease to function. Most households have three days of food available and no stored potable water. Hospitals would continue to function for a few days. National Guard and law enforcement agencies have stated on the record that they believe their employees would stop coming to work after less than a week. Disease and starvation would set in within days.[469]

The devastation and loss of life is predictable. America saw the results of the loss of electric power in the wake of past hurricanes. Imagine the impact if an entire region of the US or the entire nation lost power due to a cyber attack.

Economic Infrastructure

The US lacks a coherent policy to defend against cyber threats designed to undermine our economy, and such attacks do cause significant economic harm. In fact, we are facing a "crime wave," according to IBM Corporation's chairman, CEO, and president, Ginni Rometty, who says cyber crime may be the greatest threat to every company in the world.[470]

The cost of cyber crime keeps going up. Five years ago, according to the *Wall Street Journal,* the cost of cyber crime to the United States was $100 billion. Juniper Research predicts the global cost of this type of criminal activity will reach $2.1 trillion by 2019, four times the estimated cost of breaches in 2015.[471]

Cyber crime is terrible, but nation-on-nation cyber attacks are worse.

A 2017 report, *Framework and Terminology for Understanding Cyber-Enabled Economic Warfare,* defines cyber-enabled economic warfare (CEEW) as a "hostile strategy involving attack(s) against a nation using cyber technology with the intent to weaken its economy and thereby reduce its political and military power." A cyber campaign must meet four criteria. The attack(s) must: 1) be cyber enabled; 2) be intended to cause economic harm; 3) result in economic damage that is "significant enough to potentially degrade national security capabilities"; and 4) be the result of that intent.[472]

The report indicates that China's economic theft of intellectual property is considered CEEW, along with Russia's cyber attack on nation states like Estonia (2007) and Georgia (2008). Further, the breach of the US Office of Personnel Management (in 2015, which resulted in the loss of 21.5 million records) and Russia's frequent hacks of United States government agencies are CEEW tactics, according to the report.

Much of CEEW attacks are supported by nation states like Russia. Russian intelligence reportedly hires cyber proxies, "trolls," to conduct offensive cyber operations. Evidently, former Soviet states boast very capable and underemployed citizens willing to act as cyber proxies, "trolls" for a price.

Alexei Borodin, a hacker for hire, explained: "People think: I've got no money, a strong education and law enforcement's weak. Why not earn a bit on the side?" Russian intelligence found plenty of cyber talent for hire to do its bidding. Also, perhaps not surprising, the Russian government turns a blind eye when the subject of these "troll" attacks is other than Russian.[473]

State-sponsored Interference in the Democratic Process

Britain's former spy chief, Robert Hannigan, warned his countrymen that Russia is causing a "disproportionate amount of mayhem" in cyberspace that threatens democracy. Hannigan told a *Radio 4* audience that Putin's Russia was a threat to the democratic process, and he noted that President Emmanuel Macron of France and Angela Merkel, the German chancellor, already challenged Russia over its cyber activities, including during the French presidential election.[474]

The 2016 US presidential election was a Russian cyber target as well. Jeanette Manfra, head of cybersecurity at the United States Department of Homeland Security (DHS), said that several states' voter registration rolls were "successfully penetrated" by Russians during the 2016 election cycle.[475]

"We saw a targeting of 21 states and an exceptionally small number of them were actually successfully penetrated," Manfra said, and she added that the Russians were responsible.[476]

Obama's DHS Secretary Jeh Johnson agrees with Ms. Manfra. The situation is a "wake-up call," and he calls on "states and the feds to do something about it before our democracy is attacked again."[477]

Mr. Dan Coats, director of national intelligence, warned the Senate Intelligence Committee in February 2018 to expect more Russian interference in the 2018 midterm elections. "There should be no doubt that Russia perceived its past efforts as successful and views the 2018

U.S. midterms as a potential target for Russian influence operations," he said.[478]

"I believe that President [Vladimir] Putin has clearly come to the conclusion that there's little price to pay [for interfering in U.S. elections] and therefore, 'I can continue this activity,'" Admiral Mike Rogers, the director of both the US Cyber Command and the National Security Agency, told Congress in February 2018. Rogers went on to state, "Clearly what we have done hasn't been enough.... [because] It certainly hasn't generated the change in behavior that, I think we all know we need."[479]

Britain's Ciaran Martin, chief executive of the National Cyber Security Centre, warned leaders of all British political parties about the Russian threat, which applies to America as well. "This is not just about the network security of political parties' own systems," Martin said. "Attacks against our democratic processes go beyond this and can include attacks on Parliament, constituency offices, think tanks and pressure groups and individuals' email accounts."[480]

The cyber attacks against our democratic processes could get worse, thanks to the emergence of artificial intelligence (AI). Combining the power of artificial intelligence and information could pose an existential threat against our democracy, argues Doug Wise, the former deputy director of the Defense Intelligence Agency. Wise warns that our adversaries already used cyber-hosted "fake news" to trigger "a digital rot within our social and political structures which can have a significant effect as full scale war."[481]

Wise sees a time in the not-so-distant future "when these attacks are driven and enabled by very sophisticated AI systems." He contends, "This is the existential threat to us...in the foreseeable future; I fear this far more than being targeted by self-aware autonomous weapons systems.... AI systems will allow adversaries to exponentially expand the scale of the attacks, the rate of the attacks, and the number of targets including the ability to link attacks among multiple targets."[482]

Let there be no doubt: China and Russia have weaponized the Internet, making it a dangerous and dark place that will get worse as the new dual Cold War heats up. As one cyber expert put it, once information is weaponized, nothing is safe.[483]

In conclusion, only three things can happen if the new dual Cold War totally weaponizes the Internet: 1) The rules of Internet behavior will be changed so we can continue to operate (unlikely); 2) Walled-off cyber networks like North Korea will be created (more likely but very expensive); or 3) Cyber wars will grow into shooting conflicts (unfortunately, most likely).

It is noteworthy that Russia has already moved in the direction of a walled-off cyber network. In 2016, the Russian government began to operate the Closed Data Transfer Segment, an internal intranet for military and official use. Herman Klimenko told Russian television on March 6, 2018, "Technically, we are ready for any action now." The implication is that Moscow intends to reduce Russia's dependence on foreign information technology (read "Internet"), which Putin calls a CIA project.[484]

Not only has Moscow pursued a closed network, but it has also created a Linux-based operating system to wean the Russian government from Microsoft products, a perceived vulnerability.[485]

New Dual Cold War's Economic Battleground

Third, economic competition is a new battleground because it's about jobs, talent, fair trade, and access to natural resources and intellectual property. Unfortunately, China and Russia don't like to play by the rules—besides, the US is in serious trouble.

America has acted stupidly when it comes to dealing with China and Russia economically, according to Dr. Chodakiewicz:

> They lure Western capital in. We bankroll their development;
> we are compelled to hand over our technology; and then we

get kicked out. There is no free market either in China or Russia. You can only do business if the government blesses you with a secret policeman who becomes your open or hidden partner. And then he forces you to lobby on his country's behalf, if you want to continue to operate either in Russia or in China. The Chinese are much better at it than the Russians. They are not as ham fisted. One thing is clear, though. There is a double standard at work. Both Moscow and Beijing demand free market and freedom of academia and media and speech for their nationals/agents and their lobbyists and enablers in the United States and elsewhere in the West. At the same time, both Russia and China deny the United States and its allies the same under their jurisdiction. There are no free markets, no free speech, no free media, no free system in China and Russia.[486]

That's quite an indictment, but a view shared by others who know the economic scene. Folker Hellmeyer, the chief economist at Bremer Landesbank, told *German Economic News* in 2015 that the global economic conflict "has already been decided." He elaborated:

The axis Moscow-Beijing-BRICS [Brazil, Russia, India, China, and South Africa] wins. The dominance of the West is through. In 1990 those countries accounted for only about 25% of world economic output. Today, they represent 56% of world economic output, and 85% of world population. They control about 70% of the world's foreign exchange reserves. They grow annually by an average of 4%–5%. Since the United States was not prepared to share power internationally (e.g., by changing the voting-apportionments in the IMF and World Bank), the future rests with those countries themselves, to build in the emerging markets sector on their own financial system. There lies their future.[487]

President Trump understands the seriousness of the economic threat. He used his 2017 National Security Strategy (NSS) to call out China and Russia for their threats to our national security, which includes our economic security. China and Russia "are determined to make economies less free and less fair," states Mr. Trump. He commits to "promote American prosperity…for the benefit of American workers and companies…[and] we will insist upon fair and reciprocal economic relationships to address trade imbalances."[488]

The president states in his NSS that "for decades, the United States has allowed unfair trading practices to grow." Other countries have "used dumping, discriminatory non-tariff barriers, forced technology transfers, non-economic capacity, industrial subsidies, and other support from governments and state-owned enterprises to gain economic advantages."

Mr. Trump explicitly calls out China for stealing. "Every year, competitors such as China steal U.S. intellectual property valued at hundreds of billions of dollars," states the NSS. "Stealing proprietary technology and early-stage ideas allows competitors to unfairly tap into the innovation of free societies."

For these and more reasons, Mr. Trump's former chief strategist said the United States is in an economic war with China, and Mr. Steve Bannon warned that Washington is losing that fight.[489]

The evidence that the US is losing the economic war with China abounds. American stores are full of products made in China, which explains the 2016 US trade deficit with China totaling $347 billion, and in June 2017, the US debt to China amounted to $1.14 trillion.[490]

Michael Sekora, founder of Project Socrates, the Reagan-era intelligence community program used to determine the underlying cause of America's declining competitiveness and to reverse same, says the US is "losing the economic war with China and nothing that is being proposed by the present [Trump] administration or Congress has the ability to turn the situation around."[491]

Of course, the Chinese government disputes that claim. Chinese foreign ministry spokesman Hua Chunying said the China-US trade relationship is mutually beneficial. She continued, "We have also said before, a trade war has no future. A trade war does not serve the interests of any party, as fighting a trade war will not produce a winner. We hope that relevant parties can stop viewing issues of the 21st century with a 19th- or 20th-century mentality."[492]

Consider the evidence of the current economic battleground between the United States and China.

The US and Japan claim that Beijing is not a market economy as it pretends to be, a key requirement for accession to the World Trade Organization, which China joined in 2001, thanks to America's endorsement. That status makes it harder for competing countries to impose anti-dumping duties on Chinese goods. But China does flood world markets with cheap steel, toys, bicycles, ceramics, and textiles way below the price of production, thanks to Beijing's subsidies.

China is also stealing American manufacturing jobs, said then presidential candidate Donald Trump in July 2016. He declared that "disastrous trade deals" hurt America's manufacturing sector, and in part, it's our fault because we supported China's so-called embrace of free trade, which ended up being a "colossal" mistake.

It is true that China attracted millions of American manufacturing jobs to those firms seeking to reduce costs and bolster profitability, according to a study in the *Journal of Labor Economics*. Unfortunately for China, many of its workers are now losing their jobs to a slowing domestic economy and stiff foreign competition, but the jobs are not returning to America yet.[493]

Manufacturing jobs are leaving China because of higher wages needed to attract workers pulled to other sectors by an expanded economy. Meanwhile, as competition for workers increased, so did the pressure to produce more expensive, high-value products. This combination made China a less desirable labor market. After all, factory workers in Vietnam, for example, earn less than half the salary of a Chinese worker, and workers in Bangladesh earn less than a quarter as much. No wonder factories are leaving China.

No doubt higher wages in China are sending some American manufacturers back to the States as well, especially now in the wake of Mr. Trump's 2017 corporate tax cut. As one corporate leader said, "It just makes economic sense" to return to the states. "The U.S. right now is in a very favorable position."

Unfortunately, many manufacturers aren't even looking back at the United States for their next move. Vietnam, Indonesia, and Ethiopia are attracting footwear factories. Taiwan's Foxconn, known for making Apple iPhones in China, is relocating its manufacturing to India, creating an estimated million new jobs.

As jobs flee China searching for lower wage markets, Beijing aggressively seeks to find new opportunities for its expanding workforce. That expansion is in part fed by China's stealing of American intellectual property (IP), as Mr. Trump states in the NSS.

The *New York Times* confirms that view in a report that found Chinese companies, some with official Beijing endorsement, are pillaging the IP of American companies working in China. Gary Cohn, Mr. Trump's former economic adviser, said China forces US companies to transfer their IP to China in order to do business in that country.

The forced transfer or otherwise loss of American IP costs the United States up to $600 billion a year, "the greatest transfer of wealth in history." The *Times* claims that China accounts for most of that loss, which includes everything from counterfeiting American fashion to pirating video games and stealing proprietary technology.

The damage incurred by Chinese theft of IP costs American jobs, weakens our military technological edge, and hurts our competitive advantage.

China and the West are also engaged in a vicious global resource (raw materials) war. The resource war is especially pronounced regarding Chinese export restrictions on rare earth minerals—those used to make high-technology devices like iPhones and sophisticated weapons. "China restricts its exports [of rare earth minerals] but allows local [China-based] companies to use and transform them into finished products—that's what the conflict is about," explained Mogens Peter Carl, former director-general of the European Commission's trade department.[494]

Those export restrictions give Chinese factories a competitive edge on world markets. Further, German companies complained they were pressured by Beijing to boost their investment in China if they want access to rare earth minerals, evidence of yet more unfair trade practices.

At the macro level, the economic battleground is especially problematic for China and the United States, because it is a fight for dominance and wealth, but neither side wants the other to suffer a complete defeat. Why? China and the US need one another. Beijing needs the economically stable consuming US, and we need a cash-abundant China.

Victory on the new dual Cold War economic battleground never removes one or the other from the fight. That would be certain defeat for both.

Time will tell whether China does become the world's leading economy and if that status translates into different rules on the economic battleground. Likely, what will happen as the new dual Cold War evolves is that China will leverage its expansive overseas assets to control global manufacturing and therefore seek to dominate all sectors of the world marketplace if not entire countries.

There is evidence of China's global reach and its ambition to take over entire countries. Columnist David Goldman spoke at Hillsdale College in February 2018 on the topic of China's economic goals when he explained about his visit to the headquarters of Huawei Technologies, China's telecommunications company—the biggest in the world, which owns 70 percent of the world market. "How did Huawei do that? It cut prices and got massive subsidies from the government," Goldman explained. Then he said something very revealing: "After a three-hour tour, the Chinese sat the Latin Americans I was with down in a little amphitheater and said, 'If you turn your economy over to us, we will make you like China. We'll put in telecommunications. We'll put in broadband. We'll bring in e-commerce. We'll bring in e-finance. You'll be advanced like we are."[495] Goldman said the Latin Americans turned down the deal, but the Turks have taken it.

Huawei is also allegedly sidestepping trade prohibitions and selling US technology to Iran, another indicator of its economic ambition. On April 25, 2018, *Reuters* reported that the US Justice Department was investigating China's Huawei Technologies for allegedly violating US sanctions against Iran. The alleged violation reported by *Reuters* indicated Huawei is suspected of shipping US-origin products to Iran and other countries in violation of American export and sanctions laws. In 2016, the United States imposed an export ban on Huawei's Chinese rival, ZTE Corporation, for directly exporting US-produced technology to Iran and North Korea.[496]

Clearly, China is the focus of this contemporary economic battleground, because it is the most threatening economic adversary in the new dual Cold War. However, Russia by comparison has a weak economy that depends mostly on energy exports for foreign exchange. Further, and to put the issue in perspective, Russia-US trade totaled $20.31 billion in 2016, according to the United States Census Bureau. That's not much for a country like the US, with $3.64 trillion in annual trade.

Of course, America's economic equation could change should Russia and China join economic forces, an unlikely future outcome. But stranger things have happened, and if Beijing were to offer its significant manufacturing know-how to Moscow, and Russia were to contribute raw materials, then the duo could have a bright economic future together.

For now, Moscow's economy creeps along on returns from its energy supplies and a weak manufacturing sector. Of course, it doesn't help that Putin's focus on building a modern military robs the rest of his economy of precious resources, as do his misadventures into places like Crimea and Syria.

Kirill Martynov, the political editor for the *Novaya Gazeta*, painted a dire economic situation facing Russia in his February 2018 article titled

"Deadline for Doves." He said that even though Russia plays the role of superpower, its share of the global economy amounts to only 3.5 percent and continues to decline. "Our GDP is already only half that of California, to say nothing of the entire US or China. In but a few years, our economy's share in the world may shrink to the historical minimum of 2.5 percent. Never has such a big country as Russia produced so little—throughout all of contemporary history."[497]

He continued:

A significant part of Russia's current elite sees the problem perfectly. If one sets aside ideology, it becomes clear: our resources are running low. Russia today is a stagnating regional economy, which claims the status of a superpower due to its nuclear potential, bequeathed by the USSR, and its readiness to get involved in escapades beyond its borders.

The economic battleground will be a significant front in the new dual Cold War. The US and West by association will constantly battle mostly China for fair treatment, and no one should be surprised that Beijing continues to play its cards from the bottom of the deck.

Arms and Technology Battleground

The old Cold War cost a fortune and ultimately broke the former Soviet Union, but this time around, there will be at least one more big player chasing the latest weapons and technologies to outpace the other side. That race will be incredibly expensive, and proxy battlefields will become the ultimate test beds for the latest killing technologies.

Arms merchants are already celebrating the new dual Cold War because it is expected to radically increase global demand for every sort of weapon and defense-related technology.

Retired US Army General Richard "Dick" Cody, former Vice Chief of Staff for the US Army and now a vice president at L-3 Communications, the seventh-largest US defense contractor, said the defense industry faces a historic opportunity. Cody said at the end of the old Cold War peace had "pretty much broken out all over the world," with Russia in decline and NATO nations cashing in on the victory and as a result "all defense budgets went south."[498]

Now, Cody said, Russia "is resurgent" around the world, which puts pressure on NATO nations to reinvest in defense, a view shared by President Trump, who repeatedly calls on the twenty-nine NATO allies to spend the mandated 2 percent of their GDP on defense.[499] At present, only five of the twenty-nine NATO allies spend at least 2 percent of their GDP on defense.[500]

China's aggressiveness and consistent, decades-long, double-digit increases in defense spending is persuading her neighbors to double down on defense spending, especially its arch enemy in Tokyo. Japan increased defense spending by 2.5 percent in 2018 over the previous year. Much of that new money goes to missile defense systems intended to defend against the North Korean threat (SM-3 Block 2a intercept missiles; PAC-3 MSE missiles), but some of the new defense money comes in response to the growing threat from China as well.

The Tokyo government expressed "strong concerns" over China's activities in the East and South China Seas, where China "continues to display what may be described as a heavy-handed attitude, including its attempts to alter the status quo by force." Predictably, Beijing dismisses Tokyo's concern. Hua Chunying, a Chinese ministry of foreign affairs spokesman, acknowledged Japan's increased defense spending: "We are aware of the reports [about Japan's defense spending] and are concerned about this." He claims that Japan has exaggerated the "China threat" to increase military spending, and then he volunteered that China will be on high alert to Japan's military moves and its real motives.[501]

There is no doubt in this author's mind that the new dual Cold War will lead to an arms race and efforts to constrain that effort because of the expense. Thus, arms control eventually becomes the cry of nations challenged by the sky-is-the-limit defense hawks. After all, defense spending will increase because of the increased tensions associated with the new dual Cold War. Global defense spending for 2016 reached $1.686 trillion, a .4 percent increase over 2015.[502]

Consider past efforts to constrain the proliferation of dangerous weapons and their associated costs. Early arms-control efforts were basically rules of battle protecting sanctuaries dating back to the Amphictyonic League in the seventh century B.C. Greece. Today, arms control is very different, primarily because of the killing potential of modern weapons.

The victors of World War I tried to regulate naval construction as a means of arms control. In February 1922, the Washington Naval Treaty imposed tonnage limitations on capital ships and aircraft carriers. Ultimately, the treaty failed to temper growing ambitions in Japan and Italy, and by the late 1930s, the treaty died thanks to widespread violations.[503]

The forty-six-year-old Cold War was the heyday of arms control, primarily because of the balance of power—mostly nuclear. Then the end of the old Cold War brought about significant new arms-control results, such as the 1993 Chemical Weapons Convention, the 1996 Comprehensive Nuclear-Test-Ban Treaty, the 1991 Strategic Arms Reduction Treaty (START), and the 2010 New START.

Other efforts included constraints on conventional arms as well.

NATO and Russia agreed in 1990 to the Treaty on Conventional Armed Forces in Europe (CFE Treaty), but that process remains deadlocked over Russia's noncompliance with the commitments it made at the 1999 Organization for Security and Cooperation in Europe (OSCE) Istanbul Summit. For Moscow, the sticking point with OSCE was the requirement for Russian military forces to withdraw from Georgia and Moldova, where they remain today.[504]

A few years later, enthusiasm for arms control began to fade, thanks to new technology, which led the United States to withdraw from the 1972 Anti-Ballistic Missile Treaty in 2002. About that time, China entered the military power scene with a large, sophisticated military, and soon a resurgent Russia reintroduced the world to the complications of a new arms race.

Today, any effort to impose arms restrictions on Russia and China would likely be rejected with accusations that the US wants the world all to itself. Besides, advanced technology makes arms control very complex, if not geopolitically challenging, given the plethora of nations with sophisticated arsenals.

Consider a brief military profile of China and Russia before considering the frightening technological advances that promise to make the new dual Cold War a daunting reality.

President Trump's security strategies mince no words about the threat posed by China and Russia. His National Security Strategy states, "China and Russia are developing advanced weapons and capabilities that could threaten our critical infrastructure and our command and control architecture." Secretary of Defense Jim Mattis warns that the United States must step up to this arms challenge.[505]

Mattis writes in the 2018 National Defense Strategy: "The costs of not implementing this strategy are clear.... Without sustained and predictable investment to restore readiness and modernize our military to make it fit for our time, we will rapidly lose our military advantage, resulting in a joint force that has legacy systems irrelevant to the defense of our people."[506]

Marine Corps General Joseph Dunford, the Chairman of the US Joint Chiefs of Staff, echoes Secretary Mattis' concern that our long-held military advantage against near-peer competitors China and Russia is eroding, and fast. General Dunford told a Tufts University forum that "in the last 10 or 15 years, that competitive advantage has eroded, and it's no longer as decisive as it was some years ago." Why did it erode?[507]

Answer: The United States under-invested in its military while our adversaries stepped up their investment. The Chairman explained that China and Russia studied our 1990–91 Persian Gulf War operations against Iraq and then invested heavily in capabilities and devised strategies and doctrine to counter our advantages such as electronic warfare, cyber capabilities, anti-space capabilities, anti-ship cruise missiles, and anti-ship ballistic missiles. These systems, according to General Dunford, have "the express purpose of keeping us [the U.S.] from projecting power into the Pacific, or into Europe as the case may be, and meeting our alliance commitments."[508]

The general said our adversaries have an advantage over us. They have "the form of government in Russia [and China], they're much more…able to combine all elements of national power to advance their interests." He continued, "They're actually conducting activities and employing capabilities [like cyber-attacks] that we may associate with war, but they're doing it on a day-to-day basis in the context of this adversarial [read "dual Cold War"] competition."[509]

The 2017 US-China Economic and Security Review Commission's annual report echoes General Dunford's warnings. The report states that China will continue to modernize strategic air and sea lift capabilities, which include its ability to deliver combat troops abroad and conduct expeditionary operations beyond the first island chain, which means it intends to contest international shipping lanes used by the United States and the economic zones of ally Japan, our friend Taiwan, and new friend Vietnam and the Philippines. These advances mean, according to the commission, that China's increasing capability intends to "erode" America's ability to operate freely in the region.[510]

China is also pursuing very advanced weapon systems to match or outpace the United States. Beijing's new weapons platform investments include modern aircraft carriers, maneuverable re-entry vehicles, hypersonic weapons, directed energy weapons, electromagnetic railguns, counter-space weapons, and unmanned and artificial intelligence equipped weapons, according to the commission.

Let there be no doubt, based on these new technologies, that Beijing seeks a global military capability. Specifically, last year China conducted sea trials with its first homegrown aircraft carrier, and now it is deploying its second carrier. This carrier will include an electromagnetic catapult for launching fighter jets, rather than the current ski-jump system; the

3rd carrier is under construction. Meanwhile, China is developing the Shaanxi KJ-600, a carrier-borne early-warning aircraft that is necessary for tracking enemy aircraft at long range, which indicates that Beijing is planning for global sea operations.[511]

In February 2018, one of China's largest shipbuilders made a surprising announcement that it plans to develop China's first nuclear-powered aircraft carrier and its fourth, part of Beijing's ambitious plan to transform its navy into a global force by the middle of the next decade.[512]

Beijing is very open about its military ambitions. The state-owned China Shipbuilding Industry Corporation said in a news release that it will "redouble efforts to achieve technological breakthroughs in nuclear-powered aircraft carriers, new nuclear-powered submarines, quieter conventionally powered submarines, underwater artificial intelligence-based combat systems and integrated network communications systems." The company said those breakthroughs are required by China's People's Liberation Army Navy, or PLAN, to "enhance its capability to globally operate in line with the service's aim to become a networked, blue-water navy by 2025."[513]

China already has a new underwater surveillance network of buoys, surface vessels, satellites, and underwater gliders, which allows China to monitor waters virtually anywhere in the world—something not lost on the US Navy. It is noteworthy that Beijing initially insisted its construction at Mischief Reef in the South China Sea was a fisherman's shelf, while recent observations of the facility found significant military facilities with jet fighters, warships and cruise missiles.[514]

On other fronts, the average Chinese soldier is also becoming a superman. In February 2018, Norinco, a Chinese state-owned maker of armored vehicles, introduced a second-generation exoskeleton for Chinese infantrymen. The device will allow a soldier to carry one hundred pounds of weapons, ammunition, and supplies. This is an interesting development for a nation that insists it has no overseas offensive ambitions. Why might a home-defense soldier need to carry such a heavy load?[515]

Russia is a growing and serious military threat as well. In June 2016, the US Sixth Fleet commander, Vice Admiral James Foggo, said the Fourth Battle of the Atlantic might be under way. What does the admiral mean?

Parenthetically, it is helpful for the reader to understand the history associated with the historic Battles of the Atlantic. The First Battle of the Atlantic took place during World War I when U-boats of the German Empire used new technologies to blockade the British Isles and sink many Allied vessels. The Second Battle of the Atlantic began again with German U-boats threatening Allies in World War II, but this time the Germans overcame the antisubmarine warfare advantages of the Allies. Fortunately, the Allies prevailed in the end to win that second encounter. The Third Battle of the Atlantic took place during the old Cold War, whereby Allied forces played constant games of cat and mouse with Soviet submarines, and that battle ended without a shooting war.[516]

Admiral Foggo warned about the Fourth Battle of the Atlantic, which is about the re-emergence of the Russian fleet. He explained that "Russia is rapidly closing the technological gap with the United States" and is speedily "building and deploying more advanced and significantly quieter attack submarines and frigates armed with long-range Kaliber cruise missiles."[517]

DIA Director Lieutenant General Ashley confirmed this new wave of Russian arms advances in his March 2018 Senate testimony:

> Moscow is improving its strategic naval forces by building and deploying the Dolgorukly class nuclear-powered ballistic missile submarine with the SS-N-32 Bulava submarine-launched ballistic missile. Russia is also refurbishing its long-range strategic bombers to carry the newest air-launched cruise missiles, the AS-23a conventional variant and the AS-23b nuclear variant.[518]

In 2014, then Chief of Naval Operations (CNO), Admiral Jonathan Greenert, echoed Admiral Foggo's warning about Russia: "There are competitors that are pursing us. We know about China. That is very well spelled out, but not as many people know what the Russians are up to…[they] spend a lot of money." The fact is that Russia's nuclear-powered ballistic missile and attack submarines are the single greatest concern for the US Navy. They can threaten the continental United States, and their attack submarines present a real risk to our carriers. Further, undersea modernization programs will continue to improve Russia's submarine forces into the future, which explains why in 2016 Admiral Harry Harris Jr., then head of the US Pacific Command, testified to the House Armed Services Committee that Russia "has the most capable submarine force in the world after ours."[519]

The Russian ballistic missile submarine force is especially impressive and growing both in numbers and capability. In 2018, Russia's submarine fleet included three Delta II-, six Delta IV-, and three Borei-class SSBNs (ballistic missile submarine), each capable of carrying sixteen nuclear-tipped, submarine-launched ballistic missiles. Russia, according to the DIA, is dedicated to a stable funding stream for SSBN modernization that includes fielding eight new Borei II-class boats by the 2020s.[520]

The current Chief of Naval Operations (CNO), Admiral John Richardson, wrote in 2016 that "for the first time in 25 years, the United States is facing a return to great power competition. Russia and China both have advanced their military capabilities to act as global powers." Further, Admiral Richardson wrote, the Russian navy is "operating with a frequency and in areas not seen for almost two decades."

The increased military threat posed by Russia and China create special challenges for the United States. Specifically, Air Force General Paul Selva, the Vice Chairman of the Joint Chiefs of Staff, addressed the issue of "redesigning the [U.S.] force" around the challenges presented by Russia and China. The dual nature of the new great power threat creates competing tensions.[521]

"Here's why they will be in competition with each other: they are not the same," Selva explained. "There are two unique competitions that we have to deal with, and the elements are overlapping but not the same." The issue is the nature of any fight with either or both China and Russia.[522]

"Any fight with China, if it were to come to blows, would be a largely maritime and air fight," Selva said. "It doesn't mean the Army and the Marine Corps don't have a place. But when you think about how a potential conflict with China would evolve, it very likely involves a substantial contribution from the naval and air forces, and the Army and Marine Corps would be supporting elements in that fight."[523]

Russia presents a very different problem because that fight would be largely an air and ground battle. The general admits there would be a maritime component to any Russian fight, which is basically getting our forces across the North Atlantic to Europe. (America has only two combat brigades and other units totaling sixty-two thousand personnel now permanently stationed in Europe today, down from more than four hundred thousand troops during the height of the old Cold War.) Further, Selva notes in the National Defense Strategy, Russia, like China, is identified as a "global challenge, a deliberate move by the [Pentagon] planner's part to try and move away from the idea that Russia is primarily a challenge for Europe to deal with."

Selva said the Pentagon is building a "global campaign plan" to fight both Russia and China, and is looking across the military's assets to decide who will apportion to that effort. That challenge will be outlined in the classified National Military Strategy later in 2018. However, what's clear is that there isn't enough funding to prepare to fight both China and Russia at the same time. Therefore, any military pact between those two countries, while unlikely today, could be difficult to overcome.

We face a tough challenge other than the cost of preparing to fight both China and Russia, either simultaneously or separately. All three nations are in a technological race as well, and the winner could very well dominate the world.

The 2018 National Defense Strategy confirms the seriousness of that challenge:

For decades the United States has enjoyed uncontested or dominant superiority in every operating domain. We could generally
deploy our forces when we wanted, assemble them where we
wanted, and operate how we wanted. Today, every domain is
contested—air, land, sea, space, and cyberspace.

This threat is no longer science fiction. Jeff Tomczak, deputy director of the Science and Technology Division at the Marine Corps Warfighting Laboratory, said, "Our adversaries continue to evolve and move
in different directions much more rapidly than what we have seen in the
past."

Tomczak continued, "It is presenting a problem to our fighting
forces because we are not only facing state actors as a threat, [but] we
are facing irregular organizations and hybrid enemies. They are taking
advantage of something that enemies in the past have not taken advantage of and that is the proliferation of technology."[524]

"We face an ever more lethal and disruptive battlefield," says Tomczak, that reflects the rapid technological advancements and the changing character of war. In fact, the drive to develop new technologies is
relentless, such as the global race to harness artificial intelligence (AI) for
many uses to include defense-related applications. Success in creating
"AI would be the biggest event in human history," said Stephen Hawking, a world renowned theoretical physicist and director of research at
the Centre for Theoretical Cosmology at the University of Cambridge.
Then Hawking, who died in 2018, warned "it might also be the last,
unless we learn how to avoid the risks."[525]

There is no doubt that the new dual Cold War adversaries will pursue technologies that were unfathomable just a few years ago. Besides the
AI and big data platforms, the new cold warriors are heavily investing in
bionics, drones, nanotechnologies, neuroscience such as genetic modification technologies, and much more. To what end?

Consider the AI threat. A 2018 report, *The Malicious Use of Artificial Intelligence: Forecasting, Prevention and Mitigation*, warns about the

coming "dark side" of AI. The report raises concerns that NATO allies are unprepared for the threats posed by AI that target security domains: digital, physical, and political.[526]

Briefly, according to the 2018 report produced by twenty-six Cambridge University experts, states: "The use of AI to automate tasks involved in carrying out cyberattacks will alleviate the existing trade-off between the scale and efficacy of attacks." Specifically, cyber criminals will weaponize AI to design competent and realistic chat-bots that masquerade as a real person and then cultivate trust to gain access to critical data.[527]

AI is also quickly becoming capable of killing. The Islamic State demonstrated attacks using autonomous drones, and in early 2018, Russian ground troops in Syria were attacked by a swarm of thirteen small, drone-killing platforms. Further, future AI-controlled platforms will remotely hack service robots and compel them to turn on their "masters."[528] The threat of out-of-control AI-run platforms gets worse yet.

A 2018 RAND Corporation report states AI could destabilize the delicate balance of nuclear deterrence, thus bringing the world closer to a catastrophe. The RAND study indicates that new smarter, faster intelligence analysis from AI agents linked to more sensor and open-source data might convince countries that their nuclear arsenals are increasingly vulnerable and thus prompt them to take more drastic steps. The study includes the results of 2017 workshops hosting experts from nuclear security, AI, government, and industry. Those workshops produced a report that underlines how AI promises to rapidly improve a country's ability to target another country's nuclear weapons. That result may cause one or the other country to rethink the risks and rewards of acquiring more nuclear weapons or even launching them in a first strike. "Even if AI only modestly improves the ability to integrate data about the disposition of enemy missiles, it might substantially undermine a state's sense of security and undermine crisis stability," the report states.[529]

The even darker side of AI is what happens when robots powered by AI make other and more sophisticated robots. That has already happened at Cambridge University, which begs the question: What do you call a robot that can make copies of itself, with each one more advanced than its predecessor? The Terminator.[530]

Also, as an aside, AI will remake social media more extreme and create entirely new political dynamics around the globe. The AI report indicates it will be used to create fake videos "of politicians issuing terrifying statements or acting in appalling ways. The phrase 'fake news' will take on an entirely new meaning."[531]

Sundar Pichai, Google's CEO, claims AI is "more profound than... electricity or fire." It will revolutionize our lives and our militaries at least as much as did the Internet, and will eventually drive tanks, ships, submarines, aircraft, and robotic soldiers. It will provide a complete picture of the future battlefield to include the enemy's location and activities.[532]

"An unmanned [AI driven] systems future is inevitable," Brigadier General Frank Kelly, the deputy assistant secretary of the Navy for Unmanned Systems, said at an AI conference on March 7, 2018. "The magic wand has already been waved." The key question, according to Kelly, is: How much autonomy do we grant robots powered by artificial intelligence?[533]

"When you give a system autonomy, you are making a choice to give another agent the freedom to make decisions on your behalf," said John Paschkewitz, a director at the Pentagon's research and development arm, the Defense Advanced Research Projects Agency (DARPA). "You have to ask in every context 'am I comfortable letting a machine make this decision on my behalf?'"[534]

In 2012, the Pentagon established formal doctrine for robots mandating the necessity for a "human in the loop" to authorize the use of lethal force. The Chinese and Russians do not have such a formal doctrine, which raises questions whether the advantages gained by our adversaries might pressure the US to abandon the human in the loop policy.[535]

It is noteworthy and possibly a ruse to deflect attention away from

ongoing AI efforts that, in April 2018, China called on nations "to negotiate and conclude a succinct protocol to ban the use of fully autonomous weapon systems." China is the first permanent member of the
UN Security Council to call for a ban on "lethal autonomous weapons
systems" (LAWS). This recommendation was made on the final day of
a Group of Government Experts (GGE) meeting on LAWS held at the
UN office in Geneva under the aegis of the Convention on Certain
Conventional Weapons.[536]

Let there be no doubt that China is catching up if it's not already
ahead of the US in the high-technology race, and likely is rapidly catching up in several critical emerging technologies, especially in AI.

"There might be an artificial intelligence arms race, but we're not
yet in it," Dr. Michael Griffin, the US under-secretary of defense for
research and engineering, said April 9, 2018, at a Future Wars conference. "Our adversaries understand very well the possible future utility of
machine learning [AI]," Griffin continued. "I think it's time we did as
well."[537]

Secretary Griffin's concern that "it's time" the US joined the AI arms
race, which explains why the Pentagon is standing up an AI center. On
April 12, 2018, Secretary of Defense James Mattis testified before the
House Armed Services Committee that "we're looking at a joint office
where we would concentrate all of DoD's efforts, since we have a number of AI efforts underway right now. We're looking at pulling them all
together."[538]

Mr. Griffin elaborated on the proposed Joint Artificial Intelligence
Center, or JAIC. He said, "I'm working right now with folks on my staff
to answer questions like 'who should lead it, where should it be, what
projects should it do, and most importantly how does such a center fit
into the overall AI strategy for the department and the nation?'" The
Pentagon counts 592 projects that involve AI, but not all are expected to
tie into the proposed JAIC.[539]

Eric Schmidt, the former Google executive who chairs the Pentagon's Defense Innovation Board, recommends that the proposed AI

center be stood up with a university to maximize the intellectual rigor behind the effort. He also suggested that the biggest benefit of such a center is the creation of a clearinghouse of information, which can help with AI training.[540]

Secretary Griffin admits the new emphasis on AI is a result of the reality that Russia and particularly China have made whole-of-government efforts to invest in developing AI capabilities. Further, Griffin warned that by 2025, China is expected to surpass the US in AI capabilities, which he calls a "Sputnik moment" for AI, a reminder that the US didn't join the space race until the Soviet Union put the first satellite [Sputnik] in orbit.[541]

The Chinese are making rapid progress on the AI front, according to SparkCognition CEO Amir Husain, who presented a brief at the Center for a New American Security in March 2018. "The Chinese are spending $150 billion [on AI] by 2030…hopefully we will spend more than the $1.2 billion we spend now," Mr. Husain said. He warned that the fundamental difference is how China and the US approach restrictions regarding AI systems.[542]

"The issue is…China is more liberal in allowing large scale experiments," Husain explained. "The level of data you can gather when you've got 5 million cameras deployed and the kinds of objects and situations you see will allow you to build better training systems…. They will have a leg up on [the U.S.]."[543]

Robert Work, the former Pentagon deputy secretary, elaborated that China's centralized government and civil-military fusion across the defense industry makes it easier for Beijing to "really drive the fusion at the national level."[544]

One of the reasons the US may lag behind China, Work said, is that, "as a democracy, I don't ever imagine something like that. The United States just needs to think through how we do this as a nation."[545]

It is important to understand that Chinese President Xi made technological development a priority, and we are seeing progress. In the last couple of years, Beijing made impressive advancements in developments in hypersonic missiles, human gene editing, and quantum satellites. But perhaps the most disconcerting advancement is in the realm of artificial intelligence.

China is serious about harvesting AI benefits ahead of all other nations. China's ministry of industry and information technology launched a three-year development plan for AI in July 2017 that includes goals for technologies like artificial neural network processing chips, intelligent robots, automated vehicles, intelligent drones, and more.[546]

The AI competition is taken seriously at the Pentagon as well. Secretary Mattis supports the Pentagon's Defense Innovation Unit Experimental, located in Silicon Valley, and aims to ensure that the military can quickly adapt and integrate AI-related innovations.

China's rapid progress in AI technologies explains in part why Secretary Mattis made Beijing's rise in technology the centerpiece of his National Defense Strategy. The Chinese AI threat is very, very serious.

Therefore, we must not get cocky, because China is no old Cold War Soviet Union. During the old Cold War, the United States vied with the Soviets for many technical innovations, and generally the US won because it outstripped Russia in the breadth of our critical industries. Now China, like the former Soviet Union, is interested in national security more than the commercial sector—but the difference between China and the former Soviet Union is in size and wealth.

China can match the US in terms of developing emerging technologies because it has a giant population—1.3 billion people—and Beijing incentivizes AI development to push the boundaries. In fact, Beijing is becoming as innovative as Silicon Valley, according to Ms. Elsa Kania, Adjunct Fellow, Technology and National Security Program, Center for a New American Security (CNAS).

Ms. Kania addressed China's initiatives that seek to change military power paradigms in key technologies at the Bio Convergence and Soldier 2050 Conference in March 2018. A few of her findings follow.

President Xi leads China's Central Military-Civil Fusion Development Commission, which set priorities that include intelligent unmanned systems through the implementation of a "whole of nation" strategy. Thus, it is expected, according to Ms. Kania, that by 2030 China will be the world's premier AI innovation center by building upon the successes with AlphaGo [a computer program that plays the board game "Go"] to leverage AI potential in areas such as planning, operational command and control, decision-support tools, war-gaming and brain-computer interfaces controlling unmanned systems. Therefore, according to Ms. Kania, "AI is seen as a potential game-changer by the Chinese, a way to augment perceived military shortcomings."[547]

This surge in Chinese innovation may result in China's First Offset, a true leap forward in technology that integrates quantum satellites with fiber-optic communication networks; human-machine interfaces; drone swarms able to target aircraft carrier task forces; naval rail guns; and quantum computing. Potential areas for AI development include: brain-computer interfaces; military exoskeletons; Chinese superintelligence; and "intelligentized" command decision-making.[548]

Russia is anxious not to be left behind on the AI front. In March 2018, Russia's Foundation for Advanced Studies, the parallel to the Pentagon's DARPA, announced proposals to standardize AI development along four lines of effort: image recognition, speech recognition, control of autonomous military systems, and information support for weapons' life cycle. At the time, Deputy Minister of Defense Nikolai Pankov said Russian military universities were engaged in research and development related to "artificial intelligence, robotics, military cybernetics and other promising areas."[549] Two technologies, one old and one new, further demonstrate the significance of the new technology race undertaken by the world's great powers. The first is the new nuclear arms race, and it has already begun in earnest.

"The new arms race has already begun," said former Defense Secretary William Perry. "It's different in nature than the one during the [old] Cold War, which focused on quantity and two superpowers producing absurd numbers of weapons. Today it is focused on quality and involves several nations instead of just two. The risk for nuclear conflict today is higher than it was during the Cold War."[550]

As outlined earlier, the US led the world in efforts to reduce the role of nuclear weapons, but now it seems as if all that effort was for naught. Nuclear weapons are proliferating once again, and China and Russia are in the lead, with many other nations (United Kingdom, Pakistan, North Korea, India, France, Israel, North Korea, and perhaps others) pursuing nuclear arsenals of their own.

President Trump's 2018 Nuclear Posture Review (NPR) focuses like a laser on the nuclear threat posed by China and Russia. He states: "While the United States has continued to reduce the number and salience of nuclear weapons, others, including Russia and China, have moved in the opposite direction. They have added new types of nuclear capabilities to their arsenals, increased the salience of nuclear forces in their strategies and plans, and engaged in increasingly aggressive behavior."[551]

The NPR states that Russia "is modernizing these [nuclear] weapons as well as its other strategic systems. Even more troubling has been Russia's adoption of military strategies and capabilities that rely on nuclear escalation for their success."[552]

Russia takes a provocative position vis-à-vis nuclear weapons. Moscow over the past decade showed a willingness to use force to alter the map of Europe to its liking, and now it backs its aggressive actions with rhetoric that implicitly threatens first use of nuclear weapons. Further, it already violated its international legal and political commitments to the 1987 Intermediate-Range Nuclear Forces Treaty, the 2002 Open Skies Treaty, and the 1991 Presidential Nuclear Initiatives. You must believe Moscow when it says nuclear first use is now on the table.

The most telling of this group of violations and implicit intentions is Moscow's threat of limited nuclear escalation, what some in the West call Russia's "escalate to de-escalate" doctrine. That concept threatens the limited nuclear first use, expecting that coercive nuclear threats or limited first use could paralyze any Western response—thus quickly ending the conflict favorable to Moscow.

The Russians assert the NPR gets their "escalate-to-de-escalate" approach wrong, however. "I don't think we have lowered our nuclear threshold," said Vladimir Frolov, a foreign policy analyst in Moscow. "In fact, we are moving in the opposite direction, investing in long-range non-nuclear deterrence capabilities to give us more options before nuking you. Even then, I doubt Russia sees limited nuclear use in Europe as a viable option."[553]

In fact, the Russians are disturbed by the perceived lowering of the US threshold for use of nuclear weapons in response to non-nuclear attacks, especially a cyber attack, which Frolov says "is absurd." Pavel Podvig, author of the *Russian Forces* blog on nuclear issues, said, "NPR got the basic Russian strategy wrong." Russia really seeks to project uncertainty as a deterrent, not early use [of nuclear weapons] or escalate to de-escalate.[554]

The NPR confirms for the Russians that their investment in non-strategic nuclear weapons deeply concerns US policy and military officials. Michael Kofman, an expert on the Russian military with the Virginia-based CAN think tank, said, "It is hard to read the NPR and not feel that the United States is desperately afraid of nuclear weapons. Why we would wish to communicate this so loudly is a mystery." He continued, "It suggests their use by Russia would strategically alter the nature of any conflict for Washington, and given that in almost all the cases, stakes for D.C. are likely to be much lower than for Moscow, reinforcing the efficacy of such capabilities will only encourage further Russian investment in dual-capable means of delivery and non-strategic nuclear weapons."[555]

Russia has a large and credible non-strategic nuclear arsenal.

The Center for Strategic and Budgetary Assessments (CSBA) reports in a 2018 white paper that Russia has at least two thousand operationally available, nonstrategic nuclear warheads for delivery by a wide variety of platforms. Further, CSBA indicates the Russians have integrated the use of nuclear weapons in their war plans (doctrine) and periodically threaten to use nuclear weapons "against U.S. forces and allies in Europe," a statement attributed to the General Paul Selva, the Vice Chairman, JCS.[556]

Nebraska Republican Senator Deb Fischer, chair of the Senate Armed Services Strategic Forces Subcommittee, is very much aware of Russia's threat to use non-strategic nuclear weapons. Specifically, she called out Putin's "blatant talks…on what their capabilities are…[especially Russia's] 'escalate to de-escalate' [doctrine, which the senator thinks] shows the need to keep our priority on our nuclear capabilities."[557]

Senator Fischer elaborated on the Russian "escalate to de-escalate" doctrine. She admits "we have no deterrence if that's what the Russians believe, that if they use a low-yield nuclear warhead, that we will back down."[558] That situation contributed incrementally to the US move to acquire a similar capability.

Secretary of Defense Jim Mattis "has made it abundantly clear that we must have these low-yield weapons if we are going to deter the Russians," Fischer said. "They need to understand that we will use the capabilities that we have. That is the only way that you have a deterrence, and that's really the only way you forestall any use of those weapons."[559]

The Pentagon set aside $22.6 million in fiscal year 2019 for two new generation low-yield nuclear warheads for its submarine-launched ballistic missile and a new sea-launched, nuclear-capable cruise missile.[560] It's about time the US take the threat seriously.

On March 1, 2018, President Putin responded to the United States' NPR in his State of the Nation speech touting Russia's new nuclear weapons as "invincible" and boasting they can defeat any missile defense system, a direct slap at the United States' fledgling anti-ballistic missile program. Further, Putin used the speech to show off a video and animations of Russia's new RS-28 Sarmat ICBM and teased his allegedly new nuclear-powered intercontinental cruise missile as well.[561]

President Putin claimed the Sarmat cannot be intercepted and has a greater range than the Soviet-era Voyevoda ICBM, known as "Satan" in the West, which the Sarmat replaces. Further, according to Putin, the Sarmat can strike targets anywhere in the world and carries a larger number of nuclear warheads than "Satan."[562]

Putin said in the speech that Russia developed these new systems because America pulled out of the 1972 Anti-Ballistic Missile Treaty. "You didn't listen to our country then. Listen to us now," Putin said. He boasted these capabilities are "not a bluff."[563]

Bluff or not, the Russians aim to short circuit America's nuclear modernization program much as they did in the old Cold War.

A prominent congressional leader says Moscow is preparing to gin up opposition to America's nuclear modernization plans, much as it did in the old Cold War. "There are well-meaning, very sincere opponents to all of the things [nuclear weapons programs] we talked about today," said Representative Mac Thornberry (R-TX), chairman of the House Armed Services Committee spoke on March 1, 2018 at the Center for Strategic and International Studies. "But after what we've seen the past year or two, we better look under the hood and make sure that the Russians are not fueling our controversies in the way that we have seen them do in recent months."[564]

"I suspect we're going to see much more sophisticated methods coming from Russia to try and influence the decisions that are required to implement this Nuclear Posture Review," Thornberry said. "So it's a big deal."[565]

The chairman put his warning in historical context by citing declassified CIA files that showed Russia funded movements against nuclear weapons in the 1970s and 1980s. "What they [the Russians] did in the '80s was they provided propaganda themes, they provided organizational support, they forged U.S. military documents, they gave them money," Thornberry said. "Add social media and all the new tools that are available that we saw them just use in the last [2016] election—I think we need to be much more alert than we have been on how they are trying to influence our defense decisions."[566]

China is modernizing and expanding its nuclear forces, and like Russia, Beijing pursues new nuclear capabilities focused on particular security objectives, especially its concern about US naval operations in the western Pacific. This new push parallel's Chinese President Xi's statement at the October 2017 19th Party Congress, where he said the

People's Liberation Army will be "fully transformed into a first tier force" by 2050, which includes its nuclear forces.

Beijing's nuclear modernization program raises serious questions about its long-term intentions. Specifically, it developed the DF-41 road-mobile strategic intercontinental ballistic missile, a new multi-warhead version of the DF-5 silo-based ICBM. The PLA Navy also operates JL-2 SLBMs that range 8,000 kilometers and are capable of MIRVs or single nuclear warheads, which gives China the ability to conduct nuclear strikes from sea.[567] Beijing rounds out its nuclear triad of platforms with a new nuclear-capable strategic bomber. Add to this mix a nuclear-capable, DF-26, intermediate-range ballistic missile thought to be quite capable of attacking naval targets such as aircraft carriers.

China, by comparison to the United States and Russia, has a very small nuclear arsenal. Specifically, the US is said to have approximately 6,800 warheads, Russia has approximately 7,000 warheads, and China has an estimated 270 nuclear warheads in its arsenal.[568]

Other ingredients in the nuclear standoff are support facilities for a future war.

It is noteworthy that both China and Russia operate extensive underground facilities (UGF), an aspect of their missile defense architecture. For example, "China's extensive network of hardened UGFs, which has been called the 'Second Great Wall,' consists of approximately 3,000 miles of tunnels. China's aggressive UGF program has also led to speculation that it may be using these facilities, together with other denial and deception practices, to conceal the true size of its nuclear forces," a perspective reported by the Center for Strategic and Budgetary Assessments.[569] The Trump administration concluded in its NPR that the best way to respond to the proliferation of nuclear weapons and related platforms, especially in China and Russia, is to expand and advertise its ability to annihilate our enemies. Therefore, in response to the growing threat, President Trump signed off on a $1.2 trillion plan to overhaul the entire nuclear-weapons complex and to authorize a new nuclear warhead.[570]

"We must modernize and rebuild our nuclear arsenal, hopefully never having to use it, but making it so strong and powerful that it will deter any acts of aggression," Mr. Trump said in his January 30, 2018, State of the Union address. "Perhaps someday in the future there will be a magical moment when the countries of the world will get together to eliminate their nuclear weapons. Unfortunately, we are not there yet."[571]

The new dual Cold War technology race includes a truly new weapons platform with revolutionary overtones—some that potentially harness nuclear warheads as well. Specifically, the US, China, and Russia are all developing hypersonic missile technology, a new capability that is extremely hard to defend against and may well transform the globe's security environment.

Hypersonic missiles are less than a decade away from full deployment. They are both accurate and extremely fast, and promise to change the face of modern warfare by rendering most anti-ballistic missile defense systems ineffective. All three great powers are in a race to be the first to deploy hypersonic missiles.

Hypersonic missiles travel at least five times the speed of sound, flying a path close to the Earth's surface and armed with either a conventional or nuclear warhead. More testing is needed to enable the warhead to endure the stress and extreme temperatures of hypersonic flight and the need to condition the vehicle to changes in flight conditions along its path. These obstacles will be overcome.

Last year, US Air Force Major General Thomas Masiello announced the United States' plans to have an operational prototype of the hypersonic system ready for testing by 2020, after two successful tests of an experimental X-51 hypersonic cruise missile earlier this decade. However, the development of hypersonic capabilities may in fact be accelerated if we are to believe Michael Griffin, the Pentagon's undersecretary of defense for research and engineering.

In late February 2018, Mr. Griffin said hypersonic capabilities have become our "highest technical priority." That's a necessity, Griffin explained, because hypersonic weapons in the hands of our enemies put at risk America's ability to project power.[572]

"When the Chinese can deploy [a] tactical or regional hypersonic system, they hold at risk our carrier battle groups. They hold our entire surface fleet at risk. They hold at risk our forward-deployed forces and land-based forces," Griffin said. That risk explains why appropriations for hypersonics jumped 27 percent in fiscal year 2018 and 136 percent in fiscal year 2019.[573]

What's the rush? Lieutenant General Samuel Greaves, the director of the Missile Defense Agency, said the pace at which Russia and China are "researching, developing, testing, [and] delivering weapons systems" requires his agency to take the hypersonic threat seriously and to hurry the pace of development.[574]

"The hypersonic threat is real and it's coming.... It's just a matter of time before [Russia and China] have fully developed that capability," General Greaves continued. "The concern is that technology leaking into the space that we have to deal with rogue nations like North Korea and Iran."[575]

Other senior uniformed leaders agree with General Greaves. The US Army's Chief of Staff, General Mark Milley, acknowledged the seriousness of the hypersonic threat in congressional testimony in March 2018. "As you rightly point out [Congressman], two significant adversaries, China and Russia, are moving out in the development of hypersonic weapons. We acknowledge that," Milley said.[576]

Navy Admiral Harry Harris, then commander of US Pacific Command (PACOM), testified before the Senate Armed Services Committee that China is "heavily investing in the next wave of military technologies, including hypersonic missiles, advanced space and cyber capabilities, and artificial intelligence."[577]

"If the U.S. does not keep pace, PACOM will struggle to compete with the People's Liberation Army on future battlefields," Harris said. "I believe China's development and research into hypersonic glide weapons is one of those technologies that they're working on that could threaten us significantly."[578]

In 2014, Beijing conducted three hypersonic vehicle tests of its

DF-ZF and another three in 2015, all apparently successful. Meanwhile, Putin said in his March 1, 2018, State of the Nation speech that for the first time, Russia's newest hypersonic weapon, the Kinzhal (named after a type of dagger), would travel at ten times the speed of sound toward "its target like a meteorite." That announcement earned some skeptical comments from experts, but not all defense leaders doubt Putin's achievement.[579] In late January 2018, US Air Force General Paul Selva, the Vice Chairman of the Joint Chiefs of Staff, soberly said, "We have lost our technical advantage in hypersonics." However, he continued, "We haven't lost the hypersonics fight."[580] But we have a lot of catching up to do, according to the director for the DARPA.

DARPA director Steven Walker admits that China has built significant scientific infrastructure to support hypersonic weapons development. "If you look at some of our peer competitors, China being one, the number of facilities that they've built to do hypersonics…surpasses the number we have in this country. It's quickly surpassing it by 2 or 3 times. It is clear that China has made this one of their national priorities. We need to do the same."[581]

Putin elaborated in his speech about his nation's newest hypersonic weapon. "It is the only one of its kind in the world. Its tests have been successfully completed, and, moreover, on December 1st of last year [2017], these systems began their trial service at the airfields of the Southern Military District," Putin said.[582]

"The missile flying at a hypersonic speed, 10 times faster than the speed of sound, can also maneuver at all phases of its flight trajectory, which also allows it to overcome all existing and, I think, prospective anti-aircraft and anti-missile defense systems, delivering nuclear and conventional warheads in a range of over 2,000 kilometers," Putin added.[583]

A week after that speech, the Kremlin trotted out a defense official to declare, "This is no bluff." Russian deputy defense minister Yury Borisov described the Kremlin's hypersonic boost-glide system Avangard as one of the weapons mentioned by President Putin in his State of the Nation speech. Russia has tested hypersonic technologies since the

1980s and, according to Borisov, "Avangard is well-tested" and ready for deployment.[584]

Borisov, who oversees Russian defense procurement, said the development of the Avangard was not without stumbling blocks, but those are overcome and "we already have a contract for the mass production of this system." Further, he indicated that Russia's new heavy intercontinental ballistic missile, the two hundred-ton Sarmat, can launch a hypersonic vehicle such as Avangard as well.[585]

It is noteworthy that on May 4, 2018, Borisov announced his country armed ten of its MiG-31 fighter jets with the new air-launched hypersonic missiles. "It is a cutting-edge weapon, namely a hypersonic long-range missile capable of overcoming air and missile defenses," Borisov claimed. "It is invincible, having serious combat might and potential."[586]

U.S. Air Force General John Hyten, the head of the US Strategic Command, soberly supported the Russian claim: "You should believe Vladimir Putin [and his minions] about everything he said he's working on." The general continued, "Now, the operational status of a lot of those capabilities…that's a different issue. But everything that he's said, I know that Russia's working on, and we watch them very closely."[587]

Meanwhile, the head of the Pentagon's high-technology workshop, DARPA, says the United States is on track for a series of hypersonic prototype tests in the coming years, thanks to a big spending increase in the fiscal year 2019 budget request. However, Steven Walker, DARPA's director, warned that it is time for America to come to grips with the fact that a national push is needed if the US is to keep pace with competitors, an acknowledgement that Russia and China are poised to leapfrog the United States in the technology.[588]

The hypersonic arms race is very important because there is no known defense, especially to protect large naval warships like aircraft carriers, which are giant targets. Likely, this emerging capability will foster the development of directed-energy weapons like high-powered lasers or microwaves, something each nation pursues. Time will tell whether these capabilities become available and viable as the hypersonic arsenals come online.

Further, the introduction of hypersonic weapons to the twenty-first-century battlefield will significantly alter strategic planning by the great powers, such as calculating when to strike the weakest components of the enemy's hypersonic system—most likely the fixed command, control, intelligence, surveillance, and reconnaissance networks. Also, these weapons will alter nuclear warfare planning, because once deployed, militaries will be forced to consider preemptive strikes against countries developing hypersonic capabilities.

The hypersonic weapons race is just one aspect of the broader new space race.

The Pentagon is also preparing for war should China, Russia, and other adversaries attack our satellites and other space systems, according to senior Pentagon officials in congressional testimony.

On March 7, 2018, John Rood, undersecretary of defense for policy, testified before a House subcommittee that the administration's new defense policy calls for conducting military operations in response to space attacks, mainly by China and Russia. Rood said our space-based systems are essential for "our prosperity, security, and way of life."[589]

Secretary Rood said the Pentagon requested $12.5 billion for 2019 to build up a "more resilient defendable space architecture." Time is not on our side, according to the Joint Staff intelligence directorate, which warned in early 2018 that China and Russia will have fully developed space attack weapons in place by 2020 that will threaten all US satellites in low-Earth orbit.[590]

There are more than 780 orbiting satellites operated by 43 nations currently in space and vulnerable to attack. Keep in mind that satellites form the backbone of the US military's ability to conduct worldwide combined arms warfare and are integral to a modern society for many reasons, such as e-commerce and global communications.

Space weapons likely being developed by China, Russia, and the United States include advanced missile defense interceptors for attacking satellites, cyber warfare capabilities to disrupt or destroy anti-satellite and space weapons systems, and lasers, electronic jammers, and small satellites with robotic arms capable of grabbing or crushing satellites, something China already tested.

A study by the Secure World Foundation claims China and Russia are focusing more on space weapons that neutralize others' satellites rather than destroying payloads in orbit. The study claims it is more likely that future attacks will come in the form of electronic warfare jamming to disable space-based platforms, a view expressed by Brian Weeden, a former US Air Force officer and one of the authors of the study, titled *Global Counterspace Capabilities: An Open Source Assessment.*[591]

Mr. Weeden states: "The bad news is I think there is strong evidence we're seeing more development and testing of counterspace technologies than any time since probably the height of the Cold War." He continued, "We're seeing development of broad range, everything from kinetic destructive technologies to jamming and hacking but the operational use so far seems to be limited to the jamming and hacking types."[592]

China and Russia are big players in the space realm, a "worrisome combination of trends," according to Weeden. For example, the report states that Chinese capabilities against satellites in low-Earth orbit "is likely mature and may be operationally fielded on mobile launchers within the next few years." Further, Russia is likely building up its capabilities on the back of Cold War efforts and has invested heavily in electronic warfare capabilities, and "can likely jam communications satellites uplinks over a wide area from fixed ground stations facilities."[593]

Evidently, the United States believes the space war has already begun in earnest. Air Force General John Hyten, commander of the Omaha-based Strategic Command, testified that the Pentagon and National Reconnaissance Office are implementing a "space warfighting construct…[which is] needed to prevail in a conflict that extends into space." Further, there already exists the National Space Defense Center, located at Schriever Air Force Base, Colorado, which runs around the clock to warn of space attacks.[594]

No wonder, given the above rumblings and public statements about weaponizing space, that President Trump said in March 2018 that he would change the course of United States space policy. Mr. Trump said his National Security Strategy "recognizes that space is a war-fighting domain, just like land, air and sea" and therefore he is considering "a space force" that would be the equivalent of the Air Force, Army, and Navy.[595]

The arms and technology battleground will be one of the most important in the new dual Cold War simply because national security depends on its outcome. No doubt it will be incredibly expensive, but there is no acceptable alternative.

Conclusion

The new dual Cold War will be fought on at least four battlegrounds, which will impact every human being in some way. The ideological battleground will influence every aspect of culture from our social media, entertainment, public discourse, education, and public policy, and perhaps cast into doubt the very reliability of our democratic processes. The cyber domain provides great advantages, but that battleground imposes restrictions on our privacy, our safety, and our opportunities, and could lead to untold devastation. The economic battleground will potentially impact every wallet as the great powers compete for talent, jobs, wages, profits, and more. Finally, the arms and technology battleground is the most frightening perhaps because it promises great advancement but also threatens our very survival.

CHAPTER SIX

An American Response to the New Dual Cold War

Will America's brewing confrontation with the "Alliance of Evil"—Russia and China—become the catalyst that ushers in the final prophetic global war? The answer to that question may depend on the United States government's response to the new dual Cold War.

"Our very survival is at the stake," warns Dr. Marek Jan Chodakiewicz with the Washington, DC,-based Institute of World Politics. We must not procrastinate, and "if we do not start addressing certain issues now, including the challenges posed by Russia and China, we will reach a point where there will be nothing left but surrender or war," said Chodakiewicz.[596]

America and her allies must make a pragmatic assessment of their adversaries in the new dual Cold War and then act. Clearly the friction is real, with Russia saber-rattling—economically by using gas supplies as a geopolitical weapon and militarily by annexing Crimea, sparking an insurgency in Ukraine and aiding the Syrian dictator by pretending to launch military operations against Islamist radicals. China is doing much the same by laying claim to territorial waters in the South China Sea, building a global-capable blue-water navy, buying up port facilities across the world, and beginning to build military facilities on multiple continents. Secretary of Defense Mattis poked his imaginary finger in Beijing's chest when he said: "China has shredded the trust of nations in the region [regarding China's bullying in the South China Sea].... the point behind a rules-based international order—what those words mean—is that we all play by the rules."[597]

However, there is a caution here, because playing by the rules is subjective. America long ago shredded the trust of our neighbors as well. Yes, we Americans enjoy lecturing the Chinese and Russians to behave "more like us" by "maintaining the rules-based international order." That's a view that may come back to haunt us, because too often in history, America acted as a bully—such as in our 1903 seizure of Panama, a Colombia dependency at the time, to build the Panama Canal. Later, President Theodore Roosevelt threatened war with Canada over the borders of the "fat tail" of Alaska. He got his way only after he rigged an international tribunal's decision by threatening war with Britain if the British member of the court failed to vote in the United States' favor.[598]

President Roosevelt was quite the terror at the time. He boldly assumed in his 1904 State of the Union address responsibility for America's "geopolitical neighborhood," and promised to exercise "international police power," which over the subsequent thirty years resulted in twenty-one US troop deployments throughout Latin America under the guise of the 1832 Monroe Doctrine.

Do we really want China and Russia to be "more like us" and therefore seize, say, Hawaii or Alaska much as Russia did Crimea in 2014 and China did the islets in the South China Sea over the past decade? I don't think so.

Insisting that our new dual Cold War adversaries act "more like us" ignores history, and the duo's public goals that are starkly different from the vision outlined in President Trump's National Security Strategy. Therefore, this new era must become a learning moment for the West to avoid unnecessary confrontations, while charting a path that wins the new dual Cold War without a shot being fired.

An important aspect of this new "learning moment" must be to avoid acting as we once did under the progressive internationalist leadership of Rough Rider Teddy Roosevelt (Spanish-American War) and President Wilson (Russian Revolution) who ran roughshod over other countries without ample justification. Such behavior will be incredibly dangerous given our adversaries, but this should not become an excuse to overlook China and Russia's ruthless behavior either.

The former Soviet Union had a horrendous war crimes record from 1919 to 1991, which included acts by the Red Army and the Narodnyy Komissariat Vnutrennikh Del's (NKVD) Internal Troops. The worst came during the rule of Soviet leader Joseph Stalin, who pursued a policy known as Red Terror, a license for Soviet troops to do whatever they wanted with prisoners of war and civilians. The Red Army's well-documented record of atrocities includes summary executions, mass murder of prisoners, and millions of rapes by Soviet troops.

China has a history of massive violence against its own people as well. "Systematic violence and calculated terror [is] designed to instill fear and intimidation into anybody who comes into contact with the Communist Party of China," said Frank Dikotter, a professor at the University of Hong Kong.[599]

The Chinese Communist Party's record of atrocities is long, sobering, and in some cases ongoing—such as forced organ harvesting. The world should also remember the massacre by soldiers of protesting students in Beijing's Tiananmen Square as well as in twenty other Chinese cities at the time.

An estimated forty-five million Chinese died in China's so-called Great Famine, the result of the failure of Mao's Great Leap Forward, which ruined the country's economy. Further, Mao Zedong's so-called Cultural Revolution began in 1966, which got rid of perceived political enemies who opposed his Great Leap Forward, a campaign that cost tens of millions of other lives.

All three countries—the US, Russia, and China—have past disgraceful aspects to their histories. Therefore, we must deal with great care going forward.

Today, China and Russia openly challenge America's predominance, and any misunderstanding about our actions and intentions could lead to a deadly trap, says Graham Allison, a professor at the John F. Kennedy School of Government at Harvard. Professor Allison cited the ancient Greek historian Thucydides, who explained, "It was the rise of Athens and the fear that this instilled in Sparta that made war inevitable."[600]

The Athenian emissary told the Spartans, "It has always been the law that the weaker should be subject to the stronger." They fought and it ruined both, which came to be called "Thucydides' trap." A similar situation is described in chapter 2 when Napoleon pursued the Russians to his ruin and the loss of four hundred thousand soldiers. That need not be the outcome of the new dual Cold War.

President Donald Trump ought to respond to the challenges of an emerging dual Cold War to avoid the "Thucydides trap" by taking a lesson from President Ronald Reagan's playbook. Reagan executed a "principled realism" strategy when dealing with his old Cold War adversary, the former Soviet Union, a strategy that is appropriate for the twenty-first century Alliance of Evil as well.

A "principled realism" strategy combines the moral values of idealism and the power politics of realism. It is rightly skeptical of global institutions like the United Nations, believes in domestic politics shaping global order, and bases foreign policies on American interests. After all, Reagan's "principled realism" strategy "sought to advance the cause of human freedom by supporting democratic governments while undermining expansionistic communistic regimes." The Reagan Doctrine was decisive in averting a catastrophic conflict and led to the downfall of the former Soviet Union, thus ending the old Cold War without a shot, and it can work once again.[601]

So far, Mr. Trump is evidencing a "principled realism" strategy in terms of action and declaration in his National Security Strategy. One Trump official told reporters, "This [National Security Strategy released in December 2017] advances what I would call a principled realism." The official added that the global balance of power has shifted away from the United States. "This new strategy presents a plan of how America can regain momentum to reverse many of these trends."[602]

Trump's strategy properly focuses on four organizing principles consistent with the Reagan Doctrine: protecting the American homeland, protecting American prosperity, preserving peace through strength, and advancing US influence. The question we should ask is: Will the Trump administration follow through with its strategy, and if so, will it help America avoid Thucydides' trap?

This chapter begins by establishing Mr. Trump's vision for America as outlined in his National Security Strategy, and within the context of the four dual Cold War battlegrounds identified in chapter 5: ideology, cyber, economy, and arms and technology.

Subsequently, the chapter applies the classic elements of national power within those four battlegrounds using Mr. Trump's recommended "priority actions" as a guide to win the challenging new dual Cold War by applying a "principled realism" strategy.

Trump's "Principled Realism" Strategy

What is President Trump's philosophy of international relations and why does it matter?

In early 2017, Sebastian Gorka, a then White House national security aide, said on *Fox News*: "Our foreign policy has been a disaster. We've neglected and abandoned our allies. We've emboldened our enemies. The message I have—it's a very simple one. It's a bumper sticker…the era of the Pajama Boy is over January 20th [Trump's inauguration day] and the alpha males are back."[603]

Those are naïve words, according to former Obama international policy experts. "Tough talk is quite easy. Bullying is quite easy," says Wendy Sherman, who served as the chief negotiator for President Obama's Iran nuclear deal. "Getting something done in the world is quite complicated," Sherman said. She also said that without the Iran deal, "you'd probably be at war." Today Ms. Sherman is a senior counselor at the Albright Stonebridge Group and a senior fellow at Harvard Kennedy School's Belfer Center for Science and International Affairs.[604]

"One of the lessons for the alpha males," adds Michele Flournoy, "is to actually start with the facts." Ms. Flournoy was a top policy official in Obama's Pentagon and was considered the leading choice to become the first woman secretary of defense had Hillary Clinton won the 2016 presidential election.[605]

Ms. Flournoy explained her "alpha male" and "facts" statements:

> I can tell you as someone who was responsible for oversight of military planning in the Pentagon, had Wendy [Sherman] failed and the negotiations failed, the only option left on the table would have been to use military force to take out that [Iranian nuclear] program and we would have gone [and done that]. That would have started a third war in the broader Middle East.... So let's be fact-based and realistic about the consequences of the policy choices that were made.... Tough talk is easy, but actually advancing American interests in a way that's smart is a lot harder.

Ms. Flournoy currently serves as a senior fellow at Harvard's Belfer Center for Science and International Affairs alongside Ms. Sherman.[606]

Mr. Trump's foreign policy is more than just tough talk, and it is facts based. We know his foreign policy preferences from his 2016 campaign speeches. He said in those speeches that he wants to end globalization because of the damage being done to the American economy. He promised to be more aggressive against Islamic terrorists and to confront China, Iran, and North Korea. He also promised to work with the wily Russians and to get the grand bargain done between the Israelis and the Palestinians. That's an incredibly ambitious foreign policy agenda.

Gorka's "alpha male" comment suggested that Trump's foreign policy would be a macho foreign policy, whereby tough guys will take the reins from wimpy Obama Democrats. In fact, scholar Robert Kagan more delicately communicated the same view. Mr. Kagan is a senior fellow at the left-leaning Brookings Institution and a member of the progressive Council on Foreign Relations.

Kagan wrote that "Americans are from Mars [male-like, or alpha male-like] and Europeans are from Venus [female-like, wimpy]." The same perspective is held by many Americans who characterize Republicans as more militarized, a Mars-minded party in terms of national security, while Democrats tend to be the more diplomacy minded, and a Venus party [female-like].

What's clear about Mr. Trump from his first year plus in office is that he built his "Mars-like" national security cabinet around uniformed military officers (active and retired) and likes tough, authoritarian, strongmen leaders like Russia's Putin, China's Xi, and Abdel-Fattah el-Sisi, a former army general and the current president of Egypt.

So what does that tell us about President Trump's international relations philosophy and how he might translate his views into action regarding the new dual Cold War? It tells us that Mr. Trump is an advocate of "principled realism," one of the many schools of international relations, much like former President Ronald Reagan.

It was very appropriate that President Trump selected Washington's Ronald Reagan Building and International Trade Center to announce his first National Security Strategy (NSS) in December 2017. After all, President Reagan didn't pull punches when he demonstrated great courage by describing the former Soviet Union as an "evil empire," and then he traveled to the Iron Curtain that dissected Berlin, Germany, to call on then-Soviet President Gorbachev to "tear down this wall."

President Trump was bold as well in announcing his 2017 security strategy when he distinguished between "those who value human dignity and freedom and those who oppress individuals and enforce uniformity." Trump rightly placed China and Russia in the category of those who "oppress individuals," a declaration as bold as Reagan calling the former Soviet Union an "evil empire."

Trump also left no ambiguity in his NSS about his view of American exceptionalism. "Our founding principles," Trump declared, "have made the United States among the greatest forces for good in the world." That view is similar to Reagan's "peace through strength," an endorsement of the principle of peace and international prosperity guaranteed by strong, sovereign nations that pursue self interests. That philosophy is contrasted to President Obama's approach, which a Center for American Greatness author described: "In recent years, America has more and more abandoned that pursuit [American exceptionalism] as other countries sought to capitalize on our bureaucratic paralysis and regulatory suffocation."[607]

Mr. Trump's actions to date and his statements in the NSS reflect a clear representation of a "principled realism" international relations philosophy. He explained and called out that philosophy in the NSS, "An America first national security strategy is based on American principles, a clear-eyed assessment of U.S. interests, and a determination to tackle the challenges that we face. It is a strategy of principled realism that is guided by outcomes, not ideology."

Briefly, there are three schools of international relations philosophy: realism, idealism, and a mix of realism and idealism. Realism, which reflects a number of theories, is fundamentally the view that nation-states are motivated by the desire for military and economic power, not ideals. This view is synonymous with power politics.

Idealism is a progressive belief evidenced by the likes of Presidents Theodore Roosevelt, Woodrow Wilson, Franklin Roosevelt, and Barack Obama. Donald Markwell explains idealism in his 2006 book, *John Maynard Keynes and International Relations: Economic Paths to War and Peace*:

> The distinctive characteristic of…[idealism] was their belief in progress: the belief, in particular, that the system of international relations that had given rise to the first world war was capable of being transformed into a fundamentally more peaceful and just world order; that under the impact of the awakening of democracy, the growth of "the international mind", the development

of the league of nations, the good works of men of peace or the enlightenment spread by their own teaching, it was in fact being transformed; and that their responsibility as students of international relations was to assist this march of progress to overcome the ignorance, the prejudices, the ill-will, and the sinister interests that stood in this way.[608]

"Principled realism," Trump's international relations philosophy, combines the moral values of idealism and the power politics of realism. It is skeptical of global institutions like the United Nations and believes in domestic politics to help shape global order. It also assumes that the rule of law, constitutional government (nation-state sovereignty), and human rights should influence a nation's foreign policy.

Trump is following Reagan's foreign policy example whereby he often identified with "principled realism" by advancing the cause of human freedom to support democratic governments while opposing hegemonic communist regimes like the Soviet Union.

US Army Lieutenant General H. R. McMaster, then President Trump's national security adviser, reminded an audience at the Reagan National Defense Forum on December 2, 2017, that when "Reagan took office in 1981, many believed that Washington was not serving the American people well. Our confidence at home and our influence abroad had waned significantly over the past decade. The Soviet Union appeared to be on the rise, and America, it seemed, was in decline."[609]

He continued:

President Reagan ushered in a dramatic rethinking of America's role in the world and a dramatic renewal of American confidence. America would not only triumph in the Cold War and beyond, but also reach new heights of influence and prosperity. He described "a future of growth, opportunity, and security, anchored by the values of a people who are confident, compassionate, and whose heart is good."[610]

General McMaster told the Reagan Forum: "We are at a similar crossroads [today]. Revisionist powers—China and Russia—are subverting the post WWII political, economic, and security order to advance their own interests at our expense and at the expense of our allies."[611]

"These national security challenges…require a dramatic rethinking of American foreign policy from the previous decades," McMaster said. Then he reminded the audience that Reagan understood the need to rethink our policy. So, "in 1983, he [Reagan] signed National Security Decision Directive 75, which argued that containing and reversing Soviet influence required 'competing effectively on a sustained basis…in all international arenas.'"[612]

That's what President Trump has done with his 2017 National Security Strategy. So what does Mr. Trump call for in his strategy across the four battlegrounds of the new dual Cold War? I will identify the "what" Mr. Trump calls for and then I will outline the "elements" of national power that Mr. Trump should use to fight the new dual Cold War on the four battlegrounds identified in the previous chapter.

Trump's Call for Action on the Four Cold War Battlegrounds

President Trump indicates that the central challenge in the new dual Cold War is China and Russia's shared aim to shape the world to their authoritarian model—"gaining veto authority over other nations' economic, diplomatic [ideological], and security decisions."[613]

Just what is Mr. Trump's strategic response to China and Russia's authoritarian vision, and especially what is that vision within the context of each of the four Cold War battlegrounds outlined in chapter 5?

Ideological Battleground

First, Mr. Trump recognizes there is an ideological battleground in the dual Cold War. H. R. McMaster explained that we must understand "the values that define our nation and who we are. President Reagan described America as a 'shining city upon a hill,' and boldly spoke truth about the sufferings of people living under fear and oppression." Mr. Trump faces a similar values fight with China and Russia (the ideological battle) head-on, which began early in his administration with a number of overseas trips.

Mr. Trump understands that we are in an ideological war, as evidenced by his bold statements to foreign audiences. He told the Polish people in July 2017: "We value the dignity of every human life, protect the rights of every person, and share the hope of every soul to live in freedom." Earlier that spring, the president traveled to Riyadh, Saudi Arabia, where he chastised those who fail to control Islamic terrorists, and then he visited South Korea in November, where he rhetorically referenced the oppressive North Korean regime by stating that rogue regime "imprison[s] [its] people under the banner of tyranny, fascism, and oppression."

The president's "principled realism" international relations philosophy also showed its colors when Mr. Trump responded to the Syrian dictator's use of the most heinous (chemical) weapons on Earth to commit mass murder of innocent civilians. (More than eighty-nine people were killed on April 4, 2017, by Syrian chemical weapons in the town of Khan Sheikhoun.[614]) Mr. Trump responded to that atrocity within days by attacking Syrian President Bashar al-Assad's stronghold with a phalanx of cruise missiles, a clear message that the regime's actions will not be tolerated and a persuasive warning to other rogues like those in Tehran, Iran.[615]

President Trump did much the same again on April 14, 2018, by launching with our allies France and the United Kingdom 105 precision munitions destroying three fixed suspected chemical weapons facilities in Syria exactly a week after the Damascus regime killed fifty and wounded another five hundred innocent civilians with a suspected mixture of chemical weapons.

It is clear that Mr. Trump is a man of action, as these strikes demonstrate, and he plans to respond to the new dual Cold War's ideological battleground against Russia and China as outlined in his National Security Strategy just as boldly.

The NSS states:

> America's competitors [China and Russia] weaponized information to attack the values and institutions that underpin free societies, while shielding them from outside information. They exploit marketing techniques to target individuals based upon their activities, interests, opinions, and values. They disseminate misinformation and propaganda.

Mr. Trump elaborates on that view when he states that China "combines data and the use of AI [artificial intelligence] to rate the loyalty of its citizens to the state and uses these ratings to determine jobs and more." Russia, according to the NSS, is perhaps worse than China in that it "uses information operations as part of its offensive cyber efforts to influence public opinion across the globe. Its influence of [political] campaigns blends covert intelligence operations and false online personas with state-funded media, third-party intermediaries, and paid social media users or 'trolls.'"

Past American efforts to counter such ideological activities have been "tepid and fragmented," states the NSS. That will change under Mr. Trump's administration, because "we treat people equally and value and uphold the rule of law. We have a democratic system that allows the best ideas to flourish."

"There can be no moral equivalency between nations that uphold the rule of law, empower women, and respect individual rights and those that brutalize and suppress their people [like China and Russia]," states the NSS. "Through our words and deeds, America demonstrates a positive alternative to political and religious despotism."

Mr. Trump calls for the US to "lead and engage in the multinational arrangements that shape many of the rules that affect U.S. interests and values. A competition for influence exists in these institutions [like the

United Nations]." We will participate in these institutions while advancing American interests and values, explained Mr. Trump's NSS.

"Authoritarian actors [China and Russia] have long recognized the power of multilateral bodies and have used them to advance their interests and limit the freedom of their own citizens," states the NSS. That is why the United States must not totally abandon those bodies to our adversaries, which present "opportunities to shape developments that are positive for the United States will be lost."

The NSS provides a clear call to promote American interests and values through all mechanisms of government, something we will examine in the next section of this chapter. The ideological fight is a critical battle.

Cyber Battleground

Second, the cyber battleground is at the top of many nations' security agenda, and for good reason. Cyber, as addressed in the previous chapter, threatens our nuclear deterrence, our infrastructure, our economy, and our form of government—not to mention our individual identities. The threat comes from nations like China and Russia, but also from rogue regimes like North Korea and Iran, as well as from individuals who harvest their income from exploiting others via cyberspace.

The NSS states: "America's response to the challenges and opportunities of the cyber era will determine our future prosperity and security." Cyberspace, states the NSS, provides cyber actors the ability to "wage campaigns against American political, economic, and security interests without ever physically crossing our borders."

This low cost and deniable aggressive weapon has done and threatens to "seriously damage or disrupt critical infrastructure, cripple American businesses, weaken our federal networks, and attack the tools and devices that Americans use every day to communicate and conduct business." Further, it provides our enemies the means to "disrupt military command and control, banking and financial operations, the electrical grid, and means of communication."

Mr. Trump states in the NSS that the government and the private sector "must design systems that incorporate prevention, protection, and resiliency from the state, not as an afterthought." Then he promises to do "so in a way that respects free markets, private competition, and the limited but important role of government in enforcing the rule of law. As we build the next generation of digital infrastructure, we have an opportunity to put our experience into practice."

"The Internet is an American invention," states the NSS, "and it should reflect our values as it continues to transform the future for all nations and all generations. A strong, defensible cyber infrastructure fosters economic growth, protects our liberties, and advances our national security."

Cyberspace is a battleground that if left unchecked can frustrate freedom-loving nations because it grants our adversaries China and Russia the veil of secrecy from which they attack to do us harm while denying any culpability. Of course, our sophisticated cyber-detection capabilities often know the sources of these attacks, and in the future all freedom-loving nations led by the US must not tolerate such behavior that threatens our way of life. Mr. Trump promises we will act against such misbehavior.

Economic Battleground

Third, the economic battleground impacts every citizen and is the most contested of the four. China uses predatory economics to intimidate its neighbors while Russia pursues veto power over the economic decisions of its neighbors, such as whether they can join the European Union, an economic union of twenty-eight nations.

The Trump NSS states that "economic security is national security," an assertion that puts America's economic competitiveness front and center. It explains that a "strong economy protects the American people, supports our way of life, and sustains American power."

The president states: "American workers thrive when they are free to innovate, develop and access our abundant natural resources, and operate in markets free from excessive regulations and unfair foreign trade practices." However, he says that China and Russia challenge American prosperity by seeking to make our economy and those of our allies "less free and less fair," the economic battleground in the dual Cold War is therefore exposed.

Mr. Trump promises to "rejuvenate" the American economy by insisting "upon reciprocal economic relationships to address trade imbalances [China being the most notable culprit]." Then he states the US will preserve "our lead in research and technology and protect our economy from competitors who unfairly acquire our intellectual property [IP]," a clear reference to China which is the primary IP stealing culprit. Further, Mr. Trump indicates that "we will embrace America's energy dominance because, unleashing abundant energy resources stimulates our economy."

The Trump NSS promises to "rejuvenate the American economy" by insisting "upon fair and reciprocal economic relationships to address trade imbalances." He explains that for decades our factories, companies, and jobs moved overseas. Clearly, the 2008 global financial crisis, our overregulation of businesses at home, and our former hefty corporate tax regime produced anemic growth that pushed up our trade deficit, which is also attributed in part to unfair trading practices by China.

Mr. Trump also promises to reverse this economic bad news. The economic system "must be reformed to help American workers prosper, protect our innovation, and reflect the principles upon which that system was founded." He outlines initiatives necessary to fix the economic system to benefit the American economy, which are outlined in the following section of this chapter.

The NSS insists that "trading partners and international institutions can do more to address trade imbalances and adhere to and enforce the rules of the order." The document makes reference to economic trading systems that invited participants into membership that "did not share our values, in the hopes that these states would liberalize their economic and political practices and provide commensurate benefits to the United

States." That's an obvious reference to the United States' decision to welcome China into the World Trade Organization (WTO) and then, as the NSS states, countries like China "distorted and undermined key economic institutions [read "WTO"] without undertaking significant reform of their economies and politics."

The NSS explains that, for decades, the US "has allowed unfair trading practices to grow: …dumping, discriminatory non-tariff barriers, forced technology transfers, non-economic capacity, industrial subsidies, and other support from governments and state-owned enterprises to gain economic advantages." Once again, China is guilty of every one of these unfair trading practices, and Mr. Trump promises he will not allow that to continue.

"We will compete with like-minded states in the economic domain—particularly where trade imbalances exist—while recognizing that competition is healthy when nations share values and builds fair and reciprocal relationships." Of course this is not a description of China. However, and this applies to Beijing as well, the US "will pursue enforcement actions when countries violate the rules to gain unfair advantage. The United States will engage industrialized democracies and other likeminded states to defend against economic aggression, in all its forms, that threatens our common prosperity and security."

Mr. Trump rightly states: "Economic security is national security." He outlines in the NSS an economic call to action to return economic vitality to America while sanctioning China for its underhanded practices. This is a critical fight in the new dual Cold War and Mr. Trump is proving to be rather adept "at confronting China and getting within its decision making cycle," according to Dr. Christopher Lew, a Chinese scholar and author of two books on China.[616]

Arms & Technology Battleground

Fourth, the arms and technology battleground is old and new. It is old because the United States and the Soviet Union fought the nuclear arms race until that contest economically bankrupted Moscow, which contributed to the demise of the former communist regime. It is new because there are now three great powers competing for mind-blowing modern technologies and Star Wars-like arms that could give the nation that first perfects some of these sophisticated weapon technologies a decisive edge over the other nations.

Let there be no doubt that all three great powers—the United States, Russia, and China—understand what's at stake and are pursuing victory at all cost.

Chinese President Xi is readying his military for a greater global role by virtue of sustained, significant investment to improve the self-sufficiency and global operational range of his forces. He launched an ambitious modernization plan, which includes the creation of an equivalent to the US DARPA (the agency responsible for most of the US military's emerging technologies), which President Xi intends to help make his armed forces into "world-class forces" by midcentury—especially in the realms of space, cyber, and artificial intelligence.

Russia is a bit heady in regard to new arms and high technology as well. After all, a December 2017 poll found that three in four Russians believe their country is a great power, a significant increase from 31 percent in 1999.[617] That view is not just attributable to Putin's bluster, but to the Russian military success in Crimea, Ukraine, and the disinformation campaigns against France and the United States, as well as Moscow's Syrian incursion.

Russia spent very little money joining the Syrian civil war, and to most everyone's surprise, Moscow helped reverse the direction of that conflict, preserving President Bashir al-Assad's rogue regime, and reestablished Russia in the Middle East after abandoning the region at the end of the old Cold War.

The finesse demonstrated in such high-stakes operations should give the US pause as it considers Russia's military modernization and arms technology campaign. Even though Moscow has the GDP ($1283.20 trillion in 2017) of Spain, it continues to make substantial and cutting-edge military technological advances, in some cases equaling American capabilities.[618]

President Trump's NSS soberly warns that "Russia challenge[s] American power, influence, and interests, attempting to erode American security and prosperity." Further, that tension is not going away. Russian foreign minister Sergey Lavrov said what Russia seeks is a "post-West world order."[619] Specifically, Russia and the West will continue to clash over Moscow's quest for a "sphere of control in its neighborhood," an outcome neither the US nor NATO seems willing to accept. Further, Andrey Kortunov, director general of the Russian International Affairs Council, explained: "At this stage, there are not many compelling reasons for the Kremlin to reconsider its fundamental approaches to the West.... the current status quo is perceived as not perfect, but generally acceptable."[620]

Evidently, a significant aspect of what's acceptable about the new dual Cold War is the new arms race. All three great powers are modernizing their arsenals, and old arms-control agreements are fraying.

Moscow is pursuing "a broad range of existing and new versions of nuclear weapons [which] suggests that the real doctrine goes beyond basic deterrence toward regional war-fighting strategies—or even weapons aimed at bluntly causing terror."[621] Meanwhile, the US intends to spend almost $1.2 trillion on modernizing its nuclear forces over the next thirty years, and China is also investing in new nuclear capabilities. These advances leave in their wake past arms-control agreements.

Landmark arms-control treaties are unraveling beginning with the 1987 Intermediate-Range Nuclear Forces (INF) treaty, which is virtually dead in the water because of confirmed and repeated Russian violations. The New Strategic Arms Reduction Treaty (START), which years ago reduced the number of US and Russian deployed nuclear warheads, expires in 2021 and few anticipate it will be renewed. Specifically, as Steven Pifer, a Brookings Institution Fellow, said: "There is a prospect that, in 2021, for the first time in five decades, no negotiated agreements will be regulating the U.S.-Russian nuclear arms relationship."[622]

The nuclear arms treaties may be dead, but we still rely on our arsenal for strategic security. The NSS states that "Nuclear weapons have served a vital purpose in America's National Security Strategy for the past 70 years." It admits that "following the Cold War, the United States reduced investments in our nuclear enterprise and reduced the role of nuclear weapons in our strategy." Then it reminds the reader: "At the same time, however, nuclear-armed adversaries [read "China and Russia"] have expanded their arsenals and range of delivery systems. The United States must maintain the credible deterrence and assurance capabilities provided by our nuclear triad and by U.S. theater nuclear capabilities deployed abroad."

"Significant investment," as indicated above and stated by the NSS, "is needed to maintain a U.S. nuclear arsenal and infrastructure that is able to meet national security threats over the coming decades."

The new arms race includes additional key capabilities other than nuclear warheads. Specifically, the NSS indicates that the US "must retain overmatch—the combination of capabilities in sufficient scale to prevent enemy success and to ensure that America's sons and daughters will never be in a fair fight." But to retain military overmatch, the United States must be innovative, restore costly readiness for the possibility of major war, and grow the size of the force to sufficient scale.

Retaining military overmatch, according to the NSS, means the US needs a healthy defense industrial base in order to surge in response to an emergency. Unfortunately, as the NSS states, manufacturing over the last two decades has had a negative impact on these capabilities and threatens to undermine America's ability to meet its national security requirements. The United States must provide the necessary support to rebuild a vibrant domestic manufacturing sector, a solid defense industrial base.

The space race is back on as well. The NSS maintains that the US will ensure freedom of action in space because our communications, financial networks, military and intelligence systems, weather monitoring, and navigation of all types depend on the space domain. Specifically, according to DIA Director General Ashley, "Moscow has concluded that gaining and maintaining supremacy in space will have a decisive impact on the outcome of future conflicts and is developing counterspace systems to hold U.S. space assets at risk."[623]

Meanwhile, China has developed space-based systems as central to its modern warfare doctrine. The PLA has significant military space capabilities for intelligence, surveillance, reconnaissance, communications, navigation, meteorology, human space flight, and perhaps even interplanetary exploration.

Beijing continues to develop a variety of counter-space capabilities to prevent others' use of space-based assets during a conflict. The NSS states: "Others believe that the ability to attack space assets offers an asymmetric advantage and as a result, are pursuing a range of anti-satellite (ASAT) weapons," a capability China successfully tested.

"The United States considers unfettered access to and freedom to operate in space to be a vital interest," states the NSS. "Any harmful interference with or an attack upon critical components of our space architecture that directly affects this vital U.S. interest will be met with a deliberate response at a time, place, manner, and domain of our choosing." Count on both China and Russia being ready and able to attack our space architecture.

As if the above arms race isn't bad enough, the United States faces a very serious threat regarding cutting-edge technologies. The NSS promises to "prioritize emerging technologies critical to economic growth and security, such as data science, encryption, autonomous technologies [robots], gene editing, new materials, nanotechnology, advanced computing technologies, and artificial intelligence." China is very close to, if not leading, the US in these technologies, which presents a very serious challenge.

To win the new dual Cold War, America must renew its competitive advantages because "we face simultaneous threats from different actors across multiple arenas—all accelerated by technology." We can no longer afford to be complacent.

Starting in the 1990s, the United States became strategically complacent, assuming that "our military superiority was guaranteed and that a
democratic peace was inevitable." Time has proven that view to be dangerously naïve. "Instead of building military capacity, as threats to our national
security increased, the United States dramatically cut the size of our military
to the lowest levels since 1940" and we took a decade long "procurement
holiday," which has seriously eroded America's military dominance.

We also incorrectly assumed that our technological edge would
compensate for our reduced capacity. Meanwhile, China and Russia
"began to reassert their influence regionally and globally." They also
heavily invested in arms technologies and fielded military capabilities
specifically designed to "deny America access in times of crisis and to
contest our ability to operate freely in critical commercial zones during
peacetime. In short, they are contesting our geopolitical advantages and
trying to change the international order in their favor."

Yes, the new dual Cold War is far more complex than the old Cold
War. Our "adversaries studied the American way of war and began
investing in capabilities that targeted our strengths and sought to exploit
perceived weaknesses," states the NSS. They did their homework, and
now China and Russia have seriously eroded our previous advantages in
all domains.

The United States must recover its lost advantages and prepare for
a tête-à-tête competition with China and Russia. We must never forget
again that we are engaged in "continuous competition," and "our adversaries will not fight us on our terms."

The NSS promises:

We will raise our competitive game to meet that challenge, to
protect American interests, and to advance our values. Our
diplomatic, intelligence, military, and economic agencies have
not kept pace with the changes in the character of competition.
America's military must be prepared to operate across a full spec-
trum of conflict, across multiple domains at once. To meet these

challenges we must also upgrade our political and economic instruments to operate across these environments.

A Campaign Plan to Win the New Dual Cold War

I began this chapter by outlining President Trump's National Security Strategy, which addresses the four must-win dual Cold War fights first identified in chapter 5. Now I will introduce how Mr. Trump's strategy can use a military-style campaign-plan approach to harness US government agencies and departments, armed with the elements of national power, to win the new dual Cold War.

My aim is to make this war a bloodless victory, much like the old Cold War, and hopefully without the proxy fights like Vietnam and Korea. That is a tall order but not impossible.

Let me explain my perspective. I am a security cooperation expert at the Pentagon, and I teach security cooperation planning at the Army War College. Security cooperation represents those engagements with allied and partner militaries that aim to help those forces build capabilities to defend themselves and/or fight along side the US military in coalition operations as necessary. The US military conducts thousands of security cooperation engagements annually with more than 140 nations around the world at a considerable cost to the American taxpayer.

Security cooperation pays big dividends when it prevents war, through deterrence, building a partner's capability and aligning nations into credible interoperable coalition partners. The aim of preventing a shooting war is the pinnacle of the profession of arms, which requires a sophisticated understanding of all the elements of national power.

Sun Tzu, the ancient Chinese military strategist, wrote in *The Art of War*: "For to win one hundred victories in one hundred battles is not the acme of skill. To subdue the enemy without fighting is the acme of skill." That is what I teach my students—winning without fighting—through training our foreign partners and allies to do the fighting themselves rather than calling on US forces and/or preferably winning through the mechanism of an array of federal departments and agencies armed with the elements of national power to settle the war before it comes to physical blows.[624]

Victory in war without coming to blows is possible if all the elements of national power are smartly applied, but they must be appropriately organized within a comprehensive campaign plan like we currently use for our theaters of operations—say Europe or Asia—which are tethered to our nation's strategic guidance. Those plans are comprehensive, stretch over extended periods (multiple years), and involve many players across the federal government, not just the military forces.

A campaign plan has three purposes that apply broadly to the new dual Cold War. First, it operationalizes the president's NSS (his vision and guidance) "by organizing and aligning operations, activities, and investments with resources to achieve" his articulated goals. In the context of President Trump's NSS, a campaign plan would fix responsibility for each strategic goal to a federal department or agency and require the other federal players to render back-up support.[625]

The second purpose of the campaign plan is to translate the president's strategy into executable actions to achieve his goals. President Trump's NSS identifies "priority efforts" (goals) that are roughly aligned with the four dual Cold War battlegrounds. Responsibility for leading the pursuit of those goals must be fixed.

The third purpose of the campaign plan is to apply the nation's resources to the discrete plans designed to address each "priority effort." That translates into the application of the elements of national power managed by the designated lead federal departments or agencies.

Now consider the "elements," what some call the "instruments," of national power before I identify the lead departments and agencies that ought to assume responsibility for the president's "priority efforts" to win the new dual Cold War.

Understanding the Full Elements/Instruments
of National Power

It is critical that we understand the full elements/instruments of our national power. President Trump, as his former national security adviser H. R. McMaster claimed, "Has focused on aligning our diplomatic, economic, military, informational, intelligence, and law enforcement efforts [instruments of national power] since the first days of his administration." The president grounded his National Security Strategy in the integration of all elements/instruments of national power. Henceforth, I will use the term "element" to represent either "instrument" or "element" of national power.

What are the tangible and intangible elements of national power, and how should they be applied to win the dual Cold War?

The ability of a nation to influence other states is based on the use of these elements of national power. A state has power over another state when it can persuade the other to do something via the application of one's national power elements. For example, after the attacks on America on September 11, 2001, the United States demanded that the Taliban government in Kabul, Afghanistan, turn over al-Qaeda leader Osama bin Laden, the terror leader behind the attacks. The Taliban government refused to comply, so the Bush administration applied some of the elements of national power, beginning with military force, to "persuade" the Taliban otherwise, which resulted in the fall of that government.

The ability of a nation to use its power effectively depends on its skill at harnessing those various elements, which are classically divided into two groups: natural and social. The application of these national power groups is a relational exercise, but as the father of modern warfare Carl von Clausewitz once wrote, "Everything…is very simple, but the simplest thing is difficult."[626] That is especially true when it comes to getting things done at the national strategic level with other nations.

Retired US Army Colonel Harry Summers, a military author and former Army War College faculty member, used a simple story about the Vietnam War to illustrate Clausewitz's "simplest thing" statement.

When the Nixon administration took over in 1969, all the data on North Vietnam and on the United States was fed into a Pentagon computer—population; gross national product; manufacturing capability; number of tanks, ships, and aircraft; size of the armed forces, and the like.

The computer was then asked, "When will we win?"

It took only a moment to give the answer: "You won in 1964."[627]

Obviously, based on Colonel Summer's illustration, there is far more to winning than the simple employment of the elements of national power; otherwise, the Vietnam War would never have lasted past 1964, much less led to America's withdrawal and defeat in 1975.

National power is contextual, states retired US Army Colonel David Jablonsky, a former professor at the Army War College and a contributor to a volume on *Theory of War and Strategy*. It can "be evaluated only in terms of all the power elements and only in relation to another player or players and the situation in which power is being exercised," Jablonsky said. "A nation may appear powerful because it possesses many military assets, but the assets may be inadequate against those of a potential enemy or inappropriate to the nature of the conflict. The question should always be: Power over whom, and with respect to what?"[628]

Further, a single element of national power cannot determine national power. Jablonsky illustrates the point when he explains: "There is the huge size of Brazil, the large population of Pakistan, the industrial makeup of Belgium, and the first-class army of Switzerland. Yet none of these states is a first-rank power." No nation should define national power in terms of a single element; further, it is important that we also consider the nation's ability to convert potential power (size, population, industrial base) into operational power, which is often based on the political and psychological interrelationship of factors like government effectiveness and national unity.

National power is also relative, a very important factor in the new dual Cold War. Specifically, as Jablonsky explains, a nation has power "in relation to another actor or actors in the international arena." The alleged superiority of a nation over another is derived not just from its own qualities, but also from the actors with which it is compared. Consider a useful illustration.

In the late 1930s, France was universally considered superior to Nazi Germany, since the French armed forces outmatched the Germans in quality and quantity of armed capabilities in World War I. But, as Jablonsky explains:

> The French military power of 1919 was supreme only in the context of a defeated and disarmed Germany; that supremacy was not intrinsic to the French nation in the manner of its geographic location and natural resources. Thus, while the French military of 1939 was superior to that of 1919, a comparison of 1939 French military power to that of Germany in the same year would have shown a vastly different picture for many reasons, not the least of which was the German adoption of the military doctrine of blitzkrieg.

This argument is important, because as explained above in Mr. Trump's NSS, the United States has lost its edge in many military areas over the past two decades. Just because it has in the past been victorious and demonstrated great military prowess say in the 1991 Gulf War or even in Iraq in 2003, it should not be judged today against its contemporary adversaries (Russia and China) based on that past performance. That could prove to be a fatal flaw in national judgment because conditions change over time.

Another aspect of the application of elements of national power needs examination within the context of the new dual Cold War. Remember, the application of elements of national power is situational and won't work with all enemies. For example, the nuclear-mighty United States in 1979–80 was powerless to rescue the American hostages being held at our embassy in Tehran. As Jablonsky states, "Power, in other words, must be relevant in the existing circumstances for the particular situation."

Further, before examining the elements of power in the contemporary dual Cold War context, we need to consider a sidebar distinction made in the strategic literature between what's called "hard power" and "soft power." Those concepts are explained below.

Hard power refers to the influence, leverage, and capability that is derived and generated from direct military and economic means. This is in contrast to soft power, which refers to power that originates with the more indirect means of diplomacy, culture, and history. Hard power describes an actor's ability to induce another actor to perform or stop performing an action. This can be done using military power through threats or force. It can also be achieved using economic power relying on assistance, bribes, or economic sanctions.[629]

Soft power is a term used to describe the ability of an actor to indirectly influence the behavior of other actors through cultural, informational, or ideological means. In contrast with the primary tools of hard power, the organic and inherent ability to threaten or reward, the sources of soft power are cultural and informational: values, principles, morals, and ethics; and diplomatic and foreign policies. Soft power uses an attraction to shared values and the perceived justness and duty of contributing to the achievement of those values.[630]

The distinction between soft and hard power is not one of real consequence, however. Rather, true power is measured in terms of the elements of national power.

What are the elements of national power? Previously I explained they are divided into two categories, natural and social determinants of power. One version of the natural determinants is geography, resources, and population, and the social determinants list includes economic, political, military, psychological, and informational. These elements tend to blend when employed, however.

Briefly consider each element's contribution to the nation's power base.

Natural Elements of National Power

Geographical elements of power include size, location, climate, topography, and boundaries, which influence a nation's capacity and view of the world. For example, location is important to a country like the United States, because we are protected by large bodies of water, but nations like Poland are mostly caught between two historical antagonists, Russia and Germany.

Size is important—not just because it can accommodate a large population, but also because it provides a military advantage, as Hitler realized when attacking the Soviets in World War II. The Russians kept withdrawing into the interior of the country until winter, insurgents, and poor supply lines defeated the Germans.

Location is also important, because it is tied to climate, which dictates whether the nation can sustain itself agriculturally. Russia's historic bread basket is the Ukraine, and Crimea provides Moscow with its only warm water port to the Black Sea. Those factors contributed to Russia's decision to seize Crimea in 2014 and sustain the civil war in eastern Ukraine hoping to eventually annex the entire country.

Population is another important element of national power. A large population can make a dramatic difference in war, as we saw after the Prussian unification of German-speaking people in 1870. That unification grew Germany by twenty-seven million, thus shifting European power between the world wars.

Population size often plays a crucial role in the power of a country as well. After all, Mussolini opined, "Let us be frank with ourselves. What are 40 million Italians compared with 90 million Germans and 200 million Slavs?"[631]

The world's population will soon surpass eight billion, and more than 1.3 billion of those people live in China alone. Beijing is both blessed and cursed by such a large population. It is trying to bring it into the twenty-first century while taking advantage of its youthful population to best meet the needs of the nation's military and industry. In part, contemporary China gained great power status on the backs of its large population, while densely populated nations like Indonesia, the fourth most populous nation-state, is not considered powerful.

By comparison, Western countries tend to experience relatively low replacement birth rates, and their citizens, like here in America, live longer, which requires large healthcare expenditures for the aged in the national budget which otherwise could have gone to the defense budget. As America ages and its cohort of retired people consume an ever-increasing share of social welfare benefits, the nation's power will decline because an ever-smaller percentage of the population is vigorous enough to contribute to the workforce, much less populate its armed forces.

America is also blessed with an abundance of natural resources (minerals, energy products, uranium, coal, iron, gold, forests, and water), which are essential for winning the new dual Cold War. Those resources keep our dwindling industrial base fueled and bolsters our trade. But possessing natural resources by itself is not necessarily a source of power unless they are developed. For example, America has significant energy products, but for many years, those resources were kept off limits due to environmental concerns that led the country into significant economic and security challenges because of our growing dependence on foreign oil, especially energy products from the war-torn Middle East.

Today, the United States is not totally self-sufficient, even though it has an abundance of natural resources, especially energy. However, our near self-sufficiency is a significant strength, especially when compared to countries like Japan, which has few natural resources, making it dependent on imports—and as a result, the need for imports significantly influences its foreign policies. The same is true for both China, which needs a significant and constant infusion of energy to fuel its industries, and Russia, which is energy rich, yet lacks a mature and competitive industrial base.

Social Elements of National Power

The social determinants of national power include economic, political, military, psychological, and informational.

The nation's economic capacity and development link the nation's natural resources and social determinants of power. A nation that wants to prosper needs to connect its natural resources with its ability to convert those resources into exports, consumables, and arms. Of course, that ability is tied to other social determinants such as education and political will as well.

Economies sometimes get out of balance, such as the former Soviet Union, which spent excessively on its armed forces—arguably contributing to its downfall. That excess on military spending eroded Moscow's power at the expense of its larger economy, thus reducing the nation's ability to invest for growth.

Generally speaking, a nation with a production surplus makes it more powerful. Hans Morgenthau, a twentieth-century German political scientist and author, wrote that "the technology of modern warfare and communications has made the over-all development of heavy industries an indispensable element of national power."[632] That is true for the United States and evidently applies to modern China and Russia as well.

The logical conclusion is that production surplus builds a strong domestic economy, which is a source of national power and therefore impacts a nation's resilience and credibility. However, there is a fly in the ointment. The contemporary globalization of trade makes nations more interdependent, which tends to impact national power by limiting geopolitical options. That is a major factor in the dual Cold War with China, because Beijing depends on American trade to fuel its economy—and vice versa, America depends on Chinese products. Further, the trading world is also encumbered by myriad international intergovernmental organizations such as the International Monetary Fund and the General Agreement on Tariffs and Trade (GATT) that influence geopolitics that may disfavor a nation's interests.

Military power is the most common historical gauge of a nation's strength. Defeat in war signals decline while victory most often translates into ascent in power. A nation's military strength is not necessarily the sum total of the number of its ships, tanks, and men under arms, however. The history of warfare provides evidence for this conclusion. Consider Iraq's dismal performance in the 1991 Gulf War and, as illustrated much earlier in this volume, the Persian Empire's defeat at the hands of the much weaker Athenian force.

Technology is a vital contributor to military power, from the advent of the bow and arrow, to the machine gun of World War I, and to the atomic bomb that ended World War II. Consider the importance of the Stinger missile in the hands of Afghan mujahideen who successfully neutralized Soviet air power in 1989, resulting in Russia's withdrawal from Afghanistan. But technology does not always grant an edge over a less-advanced enemy, especially when a nation lacks political direction and a coherent strategy as evidenced in the Vietnam War debacle.

Political power depends on the form of a nation's government, the attitude of her population to that government, the strength and health of the people, and their efficiency. These are difficult factors to measure. For example, on paper, the former Soviet Union and the German Weimar Republic were strong democratically, but weak when opposed. The American Revolutionary War government was weak on paper compared to the British Empire, but the colonialists were highly motivated to defeat the British crown.

Hitler's Germany was incredibly efficient and effective at marshalling the elements of national power to launch military operations in 1939. The Nazis used human and material resources to pursue its national interests, but ultimately failed in part due to hubris, as pointed out earlier in chapter 2 of this volume. It also failed because it confronted a more capable match in terms of the United States, which although inefficient at times, mobilized many elements of national power in the largest resistance ever seen in the history of mankind to win World War II.

A state can enhance its political power by joining a military alliance like NATO. Alliances reflect shifting balances of power and permanent interests, as outlined in chapter 4. NATO, for example, has evolved into a new global security organization by expanding into Eastern Europe, the Baltics, the Balkans, and even as far away as Afghanistan. The United States is arguably stronger today because of its NATO membership, a factor not lost on China and Russia.

The psychological element of national power includes morale, character, and national cohesion. David Jablonsky states the psychological element is the "most ephemeral of the social power determinants that has repeatedly caused nations with superior economic and military power to be defeated or have their policies frustrated by less capable actors." We saw this element at work in Mao's defeat of Chiang Kai-shek, in America's loss to North Vietnam and the defeat of the Shah of Iran by the Ayatollah Ruhollah Khomeini. In each case, the former power had superior capability but lost due to the psychological element.

National character is an important psychological element in national power because it gives motive to policy. This was evident in World War I when President Woodrow Wilson argued for intervention based on his progressive internationalism, but it took the loss of American ships and lives before the nation entered that war. As Jablonsky argues, "The elevation of 'moralism' in the conduct of foreign policy, in turn, diminishes the ability of the United States to initiate a truly preemptive action."

The final social element of national power is informational, which became a factor following the twentieth century's communications revolution. The advent of what Joseph Nye calls "soft power" is a significant factor in contemporary national security.

No longer can nations deny their populations knowledge, because it is readily available even in the most remote places on the planet. Initially this bolstered America's influence, but in recent years, thanks to the proliferation of cyber networks and fake news, state and non-state actors have used information to distort truth and manipulate the masses.

Ideology is also part of the informational element of power. Although President Trump's NSS states that his strategy of "principled realism" is guided by outcomes, "not ideology," America still has a distinctive ideology, which was outlined earlier in this and the fifth chapter.

Now that I've outlined the elements of national power, let's apply those dimensions to the four battlegrounds using Mr. Trump's "priority issues," or what I identified earlier as his "goals" within a national campaign plan to win the new dual Cold War.

Campaign Plan for Dual Cold War's Battlegrounds

An underlying assumption must be stated before launching into this section: President Trump's NSS "priority issues" correctly identify the threat posed by China and Russia. Further, the following plan that harnesses each of the president's "priority issues" makes the best use of the elements of national power and will, given sufficient time, deliver America victory in the dual Cold War.

Another caveat is necessary as well. The president's strategy is not exhaustive and neither by association will be this analysis and plan. I will illustrate how to apply the elements of national power as outlined above to address only a few of the "priority issues"—goals—across each of the four battlegrounds. My point is to illustrate an approach that others may build upon.

Elements of Power across the Ideological Battleground

The ideological battleground primarily draws upon the following elements of national power: population, economic, political, psychological and informational. The United States government's key federal department in this fight should be the State Department, the agency best suited to orchestrate our ideological war with China and Russia.

Mr. Trump should call on the State Department to respond to the NSS to "be able to build and sustain relationships where U.S. interests are at stake." The Foreign Service Corps is best positioned to accomplish this effort by working through our embassies to interact with other governments and their citizens. Keep in mind that an embassy's country team—the collection of officials from across the interagency working on an ambassador' staff—includes experts on the media, intelligence, economics, politics, and much more. They are ideally equipped and positioned to "build and sustain relationships" among foreign partners.

The State Department officials must also, according to the NSS, "build and lead coalitions that advance shared interests and articulate America's vision in international forums." I've visited numerous international forums like the United Nations and heard American diplomats express progressive views that don't represent the values that elected Mr. Trump. It is my observation that the State Department has a history of being staffed by like-minded, liberal educated personnel who are frequently at odds with more conservative views represented in the Defense Department.

I believe that is changing, at least at the United Nations, with US Ambassador Nikki Haley, a refreshing voice in a sea of double speak. But more must be done. Our State Department must participate in these forums and do so with a clear voice that reflects Mr. Trump's values and calls out abusive practices, especially by the Chinese and Russians. Make no mistake, this will not be an easy or a quick change in outlook.

Mr. Trump calls out the United Nations in his NSS to "be reformed and recommit to its founding principles." He goes on to say, "We will require accountability and emphasize shared responsibility among members. If the United States is asked to provide a disproportionate level of support for an institution [like the UN, which the US pays 22 percent of the budget], we will expect a commensurate degree of influence over the direction and efforts of that institution." Clearly, in the recent past, American values have been rejected by the UN's progressive leadership, such as when that body condemned the US for announcing its intention to move our embassy from Tel Aviv to Jerusalem, Israel. (Our embassy officially relocated to Jerusalem on May 14, 2018 thanks to Mr. Trump.) Therefore, the State Department and Congress must hold the UN accountable, as Mr. Trump states, and should, if it fails to reflect more of our interests, cut back our significant financial support and/or relocate that body out of the country.

Our diplomats must also look for opportunities to encourage people-to-people exchanges that create "networks of current and future political, civil society and educational leaders." We saw a similar outreach during the old Cold War that significantly impacted former Soviet citizens' views of the West. We need to seek similar outcomes regarding both the Chinese and Russian people today.

China and Russia have weaponized information to attack our values and institutions while shielding their populations from outside information. Our State Department will empower true public diplomacy to compete with China and Russia for the hearts of freedom-seeking people by breaking through those governments' efforts to buffer their citizens from the truth. Clearly those media, informational outlets include the old standbys like the still-active Radio Free Europe, which must continue, and new Internet websites must emerge that provide truth to those living under the oppressive thumbs of Moscow and Beijing.

Mr. Trump outlines that campaign, which includes private enterprise. He calls for an effort that crafts:

> ...direct coherent communications...to advance American influence and counter challenges from the ideological threats that emanate from radical Islamist groups and competitor nations [China and Russia]. The public media and the Internet are the primary platforms through which these messages are transported which is why this must be a partnership with the

private sector (the American people) to promote our values that will inspire and grow communities of civilized groups and individuals in our adversaries' countries.

It is America's policy to advocate for our core principles across the world, an important aspect of the ideological fight by all parts of the US government. Mr. Trump's NSS reminds us that:

America's core principles, enshrined in the Declaration of Independence, are secured by the Bill of Rights, which proclaims our respect for fundamental individual liberties beginning with the freedoms of religion, speech, the press, and assembly. Liberty, free enterprise, equal justice under the law, and the dignity of every human life are central to who we are as a people.

That is why, as the NSS states, we will oppose "governments that routinely abuse the rights of their citizens" such as those that "fail to treat women equally."

America will respond to such governments by using diplomacy, sanctions, and "other tools to isolate states and leaders who threaten our interests and whose actions run contrary to our values." Certainly, Russia and China are often guilty of this allegation, and the State Department and appropriate congressional committees should punish such behavior. Further, the Department of Commerce ought to back-up those findings with meaningful sanctions that get their attention.

"We will advocate on behalf of religious freedom and threatened minorities," states the NSS. China and Russia have long histories of oppressing people of faith and gulags full of those of conscious. The State Department will use our political, psychological, and informational elements of power to encourage these persecuted groups and our Department of Commerce, and congressional oversight committees will sanction governments that limit freedom of faith.

Both Russia and China have growing, but largely suppressed, Christian populations—especially in China. While it has officially been United States policy not to use or promote Christian organizations in pursuing foreign policy, now is an opportune time to modify the rules. Christian values are Western values, and presenting the truth of Christ in any forum by any means would be a blessing to the people who hear it and the nation that promotes it. Knowing the truth of Christianity will have positive spillover effects on Chinese and Russian behavior in the long term.

The ideological battleground will be hard fought. Much as we fought the Soviet communists for the hearts and minds of their people, and eventually won, we must harness our psychological and informational arms of government supported by the private sector to keep truth and freedom flowing into China and Russia.

Elements of Power across the Cyber Battleground

The cyber threat is comprehensive, yet Russia and China want to focus international cyber efforts only on "information security," which is essentially messaging rather than on the security of infrastructure, hardware/software, and data vulnerabilities. Their opposition to a comprehensive international effort means the cyber war continues and likely gets worse.

Recognizing China and Russia's unwillingness to cooperate on establishing cyber norms and then enforce them explains why Mr. Trump calls for the US to provide "leadership and technology to shape and govern common domains" such as cyberspace, within international law. "The United States supports the peaceful resolution of disputes under international law but will use all of its instruments of power to defend U.S. interests and to ensure common domains remain free."

The NSS makes clear that cyberspace provides China and Russia low-cost "and deniable opportunities to seriously damage or disrupt critical infrastructure, cripple American businesses, weaken our federal networks, and attack the tools and devices that Americans use every day to communicate and conduct business." That must change.

China and Russia are the worst abusers of the cyber domain and routinely ignore international law to suit their interests. They violate treaties and sovereign rights of others, as seen in Eastern Europe and in the South and East China Seas. No wonder those governments continue to ignore efforts to regulate cyberspace because they aim to keep it free for their destructive mischief. That is why the United States will, as the NSS states, "promote the free flow of data and protect its interests through active engagement in key organizations, such as the Internet Corporation for Assigned Names and Numbers (ICANN), the Internet Governance Forum (IGF), the UN, and the International Telecommunication Union (ITU)."

For the reasons outlined above, America requires a significant defensive and offensive cyber capability, which are part of a strong campaign plan. The NSS identifies six critical infrastructure areas at risk from cyber attacks: national security, energy and power, banking and finance, health and safety, communications, and transportation. "We will assess where cyberattacks could have catastrophic and cascading consequences," states the NSS. That must begin with hardening critical government networks, a call heard over the years from various federal commissions, and issues that are necessarily parts of the campaign plan.

Hardening government networks is expensive, but not nearly as expensive if we wait to suffer a devastating cyber attack before taking corrective action. Therefore, the government must prioritize the networks most vulnerable to cyber attack and immediately begin to replace them with closed systems that provide "uninterrupted and secure communications and services under all conditions." This is an emergency and must be a high priority in the new dual Cold War plan.

Hardening networks may require Congress to pass laws and then appropriate sufficient funds to replace those systems. Time is short because China and Russia will not stop attacking our networks, and their effectiveness continues to improve.

Our campaign plans will do more than harden our networks from attack. They will also develop the capability to "impose swift and costly consequences on foreign governments…who undertake significant malicious cyber activities." This effort properly rests with the military element of national power and in particular the US Cyber Command, which includes the National Security Agency with other agencies in support.

Another aspect of this battleground warrants serious attention. The cyber threat includes the vulnerability of the world's vital fiber-optic cables, some resting on sea beds. Most of those cables are vulnerable to compromise, an issue for the US Navy to prioritize. Also, our constellation of satellites are vulnerable to cyber attacks as well, which is a defensive mission for the US Air Force and the Strategic Command, and other supporting government departments and agencies.

Unquestionably, the cyber threat posed by China, Russia, and other rogue actors impacts every country and device connected to the World Wide Web. That is why the US government "will work with our critical infrastructure partners to assess their informational needs and to reduce the barriers to information sharing," according to the NSS. This shared effort involves the State Department, the Department of Defense, the Justice Department, the director of National Intelligence, and various congressional committees. We will protect civil liberties and privacy while expanding "collaboration with the private sector so that we can better detect and attribute attacks."

Elements of Power across the Economic Battleground

China and Russia are determined to make America's economy "less free and less fair," according to the NSS. That's a serious security threat to America.

The economic battleground is a multiple-front zone that includes trade, hostile ideologies, the harnessing of data, energy, and much more.

Mr. Trump's NSS calls for rebuilding "our economic strength and restore confidence in the American economic model." He explains that over the last few decades, "American factories, companies, and jobs moved overseas" because of the 2008 global financial crisis and a lack of confidence in America.

Economic prosperity is a national security issue, according to the NSS. That is why America needs to take bold and quick action against those who threaten our prosperity, namely China and Russia. Corrective action begins at home.

Mr. Trump worked with Congress to reduce regulatory burdens that unleash businesses to compete. That work will continue and meanwhile, in December 2017, Mr. Trump led Congress in passing a dramatic tax reform bill that stimulated our domestic economy by giving businesses a shot in the arm through tax relief. Mr. Trump told reporters that the new tax bill reduced "business tax all the way down from 35 to 20 [percent]."[633]

Tax and regulation relief will whittle away at our over $20 trillion debt, which is a "grave threat to America's long-term prosperity and, by extension, our national security," according to the NSS.

Next, Mr. Trump must turn to rectify economic wrongs overseas:

> For decades, the United States has allowed unfair trading practices to grow. Other countries have used dumping, discriminatory non-tariff barriers, forced technology transfers, non-economic capacity, industrial subsidies, and other support from governments and state-owned enterprises to gain economic advantages.

China is the primary aggressor behind these economic infractions, and as a result it is the target of this plan. The campaign plan will direct our Trade Representative and the Department of Commerce, which, Mr. Trump says, "will pursue bilateral trade and investment agreements with countries that commit to fair and reciprocal trade and will modernize existing agreements to ensure they are consistent with those principles." Obviously, our Justice and State Departments need to help with oversight to protect our trade as well.

We will counter unfair trade practices through sanctions and international law as well as through organizations like the World Trade Organization. Clearly, we are concerned that China continues to distort markets and exercises unfair trade practices.

America is blessed with many natural resources, a very important element of national power. Fortunately, for the "first time in generations, the United States will be an energy-dominant nation." We are a leading producer and consumer and energy innovator that ensures that markets are free and access to energy is diversified.

Our energy resources give America great economic security by helping us counter an "anti-growth energy agenda" and deny the likes of Russia the use of energy as a geopolitical weapon. That reality provides the United States with leverage to apply to China's efforts to distort the energy market.

China and Russia's aim to make America's economy "less free and less fair" is a very serious threat. Our campaign plan will leverage all the elements of national power to invigorate our economy and counter all efforts to marginalize fair trade that robs us of jobs, industries and markets.

Elements of Power across the Arms & Technology Battleground

The arms and technology battleground is incredibly contentious, threatens to drain nation-state coffers, and could very well bring the two sides of the new dual Cold War into armed conflict. There are many fronts to this emerging battleground.

The first front regards innovation that promises to create jobs and improve quality of life at home and abroad. But emerging technologies are especially critical to both economic growth and security, which explains why it is a significant front.

Mr. Trump calls for America to retain its "advantages over our competitors," a challenge in the new dual Cold War. It is especially important for the Department of Defense to "establish strategic partnerships with U.S. companies to help align private sector R&D resources to priority national security applications."

America must protect our national security innovation base against competitors such as "China [which] steal U.S. intellectual property valued at hundreds of billions of dollars. Stealing proprietary technology and early-stage ideas allows competitors to unfairly tap into the innovation of free societies," states the NSS.

Mr. Trump calls on the American government to "develop a capability to integrate, monitor, and better understand the national security implications of unfair industry trends and actions of our rivals." This is clearly the work of our national intelligence, justice, and economic sectors. We must vigorously prosecute spies and sanction governments that sponsor snoops and hackers. Further, the NSS calls for Congress to "strengthen the Committee on Foreign Investment in the United States (CFIUS) to ensure it addresses current and future national security risks."

At present, CFIUS lacks the resources and legislative authorities to monitor or prevent many of the sophisticated efforts that China and other nations use to control, influence, or eliminate American economic capabilities. The fact is the Chinese communist regime is explicit about its desire for complete control of China's economy, and that includes foreign companies forced to accept intrusive demands. Meanwhile, the CFIUS process is voluntary, which means many transactions skirt that authority.[634]

The problem of an ineffective CFIUS is illustrated by the recent acquisition of the United States' only rare earth mineral mine. Evidently, foreign companies found a loophole in the CFIUS process that allowed a Chinese-affiliated consortium including rare earth miner Shenghe Resources Holding Company to acquire the only formerly operational US rare earth mine. CFIUS did not review the transaction despite the fact that rare earth minerals are critical to every major American weapon system.[635] Coupled with the sale of American Uranium to Russia during the Obama administration [Uranium One], it is easy to see that we can be our own worst enemy in retaining critical defense materials. This hole in our oversight process must be plugged to protect national security against manipulation from China.

Ellen Lord, the Pentagon's top acquisition official, said, "We have an amazing amount of dependency on China." Specifically, Ms. Lord's concern is due to China being America's "sole source for rare earth minerals." That is why she called for a whole-of-market approach to critical minerals supply chain primarily because China is the primary provider of the most important building blocks for military equipment from copper to steel to rare earth elements. America's technological superiority literally hinges on maintaining reliable access to key materials, and without that access, our precision-guided missiles won't work properly, our aircraft and submarines can't be built correctly, and worse.[636]

Our monitoring efforts must also include an effort to reevaluate our immigration policies to "reduce economic theft by non-traditional intelligence collectors." The US hosts many tens of thousands of Chinese green-card workers in this country, a source of valuable intellectual property information for Beijing. This must stop, and that includes reducing the number of permits for students from China, who take advantage of research done within our educational and government institutions.

On the second front, the United States military is in a non-shooting competition with both the Chinese and Russians over size, capability, and sophistication of our conventional forces. Specifically, the US military seeks to maintain an overmatch capability sufficient to prevent enemy "success and to ensure that America's sons and daughters will never be in a fair fight." As Mr. Trump understands, America's decades-long procurement holiday created voids in our capability and therefore makes our Joint Force vulnerable vis-à-vis the rapidly improving sophisticated Chinese and the Russians. That must be a serious concern for Congress, which should immediately fund the force to maintain a comfortable overmatch capability.

That effort includes investing in improved acquisition processes, more capacity (mostly size of the force), and more readiness investments to sustain capability. These are issues well-known to Congress and the Pentagon. However, they must be supported by the American people who register their concerns with Congress and accept the investment of their tax dollars. Also, our Commerce Department must work with the Pentagon and Congress to keep healthy our defense industrial base and the national security innovation base. Maintaining that base means we must maintain and develop skilled trades and high-technology skills through technical education programs—something not lost on China, which sends boatloads of students to American universities to learn our technical secrets.

The third front is our nuclear arsenal, which must not be allowed to atrophy, especially now that we see the Chinese and Russians building and deploying new warheads atop new sophisticated, global-reach platforms. Our nuclear arsenal is the foundation of our strategy to preserve peace and stability, according to the NSS. Unfortunately, after the old Cold War, according to the NSS, the US "reduced investments in our nuclear enterprise and reduced the role of nuclear weapons in our strategy."

The Pentagon, the Department of Energy, and Congress must work together to sustain our nuclear arsenal. Not only must we sustain the arsenal, but we need to smartly modernize our forces and infrastructure to ensure that "we have the scientific, engineering, and manufacturing capabilities necessary to retain an effective and safe nuclear triad and respond to future national security threats."

Keep in mind that maintaining, much less improving, this vital capability requires an interagency effort and smart oversight and funding by Congress. We must avoid miscalculation, and meanwhile, the State Department with the Pentagon's input must pursue new arms-control arrangements that contribute to strategic stability.

The fourth front is the space domain, which is vital to our modern way of life. It requires constant attention and ongoing investment given the tough competition emerging with China, especially the threat posed by both China and Russia's anti-satellite weapons programs. State and Defense departments must pursue agreements that maintain our "unfettered access to and freedom to operate in space," while recognizing in the dual Cold War that "freedom" will become more challenging. Part of that challenge is funding an effective space-based defense capability to protect our constellation of satellites and when deemed necessary, if not prohibited by treaty, an offensive weapons platform to counter China's growing aggressiveness in that domain.

Finally, on the fifth front, America needs a robust intelligence capability to gather, analyze, discern, and operationalize information in the dual Cold War environment. We should expect as much from the Russians and Chinese and therefore our intelligence community (IC) must modernize to continuously anticipate foreign threats and prevent surprise in all domains.

Improving our understanding of the threat through effective intelligence-gathering and analyses services requires a thorough integration of all the elements of national power that are subject to Chinese and Russian influence. We must monitor and analyze how our adversaries rob our information and manipulate our media to serve their geopolitical purposes. That's one of the roles of the IC as well as increasing our understanding of their economic policy priorities to improve our ability to detect and defeat enemy attempts to commit economic espionage. This impacts economic, military, psychological, and natural elements of national power.

Conclusion

Will America and her allies win the new dual Cold War? That will depend on whether freedom-loving governments like that in the United States understand the threat, generously invest sufficient elements of national power, and develop a national campaign plan focused on the defeat of our adversaries. It also depends on America's future leadership.

General Boykin said the dual Cold War depends on America's leadership. "If we get another Obama then the Cold War will grow in intensity and last for a long time," said Boykin. "However, if America keeps strong leaders like Mr. Trump, then he will keep China and Russia in check."[637]

Let there be no doubt that China and Russia are focused on defeating the United States and remaking the world in their totalitarian image. Failing to adequately counter their determined effort with strong American leadership may very well launch the world into the prophetic end times, the topic of the next chapter.

CHAPTER SEVEN

China and Russia and the Prophetic End Times

There is no doubt that the foreboding times of the emerging new dual Cold War could become a catalyst for the end times and a horrendous ending for all mankind. Biblical prophecy tells us the end times will be marked by fighting and dissension; the world will be filled with ceaseless, unending war. Hunger will humble millions, earthquakes will frighten everyone, and pestilence will be out of control.

Many Christians and some biblical scholars sincerely believe China and Russia are major players in the end-times prophetic scenario, which means today's new dual Cold War could be the catalyst that ushers in the end times. Others are doubtful, arguing that no one can really know for certain which contemporary countries if any other than Israel are really end-times players. In fact, it is quite possible and even likely that the biblical end times are yet far into the future.

I'm not a biblical scholar, just a student who loves God's Word, and I guess most of those reading this volume fit that description as well. Many of us study God's Word and may be persuaded by biblical scholars and others whom we respect that contemporary evidence does suggest the world is rapidly moving toward the end times—and we may even agree with them that Russia and China will play important roles in the prophetic end times. However, in our anticipation of Christ's return, we must be honest with ourselves and review the end-time prophecies and then answer a couple of tough questions about whether biblical prophecy does in fact mention or refer to contemporary China and Russia. Are we reading into God's Word things that were never intended?

This chapter is divided into four sections. First, consider a common scriptural account of the biblical end times. Consider this a scene-setter in preparation for considering a possible role for China and Russia.

Second, I provide a perspective regarding the question: Did God encrypt in His prophetic Word the identity of contemporary China and Russia for critical roles in the end of times?

Third, what is America's role if the new dual Cold War is the catalyst for the end times? After all, there is considerable disagreement that America even has a role in the prophetic end times. So, if there is no US involved at the end times, then we need to consider the question: What happens to remove America from the end-times scenario?

Fourth, what do you believe about God's Word and the contemporizing of prophetic Scripture, and what are the consequences of those views? That's the more important question in this chapter because, frankly, none of us fully understands with certitude the mysteries of God, much less whether China and Russia are indeed end-times players and when in fact the end times will occur. What we do know is God sent His Son who died on the cross for sinners, and the way to eternal salvation is by accepting Jesus Christ as our Savior. That's our message and motivation; the rest is nice to know but not necessary for salvation.

No doubt that China and Russia are important to students of prophetic Scripture, especially if, in fact, they are appearing on the world scene today to usher in the end times. That's really unknowable, but an entertaining thought and one that gets many of us excited for the Lord's return.

I will now present a view of the prophetic end times and then answer the above questions.

Prophetic End-Times Accounts

There are differences of opinion about the prophetic end times. Consider the following account, which is a blend of a number of views. Then we will examine the common arguments for identifying China and Russia as key end-times nations.

The framework of biblical prophecy is found in the Old and New Testaments. The New Testament book of Revelation details the events leading to the return of Jesus Christ, which includes seven seals, seven trumpets, and seven vials. They represent a progression of catastrophic plagues of God on mankind. Elsewhere in the New Testament, we read about the signs that will announce the coming end times.

The Bible describes what 2 Timothy 3 calls the "last days" (KJV), which identifies a long list of signs. Those signs include: "For men shall be lovers of their own selves, covetous, boasters, proud, blasphemers, disobedient to parents, unthankful, unholy, without natural affection, trucebreakers, false accusers, incontinent, fierce, despisers of those that are good, traitors, heady, high-minded, lovers of pleasures more than lovers of God."

Jesus Christ describes some of the same signs in the Gospels, such as in Matthew 24:7 (KJV), which states that "nation will rise against nation, and kingdom against kingdom."[638]

The problem with naming national conflicts (wars) as a sign of the end times is that wars are common throughout history. So there must be something especially frightening about the wars at the end of time. I believe we will understand this when in fact the time is upon us—but not until.

Jesus also warns us to watch: "For there shall arise false Christs, and false prophets, and shall shew great signs and wonders; insomuch that, if it were possible, they shall deceive the very elect" (Matthew 24:24, KJV). These false christs will corrupt those who follow them. Therefore, true believers must be cautious and heed Jesus' warning in John 14:21 (KJV): "He that hath my commandments, and keepeth them, he it is that loveth me: and he that loveth me shall be loved of my Father, and I will love him, and will manifest myself to him."

These warnings portray a perilous time ahead. It will be even worse than the terrible suffering Middle East Christians experienced at the hands of the Islamic State in 2014–2017 whereby some Christians were hung on crosses until dead, buried alive, or burned alive. The end times must be something extra special.

The problem of fixating on these signs is that we really don't know with any certainty when these indicators will usher in the prophetic end times. After all, the Gospel of Mark 13:32 (KJV) states "But of that day and that hour knoweth no man, no, not the angels which are in heaven, neither the Son, but the Father."

Christ also cautions us in Matthew 24:5–8 (KJV) about the end times:

> For many shall come in my name, saying, I am Christ; and shall deceive many. And ye shall hear of wars and rumors of wars: see that ye be not troubled: for all [these things] must come to pass, but the end is not yet. For nation shall rise against nation, and kingdom against kingdom: and there shall be famines, and pestilences, and earthquakes, in divers places. All these [are] the beginning of sorrows.

Scripture tells us there will be heavenly evidence of the end times; perhaps those signs are more reliable indicators of the true end times than the others. Luke 21:24–26 (KJV) states:

> And they shall fall by the edge of the sword, and shall be led away captive into all nations: and Jerusalem shall be trodden down of the Gentiles, until the times of the Gentiles be fulfilled. And there shall be signs in the sun, and in the moon, and in the stars; and upon the earth distress of nations, with perplexity; the sea and the waves roaring; men's hearts failing them for fear, and

for looking after those things which are coming on the earth: for the powers of heaven shall be shaken.

Some similar passages speak of the "roaring" in the heavens and seas.

We read in the Scriptures about the Great Tribulation preceded by the Rapture of the Church, the lifting-up of the believers (1 Thessalonians 4:17). Christ says: "For then shall be great tribulation, such as was not since the beginning of the world to this time, no, nor ever shall be" (Matthew 24:21, KJV). The Great Tribulation is set in motion by the Antichrist (the Beast) and brought to an end by Jesus Christ.

Richard F. Ames with *Tomorrow World* wrote an overview regarding the seven seals of Revelation that provide a perspective of the end times.[639] The following is a paraphrase from that overview to help the reader understand the sequence of end-times events from a New Testament perspective.

The great Tribulation is associated with seven seals, seven trumpets, and seven vials in the book of Revelation. Those seals reveal prophetic events ahead.

There is a scroll sealed with seven seals in Revelation 5, and only the "lion of the tribe of Judah," "the root of David" is worthy to break the seals. That being is Jesus Christ, who begins to remove the seals in their numerical order.

The first four seals in Revelation 6 are known as the four horsemen of the apocalypse. The apostle describes Jesus opening the first seal in Revelation 6:1–2 (KJV): "And I saw when the Lamb opened one of the seals, and I heard, as it were the noise of thunder, one of the four beasts saying, Come and see. And I saw, and behold a white horse: and he that sat on him had a bow; and a crown was given unto him: and he went forth conquering, and to conquer." The most common view is that the rider is the Antichrist who initially brings peace, but in reality is indwelt by Satan. One view is the white horse represents false religions as in Matthew 24:4–5.

The second seal reveals a red horse, with power over peace; and the third seal a black horse, representing lack of food and famine. The fourth rider is on a pale horse with the power to kill one-fourth of the Earth with a "sword, and with hunger, and with death, and with the beasts of the earth" (Revelation 6:8, KJV).

"And when he had opened the fifth seal, I saw under the altar the souls of them that were slain for the word of God, and for the testimony which they held" (Revelation 6:9, KJV). This is a description of the fate of those who accept Christ after the rapture and during the tribulation; they die as martyrs for their belief.

The sixth seal reveals heavenly signs, similar to what I introduced above. "And I beheld when he had opened the sixth seal, and, lo, there was a great earthquake; and the sun became black as sackcloth of hair, and the moon became as blood; and the stars of heaven fell unto the earth, even as a fig tree casteth her untimely figs, when she is shaken of a mighty wind. And the heaven departed as a scroll when it is rolled together; and every mountain and island were moved out of their places" (Revelation 6:12–14, KJV). This will be a shocking time likely with asteroids and meteorites falling from the sky, massive earthquakes the Apostle John describes as "every mountain and island were moved out of their places."

Revelation 8 describes the seventh seal as the day of the Lord, which is comprised of seven trumpet judgments. "When he opened the seventh seal, there was silence in heaven for about half an hour. And I saw the seven angels who stand before God, and to them were given seven trumpets" (Revelation 8:1-2, KJV). The trumpet sounds to announce each plague.

The first four trumpets announce great ecological disaster: earthquakes, vast fires, death of a third of sea life and poisoned water sources. The last three trumpets are called woes: "Woe, woe, woe, to the inhabiters of the Earth by reason of the other voices of the trumpet of the three angels, which are yet to sound!" (Revelation 8:13, KJV).

The fifth trumpet or first woe announces a military action as does the sixth trumpet, an intense military counterattack. "One woe is past; and, behold, there come two woes more hereafter. And the sixth angel sounded, and I heard a voice from the four horns of the golden altar which is before God, saying to the sixth angel which had the trumpet, loose the four angels which are bound in the great river Euphrates" (Revelation 9:12–14, KJV).

The waters of the Euphrates are halted for a vast army to cross to kill one-third of the Earth's population—a world war perhaps. "And the four angels were loosed, which were prepared for an hour, and a day, and a month, and a year, for to slay the third part of men. And the number of the army of the horsemen were two hundred thousand thousand: and I heard the number of them. And thus I saw the horses in the vision, and them that sat on them, having breastplates of fire, and of jacinth, and brimstone: and the heads of the horses were as the heads of lions; and out of their mouths issued fire and smoke and brimstone. By these three was the third part of men killed, by the fire, and by the smoke, and by the brimstone, which issued out of their mouths" (Revelation 9:15–18, KJV).

The seventh trumpet announces the establishment of the kingdom of God on Earth, the return of Jesus Christ. "The seventh angel sounded his trumpet, and there were loud voices in heaven, which said: 'The kingdom of the world has become the kingdom of our Lord and of his Messiah, and he will reign for ever and ever'" (Revelation 11:15, NIV).

The seventh trumpet also introduces God's wrath on rebellious nations. "And I saw another sign in heaven, great and marvelous, seven angels having the seven last plagues; for in them is filled up the wrath of God" (Revelation 15:1, KJV). This trumpet consists of "seven last plagues" (Revelation 15–16) such as painful sores, poisonous rivers, and the sun becoming hotter.

The sixth angel pours "out his vial upon the great river Euphrates; and the water thereof was dried up, that the way of the kings of the east might be prepared" (Revelation 16:12, KJV).

Then the Antichrist—the prophesied European superpower

leader—moves into the Middle East and joins ranks with the "kings of the east" to fight against Jesus Christ who returns as revealed in Revelation 11. Those forces gather at Armageddon, fifty miles north of Jerusalem to make war against Jesus Christ.

The Apostle John writes, "And I saw heaven opened, and behold a white horse; and he that sat upon him was called Faithful and True, and in righteousness he doth judge and make war. His eyes were as a flame of fire, and on his head were many crowns; and he had a name written, that no man knew, but he himself. And he was clothed with a vesture dipped in blood: and his name is called The Word of God. And the armies which were in heaven followed him upon white horses, clothed in fine linen, white and clean. And out of his mouth goeth a sharp sword, that with it he should smite the nations: and he shall rule them with a rod of iron: and he treadeth the winepress of the fierceness and wrath of Almighty God. And he hath on his vesture and on his thigh a name written, KING OF KINGS, AND LORD OF LORDS" (Revelation 19:11–16, KJV).

When Christ returns to this Earth, He will judge and conquer all His enemies. John continues: "And I saw the beast, and the kings of the earth, and their armies, gathered together to make war against him that sat on the horse, and against his army." (Revelation 19:19, KJV).

Jesus will totally conquer the greatest military ever assembled. He will return as King of Kings and Lord of Lords to bring this war-torn planet a thousand years of peace in a fulfillment of Zechariah 14:9 (KJV): "And the LORD shall be king over all the earth: in that day shall there be one LORD , and his name one."

That is the view of the end times from a New Testament perspective. However, that is only part of the prophecies regarding the end times. We need to consider an Old Testament perspective and one focused on the end-time wars, which makes it easier to understand how large foreign militaries like those presumably from Russia and China might become involved in the end times.

Dr. David Reagan wrote an article, "The Wars of the End Times," for Lamb & Lion Ministries making the case for the end times being marked by nine battles, not just the single popularized war/battle known as the Battle of Armageddon. That battle concept comes from Revelation 16:16, where armies will gather at a place called *har-magedon*, which means the "Mount of Megdeon," and refers to the present-day tourist site of the ancient fortress of Megiddo that once controlled the valley of Jezreel, in northern Israel.

As seen above in the description of the end times, there is no reference in the book of Revelation to the "valley of Armageddon," nor is there mention of "the Battle of Armageddon." In fact, Dr. Reagan makes a case that Bible prophecy reveals nine wars (battles) in the end times and Armageddon is only one of these.

Reagan states that "most prophetic scholars have long believed that the next great end time war will be the war of Gog and Magog that is described in Ezekiel 38 and 39." He states that "this war will start when Russia invades Israel with certain specified allies, all of whom are Muslim nations today." However, he identifies nine end-time prophetic wars in chronological sequence, not all involve a reference to Russia and China.

The first such war is the war of extermination mentioned in Psalm 83:4–8. This is a fight Israel wins with her neighbors.

The second war involves Gog and Magog of Ezekiel 38–39. Reagan says the Arabs who lost in the Psalm 83 war will turn to the Russians for help. Soon, Russia and her Arab allies launch an invasion to destroy Israel, and, according to Ezekiel 38:12, the Russians will come "to capture spoil and to seize plunder."

The Russian-led army will be destroyed by God "on the mountains of Israel" (Ezekiel 39:4), a feat realized through earthquakes, pestilence, hail storms, and battlefield confusion (Ezekiel 38:19–22).

The third war breaks out soon after the Tribulation begins (Revelation 6). This is a conventional war led by the Antichrist (Daniel 8:23) to conquer the world, to "overcome them: and power was given him over all kindreds, and tongues, and nations" (Revelation 13:7, KJV).

The fourth war is an escalation of the third conventional war into a nuclear holocaust, which results in the deaths of one-third of mankind

(Revelation 9:15). Reagan argues that war becomes nuclear because Revelation 8:7 says one-third of the Earth is burned up, and Revelation 16:2–11 indicates that the people will be afflicted with "loathsome and malignant" sores, the evident consequence of radiation exposure.

The fifth war is one among the supernatural realm pitting Satan and his angels against Michael and his angels (Revelation 12). Dr. Reagan indicates that once Satan realizes he can't win against Michael, he turns on the Jewish people, which leads to the next war.

The sixth war begins with Satan possessing the Antichrist (Revelation 13:2), intending to inspire him to destroy all the Jews in the "Great Tribulation" (Matthew 24:31). Two-thirds of the Jewish people are in fact killed by the Antichrist in this war.

The seventh war is described in Daniel 11:40–45 as a military campaign of the Antichrist to destroy the rest of the Jews and the saints. At this point, according to Reagan, the nations of the Middle East are led by the "king of the north" and the "king of the south" who will rebel against the Antichrist.

Just as the Antichrist gains the upper hand over his adversaries, he learns about "rumors from the east and from the north," which cause him to withdraw to the Valley of Armageddon. That news evidently points to "the kings from the east" (Revelation 16:12), who come from Asia (supposedly China) and join the reconstituted Russian army mentioned above.

The eighth war begins as the armies from the east and the north arrive in the Valley of Armageddon. At that point, the Lord God returns to the Mount of Olives to instantly destroy the armies "with the spirit of his mouth" (2 Thessalonians 2:8, KJV).

The ninth and final war comes after one thousand years of peace during the reign of Jesus from Jerusalem (Isaiah 11:4–5,9). It is a time when swords will be beaten into plowshares and spears into pruning hooks, and "nation will not lift up sword against nation" (Isaiah 2:4 KJV). During those years, Satan is bound (Revelation 20:1–3), so this is a time when sin and crime are greatly reduced.

At the end of Christ's thousand-year reign, Satan is released for one last rebellion against God (Revelation 20:7–9). This rebellion is once again led by Gog and Magog (presumably Russia) against Jesus Christ. That will be the final war of history, in which God takes the redeemed off the Earth and places them in the New Jerusalem. Then God destroys the earth with fire, and from that inferno comes the new heavens and a new earth.

Will China and Russia Really Be Part of the Prophetic End-Times War against Israel?

Did God encrypt in His prophetic Word the identity of contemporary China and Russia for critical roles in the end of times? It is an interesting exercise to search the Scriptures and try to match our views of God's Word with contemporary behaviors. However, we need to be careful not to focus on the minors and ignore the major issues at hand.

Some authors within the Christian community strongly believe God encrypted His Word for future generations, and in fact allegedly communicated that China and Russia are leaders at the end times. Therefore, according to their view, we are living in the end times.

That view is not shared by Dr. Michael S. Heiser, an American biblical scholar and author who cautions against trying to contemporize the Scriptures.

"I don't see any modern state as the focus of any biblical prophecy," Dr. Heiser explained. He acknowledged that "Israel of course plays a role because Armageddon is cast as a battle at…Mount Zion/Jerusalem, but these other modern states didn't exist. What we think of as Russia and China aren't even in the table of nations [in the biblical times], so it's doubtful people in the first century even knew they existed."[640]

"[I]f we interpret scripture in its own context [not ours] we have to look at it quite differently," Heiser writes. He continues:

You could say, "Well God knew about all those countries and countries that would become countries." Sure. God knew lots of things—like the brain is really the locus of intellect and emotions, not the kidneys or heart [as the ancients believed]; like a woman's hair had nothing to do with fecundity [capacity to produce offspring], like the Earth really wasn't round and flat with a dome over it, like Jerusalem really wasn't the actual geographical center of the Earth, though Ezekiel calls it such—but God didn't correct the men he chose to produce scripture on these matters.... So why would I presume God would encrypt modern geo-political information into a first century (or much older) text? Wasn't the whole idea that the writers were supposed to be communicating to their own audience?

This issue comes down to understanding God's intent with the Bible, according to Heiser. In a 2015 presentation available on You-Tube, *The Naked Bible,* Dr. Heiser seeks to clarify some fundamental misunderstandings about the Bible. For example, he states, "The Bible is not a paranormal event.... The writers were not zapped by God who took control over their minds in a trance and then wrote the text." God worked through human circumstances after having prepared the writers through their lives. The writing process of the Word is "a providential process," not "a paranormal event." [641]

Heiser then states that inspiration does not involve modern content, because "God's word is written for us not to us." It is also "the product of culture that produced it" to convey a theological message in the language of the day that is consistent with the ancient world." Therefore, Heiser insists, "Let the Bible be what it is and resist the urge to be what it isn't." [642]

Heiser's views do not dispute end-times prophetic Scriptures, but they caution modern man against reading into the ancient text something God unlikely intended. Frankly, even though contemporary geo-political events seem to fit what ancient prophets like Ezekiel and the Apostle John wrote, let's not be too dogmatic.

Heiser then asks:

How is it sound hermeneutical method to think prophecy was about countries and peoples the biblical writers knew nothing about? If someone can show me how that approach is sound, then it changes things. I've just never come across a coherent way to do that. I prefer to read scripture in its own context, not a foreign context. It's a simple strategy, but it's the one that is most coherently defended.

Non-seminarians like me likely are not familiar with the "hermeneutical method." So I visited compellingtruth.org, an organization that boasts its purpose is "presenting the truth of the Christian faith in a compelling, relevant, and practical way." That site explains hermeneutics with the following paragraphs.

Biblical hermeneutics is the field of study related to the interpretation of the Scriptures. Because Christians have historically lived based on the teachings of the Bible, and because "All Scripture is given by inspiration of God, and is profitable for doctrine, for reproof, for correction, for instruction in righteousness, that the man of God may be complete, thoroughly equipped for every good work." (2 Timothy 3:16–17 NKJV), a proper interpretation of the Bible's contents is vital. As the Apostle Paul wrote in 2 Timothy 2:15, the Christian's goal is to "Be diligent to present yourself approved to God, a worker who does not need to be ashamed, rightly dividing the word of truth."[643]

Biblical hermeneutics involves many principles of literature that have developed over time. For example, one principle involves first identifying the genre of that particular passage of study. Genesis included much narrative content. Many of Paul's writings are letters. The Psalms are poetic while the Proverbs are wisdom literature. Each genre is understood in unique ways that help readers better understand the meaning of the particular passage.

Three important guidelines related to biblical hermeneutics include observation, interpretation, and application. Observation focuses on what the text says—the who, what, when, why, and how? Interpretation seeks to understand the meaning of the passage along with various controversies regarding particular passages or topics. Application then applies the original, historic understanding of a biblical passage to a contemporary context.

Of great importance in this process of biblical hermeneutics is to interpret Scripture according to its original setting. This includes the historical context, grammar, genre, literary context, and more. Rather than asking, "What do these words mean to me?" proper biblical hermeneutics first seeks to understand what the passage meant when written. Only after this does the reader or interpreter look to discover how the original intent of the writing applies to one's own personal context.

In more recent years, postmodern literary theory has attacked this historic biblical hermeneutic, emphasizing "reader response" more than or instead of the author's original intent. While application and human emotion are important elements to spiritual growth, this does not negate the importance of understanding Scripture from its original perspective. Both inductive study as well as modern application must serve as part of a healthy biblical hermeneutic.

Finally, a biblical hermeneutic is of great importance because of the power of the Word of God. Hebrews 4:12 (NKJV) teaches, "For the word of God is living and powerful, and sharper than any two-edged sword, piercing even to the division of soul and spirit, and of joints and marrow, and is a discerner of the thoughts and intents of the heart." Scripture offers much power for those who would study its contents and look to apply its principles to their lives today.

Another interpretive tool is exegesis, which refers to drawing truths out of the Bible. This is like hermeneutics in that we should check the context of the verses, chapter, and the entire book of the Bible to capture a more complete understanding. Then we should consider the original language as well.

Alternatively, "eisegesis" refers to the practice of reading things into the inspired text, as opposed to drawing things out. This can be a dangerous practice because it imposes one's own preferred views upon the Bible. Although the interpretive effort may be sincere, it is influenced by the inevitable flaws of humankind and should be avoided especially if we are dogmatic about those interpretations.

Now, consider some of the scriptural interpretations pointing to China and Russia as major players in the end times. Then apply the explanation of the hermeneutical method above to either confirm or reject these interpretations.

There are two common arguments to support the view that China is involved in the end-times prophetic scenario.

China: The "Kings from the East" in Revelation 16 Who Join the Battle of Armageddon

Revelation 16:12–16 (KJV) states:

> And the sixth angel poured out his vial upon the great river Euphrates; and the water thereof was dried up, that the way of the kings of the east might be prepared. And I saw three unclean spirits like frogs come out of the mouth of the dragon, and out of the mouth of the beast, and out of the mouth of the false prophet. For they are the spirits of devils, working miracles, which go forth unto the kings of the earth and of the whole world, to gather them to the battle of that great day of God Almighty. Behold, I come as a thief. Blessed is he that watcheth, and keepeth his garments,

lest he walk naked, and they see his shame. And he gathered them together into a place called in the Hebrew tongue Armageddon.

This passage in Revelation describes the Battle of Armageddon, which occurs at the end of the Tribulation. Leading up to the battle, the Euphrates River will dry up, allowing the "kings from the east" to march toward Israel. Some people interpret the "kings from the east" to be the modern nation of China. Thus, the massive Chinese army, which is part of a global coalition, crosses the dried river bed and sweeps westward to join up with the forces of the Antichrist.

It is impossible to know for certain whether this Scripture means modern-day China. Certainly today, that nation has a massive military and is an economic world power. We know that under Chinese President Xi, the Chinese military is rapidly expanding its influence across the world—but will that expansion at some future point include an attack on Israel at the Battle of Armageddon? We just don't know.

Besides, if one studies a map of the track of the Euphrates River through present-day Syria and Iraq, it is not clear why any modern army, especially one originating in current China, would take a cross-land route to Israel. The ancient Silk Road crosses the Euphrates River north of Baghdad and presumably an army dependent on that route would have to do the same. But a modern army with ships and aircraft would not elect a ground movement.

China: A Major Contributor to the 200-Million-Man Army in the Battle of Armageddon

Revelation 9:15–17 (KJV) reads:

And the four angels were loosed, which were prepared for an hour, and a day, and a month, and a year, for to slay the third part of men. And the number of the army of the horsemen were two hundred thousand thousand [200 million]: and I heard the number of them. And thus I saw the horses in the vision, and them that sat on them, having breastplates of fire, and of jacinth, and brimstone: and the heads of the horses were as the heads of lions; and out of their mouths issued fire and smoke and brimstone.

A two hundred-million-man army is hard to image, even in the contemporary world of nearly eight billion souls. However, for those looking for an explanation of how such a massive army might be assembled, they understandably look to China, which has a large (3.3 million members—active, reserve, and paramilitary) standing armed forces, a far cry from two hundred million, however.

Interpreting this Scripture to point to contemporary China is problematic for a number of reasons, not the least of which is that it says nothing about an army from the east. Rather, the verse speaks of a demonic horde riding "horses." Further, the battle of Revelation 9 occurs after the sixth trumpet judgment, and the battle of Revelation 16, which involves the "kings of the east," occurs about three and a half years later. The timing is not right for such an interpretation.

Besides, no one has ever seen a two hundred-million-man army. I've seen and been part of large army formations and have some appreciation for the logistics associated with huge ground forces. Frankly, two hundred million men and their equipment can't fit inside the Valley of Armageddon. The triangular-shaped Plain of Jezreel (Valley of Armaggedon), is 36 miles by 15 miles, or 540 square miles, which means 370,370 soldiers and their equipment must fit into each square mile. There must be a better explanation for this Scripture.

Claims That Russia is an End-Times Player

Even the leader of the Russian Orthodox Church believes mankind is approaching the end times, and Russia is a factor. In November 2017,

Patriarch Kirill at Moscow's Christ the Savior Cathedral said, "One must be blind not to see the approach of the terrible moments of history about which the apostle and evangelist John the theologian spoke in his Revelation." He explained that the apostle's apocalyptic vision is being brought about by sinful behavior.[644]

Russian clergy are serious about the coming apocalypse. Archpriest Vesevolod Chapalin said it is Russia's God-given mission to stop America. "It is no coincidence that we have often, at the price of our own lives…stopped all global projects that disagreed with our conscience, with our vision of history and, I would say, with God's own truth," the archpriest told *Interfax* in 2014. "Such was Napoleon's project; such was Hitler's project. We will stop the American project too." Then, Chapalin said, Russia would lead the world against the forces of the Antichrist in an apocalyptic struggle. Who is that leader?

Russian philosopher Aleksandr Dugin sees Russian President Vladimir Putin as an Eastern Orthodox czar leading the war against the Antichrist in an apocalyptic struggle. In fact, Putin is our "katechon," Dugin explained. The Greek word *katechon* is used in 2 Thessalonians 2:6–7 to describe a force that holds back the "mystery of iniquity." To Dugin, the "mystery of iniquity" is the secularized West.

Does that mean that Putin is Gog?

Ezekiel's Gog and Magog Point to Russia

Ezekiel 38:1–3 (KJV) states:

And the word of the LORD came unto me, saying, Son of man, set thy face against Gog, the land of Magog, the chief prince of Meshech and Tubal, and prophesy against him, and say, Thus saith the Lord GOD; Behold, I am against thee, O Gog, the chief prince of Meshech and Tubal.

Gog is a person from the land of Magog and the leader of Tubal and Meshek and a confederacy of nations: Persia, Cush, Put, Gomer, and Beth Togarmiah (Ezekiel 38:5–6). Gog has plans to attack Israel, and it's clear that the Lord is against him and he will be defeated (Ezekiel 38:4, 19–23; 39:3–5).

"Magog" is identified as a land "in the far north" of Israel, which many Bible commentators interpret as Russia. Or it could be a general reference to barbarians near the Black and Caspian seas. It is true geographically that Russia is to Israel's north and that by association "Rosh" is a reference to Russia and "Meshek" could be Moscow or people of the Black Sea (also north of Israel) and "Tubal," could be in central Turkey.

Therefore, the area referenced in Ezekiel 38–39 is territorially now referred to as Russia.

Dr. Heiser takes great umbrage with this view. He writes in *The Unseen Realm*:

> The prophetic description in Ezekiel 38–39 of the invasion of "Gog, of the land of Magog" (Ezekiel 38:1–3, 14–15) is well known and the subject of much interpretive dispute, both scholarly and fanciful. One of the secure points is that Gog will come from 'the heights of the north' (38:15; 39:2). While many scholars have focused on the literal geographic aspects of this phrasing, few have given serious thought to its mythological associations in Ugaritic/Canaanite religion with Baal, lord of the dead.
>
> An ancient reader would have looked for an invasion from the north, but would have cast that invasion in a supernatural context. In other words, the language of Ezekiel is not simply about a human invader or human armies. An ancient reader would also have noticed that this invasion would come at a time when the tribes had been united and dwelt in peace and safety within the Promised Land—in other words, since the period of exile had ended.
>
> The battle of Gog and Magog would be something expected

after the initiation of Yahweh's plan to reclaim the nations and, therefore, draw his children, Jew or gentile, from those nations. The Gog invasion would be the response of supernatural evil against the messiah and his kingdom. This is in fact precisely how it is portrayed in Revelation 20:7–10.

Gog would have been perceived as either a figure empowered by supernatural evil or an evil quasi-divine figure from the supernatural world bent on the destruction of God's people. For this reason, Gog is regarded by many biblical scholars as a template for the New Testament anti-Christ figure.

While Magog and "the heights of the north" aren't precisely defined in the Gog prophecy, the point is not about literal geography per se. Rather, it is the supernatural backdrop to the whole "northern foe" idea that makes any such geographical reference important. For sure ancient Jews would expect that the reconstituted kingdom of Yahweh would be shattered by an enemy from the north—as it had before. But ancient Jews would also have thought in supernatural terms. A supernatural enemy in the end times would be expected to come from the seat of Baal's authority—the supernatural underworld realm of the dead, located in the heights of the north. Gog is explicitly described in such terms.

Russia Will Lead an Alliance of Nations against Israel

Ezekiel 38:13 states that when the aggressors (often identified as being led by Russia) move against Israel, other nations will join their alliance, such as "Persia (modern-day Iran), Put (modern-day Sudan), Cush (modern-day Libya), Gomer (part of modern-day Turkey), and Beth Togarmah (another portion of modern-day Turkey or possibly Syria)."[645] Some commentators believe this war is one of the events leading up to the beginning of the Tribulation. Others believe it will occur close to the midpoint of the Tribulation, since Israel will be "dwelling without walls, and having neither bars nor gates" (Ezekiel 38:11)—in other words, Israel will feel secure at that time, possibly because of the covenant they have signed with the Antichrist (Daniel 9:27). Either way, this battle is distinct from the Battle of Armageddon, which occurs at the end of the Tribulation.

God promises to destroy Gog's army: "And I will bring him to judgment with pestilence and bloodshed; I will rain down on him, on his troops, and on the many peoples who *are* with him, flooding rain, great hailstones, fire, and brimstone" (Ezekiel 38:22, NKJV, emphasis added). The bodies of the fallen army of Magog will be buried, but it will take over seven months to complete the macabre task (Ezekiel 39:12, 14). This supernatural judgment will have the effect of preserving Israel and turning many hearts to God: "Thus I will magnify Myself and sanctify Myself, and I will be known in the eyes of many nations. Then they shall know that I *am* the LORD" (Ezekiel 38:23, NKJV, emphasis added). Many will be saved during the tribulation (Revelation 7), and the fulfillment of Ezekiel 38–39 will be one means by which God will bring people to a knowledge of Himself.

There is much we do not know for certain about Ezekiel's prophecy, including the timing of these events. However, it is possible contemporary Russia could be involved and will in fact lead an end-times league of nations to seize Israel's land. The prophet Ezekiel comforts Israel in much the same way as Moses had centuries ago: "For the LORD your God *is* He who goes with you, to fight for you against your enemies, to save you" (Deuteronomy 20:4, NKJV, emphasis added).

I asked retired General Jerry Boykin about Russia and the end times. He said that he differs from many theologians regarding Russia's end-times role. He doesn't believe the prophetic Scriptures refer to Russia, but to Turkey as "the big dog" at the end times. He admits that Russia might participate in the end times, but the major power from the north will be Turkey, not Russia. Specifically, the general believes that Turkish President Recep Tayyip Erdogan intends to restore the Ottoman Empire, a view shared by other Mideast leaders.[646]

In November 2017, General Boykin had the occasion to meet with Egypt's President Abdel Fattah el-Sisi in Cairo. El-Sisi told the general that Erdogen has one objective and that is to recreate the caliphate and to become the caliph. Does that make Erdogen Gog of Magog?[647]

There are likely other Scriptures and interpretations that place both Russia and China in active roles in the prophetic end times. However, whatever those passages and their interpretations, they are based on speculation and employ questionable hermeneutic methods.

Then there is the question about America at the end times.

Where Is America in the Prophetic End Times?

What is America's role if the new dual Cold War is the catalyst for the prophetic end times? After all, the new dual Cold War described in the first six chapters of this volume clearly pits the Alliance of Evil, China and Russia, against the United States and its mostly Western allies with Israel. But, as many Bible scholars argue, America is absent from the end-times prophetic Scriptures. What happens to America, and does that necessarily impact the roles, if any, China and Russia play in the end times?

Dr. David Reagan explains that the absence of America in biblical prophecy is based on pure speculation. For example, Isaiah 18 speaks of a people "tall and smooth" who are "feared far and wide," which some authors speculate refers to a nation divided by a great river, such as the Mississippi River (the United States).[648]

One of the more popular Scriptures used by some to speculate about the demise of America before the end times is Ezekiel 38, which the prophet describes as an invasion of Israel launched by a nation "from the remote parts of the north." This nation is considered Russia by some authors, but America isn't suggested here.

Some of the same authors go on to claim that the passage at Ezekiel 38:13, "the merchants of Tarshish and all its villages," is a reference to

Britain and English-speaking nations such as the United States. Apparently, Tarshish was once a seaport town near current-day Cadiz, Spain. Many years ago, so goes the speculation, people from Tarshish moved to England and then eventually to the United States. Thus, "the young lions of Tarshish" mentioned in Ezekiel 38 is speculated to apply to contemporary America. Further, in the final conflict when Israel is invaded by "Gog of Magog," the young lions of Tarshish say, "What are you doing?" Americans are allegedly monitoring the conflict from afar and ask the question, but evidently have no influence over the war's outcome.

Other Bible speculators claim that Revelation 12:13–17 identifies the US as the "wings of a great eagle" that helps Jews escape the Tribulation. Why? The "great eagle" is, some claim, a tipoff that the United States, which is identified by the bald eagle, the emblem of the United States, rescues the Jewish remnant in Israel by an airlift out of the grip of the Antichrist.

Finally, according to Dr. Reagan, another widely used passage to identify the United States in biblical end-times prophecy is Revelation 18, specifically the phrase "Babylon the great." Dr. Reagan says that chapter is about the last Gentile empire that dominates the earth at the Lord's Second Coming and it is not the United States.

There is evidently, based on the above examples, no meaningful mention of the US in Bible prophecy. That leaves us with only generalizable prophecies applicable to all nations to include the US that will be judged at the end times and as a result cease to exist.

There are two alternative explanations as to why America falls out of the spotlight, according to Dr. Reagan: economic catastrophe and destruction. The economic destruction is not that hard to believe, given today's economic conditions and, especially, America's high debt ($21+ trillion), the ongoing issuance of fiat currency by the US Federal Reserve, the fact that America is a service-based economy that overconsumes, the rise of the giant and very competitive Chinese economy, and much more. We addressed this issue in greater detail in chapter 2 of this volume.

America could also be militarily destroyed—especially if, as I outline in chapter 2, we continue our naïve, hubristic ways. Yes, another nation, Reagan suggests Russia, launches a preemptive nuclear attack on America, allegedly because our country is the only one willing to defend Israel in the end times. He suggests that Ezekiel 39:6 is key here in that the fire—perhaps the nuclear-tipped ballistic missiles launched from Russian submarines—falls on "those who inhabit the coastlands in safety," to wit the United States. Once again, that's possible, but what mitigates against such a view is that Russia would cease to exist given the certainty that the US would utterly destroy Russia with nuclear weapons as well.

There is also the possibility that the Rapture (1 Thessalonians 4:17) removes such a large number of American Christians that it quickly leads to the demise of the United States. The logic goes something like the following: All American, born-again Christians, who make up perhaps a third of the US population, or one hundred million souls, suddenly disappear from the face of the Earth. That event causes the American economy to implode, and suddenly the country is militarily weakened to the point of impotence. This theory depends on born-again Christians being in many of the critical national security roles and their sudden disappearance results in the collapse of America's national defense.

Are these rational explanations? You decide. However, no one really knows.

The analysis of the Scripture outlined above should create enough doubt for you to question the reliability of those arguing with great confidence that China, Russia, and the United States are end-times players. Further, whatever you conclude after reviewing this analysis has no bearing on the ultimate reliability of the Scriptures. None. What this analysis suggests is that mankind, no matter how smart and in tune with the Scriptures, just doesn't know the details of the end times—concerning what nations, time, and events will be involved.

Yes, I believe the Scripture will be fulfilled exactly as it states. I don't know with any precision the details of the end times, and I sincerely doubt any other human does, either. So what then must we do?

What Is an Alternative Approach When Prophetic Scriptures Are Not Clear about End-Time Players?

What do you believe, and what are the contemporary consequences of those views? That's the more important question, because, frankly, none of us understands with certitude the mysteries of God—much less the details of the end times other than what the plain text of the Scriptures reveals. We do know that God sent His Son to die on the cross for sinners, and the only way to eternal salvation, as stated earlier, is by accepting Jesus Christ's sacrifice and Him as our Savior. That's our message and motivation.

We should also expect that if we live long enough, we might experience some of the end-times signs outlined at the beginning of this chapter. It will be horrible, and Christians especially will suffer for their faith. But Christians will be spared from the worst part, and Jesus will return and call us to meet Him in the air in the Rapture event. Exactly at what stage that will be is not clear; we are simply commanded to be watching.

What about the Christian Church and the end times? Expect Christians to suffer more than all others because of their faith. The end times will usher in a time of great antagonism, serious persecution for Christians, worse than what fellow believers experienced at the bloody hands of the Islamic State of Iraq and Syria between 2014 and 2017, where some were crucified on crosses, others buried alive or burned at the stake—and no one escaped the most horrendous treatment known to man.

For the Christian, the era leading up to the prophesied end times should be full of great expectation because God promises to rapture—lift up to heaven—true believers just before the start of the coming final world war. Premillennialist Christians like me believe the Christian Church, the earthly body of Christ, will be raised in the twinkling of an eye to heaven (1 Thessalonians 4:17). Our Lord Jesus told us to "take heed"—to literally look around for signs of the coming end times and not to be fooled by false prophets.

Until that time there are a number of things Christians ought to do.

We should get to know the Scriptures to include the prophetic Word, but avoid unnecessary speculation that isn't based on sound hermeneutics. It is human nature to wonder, but we must be especially careful not to deceive the innocent and those easily influenced about the Scriptures (1 Timothy 1:3–7; 2 Peter 1:20–21).

Remember, we are still subject to error even though we may exercise a sound hermeneutic method. When that occurs, we must acknowledge the error and then make quick corrections informing those who might be influenced. Believers who see error must call it out and warn others, lest the weak fall prey and tarnish our witness to the unbelieving world.

We must also find a balance in our Christian lives. Christians are followers of Jesus Christ, which must become our message to a lost world—focus on the Great Commission. We should not make our primary emphasis Bible prophecy speculation, but we should call out what is tangible and knowable that yields fruit. Never forget that Jesus admonishes us in Matthew 24, Mark 13, and Luke 12 to watch and be ready—for His return.

Conclusion

No human knows for certain that China and Russia will be critical players in the prophetic end times. Further, the United States may or may not survive as a global power to participate as a factor in the end-times scenario, either. What is certain today is that the contemporary geopolitical situation presents many markers that seem to fit popular interpretations of end-times Scriptures, but at best those views are based on speculation clouded with uncertainty. Therefore, although we should be mindful of those Scriptures, our primary effort in the twenty-first century ought to be focused on the Great Commission (Matthew 28:16–20) while remaining watchful for the signs of the end times outlined in 2 Timothy 3 and heed what the Lord Jesus states in Matthew 24:36 (kjv): "But of that day and hour knoweth no man, no, not the angels of heaven, but my Father only."

Epilogue

The Alliance of Evil establishes that without a doubt the world is locked in a new dual Cold War pitting Russia and China against the US and her allies. In seven chapters, this volume details evidence for the new dual Cold War, but as yet has not suggested how that war might end. There is a chance that the dual Cold War and America's dual containment policy regarding China and Russia are indeed the catalysts that lead to the prophetic end times, or it might end with a whimper like the old Cold War, then history proceeds to a different time as we wait for the Lord's return. No one knows the future but God.

Remember, no one knew during the worst times of the old Cold War how that conflict might end. Providentially, that war concluded without a world war or a shot fired. However, at various points during those decades, tensions rose to a fever pitch and seemed at times as if we were on the brink of a nuclear holocaust. Fortunately, the leadership on both sides quickly managed to cool the strain before people died and the Earth went up in nuclear dust.

Today, many international affairs experts argue that the current stress between the United States and Russia and China could get worse, but they disagree that it may ever come to a shooting war, much less prompt the end times. That's a naïve view, given the history of man and the view that, historically, war inevitably finds a way in spite of man's best intensions.

The principal reason some skeptics see war as unlikely today is because both sides have so much to lose by reverting to hostilities, especially because of the shadow of nuclear escalation. After all, history tells us that nation-states almost always try to avoid the risks that might snowball them into the arms of destructive hostilities, but mankind throughout history hasn't been very successful at sidestepping war.

Look back through 3,400 years of recorded history to find only 268 years of peace, or about 8 percent of the time the world was supposedly war-free. Then consider the fact that more than 108 million people died in wars in the twentieth century alone, and modern war is becoming more deadly due to sophisticated weaponry. How likely is it that mankind will avoid another war?[649]

The present times are filled with many risks, and wars are likely on our horizon. However, some experts argue that a shooting war in the twenty-first century is remote of the historical precedent. After all, the United States sanctions Russia for seizing Crimea, but Washington doesn't care enough about things Russia cares a lot about to opt into a real shooting war, much less a nuclear holocaust. Regarding China, the argument goes that the economic disincentives for a shooting conflict are enormous, enough to keep our collective barrels cool.

The problem with these arguments is that similar conditions have been present before in recorded history and war ensued anyway. History teaches us as well that because war finds a way, there are plenty of international-relations theorists who already recognize the uncertainties and dynamism of power structures today, and they see lots of risk of military conflict well into the future.

Let me paint a scenario that leads to a shooting war using the material in this volume—the uncertainties and dynamism of power structures. The prophecy followers will find the scenario especially compelling, but a warning here is appropriate. This is one strategist's speculation, although informed by the material in this book. However, no one really knows how current events might play out on the world stage, much less the twists and turns the nation-state players take as the new dual Cold War tracks through the future.

Consider what we know about the dueling sides of the new dual Cold War from this volume.

Chapter 1 identifies sixteen indicators of a new dual Cold War. Those indicators demonstrate significant tension between the sides; and those stresses are building and could eventually explode into a real kinetic conflict. The second chapter addresses American arrogance, hubris. We Americans tend to be cocky in our international relations behaviors, which irritates our allies and angers our enemies, notably the Russians and Chinese. We better wake up to the fact that we are no longer the king of the global roost; our actions have real consequences in the new dual Cold War environment.

Chapter 3 dissects important aspects of the old Cold War. It focuses on two nations—the Soviet Union and the United States—and the tension between those nations which started in the early twentieth century with the Russian Revolution and significantly diminished on Christmas Day 1991 with the collapse of the former Union of Soviet Socialist Republics. Of course, conditions between the sides today are very different, but there are lessons from the old Cold War for the new dual Cold War.

Some of the differences between then and now include the fact that Russia's geopolitical influence outside its own neighborhood is much less than it was during the Soviet Union era. Although Moscow is pushing to reestablish itself in the Middle East, the Balkans, and a few other locations, it is "unlikely" to regain its former influence. Evidently, it is rebuilding a smaller, albeit high-technology, armed forces compared to the significant military of the USSR, yet Moscow retains a robust nuclear backbone equal to our own triad force. Further, the Russian Federation is led by a very popular authoritarian, President Putin, who aims to reestablish Russia as a great power and is willing to take great risks to reach that goal.

China is a very different threat today than during the old Cold War era because it is now a global political and economic power and rapidly growing a global-capable superpower with a joint, all-domain expeditionary military force. Also, Chinese President Xi is, like Putin, an autocrat who, thanks to the Communist Party's 19th Congress and the National People's Congress, will likely rule for life to pursue his goal of world dominance.

Yes, as some argue, the complex interdependence between the United States and China economically serves as a stabilizing force and provides a basis for expanding cooperation. However, that "strategic competition" and interdependence could lead to missteps that bring the countries to blows.

Chapter 4 addresses the implications of the new dual Cold War that demonstrate both China and Russia are in fact modern great powers, and there is compelling evidence they are cooperating on many fronts. That cooperation may lead to the formation of a formal alliance or something similar that creates a mighty global armed force coalition and spawns an undisputed global economic powerhouse. Further, already countries around the world are beginning to align with one side or the other, while true neutrality is becoming less of an option as were the years of the old Cold War.

Chapter 5 outlines four "battlegrounds," a metaphorical term that doesn't necessarily mean hostile action—a shooting war—but certainly represents an intense state of strategic competition between the new dual Cold War adversaries. Clearly, these adversaries will compete at a high level ideologically, across the cyber domain, economically, and in terms of sophisticated arms and security technologies. Any of these "battlegrounds" could spawn the sparks that lead to actual physical blows. How likely is that outcome? I give it a 6 on a 10-point scale.

Chapter 6 addresses the US government's plan to address the challenges posed by China and Russia across four battlegrounds. The Trump administration's approach, outlined in the National Security Strategy and National Defense Strategy, aims at shaping the international environment to avoid kinetic conflict among the dueling nations that might become the catalyst that leads to the biblical end-times scenario outlined in chapter 7. That strategy seems logical, measured but is no guarantee of future peace.

I express skepticism in chapter 7 that God encrypted in the prophetic Scriptures to identify Russia and China as critical end-times players. It is also uncertain as to whether the United States plays a role leading up to and or during the end times as well. Frankly, no one knows whether any one of these three nations will even exist when the time arrives, because only God knows the ultimate final-days scenario, much less the players. We can speculate and try to template Scriptures to fit contemporary geopolitical times, but that's at best a risky, presumptuous undertaking.

What is clear in the Scriptures is that the end times will be a terrible era that pits the world against Israel. It will involve many nations with mighty capabilities and will lead to a final series of battles and the Second Coming of Jesus Christ.

Speculative Scenario Leading to World War III

How might World War III find a way from the new dual Cold War era, if at all, to an end-times scenario? The following perspective is totally speculative, rather presumptuous on my part but based on the nonfiction material in this volume.

Let's think ahead in time to the year 2040. Consider the four lines of effort, what I previously label as "battlegrounds," that link the present time with the future. As we saw in chapter 5, the battlegrounds are primary venues of confrontation in the new dual Cold War and perhaps will host the sparks that trigger the end-times scenario outlined in the Scriptures.

Here is how actions upon each battleground could lead to China, and by association Russia in an alliance, to dominate the world and thus usher in the end times against tiny Israel and her geopolitical partners.

The global economic battleground could easily end up favoring China and her twenty-first-century allies. It begins with the autocrats Xi and Putin forming a security and economic alliance that provides China access to significant and dependable energy resources from Russia via the Siberian pipeline and giant liquefied natural gas supplies from Arctic reserves in Yama, Russia. China uses that reliable source of energy supplemented with other energy supplies from the Middle East, notably Iran and the newly tapped wells in the South China Sea to emerge as the world's leading economic powerhouse.

China becomes the globe's dominant economy—a foregone conclusion by 2018—and thus controls most markets as well. Thanks to Beijing's multi-trillion-dollar investment beginning in 2013 vis-à-vis President Xi's "One Belt, One Road" global initiative, China interconnects every continent's markets and raw material resources. Much of the world ends up economically aligned with Beijing, which controls production, trade, and the Chinese yuan renminbi becomes the world's reserve currency, supplanting the American dollar.

The world's financial network is realigned to Beijing's orders and regulated via Chinese-controlled cyber networks. The World Trade Organization and World Bank, as well as new regulatory world financial institutions, take orders from Chinese chiefs, who follow a script written in communist Beijing. In 2018, China is home to the world's largest banks that grow in influence through the subsequent decades.

A world dominated economically by autocratic Beijing squeezes wealth out of the West and transfers ever more of that wealth each year to China and her surrogates. That results in significant discontent across the formerly wealthy West and creates tension at every turn: less access to raw materials, drained banks, plummeting standard of living, and—in the West especially—an acceleration of the moral collapse that began in the late twentieth century. Major unrest disrupts everyday life, contributing to great anxiety across the West especially. This leads political secular

Western leaders to make geopolitically risky decisions to recapture the West's lost luster of the late twentieth and early twenty-first centuries.

The arms and technology battleground ends up favoring China by 2040. Chinese and Russian armed forces jointly work across all domains—land, cyber, space, air, and sea. They equip a growing list of partner countries around the world with Chinese-made arms. These countries become surrogates to a certain extent, and the China-Russia security alliance annually conducts interoperable, all-domain exercises across the world, while most non-Western nations long ago understood the global power shift away from the US and therefore aligned their security interests with the new world order headed by the autocrats in Beijing and Moscow. Clearly, the military balance shifts in favor of China by 2030, although the West clings to its nuclear triad as insurance against the rising giant in Beijing.

The cyber domain (battleground) accelerates in the 2020s to be hotly contested in spite of a host of global cyber-space security agreements. Although most nations will have to create private cyber networks, the Chinese, through a variety of sophisticated AI-related means, continue to successfully hack all but a very few secret government networks and thus they hold sway over every aspect of modern life tethered to cyber-space. Specifically, Beijing is widely known to possess the capability to manipulate financial markets and critical infrastructure of any country tethered to the porous global World Wide Web.

Beijing also dominates outer space with hundreds of Earth-orbiting satellites and weaponized defense platforms that protect the alliance's assets using kinetic laser and cyber infiltration weapons. Space is a critical component of China's economic and security operations, harnessed to AI and "big data" platforms that act autonomously although overseen by Chinese Earth-based "pilots." Western platforms are routinely threatened or secretly disabled by suspected Chinese AI platforms, which plagues confidence in technology and Western governments.

China and her alliance partners, which include Russia, dominate the world's oceans as well. Their blue-water navy boasts a fleet of aircraft carrier task forces armed with the latest hypersonic missiles, sixth-generation robotic jet fighters, and the mostly robot-controlled nuclear submarine fleet armed with nuclear-tipped hypersonic cruise missiles that constantly monitor every sea lane, underwater cables, and vessels afloat. By 2025, the US and its Western allies reduce their presence except within their regions because of Chinese anti-access threats that predictably hamper Western trade and undermine Western geopolitical influence.

The ideological battleground favors China and her global alliance by 2030 as well. The Chinese global alliance's massive population across more than half of all countries long ago will have forfeited its civil liberties in exchange for security and government-guaranteed quality of life—jobs, social services, housing, and medical care. Beijing holds all the power to prescribe every aspect of life from cradle to grave and suppresses all dissent and non-state-condoned expressions of faith in God.

The power of global media controlled by Chinese AI proxies uses a variety of humanoid "bots" and "big data" to monitor and manipulate social media messaging. Even global entertainment can't escape the behind-the-scenes psychological manipulation of the powers in Beijing. Much as religion is known as the opiate of the masses, Beijing's masters of psychological manipulation have grabbed the reins of global communication platforms to feed the masses in order to control them, especially the West, which tries to cling to democratic traditions.

What happens to the United States as China emerges to run the world by 2040? The United States will have long ago begun to decline as a global force because of a self-imposed cultural, moral implosion. Although it remains a force to be reckoned with even in 2040 at least economically, the American left, the progressives, will have retaken control of the political reins in Washington after eight years under the stewardship of populist President Donald Trump. He was a mere momentary blip in the nation's long decline, to be quickly followed by progressives who took a wrecking ball to our national sovereignty, our security, our secure borders, and nationalist policies. Those progressive globalists were duped by the Chinese into surrendering our sovereignty to international institutions like the United Nations, which Beijing controls, which accelerates America's moral decline.

Turkey, which will have emerged in the 2020s as an Islamist state under the iron fist of a self-declared new caliph, joins forces with the rising Chinese to gradually consolidate control over much of the Middle East—all except tiny Israel. About that time Ankara grasps sway over the Islamic world because other erstwhile regional players begin to recede in influence for a variety of reasons. Specifically, the Saudi kingdom fades because of the collapse in demand for its only product, petroleum—and geopolitically, it splits along Sunni-Shia lines with the establishment of yet another emirate in the eastern portion of the former "kingdom" that aligns itself with Bahrain, a Shia-majority country. Meanwhile, Tehran suffers a counter revolution that displaces the Shia ayatollahs with a quasi-secular government aligned with Ankara, Beijing, and Moscow.

Meanwhile, the tiny nation of Israel continues to struggle as even the United States distances itself from Jerusalem, thanks to progressive leaders in Washington. By 2040, Israel finds itself opposed on most fronts, especially its Islamic neighbors and Turkey's new Ottoman "empire" led by a powerful caliph, a possible glimpse of the prophetic Gog of Magog.

Behind the scenes, a number of interesting developments start to emerge with Israel that really challenge not only the powers in Ankara and across the Mideast, but also in Beijing. Israel, ever since its reestablishment in 1948, prospered and secretly developed strategic capabilities (read "nuclear weapons") and nuanced alliances that kept outside opponents at bay. It seemed as if in spite of outside competition, the small Jewish nation always prospers in terms of technologies. But its outside relationship with the democratic India, the world's second-largest population, seriously antagonizes Beijing.

Long ago, during the old Cold War, India was non-aligned, but after the break-up of the Soviet Union and the 1991 Desert Storm war against Iraq, relations between the US and India, and by association Israel, warmed up and became even more strategic after India tested nuclear weapons in 1998–99. New Delhi's nuclear tests sparked a counter and albeit stronger bilateral relationship between its antagonist neighbor Pakistan and sponsor China, which supplied Islamabad with the nuclear technology to counterbalance India's strategic rise.

The Islamist attacks on America in 2001 led to a stronger US-India relationship because of the resulting global war on terror, a threat shared with India because of its own internal Islamic troubles. Evidence of that robust relationship came with the 2004 Next Steps in Strategic Partnership (NSSP), the 2005 New Framework for Defense Relationship, and by 2016, India was a major US defense partner. By 2018, American and Indian forces routinely participated in joint exercises and exchanges, and fostered interoperability in key functional military areas, a relationship that caught Beijing's attention.

In the 2020s the US-India-Israel relationship matures into an alliance seen as opposed to the Beijing-Moscow-Ankara (BMA) alliance. That is necessary from all parties' perspective as a counter-balance against the BMA's hegemonic actions in Pakistan, Myanmar, Thailand, Malaysia, and the Islamic Middle East led by Ankara and much of Eastern Africa.

Throughout the 2020s, India contests China for control of Central Asia, especially Pakistan and the passages of the underbelly of Asia through the Straits of Malacca. Not only does tension along the China-India land border frequently fester, so do their confrontations at sea—Indian Ocean and the transit zone of the South China Sea. Meanwhile, New Dehli ramps up its strategic forces to begin to counter Beijing's ambitions for that region stretching to the east coast of Africa to China's so-called second island chain that includes the Philippines, Japan, and Malaysia.

Predictably, Ankara's new Ottoman "empire" led by the self-appointed caliph seeds growing confrontations against Israel, which begin to appear to be the set-up for the war described in Psalm 83, the "Gog of Magog" armed conflict prophesied in Ezekiel 38–39, and the "king of the north" joined by ally "kings of the east" scenario presented in Revelation 6.

Certainly by 2040, the world begins to see the signs of the prophetic end times playing out exactly as outlined in the Scriptures. Just how those times play out geopolitically and what current nations, if any, participate, is not for us to know. It is possible that we are rapidly approaching the end times—and yes, China and Russia might be key players, but so might Turkey and India, as proposed above. However, those secrets are only known by God, and so is the timing of the promised Rapture of the Church, the final battle, and the return of Christ.

How realistic is this end-times scenario? I don't know and neither do you. So, for now, our best course of action is to answer God's call to obedience to Christ and keep looking up.

Yes, my proposed scenario is disturbing, yet it, or some variant, is very possible. What we do know and can count on are two things. First, God has a plan to bring history to a close, and it seems unlikely that it is in the distant future. We can already see and feel the birth pangs of the catastrophes that will plague the planet during the Tribulation and we can see geopolitical movement toward the alliances that will bring the world against Israel in the final battle.

Second, radical progressive politics in America are a threat to our very existence. We should be concerned that its presence and potential for taking over our government again is the very reason that America is nowhere to be found in prophecy; the US will become an irrelevant blip in world history. That's why God-fearing people who care about their children and grandchildren had better oppose radical progressives and their lust to control our lives (feudalism), which includes suppressing any expression of our faith and the willing surrender of our sovereignty to other nations and international fora like the United Nations.

America must maintain a principled realism foreign policy such as that embraced so far by President Trump and sustain a pro-America, nationalist domestic policy constrained by conservative Judeo-Christian moral and economic values.

America must turn back to God; He promises that any nation that does so will be blessed and their land will be healed. Make no mistake, however: God has a plan and He knows the exact hour that His prophecies will come to pass. Anything America does will not alter that plan. But that is not the issue. A revived Christian America can make a difference in terms of how we are used by God as the end times approach. We have a choice to serve evil or good. The right choice will ensure that we remain the "shining city on the hill" even when the world is going in the opposite direction. Not only will America be protected to some degree if we are obedient to God, but she can mitigate the horror facing the end-times world.

Notes

1. Stephen Collinson, "Trump Warns of 'Dangerous Low' in Russia Relations," CNN, October 25, 2017, http://www.cnn.com/2017/08/03/politics/russia-us-trump-putin-sanctions/index.html.
2. Ibid.
3. "We Are Seeing What Happens When the U.S. Pulls Back," Spiegel Online, January 8, 2018, http://www.spiegel.de/international/germany/sigmar-gabriel-we-are-seeing-what-happens-when-the-u-s-pulls-back-a-1186181.html?utm_source=Sailthru&utm_medium=email&utm_campaign=New%20Campaign&utm_term=Editorial%20-%20Early%20Bird%20Brief.
4. Gurpreet S. Khurana, "Trump's New Cold War Alliance in Asia Is Dangerous," Washingtonpost.com, November 14, 2017, https://www.washingtonpost.com/news/theworldpost/wp/2017/11/14/trump-asia-trip/?utm_term=.28980e6041ae.
5. Tara Copp, "INDOPACOM, It Is: US Pacific Command Gets Renamed," *Military Times*, May 30, 2018, https://www.militarytimes.com/news/your-military/2018/05/30/indo-pacom-it-is-pacific-command-gets-renamed/?utm_source=Sailthru&utm_medium=email&utm_campaign=ebb%2031.05.18&utm_term=Editorial%20-%20Early%20Bird%20Brief.
6. Patrick Buchanan, "Is Scarborough Shoal Worth a War?" creators.com, May 24, 2016, https://www.creators.com/read/pat-buchanan/05/16/is-scarborough-shoal-worth-a-war.

7. "What Beijing Is Building in the South China Sea," STRATFOR, April 30, 2018, https://worldview.stratfor.com/article/what-beijing-building-south-china-sea?id=743c2bc617&e=99971e0a2b&uuid=1f434fa6-6561-47dc-bfb0-73db0d708b91&utm_source=Topics%2C+Themes+and+Regions&utm_campaign=6f04d04672-EMAIL_CAMPAIGN_2018_04_30&utm_medium=email&utm_term=0_743c2bc617-6f04d04672-53692653&mc_cid=6f04d04672&mc_eid=[UNIQID].

8. Ibid.

9. "China: Beijing Reportedly Deploys Cruise Missiles to Spratly Islands," STRATFOR, accessed May 3, 2018. https://www.stratfor.com/situation-report/china-beijing-reportedly-deploys-cruise-missiles-spratly-islands.

10. "China 'Crosses Threshold' with Missiles at South China Sea Outposts," *Asia Times*, May 4, 2018. http://www.atimes.com/article/china-crosses-threshold-with-missiles-at-south-china-sea-outposts/?utm_source=Sailthru&utm_medium=email&utm_campaign=ebb%2004.05.18&utm_term=Editorial%20-%20Early%20Bird%20Brief.

11. Mike Yeo, "How Far Can China's Long-Range Missiles Reach in the South China Sea?" *Defense News*, May 4, 2018. https://www.defensenews.com/naval/2018/05/04/how-far-can-chinas-long-range-missiles-reach-in-the-south-china-sea/?utm_source=Sailthru&utm_medium=email&utm_campaign=ebb%2007.05.18&utm_term=Editorial%20-%20Early%20Bird%20Brief.

12. David Hutt, "Vladimir Putin Is Also Heading to Vietnam, But with Little to Offer," *Forbes*, November 5, 2017, https://www.forbes.com/sites/davidhutt/2017/11/05/vladimir-putin-is-also-heading-to-vietnam-but-with-little-to-offer/#13586e7a457a.

13. Ibid.

14. Philip Elliott, "7 Questions: Condoleezza Rice," *Time*, May 14, 2018, page 64.

15. Stephen W. Walt, "I Knew the Cold War. This Is No Cold War," *Foreign Policy*, March 12, 2018, http://foreignpolicy.com/2018/03/12/i-knew-the-cold-war-this-is-no-cold-war/.

16. Interview with Dr. Marek Jan Chodakiewicz on March 14, 2018. Doctor Marek Jan Chodakiewicz is the holder of the Kosciuszko Chair professor

of history with the Washington, DC,-based Institute of World Politics. Previously he served as an assistant professor of history at the Miller Center of Public Affairs, University of Virginia. Professor Chodakiewicz's interests include the post-Soviet zone, the Second World War and its aftermath, Europe in the nineteenth and twentieth centuries, Western civilization, and its intellectual tradition and comparative civilizations.

17. Ibid.

18. "Russia Military Power, Building a Military to Support Great Power Aspirations," Defense Intelligence Agency, 2017, p. 41, http://www.dia. mil/Portals/27/Documents/News/Military%20Power%20Publications/ Russia%20Military%20Power%20Report%202017.pdf.

19. "Prosecutors Ban Soros Foundation as 'Threat to Russian National Security'," Russian Television, November 30, 2015, https://www.rt.com/ politics/323919-soros-foundation-recognized-as-undesirable/.

20. "Russia Military Power, Building a Military to Support Great Power Aspirations," Defense Intelligence Agency, 2017, p. 39, http://www.dia. mil/Portals/27/Documents/News/Military%20Power%20Publications/ Russia%20Military%20Power%20Report%202017.pdf.

21. Francesca Ebel, "Meet Russia's Trolls: From Standup Comic to a Siberian Jay Z," Associated Press, March 3, 2018, https://www.fifthdomain.com/ international/2018/03/02/meet-russias-trolls-from-standup-comic-to- a-siberian-jay-z/?utm_source=Sailthru&utm_medium=email&utm_ campaign=ebb%2003.05.18&utm_term=Editorial%20-%20Early%20 Bird%20Brief.

22. Ibid.

23. Ibid.

24. Eytan Halon, "Putin: Jews Might Have Been behind U.S. Election Interference," *Jerusalem Post*, March 10, 2018, http://www.jpost. com/International/Putin-Jews-might-have-been-behind-US-election- interference-544708?utm_source=newsletter&utm_campaign=11-3- 2018&utm_content=putin-jews-might-have-been-behind-us-election- interference-544708.

25. "Trump Administration Hits Russia with New Sanctions for Election Meddling, Cyber-attacks," *Duetche Welle*, March 15, 2018, http:// www.dw.com/en/trump-administration-hits-russia-with-new-

sanctions-for-election-meddling-cyber-attacks/a-42993524?utm_
source=Sailthru&utm_medium=email&utm_campaign=ebb%20
03.16.18&utm_term=Editorial%20-%20Early%20Bird%20Brief.

26. Robert L. Kuhn, "Xi Jinping's Chinese Dream," *New York Times*, June 5, 2013, http://www.nytimes.com/2013/06/05/opinion/global/xi-jinpings-chinese-dream.html.

27. Interview with Dr. Christopher Lew on March 8, 2018.

28. Interview with Dr. Steven W. Mosher on March 18, 2018.

29. Interview with Dr. Chodakiewicz on March 14, 2018.

30. Randolph A. Kahn, "Economic Espionage in 2017 and Beyond: 10 Shocking Ways They Are Stealing Your Intellectual Property and Corporate Mojo," *Business Law Today*, May 2017, https://www.linkedin.com/pulse/business-law-today-march-18-2017-randolph-kahn/.

31. Blake Clayton & Adam Segal, *Addressing Cyber Threats to Oil and Gas Suppliers,* Council on Foreign Relations (June 2013), https://www.cfr.org/report/addressing-cyber-threats-oil-and-gas-suppliers.

32. Matt Spetalnick and Michael Martina, "Obama Announces 'Understanding' with China's Xi on Cyber Theft but Remains Wary," Reuters, September 25, 2015, https://www.reuters.com/article/us-usa-china/obama-announces-understanding-with-chinas-xi-on-cyber-theft-but-remains-wary-idUSKCN0RO2HQ20150926.

33. Bill Gertz, "China's Intelligence Networks in United States Include 25,000 Spies," *Washington Free Beacon*, July 11, 2017, http://freebeacon.com/national-security/chinas-spy-network-united-states-includes-25000-intelligence-officers/.

34. Ibid.

35. Ibid.

36. Ibid.

37. Ibid.

38. Robert Delaney, "US Government Quiet as Chinese Agents Cripple Spy Operations in Beijing," *South China Morning Post*, October 12, 2017, http://www.scmp.com/news/china/diplomacy-defence/article/2114983/us-government-quiet-chinese-counter-agents-cripple-spy.

39. Bill Gertz, "Party Directive Reveals Increased Chinese Theft of U.S. Technology," *Washington Free Beacon*,

April 2, 2018, http://freebeacon.com/national-security/
party-directive-reveals-increased-chinese-theft-u-s-technology/.

40. Natalie Johnson, "CIA Warns of Extensive Chinese Operation
to Infiltrate American Institutions," *Washington Free Beacon*,
March 7, 2018, http://freebeacon.com/national-security/
cia-warns-extensive-chinese-operation-infiltrate-american-institutions/.

41. Karen Jowers, "Exchanges Pull Certain Chinese Cellphones, Other
Devices over Security Concerns," *Military Times,* May 2, 2018, https://
www.militarytimes.com/pay-benefits/2018/05/02/exchanges-pull-
certain-chinese-cellphones-other-devices-over-security-concerns/?utm_
source=Sailthru&utm_medium=email&utm_campaign=ebb%20
03.05.18&utm_term=Editorial%20-%20Early%20Bird%20Brief.

42. Ibid.

43. Ibid.

44. Bill Ertz, "Russian Spy Ship off Georgia Coast," *Washington Free
Beacon*, March 8, 2018. http://freebeacon.com/national-security/
russian-spy-ship-off-georgia-coast/.

45. Ibid.

46. Ibid.

47. "Russian Spy: Highly Likely Moscow behind Attack, Says Theresa May,"
BBC, March 13, 2018, http://www.bbc.com/news/uk-43377856

48. Ibid.

49. Ibid.

50. Daniel Arkin, "Nikki Haley Tells UN Russia Responsible for Chemical
Attack," NBC News, March 15, 2018, https://www.nbcnews.com/
news/world/nikki-haley-tells-u-n-russia-responsible-chemical-attack-
n856701?utm_source=Sailthru&utm_medium=email&utm_
campaign=ebb%2003.15.18&utm_term=Editorial%20-%20Early%20
Bird%20Brief.

51. Aaron Mehta, "EUCOM Head: Alleged Russian Chemical Attack
Shows 'What They're Willing To Do,'" *Defense News*, March 16, 2018,
https://www.defensenews.com/global/europe/2018/03/16/eucom-head-
alleged-russian-chemical-attack-show-what-theyre-willing-to-do/?utm_
source=Sailthru&utm_medium=email&utm_campaign=ebb%20
03.16.18&utm_term=Editorial%20-%20Early%20Bird%20Brief.

52. Ibid.

53. "Russia: West Just Angry over Advances in Syria," Associated Press, March 19, 2018, https://www.militarytimes.com/news/2018/03/17/russia-west-just-angry-over-advances-in-syria/?utm_source=Sailthru&utm_medium=email&utm_campaign=ebb%20 03.19.18&utm_term=Editorial%20-%20Early%20Bird%20Brief.

54. Vadim Grishin, "U.S.-Russia Economic Relations," CSIS, October 24, 2017, https://www.csis.org/analysis/us-russia-economic-relations.

55. Chris Miller, "Russia's Energy Leverage on Europe: Declining but Still Troubling," *Global Issues*, Aspen Institute, March 22, 2016, https://www.aspeninstitute.it/aspenia-online/article/russia%E2%80%99s-energy-leverage-europe-declining-still-troubling.

56. Ibid.

57. Amie Ferris-Rotman, "Cold War Two? Russians Say New U.S. Sanctions Could Push Ties to 'Uncharted Waters'," *Haaretz*, July 26, 2017, https://www.haaretz.com/world-news/.premium-1.803638.

58. National Security Strategy, White House, December 2017, https://www.whitehouse.gov/wp-content/uploads/2017/12/NSS-Final-12-18-2017-0905.pdf.

59. Susan Shirk, "Trump and China," *Foreign Affairs*, Mar/Apr 2017, https://www.foreignaffairs.com/articles/2017-02-13/trump-and-china.

60. David Lynch, "Trump Readies Tougher 'America First' Line for China Trade in 2018," *Washington Post*, December 27, 2017, https://www.washingtonpost.com/news/wonk/wp/2017/12/27/trump-readying-shock-and-awe-response-on-china-trade-for-2018/?utm_term=.58678022e403.

61. Bill Gertz, "After Tariffs, Trump to Punish China for Intellectual Property Theft," *Washington Free Beacon*, March 12, 2018, http://freebeacon.com/national-security/tariffs-trump-punish-china-intellectual-property-theft/.

62. Ibid.

63. Ibid.

64. David P. Goldman, "How to Meet the Strategic Challenge Posed by China," IMPRIMIS, a publication of Hillsdale College, Vol. 47, No. 3, March 2018.

65. "For the U.S. and China, the Economic Fight of the Century Begins," Stratfor, May 10, 2018, https://worldview.stratfor.com/article/us-and-china-economic-fight-century-begins.

66. Christian Shepherd and Michael Martina, "China Boosts Defense Spending, Rattling Its Neighbors' Nerves," Reuters, March 5, 2018, https://www.reuters.com/article/us-china-parliament-defence/china-boosts-defense-spending-amid-military-modernization-idUSKCN1GG072?utm_source=Sailthru&utm_medium=email&utm_campaign=ebb%20 03.05.18&utm_term=Editorial%20-%20Early%20Bird%20Brief.

67. Ibid.

68. *Annual Report to Congress, Military and Security Developments Involving the People's Republic of China*, Office of the Secretary of Defense, May 15, 2017, P.39, https://www.defense.gov/Portals/1/Documents/pubs/2017_China_Military_Power_Report.PDF.

69. Sydney J. Freeberg Jr., "US Defense Budget Not That Much Bigger Than China, Russia: Gen. Milley," *Breaking Defense*, May 22, 2018, https://breakingdefense.com/2018/05/us-defense-budget-not-that-much-bigger-than-china-russia-gen-milley/?utm_source=Sailthru&utm_medium=email&utm_campaign=ebb%20 5/22/18&utm_term=Editorial%20-%20Early%20Bird%20Brief.

70. "Russia: Military Spending Falls for First Time in 19 Years," STRATFOR, accessed May 2, 2018, https://www.stratfor.com/situation-report/russia-military-spending-falls-first-time-19-years.

71. "World Military Spending: Increases in the USA and Europe, Decreases in Oil-Exporting Countries," Stockholm International Peace Research Institute, April 24, 2017, https://www.sipri.org/media/press-release/2017/world-military-spending-increases-usa-and-europe.

72. "Japan Defense Chief Hints at Need to Bring Down Chinese Cruise Missiles," *Asia Times*, January 12, 2018, http://www.atimes.com/article/japan-defense-chief-hints-need-bring-chinese-cruise-missiles/.

73. "World Military Spending: Increases in the USA and Europe, Decreases in Oil-Exporting Countries," Stockholm International Peace Research Institute, April 24, 2017, https://www.sipri.org/media/press-release/2017/world-military-spending-increases-usa-and-europe.

74. "Denmark Will Increase Defense Spending to Counter Russia: PM," Reuters, January 15, 2018, https://www.reuters.com/article/us-russia-security-denmark/denmark-will-increase-defense-spending-to-counter-russia-pm-idUSKBN1F42LT?utm_

source=Sailthru&utm_medium=email&utm_campaign=ebb%20
01.16.2018&utm_term=Editorial%20-%20Early%20Bird%20Brief.

75. *Annual Report to Congress, Military and Security Developments Involving the People's Republic of China*, Office of the Secretary of Defense, May 15, 2017, P.39. https://www.defense.gov/Portals/1/Documents/pubs/2017_China_Military_Power_Report.PDF.

76. "China Has Started Building its Third Aircraft Carrier, Military Sources say," *South China Post*, January 4, 2018, http://www.scmp.com/news/china/diplomacy-defence/article/2126883/china-has-started-building-its-third-aircraft-carrier?utm_source=Sailthru&utm_medium=email&utm_campaign=DFN%20EBB%2008.01.2018&utm_term=Editorial%20-%20Early%20Bird%20Brief.

77. Bill Gertz, "China Rapidly Building Advanced Arms for Use against U.S.," *Washington Free Beacon*, May 11, 2018, http://freebeacon.com/national-security/china-rapidly-building-advanced-arms-use-u-s/.

78. "Russia Military Power, Building a Military to Support Great Power Aspirations," Defense Intelligence Agency, 2017, p. 25. http://www.dia.mil/Portals/27/Documents/News/Military%20Power%20Publications/Russia%20Military%20Power%20Report%202017.pdf.

79. Jess Macy Yu and Greg Torode, "Taiwan Plans to Invest in Advanced Arms as China Flexes Its Muscles," Reuters, January 11, 2018, https://www.reuters.com/article/us-taiwan-defence-spending/taiwan-plans-to-invest-in-advanced-arms-as-china-flexes-its-muscles-idUSKBN1F00PC.

80. Rezaul H Laskar, "India Is Fifth Largest Military Spender with Outlay of $55.9 Bn: SIPRI," *Hindustantimes*, April 24, 2017. https://www.hindustantimes.com/world-news/india-is-fifth-largest-military-spender-with-outlay-of-55-9-bn-sipri/story-bOH1JVFUcnOxKH3XTdncSM.html.

81. "What Is India's Military Strength?," *Indian Express*, July 16, 2017, http://indianexpress.com/article/what-s/what-is-indias-military-strength-4748511/.

82. "Chinese Military Waging a Cold War at the Roof of the World," *Asia Times*, May 7, 2018, http://www.atimes.com/article/chinese-military-waging-a-cold-war-at-the-roof-of-the-world/?utm_source=Sailthru&utm_medium=email&utm_campaign=ebb%20 08.05.18&utm_term=Editorial%20-%20Early%20Bird%20Brief.

83. "Russia Military Power, Building a Military to Support Great Power

Aspirations," Defense Intelligence Agency, 2017, p. 15, http://www.dia.mil/Portals/27/Documents/News/Military%20Power%20Publications/Russia%20Military%20Power%20Report%202017.pdf.

84. Bill Gertz, "DIA: China, Russia Engaged in Low-Level Warfare against U.S.," *Washington Free Beacon*, March 7, 2018, http://freebeacon.com/national-security/dia-china-russia-engaged-in-low-level-warfare-against-u-s/.

85. Lucas Robinson, "The New Cold War Is On," UWIRE, August 18, 2016, p.1, http://www.idsnews.com/article/2016/08/new-cold-war-is-on.

86. "Analysts: Russia's Military Threats Mainly Bluster, but Conflict Risk Rising," *Voice of America*, March 7, 2018, https://www.voanews.com/a/analysts-russia-military-threats-mainly-bluster-conflict-risk-rising/3913524.html.

87. "What is Atlantic Resolve?" US Army Europe website, accessed May 26, 2018, http://www.eur.army.mil/AtlanticResolve/.

88. "List of Russian Military Bases Abroad," Wikipedia, accessed March 8, 2018, https://en.wikipedia.org/wiki/List_of_Russian_military_bases_abroad.

89. Michael Wilner and Herb Keinon, "Allied Strike Reveals Robust, 'Clandestine' Chemical Program in Syria," *Jerusalem Post*, April 14, 2018, http://www.jpost.com/International/Allied-strike-reveal-robust-clandestine-chemical-program-in-Syria-549811?utm_source=newsletter&utm_campaign=15-4-2018&utm_content=allied-strike-reveal-robust-clandestine-chemical-program-in-syria-549811.

90. Robert Ashley, DIA Director, testimony before the Senate Armed Services Committee, March 6, 2018, http://www.dia.mil/DesktopModules/ArticleCS/Print.aspx?PortalId=27&ModuleId=24601&Article=1457815.

91. Todd South, "Top General Says Balkans, Not Baltics, the Most Vulnerable to Russian Influence," *Army Times*, March 8, 2018, https://www.armytimes.com/news/your-army/2018/03/08/top-general-says-balkans-not-baltics-the-most-vulnerable-to-russian-influence/?utm_source=Sailthru&utm_medium=email&utm_campaign=ebb%2003.09.18&utm_term=Editorial%20-%20Early%20Bird%20Brief.

92. Morgan Chalfant, "Russia Claims North Pole for Itself, Plants Titanium Russian Flag on Floor of Arctic Ocean," *Washington Free Beacon*, August 5, 2015, http://freebeacon.com/national-security/russia-claims-north-pole-for-itself-plants-titanium-russian-flag-on-floor-of-arctic-ocean/.

93. Sebastien Roblin, "Why Russia's Enemies Fear the Kalibr Cruise Missile," *National Interest*, January 22, 2017, http://nationalinterest.org/blog/the-buzz/why-russias-enemies-fear-the-kalibr-cruise-missile-19129.

94. *Annual Report to Congress, Military and Security Developments Involving the People's Republic of China*, Office of the Secretary of Defense, May 15, 2017, P.39, https://www.defense.gov/Portals/1/Documents/pubs/2017_China_Military_Power_Report.PDF.

95. Jean-Marc Blanchard, "The Security Implications of China's Overseas Investment Boom," *The Diplomat*, April 14, 2017, https://thediplomat.com/2017/04/the-security-implications-of-chinas-overseas-investment-boom/.

96. Ibid.

97. Logan Pauley, "As the US and Russia Spar over Syria, China sits Strategically on the Sidelines," *World Politics*, Review, April 17, 2018, https://www.worldpoliticsreview.com/articles/24580/as-the-u-s-and-russia-spar-over-syria-china-sits-strategically-on-the-sidelines.

98. Ibid.

99. Ibid.

100. Ibid.

101. "US revising missile defense policy to include threats from Russia, China: Report," *Army Times*, March 3, 2018, http://www.atimes.com/article/us-revising-missile-defense-policy-include-threats-russia-china-report/?utm_source=Sailthru&utm_medium=email&utm_campaign=ebb%2003.05.18&utm_term=Editorial%20-%20Early%20Bird%20Brief.

102. Juri Luik and Tomas Jermalavicius, "A Plausible Scenario of Nuclear War in Europe, and How to Deter It: A Perspective from Estonia," *Bulletin of the Atomic Scientists*, 2017, Vol 73, No. 4, 233–239, www.tandfonline.com/doi/abs/10.1080/00963402.2017.1338014.

103. "Russia Military Power, Building a Military to Support Great Power Aspirations," Defense Intelligence Agency, 2017, p. TBD, http://www.dia.mil/Portals/27/Documents/News/Military%20Power%20Publications/Russia%20Military%20Power%20Report%202017.pdf.

104. Ibid.

105. Ibid.

106. Tom O'Connor, "Russia Conflict with NATO and U.S. Would Immediately Result in Nuclear War, Russian Lawmaker Warns," *Newsweek*, May 30, 2017, http://www.newsweek.com/russia-politician-nuclear-weapons-us-nato-crimea-617613.

107. Ibid.

108. Tom O'Connor, "Russia Conflict with NATO and U.S. Would Immediately Result in Nuclear War, Russian Lawmaker Warns," Newsweek, May 30, 2017, http://www.newsweek.com/russia-politician-nuclear-weapons-us-nato-crimea-617613.

109. Carlos Ballesteros, "Russia Has Underwater Nuclear Drones, Leaked Pentagon Documents Reveal," *Newsweek*, January 15, 2018, https://www.msn.com/en-us/news/world/russia-has-underwater-nuclear-drones-leaked-pentagon-documents-reveal/ar-AAuFOuP?li=AA4Zpp&ocid=spartandhp.

110. *Annual Report to Congress, Military and Security Developments Involving the People's Republic of China*, Office of the Secretary of Defense, May 15, 2017, P.60, https://www.defense.gov/Portals/1/Documents/pubs/2017_China_Military_Power_Report.PDF.

111. "Revealed: China's Nuclear-Capable Air-Launched Ballistic Missile," *The Diplomat,* April 2018, https://thediplomat.com/2018/04/revealed-chinas-nuclear-capable-air-launched-ballistic-missile/?utm_source=Sailthru&utm_medium=email&utm_campaign=ebb-4-11&utm_term=Editorial%20-%20Early%20Bird%20Brief.

112. Robert Ashley, DIA Director, testimony before the Senate Armed Services Committee, March 6, 2018, http://www.dia.mil/DesktopModules/ArticleCS/Print.aspx?PortalId=27&ModuleId=24601&Article=1457815.

113. Elizabeth Chuck, "Fact Sheet: Who Has Nuclear Weapons, And How Many Do They Have?," NBC News, March 31, 2016, https://www.nbcnews.com/news/world/fact-sheet-who-has-nuclear-weapons-how-many-do-they-n548481.

114. Ibid.

115. Robert Ashley, DIA Director, testimony before the Senate Armed Services Committee, March 6, 2018, http://www.dia.mil/DesktopModules/ArticleCS/Print.aspx?PortalId=27&ModuleId=24601&Article=1457815.

116. *Russia Military Power, Building a Military to Support Great Power Aspirations*, DIA, 2017, p.15.

117. Robert Burns, "Intelligence report: The Kremlin Believes the US Wants Regime Change in Russia," Associated Press, June 28, 2017. http://www.businessinsider.com/report-kremlin-believes-us-wants-regime-change-in-russia-2017-6

118. Ibid.

119. Ibid.

120. *Annual Report to Congress, Military and Security Developments Involving the People's Republic of China*, Office of the Secretary of Defense, May 15, 2017, P.39, https://www.defense.gov/Portals/1/Documents/pubs/2017_China_Military_Power_Report.PDF.

121. Ibid, p.50.

122. Ray Smith, "Yes, It Is a New Cold War. What Is to Be Done?" *War on the Rocks*, April 25, 2018, https://warontherocks.com/2018/04/yes-it-is-a-new-cold-war-what-is-to-be-done/?utm_source=Sailthru&utm_medium=email&utm_campaign=ebb%2026.04.18&utm_term=Editorial%20-%20Early%20Bird%20Brief.

123. Ibid.

124. Meghan Friedmann, "Prof. Declares Emergence of Second Cold War," *Brown Dailey Herald*, April 1, 2014, http://www.browndailyherald.com/2014/04/01/prof-declares-emergence-second-cold-war/.

125. An Baijie, "China, Russia Note Strategic Importance Tied to Relationship," *China Daily*, April 28, 2017, http://usa.chinadaily.com.cn/world/2017-04/28/content_29128332.htm.

126. "Russian Defence Minister Had an Appointment with Vice Chairman of the Central Military Commission of the People's Republic of China," Ministry of Defense Russian Federation, accessed March 10, 2018, http://eng.mil.ru/en/army2016/news/more.htm?id=12054707@egNews.

127. "Chinese Naval Fleet Departs for Joint Drill in Russia," *Xinhuanet*, June 18, 2017. http://www.xinhuanet.com/english/2017-06/18/c_136375277.htm.

128. Ethan Meick, "China-Russia Military-to-Military Relations: Moving toward a Higher Level of Cooperation," U.S.-China Economic Security Review Commission, March 20, 2017, https://www.uscc.gov/sites/default/

files/Research/China-Russia%20Mil-Mil%20Relations%20Moving%20
Toward%20Higher%20Level%20of%20Cooperation.pdf.

129. Gabriel Domingue, "China, Russia Experiencing 'Highest Period of
Military Co-operation', Says US Report," *Jane's 360*, March 21, 2017,
http://www.janes.com/article/68856/china-russia-experiencing-highest-
period-of-military-co-operation-says-us-report.

130. Vladimir Isachenkov, "China's Defense Chief Calls His
Moscow Trip a Signal to U.S.," ABC News, April 3,
2018, http://abcnews.go.com/International/wireStory/
chinas-defense-chief-moscow-trip-signal-us-54205721.

131. Tom O'Connor, "Russia, China Pledge New Military Ties, Challenge
U.S.," *Newsweek*, April 25, 2018, http://www.msn.com/en-us/
news/world/russia-china-pledge-new-military-ties-challenge-us/
ar-AAwibTl?ocid=ientp.

132. Bill Gertz, "Trump to Sign Taiwan Bill Opposed by Beijng," *Washington
Free Beacon*, March 2, 2018, http://freebeacon.com/national-security/
trump-sign-taiwan-bill-opposed-beijing/.

133. Ibid.

134. Adela Lin and Ezra Fieser, "Dominican Republic Establishes China Ties in
Taiwan Blow," *Bloomberg*, April 30, 2018, https://www.bloomberg.com/
news/articles/2018-05-01/dominican-republic-establishes-ties-with-china-
in-blow-to-taiwan?utm_source=Sailthru&utm_medium=email&utm_
campaign=ebb%205/1/18&utm_term=Editorial%20-%20Early%20
Bird%20Brief and "Burkino Faso: Ougadougou Cuts Deplomatic Ties
with Taiwan," Stratfor, accessed May 26, 2018, https://www.stratfor.com/
situation-report/burkina-faso-ouagadougou-cuts-diplomatic-ties-taiwan.

135. Tom O'Connor, "U.S. War with China May Be More Likely,
Deadlier," *Newsweek*, October 4, 2017, http://www.newsweek.com/
us-war-china-more-likely-deadlier-report-677696.

136. Interview with Dr. Christopher Lew on March 8, 2018.

137. Hannah Hartig, John Lapinski and Stephanie Perry, "Poll: Majority of
Americans Worried about War, Feel Favorably Toward NATO," NBC
News, February 22, 2017, https://www.nbcnews.com/feature/data-points/
poll-majority-americans-worried-about-war-feel-favorably-toward-
nato-n723931.

138. Greg Price, "U.S. Is Russia's Biggest Enemy, According to Majority of Russians in New Poll," *Newsweek*, January 10, 2018, http://www. newsweek.com/cold-war-russia-us-enemy-776772.

139. Marc Champion, "New Cold War Chills Annual Kremlin Gathering of Foreign Experts," *Bloomberg*, October 26, 2016, https://www.bloomberg.com/news/articles/2016-10-26/ new-cold-war-chills-annual-kremlin-gathering-of-foreign-experts.

140. Cited in David Ignatius, "America Ignores Russia at Its Peril," *Washington Post*, March 6, 2018. https://www.washingtonpost.com/opinions/ global-opinions/america-ignores-russia-at-its-peril/2018/03/06/0fad7f52-218e-11e8-94da-ebf9d112159c_story.html?utm_campaign=EBB%20 3.7.18&utm_medium=email&utm_source=Sailthru&utm_ term=.8739a6e37c55.

141. "Analysts: Russia's Military Threats Mainly Bluster, but Conflict Risk Rising," *Voice of America*, March 7, 2018. https://www.voanews. com/a/analysts-russia-military-threats-mainly-bluster-conflict-risk-rising/3913524.html.

142. Ibid.

143. Meghan Friedmann, "Prof. Declares Emergence of Second Cold War," *Brown Dailey Herald*, April 1, 2014, http://www.browndailyherald. com/2014/04/01/prof-declares-emergence-second-cold-war/.

144. Ibid.

145. Cited in "Russian Commentators Criticize Putin's State of the Nation Address for Strengthening U.S. Hawks Rather Than Paving Way for Negotiations Part II," MEMRI Special Dispatch No. 7372, March 8, 2018, https://www.memri.org/reports/russian-commentators-criticize-putins-state-nation-address-strengthening-us-hawks-rather.

146. Ibid.

147. Ibid.

148. Cited in "Reactions to Putin's State of the Union Address: If What the U.S. Wants Is the Cold War, So Let It Be the Cold War—Part I," MEMRI Special Dispatch No. 7367, March 6, 2018, https://www.memri.org/ reports/reactions-putins-state-union-address-if-what-us-wants-cold-war-so-let-it-be-cold-war-%E2%80%93-part.

149. Kor Kian Beng, "China Warming to New Cold War?," *Strait*

Times, August 22, 2016, http://www.straitstimes.com/opinion/ china-warming-to-new-cold-war.

150. Ibid.

151. James Griffiths and Serenitie Wang, "China Says Trump's New Security Policy Shows 'Cold War Mentality,'" CNN, December 19, 2017, http:// www.cnn.com/2017/12/19/politics/china-trump-national-security-strategy-intl/index.html.

152. Ibid.

153. Interview with Dr. Steven W. Mosher on March 18, 2018.

154. "National Security Strategy," The White House, December 2017. Accessed March 10,2018, p. 25, https://www.whitehouse.gov/wp-content/ uploads/2017/12/NSS-Final-12-18-2017-0905.pdf.

155. James Griffiths and Serenitie Wang, "China Says Trump's New Security Policy Shows 'Cold War Mentality,'" CNN, December 19, 2017, http:// www.cnn.com/2017/12/19/politics/china-trump-national-security-strategy-intl/index.html.

156. Ibid.

157. Diana Stancy Correll, "H. R. McMaster: US Has 'Failed to Impose Sufficient Costs' on Russia," *Washington Examiner*, April 3, 2018, https://www.washingtonexaminer.com/news/ hr-mcmaster-us-has-failed-to-impose-sufficient-costs-on-russia.

158. "Kremlin Denounces 'Imperialist Character' of US Strategic Report," *Sun Daily*, December 19, 2017, http://www.thesundaily.my/news/2017/12/19/ kremlin-denounces-imperialist-character-us-strategic-report.

159. Simon Shuster, "Exclusive: Russia's Prime Minister on Syria, Sanctions and a New Cold War," *Time*, February 15, 2016, http://time.com/4224537/ russia-syra-civil-war-dmitri-medvedev-interview/.

160. MEMRI Special Dispatch No. 6802, Munich Security Conference— Russian FM Lavrov's Call for a New World Order to Counter U.S. Influence in Europe, February 24, 2017.

161. Andrew Kaczynski, "Senate Intel Chair Says US Is in a New Cold War with Russia," CNN, April 25, 2017, https://www.cnn.com/2017/04/25/ politics/kfile-richard-burr-new-cold-war/index.html.

162. "Ex-CIA Chief Warns of New Cold War with Russia, WMD Threat from ISIS," CBS News, March 1, 2018, https://www.cbsnews.com/

news/michael-morell-cold-war-russia-putin-nuclear-weapons/?utm_source=Sailthru&utm_medium=email&utm_campaign=ebb%20 03.01.18&utm_term=Editorial%20-%20Early%20Bird%20Brief.

163. Ibid.

164. Bradford Betz, "'There's a War Coming,' Marine Corps General Warns US Troops," Fox News, December 23, 2017, http://www.foxnews.com/us/2017/12/23/theres-war-coming-marine-corps-general-warns-us-troops.html.

165. Jack Maidment, "Relationship between Russia and US Most 'Dangerous' Since Cold War, Says Former UK Ambassador to Moscow," *Telegraph*, July 7, 2017, http://www.telegraph.co.uk/news/2017/07/07/relationship-russia-us-dangerous-since-cold-war-says-former/.

166. Ibid.

167. Ibid.

168. Christina Anderson and Rick Gladstone, "If War Comes? Stock Up on Tortillas and Wet Wipes, Sweden Suggests," New York Times, May 21, 2018, https://www.nytimes.com/2018/05/21/world/europe/sweden-disaster-handbook.html.

169. "The New Cold War, *Maclean's*, October 24, 2016, p.9.

170. Robert Ashley, DIA Director, testimony before the Senate Armed Services Committee, March 6, 2018, http://www.dia.mil/DesktopModules/ArticleCS/Print.aspx?PortalId=27&ModuleId=24601&Article=1457815.

171. Maggis Tenis, "U.S. May Act on Russian INF Violation," Arms Control Association, July/August 2017, https://www.armscontrol.org/act/2017-07/news/us-may-act-russian-inf-violation.

172. David Welna, "Pentagon Confirms Russia Violated Nuclear Arms Treaty," NPR, March 9, 2017. https://www.npr.org/2017/03/09/519499961/pentagon-confirms-russia-violated-nuclear-arms-treaty.

173. Ibid.

174. "Trust, But Verify," Wikipedia. Accessed March 18, 2018, https://en.wikipedia.org/wiki/Trust,_but_verify.

175. "We're on the Road to a New Cold War," Editorial Board, *Washington Post*, July 31, 2017, https://www.washingtonpost.com/opinions/were-on-the-road-to-a-new-cold-war/2017/07/31/213af6be-7617-11e7-8839-ec48ec4cae25_story.html?utm_term=.5abdac401f1d.

176. "Putin Ally's Private Army behind Attack on U.S.-Backed Forces?," CBS News, February 23, 2018, https://www.cbsnews.com/news/russia-vladimir-putin-yevgeny-prigozhin-wagner-group-attack-us-allies-syria/.

177. Paul Crookston, "Mattis on Russian Mercenaries in Syria: I Ordered Their Annihilation," *Washington Free Beacon*, April 26, 2018. http://freebeacon.com/national-security/mattis-russian-mercenaries-syria-ordered-annihilation/.

178. Ibid.

179. Richard Engel, "U.S. Troops Who Repelled Russian Mercenaries Prepare More Attacks," NBC News, March 15, 2018, https://www.nbcnews.com/news/world/u-s-troops-who-repelled-russian-mercenaries-prepare-more-attacks-n855271?utm_source=Sailthru&utm_medium=email&utm_campaign=ebb%2003.16.18&utm_term=Editorial%20-%20Early%20Bird%20Brief.

180. Ibid.

181. "Russian Civilians Helping Assad Use Military Base Back Home—Witnesses," Reuters, April 25, 2018, https://www.reuters.com/article/us-mideast-crisis-syria-russia-military/exclusive-russian-civilians-helping-assad-use-military-base-back-home-witnesses-idUSKBN1HW0LX?utm_source=Sailthru&utm_medium=email&utm_campaign=EBB%20 4.25.18&utm_term=Editorial%20-%20Early%20Bird%20Brief.

182. "Russia Revisits an Old Cold War Battleground," STRATFOR, January 15, 2018, https://worldview.stratfor.com/article/russia-revisits-old-cold-war-battleground?id=743c 2bc617&e=99971e0a2b&uuid=411c1f4b-11c3-49b6-ba68-27274f7bc472&utm_source=Topics%2C+Themes+and+Regions&utm_campaign=eb057bce7a-EMAIL_CAMPAIGN_2018_01_15&utm_medium=email&utm_term=0_743c2bc617-eb057bce7a-53692653&mc_cid=eb057bce7a&mc_eid=99971e0a2b.

183. Abigail Norris, "North Korea THREAT: US General Warns China Is Fighting a Proxy War with US amid WW3 Fears," *Express*, December 28, 2017, https://www.express.co.uk/news/world/897370/North-Korea-news-China-Kim-Jong-un-Donald-Trump-World-War-3-latest.

184. Katsuji Nakazawa, "Project 2035: Xi Tells Kim Why China Is a Better Bet Than Trump," *Nikkei Asian Review*, April 16, 2018,

https://asia.nikkei.com/Editor-s-Picks/China-up-close/Project-2035-Xi-tells-Kim-why-China-is-a-better-bet-than-Trump?utm_source=Sailthru&utm_medium=email&utm_campaign=EBB%20 4/17/18&utm_term=Editorial%20-%20Early%20Bird%20Brief.

185. David C. Gompert, Astrid Stuth Cevallos and Cristina L. Garafola, "War with China Thinking through the Unthinkable," RAND, 2016, https://www.rand.org/pubs/research_reports/RR1140.html.

186. Nafeez Ahmed, "Pentagon Study Declares American Empire Is 'Collapsing'," *Insurgeintelligence*, July 17, 2017, https://medium.com/insurge-intelligence/pentagon-study-declares-american-empire-is-collapsing-746754cdaebf.

187. Nathan P. Freier et al, "At Our Own Peril: DoD Risk Assessment in a Post-Primacy World," Strategic Studies Institute, U.S. Army War College, June 2017, https://ssi.armywarcollege.edu/pdffiles/PUB1358.pdf.

188. Cited in "President Reagan's "Evil Empire" Speech to the National Association of Evangelicals," accessed March 14, 2018, http://chnm.gmu.edu/1989/items/show/64.

189. English Oxford Living Dictionaries, accessed March 14, 2018, https://en.oxforddictionaries.com/definition/us/empire.

190. Henry Kissinger, *World Order*, Penguin Press, New York, 2014, p. 140.

191. J.R. Fears, "Reflections on the Rise and Fall of Empires," Big Think, accessed March 14, 2018, http://bigthink.com/learning-from-the-past/reflections-on-the-rise-and-fall-of-empires.

192. Ibid.

193. "Baby Boomer Excess Led to Hubris, Cultural Decay," *National Review*, November 14, 2017, https://www.nationalreview.com/2017/.../baby-boomer-excess-led-hubris-cultural-dec.

194. Ben Shapiro: Hundreds of People Were Turned Away from Attending UConn Speech, Fox News, January 24, 2018, http://insider.foxnews.com/2018/01/24/ben-shapiro-uconn-speech-writer-reacts-restricted-access-student-counseling.

195. David P. Goldman, "How to Meet the Strategic Challenge Posed by China," IMPRIMIS, a publication of Hillsdale College, Vol. 47, No. 3, March 2018.

196. Aaron Mehta, "America's Industrial Base Is at Risk, and the Military May

Feel the Consequences," *Defense News*, May 21, 2018, https://www. defensenews.com/pentagon/2018/05/22/americas-industrial-base-is-at- risk-and-the-military-may-feel-the-consequences/.

197. J. R. Fears, "Reflections on the Rise and Fall of Empires," Big Think, accessed March 14, 2018, http://bigthink.com/learning-from-the-past/ reflections-on-the-rise-and-fall-of-empires.

198. "Ancient Persia Dreier Lyons," accessed March 14, 2018, https:// sites.google.com/a/jeffcoschools.us/ancient-persia-dreier-lyons/ reasons-for-its-decline-and-fall.

199. N. S. Gill, "The Fall of Rome: How, When and Why Did It Happen?," Thoughtco.com, March 13, 2017, https://www.thoughtco.com/ what-was-the-fall-of-rome-112688.

200. N. S. Gill, "Economic Reasons for the Fall of Rome," Thoughtco.com, March 8, 2017, https://www.thoughtco.com/ economic-reasons-for-fall-of-rome-118357.

201. Jim Dexter, "CNN Fact Check: The Last President to Balance the Budget," CNN, February 3, 2010, http://politicalticker.blogs.cnn.com/2010/02/03/ cnn-fact-check-the-last-president-to-balance-the-budget/.

202. David M. Smick, "The Death of Economics; a Fatal Case of Hubris," *Weekly Standard*, July 8, 2013, http://www.weeklystandard.com/ the-death-of-economics/article/738065.

203. Kenneth Rogoff, "Don't Blame the Federal Reserve for Not Predicting the Financial Crisis," *Guardian*, February 11, 2013, https://www.theguardian. com/business/2013/feb/11/federal-reserve-blame-financial-crisis.

204. Andrew Clark and Jill Treanor, "Greenspan—I Was Wrong about the Economy. Sort Of," *Guardian*, October 24, 2008, https://www.theguardian.com/business/2008/oct/24/ economics-creditcrunch-federal-reserve-greenspan.

205. David Ronfeldt, "Beware the Hubris-Nemesis," RAND, 1994, p.2, https://www.rand.org/pubs/monograph_reports/MR461.html.

206. Amy Davies, "Read an Extract from Hubris by Alistair Horne," October 23, 2015, https://www.wnblog.co.uk/2015/10/ read-an-extract-of-hubris-by-alistair-horne/.

207. "Napoleon Retreats from Moscow, *This Day in History*, History,

Accessed March 14, 2018, http://www.history.com/this-day-in-history/napoleon-retreats-from-moscow.

208. Roger Moorhouse, "Hitler's Willing Warriors; The German Army Was Quickly Seduced by Nazi Fantasy," *Times*, June 18, 2016.

209. Review by Roger Moorehouse, "Hitler's Soldiers: The German Army in the Third Reich by Ben H Shepherd," *Times*, June 18, 2016, https://www.thetimes.co.uk/article/hitlers-soldiers-the-german-army-in-the-third-reich-by-ben-h-shepherd-89kzhhfw9.

210. Ibid.

211. David Halberstam, *The Coldest Winter, Reviewed by Stanley Weintraub, washingtonpost.com,* September 23, 2007, http://www.washingtonpost.com/wp-dyn/content/article/2007/09/20/AR2007092002084.html.

212. Ibid.

213. Donald J. Farinacci, *Truman and MacArthur: Adversaries for a Common Cause*, Lulu.com, p. 151.

214. David Halberstam, *The Best and the Brightest*, Random House Publishing, March 26, 2002.

215. Robert S. McNamara, "'We Were Wrong, Terribly Wrong'," *Newsweek*, April 16, 1995, http://www.newsweek.com/we-were-wrong-terribly-wrong-181794.

216. Robert McNamara, *In Retrospect: The Tragedy and Lessons of Vietnam*, Knopf Doubleday Publishing Group, September 6, 2017, p.22.

217. Janet Landman, "The Confessions of a War Maker and a War Resister," *Michigan Quarterly Review*, Volume XXXVIII, Issue 3, Summer 1999.

218. T. Christopher Jespersen, "Analogies at War: Iraq and Vietnam," *OAH Magazine of History*, January 2013, Vol. 27, No. 1, pp. 19–22.

219. Michael Isikoff and David Corn, *Hubris: The Inside Story of Spin, Scandal and the Selling of the Iraq War*, review by Major Georffrey S. DeWeese, *Military Law Review*, Vol. 194, Winter 2007.

220. T. Christopher Jespersen, "Analogies at War: Iraq and Vietnam," *OAH Magazine of History*, January 2013, Vol. 27, No. 1, pp. 19–22.

221. Ibid.

222. Ibid.

223. Paul Pillar, "Intelligence, Policy and the War in Iraq," *Foreign Affairs*, Mar./Apr. 2006, *available at* http://www.foreignaffairs.

org/20060301faessay85202-p0/paul-r-pillar/intelligence-policy-and-the-war-in-iraq.html.

224. "Bush Cchastised for Vietnam Analogy," *Politico*, CBS News, August 24, 2007, https://www.cbsnews.com/news/bush-chastised-for-vietnam-analogy/.

225. Williamson Murray, *War Strategy and Military Effectiveness*, Cambridge University Press, September 30, 2011, p. 68.

226. Ibid., p. 69.

227. Ibid.

228. Paul D. Shinkman, "Army Chief Chafes at New Reliance on Technology," *US News*, October 23, 2013, https://www.usnews.com/news/articles/2013/10/23/army-chief-chafes-at-new-reliance-on-technology.

229. Charles Smith, "When the Aristocracy Leaves the Commoners in the Dust, the Empire Is Doomed," Two Minds.com, October 2015, http://charleshughsmith.blogspot.com/2015/10/when-aristocracy-leaves-commoners-in.html.

230. Ibid.

231. Charles Hugh Smith, "When the Aristocracy Leaves the Commoners in the Dust, the Empire Is Doomed," washingtonblog.com, October 2015, http://www.washingtonsblog.com/2015/10/when-the-aristocracy-leaves-the-commoners-in-the-dust-the-empire-is-doomed.html.

232. Ibid.

233. Lord David Owen, "Hubris and Nemesis in Heads of Government," *Journal of the Royal Society of Medicine*, 2006 Nov; 99(11): 548–551, https://www.ncbi.nlm.nih.gov/pmc/articles/PMC1633549/.

234. Steven M. Walt, "The Myth of American Exceptionalism," *Foreign Policy*, October 11, 2011, http://foreignpolicy.com/2011/10/11/the-myth-of-american-exceptionalism/.

235. Ibid.

236. Stanley Hoffman, "The High and the Mighty," *American Prospect*, December 19, 2002, http://prospect.org/article/high-and-mighty.

237. Nichlos Clairmont, "'Those Who Do Not Learn History Are Doomed to Repeat It.' Really?," Bigthink.com, accessed March 14, 2018, http://bigthink.com/the-proverbial-skeptic/those-who-do-not-learn-history-doomed-to-repeat-it-really.

238. Joseph M. Siracusa, "The 'New' Cold War History and the Origins of the
      Cold War," *Australian Journal of Politics and History*: Volume 47, Number
      1, 2001, pp. 149–155.

239. Cited in Leon Hadar, "A New Perspective on Cold War History," a book
      review, *The American Conservative,* 17.1 (January-February 2018): p53+.

240. Ibid.

241. Cited in Jeremy Kuzmarov and John Marciano, "The Russians Are
      Coming, Again," *Monthly Review*, September 2017.

242. Ibid.

243. Cited in Michael J. Carley, Review of Foglesong, David S., *America's
      Secret War Against Bolshevism: U.S. Intervention in the Russian Civil War,
      1917–1920*. H-Russia, H-Net Reviews. June, 1996, http://www.h-net.
      org/reviews/showrev.php?id=489.

244. Ibid.

245. Ibid.

246. "Allied Intervention in the Russian Civil War," Wikipedia.
      org, accessed March 14, 2018, https://en.wikipedia.org/wiki/
      Allied_intervention_in_the_Russian_Civil_War.

247. Cited in Jeremy Kuzmarov and John Marciano, "The Russians Are
      Coming, Again," *Monthly Review*, September 2017.

248. D. F. Fleming, "The Western Intervention in the Soviet Union, 1918–
      1920," *New World Review*, Fall 1967; D. F. Fleming, *The Cold War and Its
      Origins, 1917–1960*, vol. 1 (New York: Doubleday, 1960); William Blum,
      Killing Hope (Monroe, ME: Common Courage, 1998), 8.

249. William Appleman Williams, *American Russian Relations 1781–1947*
      (New York: Rhinehart, 1952), 83.

250. Cited in Jeremy Kuzmarov and John Marciano, "The Russians Are
      Coming, Again," *Monthly Review*, September 2017.

251. Ibid, p.19.

252. Ibid.

253. Neil Carey, ed., *Fighting the Bolsheviks: The Russian War Memoir of Private
      1st Class Donald E. Carey, U.S. Army, 1918–1919* (Novato, CA: Presidio,
      1997), x; David Foglesong, *America's Secret War Against Bolshevism* (Chapel
      Hill, NC: University of North Carolina Press, 2001), 7.

254. Cited in Leon Hadar, "A New Perspective on Cold War History," *The*

American Conservative. 17.1 (January–February 2018): p53+.

255. Ibid.

256. "A New Perspective on Cold War History," Leon Hadar *The American Conservative*. 17.1 (January-February 2018): p53+.

257. "Stalin's Cold War: The Soviet Dictator All by Himself Was the Cause Ronald Radosh," *The Weekly Standard,* 19.5 (Oct. 7, 2013).

258. Ibid.

259. Ibid.

260. Ibid.

261. Ibid.

262. Ibid.

263. Ibid.

264. Joseph M. Siracusa, "The 'New' Cold War History and the Origins of the Cold War," *Australian Journal of Politics and History*, Vol. 47, No. 1, 2001.

265. Ibid.

266. Ibid.

267. Ibid.

268. "2,400 Year Old "Enemy of My Enemy Is My Friend" Myth Has Led to Insanely Stupid U.S. Foreign Policy," washingtonsblog.com, September 2014, accessed March 14, 2018, http://www.washingtonsblog.com/2014/09/americas-strategy-failing-world-complex-use-enemy-enemy-friend-strategy.html.

269. Cited in Michael J. Carley, Review of Foglesong, David S., *America's Secret War Against Bolshevism: U.S. Intervention in the Russian Civil War, 1917–1920*. H-Russia, H-Net Reviews. June, 1996, http://www.h-net.org/reviews/showrev.php?id=489.

270. Robert Newman, "Remember the Smithsonian's Atomic Bomb Exhibit? You Only Think You Know the Truth," History News Network, August 6, 2004, p.81. https://historynewsnetwork.org/article/6597.

271. Robert P. Newman, *Enola Gay and the Court*, Peter Lang Publishing, Inc., New York, NY, 2004, p. 91.

272. "NSC-68, 1950," U.S. State Department, Office of the Historian, accessed March 16, 2018, https://history.state.gov/milestones/1945-1952/NSC68.

273. "McCarran Internal Security Act, Wikipedia, accessed March 16, 2018, https://en.wikipedia.org/wiki/McCarran_Internal_Security_Act.

274. Odd Arne Westad, "The New International History of the Cold War: Three (Possible) Paradigms," *Diplomatic History*, Volume 24, Issue 4, 1 October 2000, Pages 551–565. https://doi.org/10.1111/0145-2096.00236.

275. Ibid.

276. Ibid.

277. Ibid.

278. Ibid.

279. "Marshall Plan," History.com, accessed March 16, 2018, http://www.history.com/topics/world-war-ii/marshall-plan.

280. Melvyn P. Leffler, "Inside Enemy Archives: The Cold War Reopened," *Foreign Affairs*, Vol. 75, July/August 1996, pp. 120–135.

281. "The Truman Doctrine, 1945," U.S. Department of State, Office of the Historian, accessed March 16, 2018, https://history.state.gov/milestones/1945-1952/truman-doctrine.

282. Odd Arne Westad, "The New International History of the Cold War: Three (Possible) Paradigms," *Diplomatic History*, Volume 24, Issue 4, 1 October 2000, Pages 551–565. https://doi.org/10.1111/0145-2096.00236.

283. Stephen Kinzer, "The CIA's Holy War," American History, Watson Institute, Brown University, June 2016, p. 46–53, http://watson.brown.edu/news/2016/cias-holy-war-written-stephen-kinzer.

284. Ibid.

285. Ibid.

286. Ibid.

287. Victor Navasky, "The Roads Not Taken," *Nation*, April 6, 2015, p. 109f.

288. Joseph McCarthy, history.com, accessed March 16, 2018, http://www.history.com/topics/cold-war/joesph-mccarthy.

289. Victor Navasky, "The Roads Not Taken," *Nation*, April 6, 2015, p. 109f.

290. Ibid.

291. Oleg Riabov, "Gendering the American Enemy in Early Cold War Soviet Films (1946-1953), *Journal of Cold War Studies*, MIT Press, Volume 19, Issue 1, Winter 2017 p.193–219.

292. Ibid.

293. Ibid.

294. Ibid.

295. Ibid.

296. Ibid.

297. Melvyn P. Leffler, "Insider Enemy Archives: The Cold War Reopened," *Foreign Affairs*, Vol. 75, July/August 1996, pp. 120–135.

298. Odd Arne Westad, "The New International History of the Cold War: Three (Possible) Paradigms," *Diplomatic History*, Volume 24, Issue 4, 1 October 2000, Pages 551–565. https://doi. org/10.1111/0145-2096.00236.

299. Richard Jensen, "The First Space Race," *Aviation History*, May 2016, p.82.

300. Ibid.

301. David Reynolds, *One World Divisible: A Global History Since 1945*, W. W. Norton & Company, 2001, p. 496.

302. Richard Jensen, "The First Space Race," Aviation History, May 2016, p.82.

303. Odd Arne Westad, "The New International History of the Cold War: Three (Possible) Paradigms," *Diplomatic History*, Volume 24, Issue 4, 1 October 2000, Pages 551–565, https://doi. org/10.1111/0145-2096.00236.

304. Melvyn P. Leffler, "Insider Enemy Archives: The Cold War Reopened," *Foreign Affairs*, Vol. 75, July/August 1996, pp. 120–135.

305. Desmond Ball, *Politics and Force Levels*, University of California Press, 1980, p. 187.

306. Odd Arne Westad, "The New International History of the Cold War: Three (Possible) Paradigms," *Diplomatic History*, Volume 24, Issue 4, 1 October 2000, Pages 551–565, https://doi. org/10.1111/0145-2096.00236.

307. Ibid.

308. Ibid.

309. Melvyn P. Leffler, "Insider Enemy Archives: The Cold War Reopened," *Foreign Affairs*, Vol. 75, July/August 1996, pp. 120–135.

310. William Wohlforth, "Superpowers, Interventions and the Third World," *Cold War History*, Vol. 6, No. 3, August 2006, pp. 365–371.

311. Ibid.

312. Ibid.

313. Melvyn P. Leffler, "Insider Enemy Archives: The Cold War Reopened," *Foreign Affairs*, Vol. 75, July/August 1996, pp. 120–135.

314. Kimberly Amadeo, Korean War Facts, Costs and Timeline, The Balance, accessed March 3, 2018, https://www.thebalance.com/korean-war-facts-definition-costs-and-timeline-4153091

315. "180,000 Chinese soldiers killed in Korean War," china.org.cn, June 28, 2010, http://www.china.org.cn/china/2010-06/28/content_20365659.htm.

316. Ibid.

317. Ibid.

318. Peter Robinson, "How Top Advisers Opposed Reagan's Challenge to Gorbachev—But Lost," *Prologue*, Summer 2007, https://www.archives.gov/publications/prologue/2007/summer/berlin.html.

319. Michael Parks, "Reforms at Stake: Gorbachev's Test: Taming Huge Party," *Los Angeles Times*, July 26, 1991, http://articles.latimes.com/1991-07-26/news/mn-229_1_party-organization/2.

320. Ibid.

321. "The Collapse of the Soviet Union," Office of the Historian, U.S. Department of State. Accessed March 17, 2018, https://history.state.gov/milestones/1989-1992/collapse-soviet-union.

322. Francis X. Clines, "End of the Soviet Union; Gorbachev, Last Soviet leader, Resigns; U.S. Recognizes Republic's Independence," *New York Times*, December 26, 1991, http://www.nytimes.com/1991/12/26/world/end-soviet-union-gorbachev-last-soviet-leader-resigns-us-recognizes-republics.html?pagewanted=all&pagewanted=print.

323. Ibid.

324. "The Collapse of the Soviet Union," Office of the Historian, U.S. Department of State. Accessed March 17, 2018, https://history.state.gov/milestones/1989-1992/collapse-soviet-union.

325. "National Security Strategy of the United States of America," The White House, December 2017, p.2, https://www.whitehouse.gov/wp-content/uploads/2017/12/NSS-Final-12-18-2017-0905.pdf.

326. Ibid, p.25.

327. Jeffrey Goldberg, "The Lessons of Henry Kissinger," *The Atlantic*, Vol.

318, Issue 5, November 10, 2016, https://www.theatlantic.com/magazine/archive/2016/12/the-lessons-of-henry-kissinger/505868/.

328. Ibid.

329. "Kremlin Hardliners Rule in Putin's Russia," *Deutche Welle*, September 18, 2014, http://www.dw.com/en/kremlin-hardliners-rule-in-putins-russia/a-17932564.

330. Bill Gertz, "China 'Dream' Is Global Hegemony," *Washington Free Beacon*, May 17, 2018, http://freebeacon.com/national-security/china-dream-global-hegemony/.

331. Charlie Campbell, "China Steps Closer to Despotism as Xi becomes Leader for Life," *Time*, March 12, 2018, p. 5.

332. Ibid.

333. Interview with Dr. Steven W. Mosher on March 18, 2018.

334. Matthew Pennington, "Xi Could Rule China for Decades, says U.S. Pacific Commander," *Military Times*, March 15, 2018, https://www.militarytimes.com/news/2018/03/15/xi-could-rule-china-for-decades-says-us-pacific-commander/?utm_source=Sailthru&utm_medium=email&utm_campaign=ebb%20 03.16.18&utm_term=Editorial%20-%20Early%20Bird%20Brief.

335. Ibid.

336. Ibid.

337. Neil MacFarquhar, "Putin Says New 'Invincible' Missile Can Pierce U.S. and European Defenses," *New York Times*, March 1, 2018, https://www.nytimes.com/2018/03/01/world/europe/russia-putin-speech.html.

338. Ibid.

339. Ibid.

340. Ibid.

341. Ibid.

342. Katie Sanders, "Did Vladimir Putin Call the Breakup of the USSR 'the Greatest Geopolitical Tragedy of the 20th Century?'," *Politico*, March 6, 2014, http://www.politifact.com/punditfact/statements/2014/mar/06/john-bolton/did-vladimir-putin-call-breakup-ussr-greatest-geop/.

343. "Russia: Putin's Back for a New Term, but the Problems Are Piling Up," Stratfor, accessed May 8, 2018, https://worldview.stratfor.com/article/russia-putin-back-new-term-problems-piling-up?id=7

43c2bc617&e=99971e0a2b&uuid=4ba2e840-1b91-4d44-9828-
5342bd27adfc&utm_source=Topics%2C+Themes+and+Regions&
utm_campaign=6513bfc47c-EMAIL_CAMPAIGN_2018_05_07&utm_
medium=email&utm_term=0_743c2bc617-6513bfc47c-
53692653&mc_cid=6513bfc47c&mc_eid=[UNIQID].

344. Ibid.

345. "Provinces in Russia," Research Maniacs, accessed May 25, 2018. https://
researchmaniacs.com/Country/Provinces/List-Of-Provinces.-

346. André Laliberté, "China's Domestic Problems," *Diplomat and International
Canada*, October 4, 2016, http://diplomatonline.com/mag/2016/10/
Chinas-domestic-problems/.

347. Benjamin M. Rowland, *Charles de Gaulle's Legacy of Ideas*, Lexington
Books, 2011, p. 71.

348. Noah Feldman, "The Unstoppable Force vs. the Immovable Object,"
Foreign Policy, May 16, 2013. http://foreignpolicy.com/2013/05/16/
the-unstoppable-force-vs-the-immovable-object/.

349. "Chapter 4. Global Balance of Power," *Global Attitudes and Trends*, Pew
Research Center, July 18, 2013, http://www.pewglobal.org/2013/07/18/
chapter-4-global-balance-of-power/.

350. "2017 China Military Strength," GFP, accessed March 3, 2018,
https://www.globalfirepower.com/country-military-strength-detail.
asp?country_id=china.

351. Bill Powell, "A New Cold War, Yes. But it's with China, not Russia,"
Newsweek, May 29, 2015, http://www.newsweek.com/2015/05/29/
us-China-cold-war-333948.html.

352. "China's One Belt, One Road Strategy," *Defense News*, April
11, 2015. https://www.defensenews.com/home/2015/04/11/
china-s-one-belt-one-road-strategy/.

353. "China to Start Paying for Oil in Yuan as Early as This Year: Report,"
Asia Times, March 31, 2018. http://www.atimes.com/article/
china-start-paying-oil-yuan-early-year-source/.

354. Keith Johnson, "Why Is China Buying up Europe's Ports?" *Foreign
Policy*, February 2, 2018,http://foreignpolicy.com/2018/02/02/
why-is-China-buying-up-europes-ports/.

355. Ibid.

356. Juan de Onis, "China Pledges $35 Billion to Latin America," *World Affairs*, January 14, 2015, http://www.worldaffairsjournal.org/blog/juan-de-onis/china-pledges-35-billion-latin-america.

357. Alan Boyd, "China Scare Spreads to New Zealand," *Asia Times*, February 22, 2018, http://www.atimes.com/article/china-scare-spreads-new-zealand/?utm_source=Sailthru&utm_medium=email&utm_campaign=ebb%2002.23.18&utm_term=Editorial%20-%20Early%20Bird%20Brief.

358. Ibid.

359. Ibid.

360. Ibid.

361. Ibid.

362. Alina Polyakaova, "Russia Is a Great Power Once Again," *Atlantic*, February 26, 2018, https://www.theatlantic.com/international/archive/2018/02/russia-syria-putin-assad-trump-isis-ghouta/554270/?utm_source=Sailthru&utm_medium=email&utm_campaign=EBB%202/27/18&utm_term=Editorial%20-%20Early%20Bird%20Brief.

363. Ibid.

364. "Gen. Votel Russia Is Both arsonist and Fireman in Syria," *Military Times*, February 27, 2018, https://www.militarytimes.com/flashpoints/2018/02/27/gen-votel-russia-is-both-arsonist-and-fireman-in-syria/?utm_source=Sailthru&utm_medium=email&utm_campaign=ebb%202-28&utm_term=Editorial%20-%20Early%20Bird%20Brief.

365. Suzan Fraser, "Turkey's Erdogan Says Missile Deal with Russia Is Final," *Washington Post*, April 3, 2018, https://www.washingtonpost.com/world/europe/putin-and-erdogan-to-launch-turkeys-1st-nuclear-reactor/2018/04/03/ef7bb4b6-3712-11e8-af3c-2123715f78df_story.html?utm_term=.e7295ae6e87b.

366. Ibid.

367. James MacHaffie, "The Potential for a China-Russia Military Alliance Explored," *Turkish Journal of International Relations*, vol 10, no. 2–3 summer-fall 2011.

368. Ibid.

369. "USSR and PRC Sign Mutual Defense Treaty," History.com. Accessed March 17, 2018, http://www.history.com/this-day-in-history/ussr-and-prc-sign-mutual-defense-treaty.

370. Chen Jian, "The Sino-Soviet Alliance and China's Entry into the Korean War," State University of New York at Geneseo, Working Paper No. 1, Cold War International History Project, Woodrow Wilson International Center for Scholars, Washington, D.C. June 1992, https://www.wilsoncenter.org/sites/default/files/ACFAE7.pdf.

371. Ibid.

372. Harold P. Ford, "Calling the Sino-Soviet Split," CIA, April 14, 2007, https://www.cia.gov/library/center-for-the-study-of-intelligence/csi-publications/csi-studies/studies/winter98_99/art05.html.

373. Cited in James MacHaffie, "The Potential for a China-Russia Military Alliance Explored," *Turkish Journal of International Relations*, Vol. 10, No. 2–3 Summer–Fall 2011.

374. "Russia and China Sign Friendship Pact," *New York Times*, July 17, 2001, http://www.nytimes.com/2001/07/17/world/russia-and-China-sign-friendship-pact.html.

375. James MacHaffie, "The Potential for a China-Russia Military Alliance Explored," *Turkish Journal of International Relations*, Vol. 10, No. 2–3 Summer–Fall 2011.

376. "China-Russia Military-to-Military Relations: Moving toward a Higher Level of Cooperation," U.S.-China Economic and Security Review Commission, March 20, 2017, https://www.uscc.gov/sites/default/files/Research/China-Russia%20Mil-Mil%20Relations%20Moving%20Toward%20Higher%20Level%20of%20Cooperation.pdf.

377. "Russia-China Trade Volume Exceeds Expectations, Hitting $84bn," RT, January 12, 2018, https://www.rt.com/business/415692-russia-china-trade-turnover/.

378. Keith Johnson and Reid Standish, "Putin and Xi Are Dreaming of a Polar Silk Road," *Foreign Affairs*, March 8, 2018, https://foreignpolicy.com/2018/03/08/putin-and-xi-are-dreaming-of-a-polar-silk-road-arctic-northern-sea-route-yamal/?utm_source=Sailthru&utm_medium=email&utm_campaign=ebb%2003.09.18&utm_term=Editorial%20-%20Early%20Bird%20Brief.

379. David M. Herszenhorn and Chris Buckley, "Xi Jinping Visits Russia on First Trip Abroad," *New York Times*, March 23, 2013, http://www.nytimes.com/2013/03/23/world/asia/xi-jinping-visits-russia-on-first-trip-abroad.html.

380. Ibid.

381. "China-Russia Military-to-Military Relations: Moving toward a Higher Level of Cooperation," U.S.-China Economic and Security Review Commission, March 20, 2017, https://www.uscc.gov/sites/default/files/Research/China-Russia%20Mil-Mil%20Relations%20Moving%20Toward%20Higher%20Level%20of%20Cooperation.pdf.

382. Ibid.

383. Charles Krauthammer, "Who Made the Pivot to Asia—Putin," *Washington Post,* May 22, 2014, https://www.washingtonpost.com/opinions/charles-krauthammer-who-made-the-pivot-to-asia-putin/2014/05/22/091a48ee-e1e3-11e3-9743-bb9b59cde7b9_story.html?utm_term=.c984d5fae679.

384. "China-Russia Military-to-Military Relations: Moving toward a Higher Level of Cooperation," U.S.-China Economic and Security Review Commission, March 20, 2017, p.5, https://www.uscc.gov/sites/default/files/Research/China-Russia%20Mil-Mil%20Relations%20Moving%20Toward%20Higher%20Level%20of%20Cooperation.pdf.

385. Ibid, p.20.

386. Leslie H. Gelb, Dimitri K. Simes, "Beware Collusion of China, Russia," *National Interest,* July/August 2013, http://nationalinterest.org/article/beware-collusion-China-russia-8640.

387. Yan Xuetong, "Intertia of History: China and the World in the Next Ten Years," *Chinascope.* Nov/Dec2013, Issue 66, p. 28–28.

388. Ibid.

389. Mansur Mirovalev,"A Sino-Russian Alliance to Rival Europe," Al Jazeera.com, July 26, 2015, http://www.aljazeera.com/indepth/features/2015/07/sino-russian-alliance-rival-europe-150719085829977.html.

390. "Cold War Alliances," *Alpha History*, accessed March 17, 2018, http://alphahistory.com/coldwar/cold-war-alliances/.

391. "Collective Defence–Article 5," North Atlantic Treaty Organization, accessed March 17, 2018, https://www.nato.int/cps/ua/natohq/topics_110496.htm.

392. Allen McDuffee, "Europe Badly Needed the U.S. to Join NATO to Battle the Russian Threat, but It Was a Tough Sell," Timeline.com, April 21, 2017, https://timeline.com/europe-badly-needed-the-u-s-to-join-nato-to-battle-the-russian-threat-but-it-was-a-tough-sell-bf9142d74664.

393. John Grady, "Panel: China Investing in Infrastructure Near the Arctic," *USNI News*, April 27, 2018, https://news.usni.org/2018/04/27/panel-china-investing-infrastructure-near-arctic?utm_source=Sailthru&utm_medium=email&utm_campaign=ebb%20 30.04.2018&utm_term=Editorial%20-%20Early%20Bird%20Brief.

394. Ibid.

395. Ibid.

396. "Latin America Should Not Rely on China: U.S. Secretary of State Tillerson," Reuters, February 1, 2018, https://www.reuters.com/article/us-usa-diplomacy-latam-China/latin-america-should-not-rely-on-China-u-s-secretary-of-state-tillerson-idUSKBN1FL6D5.

397. Ibid.

398. "Pakistan Finds a Friend in Russia," STRATFOR, accessed May 8, 2018, https://worldview.stratfor.com/article/pakistan-finds-friend-russi a?id=743c2bc617&e=99971e0a2b&uuid=434c1351-6bc4-4c15-8fd2-cf5446ea5c93&utm_source=Topics%2C+Themes+and+Regions&utm_campaign=5077403132-EMAIL_CAMPAIGN_2018_05_08&utm_medium=email&utm_term=0_743c2bc617-5077403132-53692653&mc_cid=5077403132&mc_eid=[UNIQID].

399. Max Fisher and Audrey Carlsen, "How China Is Challenging American Dominance in Asia," *New York Times*, March 9, 2018, https://www.nytimes.com/interactive/2018/03/09/world/asia/china-us-asia-rivalry.html?utm_source=Sailthru&utm_medium=email&utm_campaign=EBB%203/13/18&utm_term=Editorial%20-%20Early%20Bird%20Brief.

400. Cristina Maza, "Why Is China Building a Military Base in Pakistan, America's Newest Enemy?" *Newsweek*, January 15, 2018, http://www.newsweek.com/China-building-military-base-pakistan-america-balochistan-772092.

401. Ibid.

402. Geoff Ziezulewciz, "Top Navy and Marine Corps Officials Pan China's Expansion Plans," *Navy Times*, March 7, 2018, https://

www.navytimes.com/news/your-navy/2018/03/07/secnav-marine-corps-commandant-criticize-chinas-expansion-plans/?utm_source=Sailthru&utm_medium=email&utm_campaign=ebb%20 03.08.18&utm_term=Editorial%20-%20Early%20Bird%20Brief.

403. Ibid.

404. "China Overseas Military Base," *Voice of America*, November 3, 2017, https://www.voanews.com/a/china-overseas-military-base/4099717.html.

405. Liu Zhen, "US Warns Airmen to Beware of Laser Attacks Near China's Military Base in Djiouti," *South China Morning Post*, May 2, 2018, http://www.scmp.com/news/china/diplomacy-defence/article/2144387/us-warns-airmen-beware-laser-attacks-near-chinas?utm_source=Sailthru&utm_medium=email&utm_campaign=ebb%20 03.05.18&utm_term=Editorial%20-%20Early%20Bird%20Brief.

406. "'Significant' Consequences if China Takes over Djibouti Port, Says U.S. General," *Asia Times*, March 8, 2018, http://www.atimes.com/article/significant-consequences-china-takes-djibouti-port-says-us-general/?utm_source=Sailthru&utm_medium=email&utm_campaign=ebb%20 03.08.18&utm_term=Editorial%20-%20Early%20Bird%20Brief.

407. Ibid.

408. Max Fisher and Audrey Carlsen, "How China Is Challenging American Dominance in Asia," *New York Times*, March 9, 2018, https://www.nytimes.com/interactive/2018/03/09/world/asia/china-us-asia-rivalry.html?utm_source=Sailthru&utm_medium=email&utm_campaign=EBB%203/13/18&utm_term=Editorial%20-%20Early%20 Bird%20Brief.

409. Ibid.

410. "Xi Gives Stark Warning on Taiwan in Hands-Off Message to Trump," *Bloomberg News*, March 19, 2018, https://www.bloomberg.com/news/articles/2018-03-20/china-s-xi-begins-second-term-with-stark-warning-to-taiwan?utm_source=Sailthru&utm_medium=email&utm_campaign=EBB%203/10/18&utm_term=Editorial%20-%20Early%20 Bird%20Brief.

411. John Grady, "Panel: China Ratcheting Up Military Pressure toward Taiwan," *USNI News*, April 2, 2018, https://news.usni.org/2018/04/02/panel-china-ratcheting-military-pressure-toward-taiwan.

412. Fabian Hamacher, "Taiwan Shadows China Carrier Group after Xi Warning," Reuters, March 21, 2018, https://www.reuters.com/article/ us-taiwan-usa/taiwan-shadows-china-carrier-group-after-xi-warning-iduskbn1gx08u?utm_source=sailthru&utm_medium=email&utm_ campaign=ebb%203.21.18&utm_term=editorial%20-%20early%20 bird%20brief.

413. Ibid.

414. Ibid.

415. "70% of Taiwanese Will Fight if China Invades, Survey Finds," *Asia Times*, April 20, 2018, http://www.atimes.com/ article/70-taiwanese-will-fight-china-invades-survey-finds/?utm_ source=Sailthru&utm_medium=email&utm_campaign=ebb%20 23.04.18&utm_term=Editorial%20-%20Early%20Bird%20Brief.

416. "Cam Ranh Base," Wikipedia, accessed March 16, 2018, https:// en.wikipedia.org/wiki/Cam_Ranh_Base.

417. Tobin Harshaw, "What Happens When China Eclipses the U.S. in Asia," *Bloomberg*, February 3, 2018, https://www.bloomberg. com/view/articles/2018-02-03/what-happens-when-China-eclipses-the-u-s-in-asia?utm_source=Sailthru&utm_medium=email&utm_ campaign=ebb%2002.05.2018&utm_term=Editorial%20-%20Early%20 Bird%20Brief.

418. Ibid.

419. Ibid.

420. Telephonic interview with William G. Boykin, March 12, 2018.

421. Interview with Dr. Marek Jan Chodakiewicz on March 14, 2018.

422. "What Is America's Ideology?" *Polisci News*, November 28, 2012, https:// poliscinews.wordpress.com/2012/11/28/what-is-americas-ideology/.

423. "National Security Strategy of the United States of America," The White House, December 2017, https://www.whitehouse.gov/wp-content/ uploads/2017/12/NSS-Final-12-18-2017-0905.pdf.

424. Jochen Bittner, "The New Ideology of the New Cold War," *New York Times*, August 2, 2016, https://www.nytimes.com/2016/08/02/opinion/ the-new-ideology-of-the-new-cold-war.html.

425. Ibid.

426. Ibid.

427. T. S. Tsonchev, "The Kremlin's New Ideology," *Montreal Review*, January 2017, http://www.themontrealreview.com/2009/The-Ideology-of-Vladimir-Putin-Regime.php.

428. Ibid.

429. Ibid.

430. Cited in T. S. Tsonchev, "The Kremlin's New Ideology," *Montreal Review*, January 2017, http://www.themontrealreview.com/2009/The-Ideology-of-Vladimir-Putin-Regime.php.

431. Ibid.

432. Ibid.

433. Ibid.

434. "Popular Mood in Russia: Putin Never Gives Up!" MEMRI, Clip No. 6450, January 29, 2018, https://www.memri.org/tv/popular-mood-in-russia-putin-never-gives-up/transcript.

435. Jochen Bittner, "The New Ideology of the New Cold War," *New York Times*, August 2, 2016, https://www.nytimes.com/2016/08/02/opinion/the-new-ideology-of-the-new-cold-war.html.

436. Steven Jiang, "China Clears Way for Xi Jinping to Rule for Life," CNN, March 11, 2018. https://www.cnn.com/2018/03/11/asia/china-presidential-term-limits-intl/index.html

437. Ibid.

438. Ibid.

439. Chris Buckly, "*Xi Jinping Thought Explained: A New Ideology for a New Era,*" *New York Times*, February 26, 2018, https://www.nytimes.com/2018/02/26/world/asia/xi-jinping-thought-explained-a-new-ideology-for-a-new-era.html?mtrref=www.google.com&gwh=FF74272873A0FBE56B4537AA61CAC1AA&gwt=pay.

440. "Karl Marx a Tool to Win the Future for China, Xi Jinping Says," *Deutsche Welle*, May 4, 2018, http://www.dw.com/en/karl-marx-a-tool-to-win-the-future-for-china-xi-jinping-says/a-43650796?utm_source=Sailthru&utm_medium=email&utm_campaign=ebb%2004.05.18&utm_term=Editorial%20-%20Early%20Bird%20Brief.

441. Ibid.

442. Xi's ideology could backfire if he fails to deliver on the nationalist promise. Further, his campaign which appears to embrace a Mao-style, single-voice

of authority, seeks to cut out Western ideas and impose regime orthodoxy, which could take China backward toward repression.

443. Interview with Dr. Steven W. Mosher on March 18, 2018.

444. Teddy Ng and Mimi Lau, "Xi Jinping Places Catholic Church in China under Direct Party Control," *South China Morning Post*, March 21, 2018, http://www.scmp.com/news/china/diplomacy-defence/article/2138279/bigger-overseas-liaison-agency-fuels-fears-about.

445. Ibid.

446. Steven Mosher, "Xi Jinping Places Catholic Church in China under Direct Party Control," *One Peter Five*, April 30, 2018. https://onepeterfive.com/xi-jinping-places-catholic-church-in-china-under-direct-party-control/.

447. Natalie Johnson, "CIA Warns of Extensive Chinese Operation to Infiltrate American Institutions," *Washington Free Beacon*, March 7, 2018, http://freebeacon.com/national-security/cia-warns-extensive-chinese-operation-infiltrate-american-institutions/.

448. Stephen Gutowski, "America Should Ban Civilian Guns to Protect Human Rights, Chinese Communist Dictatorship Says Through State-Run Media," *Washington Free Beacon*, March 7, 2018, "Should Ban Civilian Guns to Protect Human Rights, Chinese Communist Dictatorship Says Through State-Run Media."

449. Ibid.

450. Ibid.

451. Ibid.

452. *Munich Security Report 2018: To the Brink—and Back?*, Munich Security Conference, p.8, https://www.securityconference.de/en/discussion/munich-security-report/munich-security-report-2018/.

453. Ibid.

454. *National Security Strategy of the United States of America*, The White House, December 2017, https://www.whitehouse.gov/wp-content/uploads/2017/12/NSS-Final-12-18-2017-0905.pdf.

455. "Statement for the Record: Worldwide Threat Assessment of the US Intelligence Community," Senate Select Committee on Intelligence, Daniel R. Coats, Director of National Intelligence May 11, 2017, https://www.dni.gov/files/documents/Newsroom/Testimonies/SSCI%20Unclassified%20SFR%20-%20Final.pdf.

456. Doug Tsuroka, "Undersea Cables Achilles Heel Lead New Cold War," *Asia Times,* January 6, 2018, http://www.atimes.com/article/undersea-cables-achilles-heel-lead-new-cold-war/?utm_source=Sailthru&utm_medium=email&utm_campaign=DFN%20EBB%20 08.01.2018&utm_term=Editorial%20-%20Early%20Bird%20Brief.

457. Ibid.

458. Bill Gertz, "China Violated Obama-Xi Agreement to Halt Cyber Theft," *Washington Free Beacon*, February 28, 2018, http://freebeacon.com/national-security/china-violated-obama-xi-agreement-halt-cyber-theft/.

459. Ibid.

460. Ibid.

461. "Yes a Cyberattack Could Spur the President to Launch a Nuclear Attack," Fifthdomain.com, February 2, 2018, https://www.fifthdomain.com/pentagon/2018/02/02/yes-a-cyberattack-could-spur-the-president-to-launch-a-nuclear-attack/?utm_source=Sailthru&utm_medium=email&utm_campaign=ebb%20 02.05.2018&utm_term=Editorial%20-%20Early%20Bird%20Brief.

462. Ibid.

463. Mark Pomerleau, "The Army's Next Question: Should Battlefield Commanders Have Cyber Capabilities?," Fifthdomain.com, March 13, 2018, https://www.fifthdomain.com/dod/army/2018/03/13/the-armys-next-question-should-battlefield-commanders-have-cyber-capabilities/?utm_source=Sailthru&utm_medium=email&utm_campaign=ebb-%203-14&utm_term=Editorial%20-%20Early%20 Bird%20Brief.

464. Ibid.

465. Ibid.

466. "Russia Mocks Gavin Williamson's Attack Warning," BBC, January 26, 2018, http://www.bbc.com/news/uk-42834662.

467. Matthew Daly, "US Says Russian Hack Did Not Compromise Power Grid, Plants," Fifthdomain.com, March 16, 2018, https://www.fifthdomain.com/critical-infrastructure/2018/03/16/us-says-russian-hack-did-not-compromise-nuclear-plants/?utm_source=Sailthru&utm_medium=email&utm_campaign=ebb%20 03.19.18&utm_term=Editorial%20-%20Early%20Bird%20Brief.

468. Ibid.

469. "Don't Ignore Cyber Threats to Power Infrastructure," by Andres, Richard B., *Power*, 00325929, Vol. 159, Issue 1.

470. Steve Morgan, "Cyber Crime Costs Projected to Reach $2 Trillion by 2019, *Forbes*, January 17, 2016, https://www.forbes.com/sites/stevemorgan/2016/01/17/cyber-crime-costs-projected-to-reach-2-trillion-by-2019/#7e8ca96e3a91.

471. Ibid.

472. Samantha F. Ravich, *Framework and Terminology for Understanding Cyber-Enabled Economic Warfare,* Center on Sanctions and Illicit Finance, February 22, 2017, http://www.defenddemocracy.org/content/uploads/documents/22217_Cyber_Definitions.pdf.

473. "Feature: Ex-Soviet Hackers Play Outsized Role in Cyber-Crime World," Reuters, August 22, 2013, https://www.reuters.com/article/russia-cybercrime/feature-ex-soviet-hackers-play-outsized-role-in-cyber-crime-world-idUSL6N0G61KM20130822.

474. Hyacinth Mascarenhas, "Ex-GCHQ Chief Says Russia Causing Cyberspace Mayhem, Urges Push Back against Russian State," *International Business Times*, July 11, 2017, http://www.ibtimes.co.uk/ex-gchq-chief-says-russia-causing-cyberspace-mayhem-urges-push-back-against-russian-state-1629744.

475. Cynthia McFadden, William M. Arkin, and Kevin Monahan "Russians Penetrated U.S. Voter Systems, Top U.S. Official Says," NBC News, February 7, 2018, https://www.nbcnews.com/politics/elections/russians-penetrated-u-s-voter-systems-says-top-u-s-n845721.

476. Ibid.

477. Ibid.

478. Matthew Rosenberg, "Russia Sees Midterm Elections as Chance to Sow Fresh Discord, Intelligence Chiefs Warn," *New York Times*, February 13, 2018, https://www.nytimes.com/2018/02/13/us/politics/russia-sees-midterm-elections-as-chance-to-sow-fresh-discord-intelligence-chiefs-warn.html?mtrref=www.google.com&gwh=77FB1DF7FDF0D7F27A1F74E309EA0294&gwt=pay.

479. "Top Intel Official Says US Hasn't Deterred Russian Meddling," Fifthdomain.com, February 27, 2018, https://www.fifthdomain.com/

critical-infrastructure/2018/02/27/top-intel-official-says-us-hasnt-deterred-russian-meddling/?utm_source=Sailthru&utm_medium=email&utm_campaign=ebb%202-28&utm_term=Editorial%20-%20Early%20Bird%20Brief.

480. "GCHQ Warns Politicians about Russian Hacking Threat," BBC, March 12, 2017, http://www.bbc.com/news/uk-39248879.

481. Doug Wise, "Could AI-driven Info Warfare Be Democracy's Achilles Heel?" *Cipher Brief*, March 11, 2018, https://www.thecipherbrief.com/column/expert-view/ai-driven-info-warfare-democracys-achilles-heel?utm_source=Sailthru&utm_medium=email&utm_campaign=ebb%2003.11.18&utm_term=Editorial%20-%20Early%20Bird%20Brief.

482. Ibid.

483. Ibid.

484. Patrick Tucker, "If War Comes, Russia Could Disconnect from the Internet. Yes, the Entire Country," *Defense One*, March 12, 2018, http://www.nextgov.com/cybersecurity/2018/03/if-war-comes-russia-could-disconnect-internet-yes-entire-country/146589/.

485. Ibid.

486. Interview with Dr. Chodakiewicz on March 14, 2018.

487. "German Banker: Russian Sanctions Are Destroying Europe," *Guardian*, June 12, 2015, https://off-guardian.org/2015/06/12/german-banker-russian-sanctions-are-destroying-europe/.

488. "National Security Strategy of the United States of America," The White House, December 2017, https://www.whitehouse.gov/wp-content/uploads/2017/12/NSS-Final-12-18-2017-0905.pdf.

489. "Trump Adviser Bannon Says U.S. in Economic War with China: Media," Reuters, August 17, 2017, https://www.reuters.com/article/us-usa-china-bannon/trump-adviser-bannon-says-u-s-in-economic-war-with-china-media-idUSKCN1AX0DE.

490. Peter Economy, "The U.S. Is Losing the Economic War with China (and What Trump Should Do About It)," INC.com, accessed March 16, 2018, https://www.inc.com/peter-economy/the-us-is-losing-the-economic-war-with-china-and-w.html.

491. Ibid.

492. "Trump Adviser Bannon Says U.S. in Economic War with China: Media,"

Reuters, August 17, 2017, https://www.reuters.com/article/us-usa-china-bannon/trump-adviser-bannon-says-u-s-in-economic-war-with-china-media-idUSKCN1AX0DE.

493. Michael Schuman, "Is China Sstealing Jobs? It May Be Losing Them Instead," *New York Times*, July 23, 2016, https://www.nytimes.com/2016/07/23/business/international/china-jobs-donald-trump.html?mtrref=www.google.com&gwh=D63DB7779F9F0F9C5E0A6F844DCE8B28&gwt=pay.

494. "Raw Materials: Towards a Global Resource War?" EURACTIV, March 3, 2011, https://www.euractiv.com/section/sustainable-dev/news/raw-materials-towards-a-global-resource-war/.

495. David P. Goldman, "How to Meet the Strategic Challenge Posed by China," *IMPRIMIS*, a publication of Hillsdale College, Vol. 47, No. 3, March 2018.

496. "U.S.: Justice Department Investigates Huawei over Alleged Iran Sanctions Violations," STRATFOR, April 26, 2018. Accessed April 26, 2018, https://www.stratfor.com/situation-report/us-justice-department-investigates-huawei-over-alleged-iran-sanctions-violations.

497. "Columnist Martynov: Russia Plays the Superpower, But with Its Puny GDP It Cannot Afford a War with the West," Novayagazeta.ru, cited in *MEMRI*, February 19, 2018, https://www.memri.org/reports/columnist-martynov-russia-plays-superpower-its-puny-gdp-it-cannot-afford-war-west.

498. Lee Fang, "U.S. Defense Contractors Tell Investors Russian Threat Is Great for Business," *Intercept*, August 19, 2016, https://theintercept.com/2016/08/19/nato-weapons-industry/.

499. Paul Szoldra, "Here's Who Is Paying the Agreed-to Share to NATO—and Who Isn't," *Business Insider*, February 16, 2017, http://www.businessinsider.com/nato-share-breakdown-country-2017-2.

500. Ibid.

501. Mina Pollman, "What's in Japan's Record 2018 Defense Budget Request?" *Diplomat*, August 2017, https://thediplomat.com/2017/08/whats-in-japans-record-2018-defense-budget-request/.

502. Niall McCarthy, "The Top 15 Countries for Military Expenditure in 2016," *Forbes*, April 24, 2017, https://www.forbes.com/sites/

niallmccarthy/2017/04/24/the-top-15-countries-for-military-expenditure-in-2016-infographic/#597a95bb43f3.

503. Omar Lamrani, "A Changing Rulebook to Tame the New Global Arms Race," STRATFOR, March 28, 2017, https://worldview.stratfor.com/article/changing-rulebook-tame-new-global-arms-race.

504. Zdzislaw Lachowski and Martin Sjogren, "Conventional Arms Control," SIPRI Yearbook 2004, SIPRI, accessed March 16, 2018, https://www.sipri.org/yearbook/2004/17.

505. National Security Strategy of the United States of America, White House, December 2017, https://www.whitehouse.gov/wp-content/uploads/2017/12/NSS-Final-12-18-2017-0905.pdf.

506. Summary of the 2018 National Defense Strategy of the United States of America, Department of Defense, 2018, https://www.defense.gov/Portals/1/Documents/pubs/2018-National-Defense-Strategy-Summary.pdf. (Note: This is an unclassified summary of a much longer classified 2018 National Defense Strategy.)

507. Jim Garamone, "Dunford: U.S. Military Advantage over Russia, China Eroding," Department of Defense, November 16, 2017, https://www.defense.gov/News/Article/Article/1374168/dunford-us-military-advantage-over-russia-china-eroding/.

508. Ibid.

509. Ibid.

510. 2017 Annual Report, U.S.-China Economic and Security Review Commission, November 15, 2017, https://www.uscc.gov/Annual_Reports/2017-annual-report.

511. Steve Mollman, "Bigger, Faster, Stronger: China's Ever-Evolving Military Tech," *Defense One*, February 20, 2018, http://www.defenseone.com/technology/2018/02/bigger-faster-stronger-chinas-ever-evolving-military-tech/146104/?oref=d-river&utm_source=Sailthru&utm_medium=email&utm_campaign=ebb-2-21&utm_term=Editorial%20-%20Early%20Bird%20Brief.

512. Mike Yeo, "China to Develop Its First Nuclear-Powered Aircraft Carrier," *Defense News*, March 1, 2018, https://www.defensenews.com/naval/2018/03/01/china-to-develop-its-first-nuclear-powered-aircraft-carrier/?utm_source=Sailthru&utm_medium=email&utm_

campaign=ebb%2003.01.18&utm_term=Editorial%20-%20Early%20 Bird%20Brief.

513. Ibid.

514. Steve Mollman, "Bigger, Faster, Stronger: China's Ever-Evolving Military Tech," *Defense One*, February 20, 2018, http://www.defenseone.com/ technology/2018/02/bigger-faster-stronger-chinas-ever-evolving- military-tech/146104/?oref=d-river&utm_source=Sailthru&utm_ medium=email&utm_campaign=ebb-2-21&utm_term=Editorial%20 -%20Early%20Bird%20Brief.

515. Ibid.

516. James Foggo III, "The Fourth Battle of the Atlantic," *Proceedings*, Vol 142/6/1,360, June 2016, https://www.usni.org/magazines/ proceedings/2016-06/fourth-battle-atlantic.

517. Ibid.

518. Robert Ashley, DIA Director, testimony before the Senate Armed Services Committee, March 6, 2018, http://www.dia.mil/DesktopModules/ ArticleCS/Print.aspx?PortalId=27&ModuleId=24601&Article=1457815.

519. Peter Dombrowski, "Peer Competition: USN Views on Russian Naval Activity Evolve," *Jane's by the Markit*, August 18, 2016.

520. Mark Gunzinger, Carl Rehberg and Gillian Evans, "Sustaining the U.S. Nuclear Deterrent: The LRSO and GBSD," Center for Strategic and Budgetary Assessments, 2018, p.16, http://csbaonline.org/uploads/ documents/CSBA6318-GBSD_LRSO_Report_web.pdf9.

521. Aaron Mehta, "The Pentagon Is Planning for War with China and Russia—Can It Handle Both?," *Defense News*, January 1, 2018, https:// www.defensenews.com/pentagon/2018/01/30/the-pentagon-is-planning- for-war-with-china-and-russia-can-it-handle-both/.

522. Ibid.

523. Ibid.

524. Kimberly Underwood, "Marine Corps Lab Imagines Weapons of the Future," *Signal*, AFCEA, January 1, 2018, https://www.afcea.org/content/ marine-corps-lab-imagines-weapons-future.

525. Stephen Hawking, Stuart Russell, Max Tegmark, Frank Wilczek "Stephen Hawking: 'Transcendence Looks at the Implications of Artificial Intelligence—But Are We Taking AI Seriously Enough?'" *Independent*,

May 1, 2014, http://www.independent.co.uk/news/science/stephen-hawking-transcendence-looks-at-the-implications-of-artificial-intelligence-but-are-we-taking-9313474.html.

526. Brandon Knapp, "The Terrifying Future of Malicious Artificial Intelligence," C4ISRNET.COM, February 22, 2018, https://www.c4isrnet.com/intel-geoint/2018/02/22/the-terrifying-future-of-malicious-artificial-intelligence/?utm_source=Sailthru&utm_medium=email&utm_campaign=ebb%2002.23.18&utm_term=Editorial%20-%20Early%20Bird%20Brief.

527. Ibid.

528. Ibid.

529. Patrick Tucker, "Experts Say AI Could Raise the Risks of Nuclear War," *Defense One*, April 24, 2018, https://www.defenseone.com/technology/2018/04/experts-say-artificial-intelligence-could-raise-risks-nuclear-war/147673/?oref=d-river&utm_source=Sailthru&utm_medium=email&utm_campaign=ebb%20 4/24/18&utm_term=Editorial%20-%20Early%20Bird%20Brief.

530. Ric Edelman, *The Truth About Your Future: The Money Guide You Need Now, Later, and Much Later*, Simon & Schuster, New York, 2017, p. 141.

531. Ibid.

532. Alanna Petroff, "Google CEO: AI Is 'More Profound than Electricity or Fire'," CNN, January 24, 2018, http://money.cnn.com/2018/01/24/technology/sundar-pichai-google-ai-artificial-intelligence/index.html.

533. Brandon Knapp, "When Should Humans Step Aside and Let AI Make Decisions?," C4ISRNET.COM, March 10, 2018, https://www.c4isrnet.com/unmanned/2018/03/10/when-should-humans-step-aside-and-let-ai-make-decisions/?utm_source=Sailthru&utm_medium=email&utm_campaign=ebb%2003.11.18&utm_term=Editorial%20-%20Early%20Bird%20Brief.

534. Ibid.

535. Ibid.

536. "China's Shock Call for Ban on Lethal Autonomous Weapon Systems," *HIS Jane's 360,* April 17, 2018, http://www.janes.com/article/79311/china-s-shock-call-for-ban-on-lethal-autonomous-weapon-systems?utm_source=Sailthru&utm_medium=email&utm_campaign=EBB%20

4/17/18&utm_term=Editorial%20-%20Early%20Bird%20Brief.

537. Brandon Knapp, "DoD official: US Not Part of AI Arms Race," C4ISRNET.COM, April 10, 2018, https://www.c4isrnet.com/it-networks/2018/04/10/dod-official-us-not-part-of-ai-arms-race/?utm_source=Sailthru&utm_medium=email&utm_campaign=ebb-4-11&utm_term=Editorial%20-%20Early%20Bird%20Brief.

538. Aaron Mehta, "Pentagon Developing Artificial Intelligence Center," *Defense News*, April 18, 2018, https://www.c4isrnet.com/intel-geoint/2018/04/18/pentagon-developing-artificial-intelligence-center/.

539. Ibid.

540. Ibid.

541. Ibid.

542. Daniel Cebul, "How Is China Developing AI Technology So Much Faster Than the US?," C4ISRNET.COM, March 15, 2018, https://www.c4isrnet.com/home/2018/03/15/how-is-china-developing-ai-technology-so-much-faster-than-the-us/?utm_source=Sailthru&utm_medium=email&utm_campaign=ebb%2003.16.18&utm_term=Editorial%20-%20Early%20Bird%20Brief.

543. Ibid.

544. Ibid.

545. Ibid.

546. Matthew Bey, "The Coming Tech War with China," STRATFOR, February 6, 2018. https://worldview.stratfor.com/article/coming-tech-war-CHINA?id=743c2bc617&e=99971e0a2b&uuid=2beccf6a-fced-4e4e-a500-26f34911c767&utm_source=Topics%2C+Themes+and+Regions&utm_campaign=416724313e-EMAIL_CAMPAIGN_2018_02_06&utm_medium=email&utm_term=0_743c2bc617-416724313e-53692653&mc_cid=416724313e&mc_eid=[UNIQID.

547. Cited in "Engaging Human-Machine Networks for Cross-domain Effects, Mad Scientist Laboratory, February 15, 2018, http://madsciblog.tradoc.army.mil/tag/peoples-liberation-army-pla-human-machine-integration/.

548. Ibid.

549. Samuel Bendett, "In AI, Russia Is Hustling to Catch Up," *Defense One*, April 4, 2018. http://www.defenseone.com/ideas/2018/04/russia-races-forward-ai-development/147178/.

550. W.J. Hennigan, "The New Nuclear Poker," *Time*, February 12, 2018, p.22.

551. "Nuclear Posture Review, U.S. Department of Defense, February 2018. P.V. https://www.defense.gov/News/SpecialReports/2018NuclearPostureReview.aspx.

552. Ibid, p.I.

553. Matthew Bodner, "Out of Moscow: Washington Got the Basics of Russian Nuclear Strategy All Wrong," February 21, 2018, https://www.defensenews.com/smr/nuclear-triad/2018/02/21/out-of-moscow-washington-got-the-basics-of-russian-nuclear-strategy-all-wrong/?utm_source=Sailthru&utm_medium=email&utm_campaign=ebb%2002.26.18&utm_term=Editorial%20-%20Early%20Bird%20Brief.

554. Ibid.

555. Ibid.

556. Mark Gunzinger, Carl Rehberg, and Gillian Evans, "*Sustaining the U.S. Nuclear Deterrent: The LRSO and GBSD*, Center for Strategic and Budgetary Assessments," 2018, p.18, http://csbaonline.org/uploads/documents/CSBA6318-GBSD_LRSO_Report_web.pdf9.

557. Joe Gould, "Interview: Senate Strategic Forces Subcommittee Chair Deb Fischer on Russia, space wars, and the state of the nuclear arsenal," *Defense One*, March 19, 2018, https://www.defensenews.com/smr/nuclear-triad/2018/03/19/interview-senate-strategic-forces-subcommittee-chair-deb-fischer-on-russia-space-wars-and-the-state-of-the-nuclear-arsenal/?utm_source=Sailthru&utm_medium=email&utm_campaign=EBB%203/10/18&utm_term=Editorial%20-%20Early%20Bird%20Brief.

558. Ibid.

559. Ibid.

560. Aaron Mehta, "Nuclear Warhead Manager Seeks FY19 Funding for New Nuke Designs," *Defense News*, March 20, 2018. https://www.defensenews.com/smr/nuclear-triad/2018/03/20/nuclear-warhead-manager-seeks-fy19-funding-for-new-nuke-designs/?utm_

source=Sailthru&utm_medium=email&utm_campaign=EBB%20
3.21.18&utm_term=Editorial%20-%20Early%20Bird%20Brief.

561. Daniel Cebul, "Coercive Tactics? Putin Touts Russia's 'Invincible' Nuclear Weapons," *Defense News*, March 1, 2018, https://
www.defensenews.com/smr/nuclear-triad/2018/03/01/coercive-tactics-putin-touts-russias-invincible-nuclear-weapons/?utm_
source=Sailthru&utm_medium=email&utm_campaign=ebb%20
03.01.18&utm_term=Editorial%20-%20Early%20Bird%20Brief.

562. "Russia Tests New Intercontinental Ballistic Missile," *Washington Post*, March 30, 2018, https://www.washingtonpost.com/world/europe/russia-tests-new-intercontinental-ballistic-missile/2018/03/30/c6cbcd94-3410-11e8-b6bd-0084a1666987_story.html?utm_term=.18384d9209ed.

563. Ibid.

564. Aaron Mehta, "Is Russia Influencing America's Nuclear Debate? Mac Thornberry Thinks They Will," *Defense News*, March 8, 2018, https://www.defensenews.com/smr/nuclear-triad/2018/03/08/
is-russia-influencing-americas-nuclear-debate-mac-thornberry-thinks-they-will/?utm_source=Sailthru&utm_medium=email&utm_
campaign=ebb%2003.09.18&utm_term=Editorial%20-%20Early%20
Bird%20Brief.

565. Ibid.

566. Ibid.

567. Mark Gunzinger, Carl Rehberg and Gillian Evans, "Sustaining the U.S. Nuclear Deterrent: The LRSO and GBSD," Center for Strategic and Budgetary Assessments," 2018, http://csbaonline.org/uploads/documents/CSBA6318-GBSD_LRSO_Report_web.pdf9

568. W. J. Hennigan, "The New Nuclear Poker," *Time*, February 12, 2018, p.23.

569. Mark Gunzinger, Carl Rehberg and Gillian Evans, "Sustaining the U.S. Nuclear Deterrent: The LRSO and GBSD," Center for Strategic and Budgetary Assessments," 2018, p. 10, http://csbaonline.org/uploads/documents/CSBA6318-GBSD_LRSO_Report_web.pdf9.

570. Ibid.

571. Ibid.

572. Aaron Mehta, "Hypersonics 'Highest YTechnical Priority' for Pentagon

R&D Head," *Defense One*, March 6, 2018, https://www.defensenews. com/pentagon/2018/03/06/hypersonics-highest-technical-priority-for-pentagon-rd-head/?utm_source=Sailthru&utm_medium=email&utm_campaign=EBB%203.7.18&utm_term=Editorial%20-%20Early%20 Bird%20Brief.

573. Ibid.

574. Ibid.

575. Brandon Knapp, "With the Rise of Hypersonics, the Missile Defense Agency Wants More Sensors," C4ISRNET.COM, April 11, 2018, https://www.c4isrnet.com/intel-geoint/sensors/2018/04/11/with-the-rise-of-hypersonics-the-missile-defense-agency-wants-more-sensors/?utm_source=Sailthru&utm_medium=email&utm_campaign=ebb%20 12.04.18&utm_term=Editorial%20-%20Early%20Bird%20Brief.

576. Matthew Cox, "Army Chief: Hypersonic Weapons 'Possible' But Early in Development," Military.com, March 16, 2018,\. https://www.military. com/dodbuzz/2018/03/16/army-chief-hypersonic-weapons-possible-early-development.html?utm_source=Sailthru&utm_medium=email&utm_campaign=ebb%2003.19.18&utm_term=Editorial%20-%20Early%20 Bird%20Brief.

577. Ibid.

578. Ibid.

579. Daniel Cebul, "Coercive Tactics? Putin Touts Russia's 'Invincible' Nuclear Weapons," *Defense News*, March 1, 2018, https:// www.defensenews.com/smr/nuclear-triad/2018/03/01/coercive-tactics-putin-touts-russias-invincible-nuclear-weapons/?utm_source=Sailthru&utm_medium=email&utm_campaign=ebb%20 03.01.18&utm_term=Editorial%20-%20Early%20Bird%20Brief.

580. Aron Mehta, "As Putin Touts Hypersonic Weapons, America Prepares Its Own Arsenal. Will It Be in Time?," *Defense News*, March 2, 2018, https:// www.defensenews.com/pentagon/2018/03/02/as-putin-touts-hypersonic-weapons-america-prepares-its-own-arsenal-will-it-be-in-time/?utm_source=Sailthru&utm_medium=email&utm_campaign=ebb%20 03.05.18&utm_term=Editorial%20-%20Early%20Bird%20Brief.

581. Daniel Gouré, "A Real Missile Gap Is Looming in Hypersonic Weapons," *National Interest*, May 1, 2018, http://nationalinterest.org/blog/the-buzz/ real-missile-gap-looming-hypersonic-weapons-25650?page=2.

582. Ibid.

583. Ibid.

584. Matthew Bodner, "Russia to World: Our New Nukes Are 'No Bluff,'" *Defense News*, March 12, 2018. https://www.defensenews.com/ industry/techwatch/2018/03/12/russia-to-world-our-new-nukes-are-no-bluff/?utm_source=Sailthru&utm_medium=email&utm_campaign=EBB%203/13/18&utm_term=Editorial%20-%20Early%20 Bird%20Brief.

585. Ibid.

586. Peter Karperowicz, "Russia Brandishes 'Invincible' Hypersonic Missiles," *Washington Examiner*, May 5, 2018. https://www.washingtonexaminer. com/news/russia-brandishes-invincible-hypersonic-missiles?utm_source=Sailthru&utm_medium=email&utm_campaign=ebb%20 08.05.18&utm_term=Editorial%20-%20Early%20Bird%20Brief.

587. Valerie Insinna, "STRATCOM head: Don't Doubt Russia's Drive to Develop 'Invincible' Hypersonic Missile," *Defense News*, April 18, 2018, https://www.defensenews.com/digital-show-dailies/ space-symposium/2018/04/18/stratcom-head-dont-doubt-russias-drive-to-develop-invincible-hypersonic-missile/?utm_source=Sailthru&utm_medium=email&utm_campaign=EBB%20 4.18.18&utm_term=Editorial%20-%20Early%20Bird%20Brief.

588. Ibid.

589. Bill Gertz, "Pentagon Gearing up for Space Warfare," *Washington Free Beacon*, March 8, 2018, http://freebeacon.com/national-security/ pentagon-gearing-space-warfare/

590. Ibid.

591. Aaron Mehta and Mike Gruss, "The Sneaky Ways China and Russia Could Threaten U.S. Satellites," C4ISMET.COM, April 11, 2018, https://www.c4isrnet.com/space/2018/04/11/how-the-threat-to-satellites-is-changing/?utm_source=Sailthru&utm_medium=email&utm_campaign=ebb%2012.04.18&utm_term=Editorial%20-%20Early%20 Bird%20Brief.

592. Ibid.

593. Ibid.

594. Ibid.

595. Seth Borenstein, "Star Wars? President Trump Proposes Military Space Force," *Military Times*, March 14, 2018. https://www.militarytimes.com/news/pentagon-congress/2018/03/14/star-wars-president-trump-proposes-military-space-force/?utm_source=Sailthru&utm_medium=email&utm_campaign=ebb-%203-14&utm_term=Editorial%20-%20Early%20Bird%20Brief.

596. Interview with Doctor Marek Jan Chodakiewicz on March 14, 2018.

597. Graham Allison, "China's Maritime Provocations Are Nothing Next to America's Adventurism A Century Ago," *Huffington Post*, July 28, 2017, https://www.huffingtonpost.com/entry/south-china-sea-america_us_5975f525e4b09e5f6cd0b1fd.

598. Ibid.

599. James Burke, "Worst Atrocities Committed by the Communist Party of China," *Vision Times*, April 23, 2017, http://www.visiontimes.com/2017/04/23/worst-atrocities-committed-by-the-communist-party-of-china.html.

600. Graham Allison, "The Thucydides Trap," *Foreign Policy*, June 9, 2017, http://foreignpolicy.com/2017/06/09/the-thucydides-trap/.

601. Adapted from Mark R. Amstutz, *International Ethics: Concepts, Theories and Cases*, pp. 58–60.

602. "Trump's National Security Strategy Unveiled with Focus on Economics," *Defense News*, December 18, 2017, https://www.defensenews.com/breaking-news/2017/12/18/trumps-national-security-strategy-unveiled-with-focus-on-economics/.

603. Susan Glasser, "Trump's Alpha Male Foreign Policy," *Politico*, February 27, 2017, https://www.politico.eu/article/donald-trumps-alpha-male-foreign-policy/.

604. Ibid.

605. Ibid.

606. Ibid.

607. Roger Kimball, "Trump's Doctrine: 'Principled Realism' Comes to the Fore," *American Greatness*, December 18, 2017, https://amgreatness.com/2017/12/18/trumps-doctrine-principled-realism-comes-to-the-fore/.

608. Donald Markwell, *John Maynard Keynes and International Relations: Economic Paths to War and Peace*, Oxford University Press, 2006, p.3.

609. "Remarks by LTG H. R. McMaster at the Reagan National Defense Forum: Reclaiming America's Strategic Confidence," White House, December 2, 2107. Accessed March 16, 2018, https://www.whitehouse. gov/briefings-statements/remarks-ltg-h-r-mcmaster-reagan-national-defense-forum-reclaiming-americas-strategic-confidence/.

610. Ibid.

611. Ibid.

612. Ibid.

613. National Security Strategy of the United States of America, The White House, December 2017, https://www.whitehouse.gov/wp-content/ uploads/2017/12/NSS-Final-12-18-2017-0905.pdf.

614. "Syria Chemical 'Attack': What We Know," BBC, April 26, 2017, http:// www.bbc.com/news/world-middle-east-39500947.

615. Michael Gordon and Helen Cooper, "U.S. Said to Weigh Military Response to Syrian Chemical Attack," *New York Times*, April 6, 2017, https://www.nytimes.com/2017/04/06/world/middleeast/us-said-to-weigh-military-responses-to-syrian-chemical-attack.html.

616. Interview with Dr. Christopher Lew on March 8, 2018. Dr. Lew is the author of *The Third Chinese Revolutionary Civil War: An Analysis of Communist Strategy and Leadership* (2009) and the second edition of the *Historical Dictionary of the Chinese Civil War* (2013).

617. "Gordost Za Stranu I Narod," Levada Center, 21 December 2017, https:www.levanda.ru/2017/12/21/17311/.

618. "Russia GDP Annual Growth Rate 1996–2018," Trading Economics. Accessed March 17, 2018, https://tradingeconomics.com/russia/ gdp-growth-annual.

619. The Ministry of Foreign Affairs of the Russian Federation, "Foreign Minister Sergey Levrov's Address and Answers to Questions at the 53rd Munich Security Conference," 18 February 2017.

620. Andrey Kortunov, "Russia's Changing Relations with the West: Prospects for a New Hybrid System," in Daniel S. Hamilton and Stefan Meister (eds.), The Russia File—Russia and the West in an Unordered World, Center for Transatlantic Relations and German Council on Foreign Relations, 2017, http://transatlanticrelations.org/wp-content/ uploads/2018/Russia_File.pdf.

621. Steven Pifer, "Will Ukraine Join NATO? A Course for Disappointment," The Brookings Institution, 25 July 2017 and Vitalii Rybak, "Ten Things You Should Know About Russian Involvement in Ukraine," Atlantic Council, 11 January 2017.

622. Steven Pifer, "Arms Control, Security Cooperation and U.S.-Russian Relations," Valdai Papers, No. 78, November 2017, http://valdaiclub.com/a/valdai-papers/arms-control-security-cooperation-and-u-s-russian/.-.3.

623. Robert Ashley, DIA Director, testimony before the Senate Armed Services Committee, March 6, 2018, http://www.dia.mil/DesktopModules/ArticleCS/Print.aspx?PortalId=27&ModuleId=24601&Article=1457815.

624. "Sun Tzu," Wikiquote. Accessed March 17, 2018, https://en.wikiquote.org/wiki/Sun_Tzu.

625. Joint Planning, Joint Publication 5-0, U.S. U.S. Department of Defense, June 16, 2017, http://www.jcs.mil/Portals/36/Documents/Doctrine/pubs/jp5_0_20171606.pdf.

626. *Clausewitz on Strategy: Inspiration and Insight from a Master Strategist*, Tiha von Ghyczy, Bolko von Oetinger, Christopher Bassford Editors, John Wiley & Sons, March 14, 2002, p. 85.

627. *The U.S. Army War College Guide to National Security Issues Volume I: Theory of War and Strategy*, 4th Edition, J. Boone Bartholomees, Jr. Editor July 2010. http://www.au.af.mil/au/awc/awcgate/ssi/guide_natsec_v1_2010.pdf.

628. Ibid.

629. Kurt Campbell and Michael O'Hanlon, *Hard Power: The New Politics of National Security* (New York, NY: Basic Books, 2006).

630. Joseph S. Nye, Jr., *Soft Power: The Means to Success in World Politics* (Jackson, TN: Public Affairs, 2004).

631. "An historical description and analysis of pronatalist policies in Italy, Germany and Sweden," VDOCUMENTS. Accessed March 17, 2018, https://vdocuments.site/an-historical-description-and-analysis-of-pronatalist-policies-in-italy-germany.html.

632. Hans Morgenthau, *Politics among Nations: The Struggle for Power and Peace*, Knopf, New York 1967, p. 31.

633. "President Donald Trump Opens the Door to 22% Corporate Tax Rate,"

Wall Street Journal, December 2, 2017, https://www.wsj.com/livecoverage/
tax-bill-2017/card/1512232645.

634. Jeff Green, "Without a Comprehensive Strategy to Regulate Foreign
     Investment, China Wins," *Defense News,* March 14, 2018, https://
     www.defensenews.com/opinion/commentary/2018/03/14/without-a-
     comprehensive-strategy-to-regulate-foreign-investment-china-wins/?utm_
     source=Sailthru&utm_medium=email&utm_campaign=ebb%20
     03.19.18&utm_term=Editorial%20-%20Early%20Bird%20Brief.

635. Ibid.

636. Jeffrey Green, "America's Critical Minerals Problem Has Gone from
     Bad to Worse," *Defense News,* May 2, 2018, https://www.defensenews.
     com/opinion/2018/05/02/americas-critical-minerals-problem-has-gone-
     from-bad-to-worse/?utm_source=Sailthru&utm_medium=email&utm_
     campaign=ebb%2003.05.18&utm_term=Editorial%20-%20Early%20
     Bird%20Brief.

637. Interview with Lieutenant General William G. Boykin, March 12, 2018.

638. Richard Ames, "The Seven Seals of Revelation," *Tomorrow's World,*
     March/April 2013, https://www.tomorrowsworld.org/magazines/2003/
     march-april/the-seven-seals-of-revelation.

639. Ibid.

640. Email from Dr. Michael Heiser, February 21, 2018.

641. Michael Heiser, "The Naked Bible: Biblical Theology, Stripped Bare of
     Denominational Confessions and Theological Confessions," YouTube,
     uploaded January 12, 2015, https://youtu.be/zgwWP1WbeZA.

642. Ibid.

643. "Biblical Hermeneutics—What Is It?" compellingtruth.org. Accessed
     March 17, 2018, https://www.compellingtruth.org/biblical-hermeneutics.
     html.

644. "Russian Orthodox Patriarch Warns of End Time Apocalypse,"
     The Trumpet.com, December 5, 2017, https://www.thetrumpet.
     com/16611-russian-orthodox-patriarch-warns-of-end-time-apocalypse.

645. "Does the Bible Say Anything about Russia in Relation to the End
     Times?" Got Questions, accessed May 15, 2018, https://www.
     gotquestions.org/Russia-end-times.html.

646. Interview with Lieutenant General William G. Boykin, March 12, 2018.

647. Ibid.

648. David R. Reagan, "America the Beautiful? The United States in Bible Prophecy," Lamb & Lion Ministries. Accessed March 17, 2018, http://christinprophecy.org/articles/the-united-states-in-bible-prophecy/.

649. Chris Hedges, "What Every Person Should Know about War," *New York Times*, July 6, 2003, http://www.nytimes.com/2003/07/06/books/chapters/what-every-person-should-know-about-war.html.